DESIGNING WEB AUDIO

DESIGNING WEB AUDIO

Josh Beggs & Dylan Thede

O'REILLY®

Beijing · Cambridge · Farnham · Köln · Paris · Sebastopol · Taipei · Tokyo

Designing Web Audio

by Josh Beggs and Dylan Thede

Printing History

January 2001:   First Edition

Editor: Richard Koman

Production Editor: Melanie Wang

Cover Designer: Edie Freedman

Library of Congress Cataloging-in-Publication Data

Beggs, Josh
  Designing web audio/Josh Beggs and Dylan Thede.--1st ed. p. cm. Includes index.
  ISBN 1-56592-353-7
  1. Computer sound processing. 2. World Wide Web. 3. Web sites--Design. I. Thede, Dylan. II. Title.

TK5105.8863 .B44 2000
006.5--dc21   00-062363

ISBN: 1-56592-353-7
[M]

CONTENTS

PREFACE

The new millennium heralds an exciting era for music and sound on the Internet. Greater bandwidth, improved browser compatibility, and simplified content creation tools are fostering a new global communications revolution. For individuals and businesses alike, web-based media distribution and broadcasting are quickly becoming the most democratic and powerful communication media in history. Web audio gives new power to the individual artist, publisher, or e-commerce entrepreneur to effectively communicate with sound and music to a worldwide audience.

Web broadcasting is relatively inexpensive and simple to implement. Compared to licensing and funding a private radio or TV station, the Web opens doors to millions of new listeners for a fraction of the cost. It is no surprise then that web audio has become a huge hit. Music is a form of universal expression that binds all cultures and people together. Sound and music entertain, inform, and inspire billions of people across the globe. As Internet technology improves and high-bandwidth connections become ubiquitous, we'll see more and more audio across the Web.

As web developers discover that sound provides a more compelling user experience, audio is finding its way on to more and more popular sites. The extensive use of sound on popular sites such as CNN, Broadcast.com, and MP3.com, and entertainment powerhouses such as Disney and Sony is a testament to the growing popularity of web audio and an indication of what is on the horizon.

The Internet is coming to life with sound. In a few short years, the majority of web sites will feature audio. Some of these sites will treat audio as a vital part of their content and brand message and will use sound effectively to enhance the visitor experience. Others will include poor-quality web audio and sound design that detracts from the visitor experience and turns visitors away. *Designing Web Audio* will show you how to capture high-quality audio and use sound intelligently to enhance your web site to and keep visitors coming back.

Audience

Designing Web Audio is an audio resource guide for Internet professionals, designers, and developers, as well as for educators, musicians, producers, and audio enthusiasts.

Individuals who want to enhance their web sites with streaming multimedia and sound will also find this book a helpful guide. The book not only shows you how to add sound files to your web site but also how to effectively produce, record, and integrate multiple audio components into an engaging web soundtrack.

We assume readers of this book have a working knowledge of HTML or have purchased a good basic HTML book. Audio professionals who know the basics of recording and editing may want to skip ahead to the specific chapters that cover their particular areas of interest.

After reading this book, you will have a thorough understanding of how digital audio is encoded from microphone to hard disk and how it is optimized for the Web using advanced compression and EQ techniques. You will also learn which format is the most appropriate for your particular project and how each format is being used in real-world professional media projects.

Chapters 1 through 5 cover the basics of professional audio production, sound design, and streaming audio. Chapters 6 through 11 take an in-depth look at the most common Internet streaming media formats: RealMedia, RealSystem G2 and SMIL, MP3, Flash and Shockwave, MIDI, and Beatnik. Two appendixes offer a buyer's guide to audio hardware and a comparison of web audio formats. A glossary defines technical terms.

Why we wrote this book

Designing Web Audio was born out of our passion for music and technology and the desire to share this knowledge with others around the world. The production of a good web soundtrack and "sonic experience" requires musical and artistic skill, a basic understanding of acoustics, and technological savvy. Our goal in writing this book was to teach and inspire the complete range of skills necessary to create a great web soundtrack and compelling user experience.

Another inspiration for writing this book was to encourage web professionals not to overlook the powerful impact that audio can and will add to a web site. Seasoned veterans of the television and film industry will be the first to tell you that audio is a key element in the success of any major production. For example, films directed by George Lucas and Steven Spielberg would not have made such an impact without the impressive soundtracks created by composers such as John Williams and sound designers such as Ben Burtt and Gary Rydstrom.

As many musicians and sound designers know, audio often takes the "back seat" to graphics and visuals. Sometimes there are good reasons for this: lean production budgets or short timelines dictate that certain elements such as text and graphics take priority over audio. Sometimes bandwidth constraints alone are simply too great to include large audio files on a web site. But in many cases, audio is not factored into the production budget because it is deemed to provide no tangible use or benefit to the audience. Worse, sound is often left out because of a lack of knowledge of how to use the tools and techniques needed to create effective soundtracks.

To educate web developers about the power of sound and about the techniques for producing high-fidelity audio became our rallying cry for the duration of this project. Fortunately, since more and more successful high-traffic web sites have integrated sound over the past year, our job has become less about convincing people to use audio, and more about teaching them how to use audio well.

How to contact us

We have tested and verified all the information in this book to the best of our ability, but you may find that features have changed (or even that we have made mistakes!). Please let us know about any errors you find, as well as your suggestions for future editions, by writing to:

O'Reilly & Associates, Inc.
101 Morris Street
Sebastopol, CA 95472
800-998-9938 (in the U.S. or Canada)
707-829-0515 (international/local)
707-829-0104 (fax)

To ask technical questions or comment on the book, send email to:

bookquestions@oreilly.com

We have a web page for the book, where we'll list errata and any plans for future editions. You can access this page at:

> *http://www.oreilly.com/catalog/sound*

For more information about this book and others, see the O'Reilly web site:

> *http://www.oreilly.com*

For audio examples and free sound effects mentioned in this book, see the authors' web site:

> *http://www.designingwebaudio.com*

Acknowledgments

This book is dedicated to enhancing the quality and creativity of interactive web audio and empowering people to share their music and sound with the rest of the world.

Thanks for the invaluable help and editorial support provided by Richard Koman, Tara McGoldrick, and Kim Brown from O'Reilly. Their vision, critiques, and attention to detail are instrumental to the quality of this book. Special thanks to Leah Goldberg for her contributions to Chapter 7, *Designing Multimedia Presentations with SMIL and RealSystem G2*, Reid Ridgway for his contributions to Chapter 11, *Designing Audio Web Sites with Beatnik*, and Jeff Essex for his technical review of many key chapters. And special thanks also to Scot Hacker, author of *MP3: The Definitive Guide* (O'Reilly & Associates) for his contributions to the MP3 chapter. A number of the sidebars in the MP3 chapter are taken from his book.

Special thanks go out to the Raspberry Media team (at *http://www.raspberrymedia.com*), especially Ethan Allen and Satya Kraus, for their technical insights, guidance, and web audio examples.

Special thanks to the individuals and companies who enriched this book with practical real-world information and tools: Peter Elsea and Gordon Mumma of UCSC Electronic Music Studios, Gary Rydstrom and Ben Burtt of Skywalker Sound, Walter Murch of Looking Glass Films, Reid Ridgway of C.S. Audio, Jeff Essex of Audiosyncrasy, Jeff Patterson of IUMA, Robert Holt of NPR, Nick DelRegno of MCIWorldcom, David Dadekian of Fox News Corp., Mike Tsang of Zone Music, David Gibson of California Recording Institute, Tim Hynes of EMI, Tim Nielson of N2K Entertainment, Steve McMillan and Kari Day of RealNetworks, John Moran and Scott Whitney of The Hollywood Edge, Tom Murphy of Liquid Audio, Paul deBenedictus of Opcode, Stuart Dubey of Sonicopia, John Grey, John Nielson, and Brian Myers.

Josh writes: Thanks to all of my friends, associates, and family who have given me the support, encouragement, and wisdom to complete this project. Special thanks to my wife, Laura Genant, who stood by with patience and love during the many late nights spent over the past three years writing this book. Much gratitude to my brothers, Ethan Allen and Kevin and Breean Beggs, for their sage advice and support along the way. Special thanks to j rain for all the words of wisdom. And most important, my thanks to the power and spirit of making and sharing music—the source of my inspiration.

Dylan writes: First and foremost, I give my thanks to God, who has inspired me all through my life. Many thanks go out to all the people who helped directly and indirectly in the creation of this book. It is my honor to give thanks to my family, especially my mother, Anita, my father, James, my grandmothers, Mary and Georgianne, and my brothers, Jeremiah and Christian. My uncles, aunts, and cousins, from California to Illinois, from New Jersey to Italy, and beyond. And to Amy Bradburn, who has inspired me to heights unimaginable. As for my extended family and friends, the list is long and the appreciation could probably fill a book in itself. The families of Thede, Ruffalo, Burgat, Manchester, Yurino, Huizenga, Robinson, Degenshein, D'Agostino, Pio, Neilson, Karst, Ruiz, Solomon, Brown, Reynolds, Barone, Stone, Macchia, Berkeley, Santa Cruz, Claremont, UCSC, UC Berkeley. The list goes on and my apologies if any are omitted. So many people who have given so much to me during my years and have inevitably been part of this project and all that I do. My heartfelt thanks to all of you. Last and certainly most of all, I wish to thank my co-author and lifelong friend, Josh Beggs. Josh, you are a talented individual and a true friend indeed!

Much love and many thanks to you all.

—Josh Beggs and Dylan Thede

THE ART OF SOUND DESIGN

This book is about adding audio to your web site. Why would you want to do that? Simply put, to enhance the user experience. If sound were not an integral part of the user experience, we'd still be sitting in silent-movie houses watching the likes of Gloria Swanson swoon and bat her eyelashes to convey a romantic interest, or Valentino beating his chest to show us the remorse of lost love. Instead, filmmakers learned to use audio technology to incorporate sound and music to transform the movie-going experience.

Just as sound and music in film and television help drive the audiences' emotions, you can provide a more engaging and compelling experience for your audience by adding audio to the text, graphics, and animation you've already developed for your site. The soundtrack of a film is often the element that makes us cry, sense fear, or feel the adrenaline of an exciting chase scene. A web soundtrack helps you communicate and connect with your audience by setting a mood that draws in visitors, makes them stay longer, helps them navigate easily using audio cues, and gives them occasion to return often. Take away the audio and you have a silent experience that is no more real or gripping than a postcard.

But while good use of sound attracts people to your web site, poor use of sound detracts from it. In fact, a badly designed soundtrack or poorly recorded audio clip may make your site sound unprofessional and even turn people away.

This chapter teaches you how to effectively use web audio to increase sales and customer satisfaction or simply how to make web content more interesting and engaging. We'll cover the basics of sound and digital audio, and show you how to apply the principles and techniques of film, television, and CD-ROM production to your site. The techniques and workarounds presented in this chapter will help you build a great web soundtrack for both low- and high-bandwidth sites and will point the way to the future where web audio rivals the quality and sophistication of film and television sound production.

A brief history of web audio

While audio is now commonplace on the web, it took the rise in commercial interest in the medium to generate the developments you see and hear today. Prior to events such as the initial public offering of Netscape in 1996, web sites were largely non-profit affairs with sparse, text-based pages and few, if any, graphical embellishments. The meteoric rise in commercial browser use created an almost clamorous demand for professional graphic designers with high-quality media production skills. In little time, huge numbers of web sites were transformed into polished corporate marketing brochures, and the once dry text pages of scientific journals were looking more like slick designer magazines.

But as much as the Web was improving in its graphic appeal, it remained a silent medium. The only audio content available other than MIDI were large *.wav* or *.au* files that took minutes or even hours to download before they could be played. The Web was far from an entertainment or broadcast medium.

In late 1996, RealNetworks broke through the silence with the intro duction of RealAudio, a monophonic streaming technology. RealAudio allowed users to click on a link and listen to audio "streaming" across the Internet. Since its inception, RealAudio has made huge advancements in its sound quality. Meanwhile, the competition in the web audio space continues to intensify with the introduction of another new technology, MP3 (see Chapter 8, *Playing, Serving, and Streaming MP3*, for more information). Streaming MP3 can provide even higher quality audio over limited bandwidths.

What you can do with sound on the Web

The advent of web audio opens up more channels for information delivery with narration, interviews, music, sound effects, and radio broadcasts. Among a huge list of benefits, web audio can be used to:

- Communicate ideas through informative dialogue, narration, and voice content

- Improve site navigation with interface-oriented sound effects such as audio button rollover cues

- Enliven your entertainment content and presentations with background music

- Generate revenue through online music sales and distribution of digitized audio clips

Here are some of the ways audio can effectively be used in web site development:

- **Webcasts**. Local radio stations are widening their audience base (and their advertising appeal) by simulcasting on the Internet. Every major league baseball game is broadcast live around the world. Concert promoters are using webcasting as a major promotional and distribution scheme. Consider for example NetAid, a multinational series of concerts and webcasts designed to raise funds for people in developing countries. The NetAid Foundation and the UN Development Program view webcasts as a way to build visibility for their web sites, which will serve as a primary, long-term fundraising vehicle. (It should be noted, however, that the concerts were webcast on the cutting-edge Internet2, and not the freely available Web. However, Internet users were able to download some footage in RealMedia format.)

- **Web soundtracks**. Audio can greatly enhance your online multimedia presentations. As more sites incorporate Macromedia's Flash technology (see Chapter 9, *Interactive Sound Design with Flash and Shockwave*, for more information) or RealNetwork's G2 technology with SMIL, a new standard multimedia markup language (see Chapter 7, *Designing Multimedia Presentations with SMIL and RealSystem G2*), audio is becoming an integral component to animation, graphics, and text on the Web.

- **E-commerce**. Online record stores such as CDNow, Tower Records, Music Boulevard, eMusic, and MP3.com as well as thousands of small, independent record labels and musicians broadcast free streaming audio previews as a shopping service to their customers. Making album clips available as samples often leads a customer to purchase the CD. These on-demand music clips not only allow users to try before they buy, but they are also a powerful tool for helping an online store to sell more.

- **On-demand audio archives**. You can use the Web to affordably categorize and rebroadcast audio content such as sounds effects, speech files, educational content, and even music clips targeted at specialized audiences. For example, *bobdylan.com* offers exclusive unreleased material available only from the web site. If the customers are diehard Dylan fans, these on-demand audio exclusives will keep them coming back.

- **Voice-over narration**. Like webcasts and interviews, rechanneling text explanations into voice-over narration frees up the visual elements to do other jobs within the site. Narration can enable more interactive storytelling. For navigational and educational purposes, narration can also serve as a guide through the site or through a tutorial.

- **Content layers**. There is only so much information a user can absorb at once. Splitting up or layering content and funneling some of it through an audio track reduces the amount of information to scroll through. Some sites tack on sound bites as column sidebars. C|net's *news.com* offers a more ambitious approach to divvying up its content: it broadcasts top stories with three daily webcasts. Readers can browse the rest of the site while a six- to twelve-minute audio show continues in the background. You can also include advertising spots in a webcast. They are less obtrusive than a rotating banner ad, but still get the URL out to the audience.

- **Audio interviews**. Another way to layer a large amount of content is with audio interviews. Instead of scrolling through lengthy Q & A documents like the author interviews at *Amazon.com*, for example, users get the information more quickly while working on other things. Because users are hearing the insider's actual voice, the audio also adds personality and makes the content more robust and enjoyable.

Two easy ways to add sound

To add a simple background sound (*.wav* or *.mid*) file to your web page, include the tags listed below: BGSOUND or EMBED. These tags are the bare minimum you need to get audio running on a web page. For anything more complex than simple playback or looping, you will need to use a plug-in-based solution such as Flash or RealAudio. The BGSOUND and EMBED tags are browser-specific and are used to ensure playback over both Netscape and Internet Explorer browsers. Internet Explorer reads the BGSOUND tag while Netscape reads the EMBED tag.

Adding a simple background sound

Here is some HTML to add a background sound to your page. The sound will begin playing as soon as the file has downloaded. This can be annoying, so use it judiciously.

```
<BGSOUND SRC="yoursound.wav">
<EMBED SRC="yoursound.wav" HIDDEN="TRUE" AUTOSTART="TRUE"></EMBED>
```

If you wish to loop the sound and provide a name for the sound link, use the following code:

```
<BGSOUND="yoursound.wav" NAME="MySound" HIDDEN="TRUE" LOOP="TRUE"
    AUTOSTART="TRUE">
<EMBED SRC="yoursound.wav" HIDDEN="TRUE" LOOP="TRUE"
    AUTOSTART="TRUE"></EMBED>
```

If you want the player console with volume control to be visible during playback, use the following tag (Netscape only):

```
<EMBED SRC="yoursound.wav" VOLUME="50" WIDTH="144" HEIGHT="60"
    CONTROLS="console"></EMBED>
```

Not all web sound has to be elaborate or complicated. A simple music loop or navigation button sound effect can enhance your site and make it a more engaging experience for the user. The following two sections discuss sound elements you can add right away, plus the scripts to get you started.

Adding a looping music soundtrack

With a looped soundtrack, you can create the right atmosphere for your site. Consider this tactic from Broderbund: as diehard Myst players awaited the sequel to Riven, the company put up a web site as a teaser. The "Riven Journals" gave users a preview of the upcoming product (or, rather, kept them at bay) while throughout the site a haunting music loop echoed the look and feel of the game to good effect.

To add a simple background sound file to your web page, include this tag:

```
<BODY BGSOUND="yoursound.wav">
```

If BGSOUND does not work with Internet Explorer, try this:

```
<CENTER><EMBED SRC="name.mid" AUTOSTART="TRUE" WIDTH="144"
    HEIGHT="56" LOOP="5"></CENTER>
```

You may use a *.mid* or *.wav* file as well. Similarly, if you wish to loop the sound, first provide a name for the link, then hide or show the browser's default player/plug-in, and set the file to autostart playback. You may set those parameters using the following code:

```
<BGSOUND="yoursound.au" NAME="click" HIDDEN="TRUE" LOOP="FALSE"
    AUTOSTART="TRUE">
```

Adding sound effects

There are several options for embedding sound effects in your web page. One of the more popular effects is a button rollover. Flash, Shockwave, Beatnik, and JavaScript all allow for interactive mouse rollover sounds. However, JavaScript is by far the easiest to implement, as it does not require plug-ins and works seamlessly on most browsers.

There are many JavaScripts available at shareware sites such as *webcoder.com* and *javascripts.com*. Here is a script by Nick Heinle, author of *Designing with JavaScript* (O'Reilly), that plays a sound when you click on a link:

```
<HTML>
<HEAD>
<SCRIPT LANGUAGE = "JavaScript">

// This function detects the ability to play LiveAudio and then
// decides whether or not to play a specified embed's sound file.

function playSound(name) {
   if (navigator.appName== "Netscape" &&
      parseInt(navigator.appVersion) >= 3 &&
      navigator.appVersion.indexOf("68k") == -1 &&
      navigator.javaEnabled() &&
      document.embeds[name] != null &&
      document.embeds[name].IsReady()) {
        document.embeds[name].play(false);
        }
}

// Turn off Netscape's error checking.

onerror = null
</SCRIPT>
</HEAD>
<BODY BGCOLOR="#FFFFFF">

<!-- Play the LiveAudio embed named "click" (when clicked). -->

<A HREF="home.html" onClick="playSound('click')">Home</A>

<EMBED SRC="click.au" NAME="click" HIDDEN="TRUE" LOOP="FALSE"
    AUTOSTART="FALSE" MASTERSOUND>
</BODY>
</HTML>
```

Audio challenges and limitations

Audio formats do not have universal browser support, nor is there widespread use of one particular format. Adoption of a single audio format has been slow due to technical challenges that include browser incompatibilities, severe bandwidth limitations, and unwieldy plug-ins:

- **Lack of standards**. The persistent incompatibilities between the latest plug-in releases, combined with a marketplace flooded with different versions of browsers, have left web designers yearning for audio format standards. These concerns may eventually disappear as older browsers go out of circulation and as more web surfers use browsers supporting audio formats such as RealAudio, Flash, MP3, and Beatnik.

- **Bandwidth limitations**. With the limited bandwidth of standard analog modems, web developers can barely afford to have a full-featured graphic interface, let alone the addition of bandwidth-intensive audio content. Building a web soundtrack in restricted bandwidth conditions is difficult and requires stringent use of graphics and audio content as well as some ingenious workarounds. One such workaround is recycling a small portion of a music loop clip to use as a button sound, as detailed in Chapter 9, *Interactive Sound Design with Flash and Shockwave*.

  Limited bandwidth also makes it difficult to work with many of the current audio technologies. Shockwave and Flash are great tools for creating interactive audio content with images and animation, but at slow modem speeds, frames come jolting to a halt and audio frequently drops out or skips ahead. The widespread use of high-speed digital modems will alleviate these problems.

  Severe bandwidth limitations also significantly reduce audio quality. Proper recording, editing, and encoding of audio files is especially important with limited bandwidth conditions. This book provides the information that will help you create high-quality audio files that are optimized for web delivery.

- **Difficult plug-in installation procedures**. The process of downloading and installing an audio plug-in is problematic for technically savvy computer users, but for novices, the process presents a whole new level of challenges. Downloading a plug-in disrupts the viewing experience, forces users to answer difficult technical questions, and generally remains far too complicated. In a professional environment that demands quality and reliability, using plug-in-dependent technology for critical content is risky at best. RealNetworks and Macromedia are in the process of developing technical solutions and marketing deals for making the plug-in download process easier. You can read more about the advantages of Macromedia's Smart-Shockwave and Aftershock plug-in download solutions in Chapter 9. Installing plug-ins is easier in IE5 and Netscape 5, but neither browser is ubiquitous.

Sound advice tips from the sound designer of the film *Titanic*

Gary Rydstrom, Academy Award–winning sound designer for *Jurassic Park*, *Terminator 2*, and *Titanic*, provides seven common film sound design techniques that also pertain to designing sound for a web site:

- Pay attention to the sounds around you in your everyday life. Imagine how you would recreate them with effects.

- Focus on sounds that have the highest emotional impact. Use sounds that help build and strengthen the character and theme of your web site.

- Use silence in your soundtrack. Remember when adding sound to your web pages that you also have the benefit of visual content to carry meaning.

- The audio elements of your presentation should have a harmonious rhythm or pattern when played in sequence. If you have a good sense of rhythm and timing, you can be a good sound designer.

- Keep your soundtrack varied. Do not use the same monotonous synth drone or music loop on every web page in your site. People quickly tune out repetitive sounds.

- Keep your soundtrack simple. Do not let it get too busy with distracting sounds; the soundtrack should pull you into the content of the web page. Only one or two sounds should be dominant in the mix at any given time.

- Try to orchestrate the sounds in your mix so that they use the entire frequency spectrum of bass, mid-range, and high-pitched tones. Avoid the simultaneous use of sounds that fill the same frequency range, such as a mid-range voice and cello or a bass guitar and baritone male voice.

Solid sound design

Sound design is about more than just adding cool effects. It must be contextual, supporting the text and the graphic content. And it must be integral to the overall purpose of the site rather than simply drawing attention to itself.

Sound can be used to induce a specific emotional reaction from an audience. Generations of filmgoers have become conditioned to certain sound associations, and a type of "aural" literacy has developed. For instance, shrill, staccato music in a horror film usually signals that the killer is nearby, even if he is offscreen; in action films, an ultra-low rumbling sound often signals the impending doom of a huge explosion or an earthquake.

Full-scale sound design came about in the late 1970s when film producers and directors realized they could put a sound signature on an entire film by hiring a single sound designer to orchestrate the dialogue, music score, and sound effects into one cohesive soundtrack. Similarly, a web sound designer can shape the various sound elements of a web site into a cohesive audio experience that is unique to that site. Since film sound design is a precursor to interactive or web sound design, it is worthwhile to take a brief look at examples of how film sound has been used in movies and television:

- **Driving action**. Hitchcock's infamous shower scene in *Psycho* was originally silent. If you watch the scene with the sound turned off, you can see why the famous director later added the chilling score. The music carries the terror and drives that entire scene. It has also lodged itself in our collective psyche as the definitive sound of horror.

- **Creating or relieving tension**. In the British film, *Distant Voices, Still Lives*, a romantic ballad plays over a scene of brutal domestic violence. Because the song plays directly against the visuals, the juxtaposition creates dramatic tension. It also comments on the scene, making it not only gruesome, but also poignant. Conversely, in a movie with a scene of a multiple car pileups underscored by comic music and effects, such as the scene in the original *Blues Brothers* film, the sound also subverts the visual's meaning, but as comic relief. What would presumably be disturbing to watch becomes funny because of the audio cues.

- **Pulling focus**. When a camera pans or zooms, it pulls the audience's focus toward a particular image. You can do the same thing with sound. One effective public service announcement on television was completely silent. When planning the sound design, the director considered not just the content, but the medium as well. In many households, people use the television as background noise, doing other things while the set is on, so the unexpected absence of sound made viewers look up to see why it was suddenly mute. In this case, the sound design supported the content by drawing the audience's attention to the serious subject matter. Silence was not only appropriate, but also captivating. Don't forget silence as a tool in sound design.

Unlike film audiences, computer users accustomed to the CD-ROM environment *engage* with interactive content. Therefore, unlike film sound, interactive sound is not necessarily sequential or continuous. This is true of the Web as well. Interactive sound designers don't have complete control over how the final product will be received by the end user because the end user can control which sounds play and when. And there are additional differences:

- **Soundtrack composition and duration**. A film has a linear soundtrack that runs from beginning to end for a predetermined period of time. Interactive media typically contains hundreds or thousands of small sound files, ranging from one second to several minutes long.

- **Audience participation**. In film, there is no audience participation, except for the reactions of the audience in the theater. (*The Rocky Horror Picture Show* is arguably an exception in which the audience, through sheer force of will, has transformed the creators' intention into a different experience.) In interactive media, the intention is for the audience to participate. You don't just sit back and watch what happens.

- **Sequence of events**. Film is strictly linear. Interactive products are generally random and unpredictable within a certain range of predetermined options.

- **Timing of audio events**. Film, again, is linear. The timing of music, environmental sound, and special effects are determined by the action on the screen. In CDs and on the Web, the timing of sounds is controlled by the audience (and by technology-created delays, such as computer and CD-ROM drive speed.)

Designing web audio

The best way to start designing web sound is to ask some basic questions. Once you've formulated your answers, you can make some concrete decisions about which tools to use to solve problems and meet project goals. Here are three things to consider in planning your sound design:

- **Overall site purpose**. Determine the purpose of your site. Will this site provide news, entertainment, or both? If you are selling a product, what's the best approach: a demo or a tutorial? RealNetworks, Macromedia, and other companies selling technology or software often have galleries that show off how customers have used their products creatively. But the galleries do more than showcase the products; they build a community of users, who are also the company's customer base.

- **Target audience**. Determine your target audience. Who will be using your site? This may influence the types of sounds or music you use. For example, extreme sports advocates may be looking for a different web experience than someone seeking health care information. Determine how much time your audience spends on a given page. Getting an average can help you decide the length of your streamed sound files. How will they be using your site? Intense gamers may be bent on immersing themselves in a site while news hounds might want to just grab headlines and move on.

- **Bandwidth limitations**. Determine your limitations before you begin the sound design process. What types of delivery machine and platform are typically used by your target audience? Working with bandwidth limitations requires a thorough understanding of your output medium and target platform.

In addition, answering these general questions before you start will help you avoid future problems:

- Will the web site audience have either slow analog modems or faster DSL, cable, or T1 connections?

- How much will you need to compress your audio to meet the bandwidth target?

- Which is more important to your audience: higher quality sound files or shorter download times?

To hear the quality of your final sound design, test the delivery machine or platform that represents the lowest common denominator. Make sure your audio sounds good over the Web and not just on your studio monitors. It is always more costly to change your soundtrack or fix mistakes at the end of the project. Don't get caught having to tell the producers that the great audio they have been hearing will not work in the final product.

Three types of sound can be incorporated into a web site:

- **Narration**. In the form of speech, interviews, voice annotations, dialogue, and newscasts, narration can be used as informative rich content. Narration as an accompaniment to text and graphics is also a great way to enrich your web content with more in-depth information.

- **Sound effects**. Interactive sound effects triggered by user actions, such as button rollovers or transition sounds, can enhance site navigation and make your content more engaging and responsive to user input. Sound effects are also commonly referred to as foley sounds (see the "What is foley?" sidebar later in this chapter).

- **Music**. Music in the form of ambient loops or long-playing streaming media clips can add life and emotional impact to your entertainment content and presentations. *Ambient loops* are short background music or audio clips that repeat, or "loop." Short sound loops are the most commonly used method for adding music to a web page in low-bandwidth conditions. A good loop downloads fast and creates the illusion of continuous music playing in the background.

Always save high-quality masters

Capturing the highest-quality source audio will improve the final output quality of your web audio, even for 8-bit sound over slow modem speeds. If you're preparing audio for low-bandwidth formats, remember to save your high-quality 44.1 kHz, 16-bit original master copies. Then when bandwidth over the Internet increases, you can reprocess your original audio with the higher quality formats.

Easy-to-use narration

Narration is one of the most popular applications of web audio because it is straightforward, easy to use, and provides a dynamic source of information and entertainment for your audience. Visitors can click on a button and listen to audio while they continue to read the rest of the web page. A small link to a streaming narration audio file can be unobtrusively placed to the side of a text column or below a picture caption. Figure 1-1 illustrates how a popular news site uses narration to enhance its text content. If users do not have the appropriate plug-in or do not wish to listen to audio, they can easily scroll past the audio link without disrupting their viewing experience. You can also offer a simple HTML page slide show with narration, graphics, and text.

Five web sound design mistakes to avoid

- *Embedding sounds on the first page of your web site with bad scripting that causes browsers to crash.* If you use audio on your home page, make sure the scripting is cross-platform. Beta-test the page thoroughly on several different systems and browsers or do not use audio on the first page.

- *Using abrasive, distracting button sounds that draw attention away from important content.* Button sounds make your site easier and more fun to navigate. Do not spoil the effect with loud obtrusive sound effects. Button sounds are triggered frequently and should be understated. A dramatic note will sound good the first time but not the second, third, and fourth time. If you saw Stanley Kubrick's last movie, *Eyes Wide Shut*, you'll remember that single piano note played repeatedly throughout the film. It offers a good example of an effective dramatic note that was overused to the point of annoyance.

- *Creating loops that are monotonous.* Unless you have a truly great groove, short loops can be annoying and aggravating. Make sure to select audio that does not offend the tastes of your target audience.

- *Using audio incessantly without silence or pauses.* If you use loops, give people's ears a rest every few pages. For instance, leave audio off the home page or fade your loops out after 15 or 30 seconds of playback. Give visitors a break from the soundtrack every time they come back to the home page. In Flash, you can specify the exact number of times a sound file loops and the rate at which it fades out.

- *Using low-quality audio with inconsistent volume.* Avoid poor source material recorded in noisy locations with less than optimal equipment. If you use narration, hire a good voice-over artist to read your content. Set consistent volume levels for all the narration on your web site.

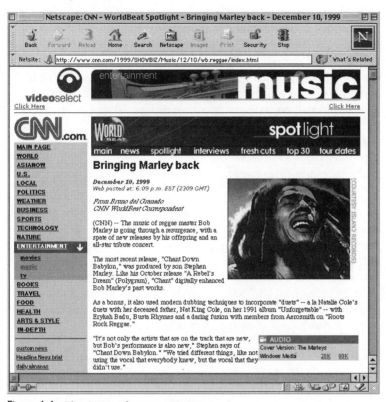

Figure 1-1. *The CNN site featuring narration*

The downside to using narration in the form of real-time streaming audio is that it may require dedicated servers, special software, and user licenses. As opposed to short sound effects and music loops that download in a few seconds then quickly play back, narration or voice clips are much longer in length and need to be broadcast in real time. Streaming to large audiences of several hundred or thousands of listeners simultaneously requires intensive bandwidth and infrastructure. If you are broadcasting to only a few hundred listeners per day, you can get away with much simpler and cost-effective solutions. For example, RealAudio's Basic RealServer will run on the same web server that serves up your web pages. See Chapter 6, *Encoding, Serving, and Streaming Sound with RealAudio*, for more information.

Capturing narration

Unlike ambient loops and sound effects, capturing high-quality narration is more a matter of practicing good general recording and editing techniques than of using special fade effects or seamless looping

What is foley?

Foley is the art of providing audio realism to visuals in post production. The Foley technique is named for Jack Foley, a sound editor at Universal Studios, who was one of the first film artists in the early 1950s to specialize in the new field of adding audio to silent film reels (*http://www.marblehead.net/ foley/jack.html*). Foley sounds are often the first sounds added to a film soundtrack and generally include footsteps, sounds of the actors clothing, and prop movements on the screen such as a closing door or an object falling to the floor. Foley artists perform in a recording room, making sounds and noises with various objects to simulate the sounds of the action on screen. A classic example of a favorite foley technique is to hit a plump cabbage in front of a microphone to simulate the sound of a fistfight.

tricks (for more about recording, see Chapter 3, *Capturing Original Source Material*; for more about editing, see Chapter 4, *Optimizing Your Sound Files*). The quality of streaming audio is determined by two factors: the condition of the source audio prior to encoding, and the compression format or encoding scheme used to encode your audio files for web delivery. If you start with low-quality audio source material, you will get poor results regardless of the speed of the users' modems or the compression format. As a web developer, you may not be able to discern your potential audience's bandwidth capabilities, but you can ensure that your audio source material is set to the proper volume level and is free of distortion and background system noise.

As we'll explain in Chapter 5, *Introduction to Streaming Media*, the amount and form of compression used to encode your source audio greatly effects the quality of the end sound. In contrast to text, audio eats up enormous amounts of bandwidth. A one-minute sound file can easily exceed the amount of digital information needed to reproduce an entire novel. In order to reduce the file size and bandwidth requirements of your audio files, encoding schemes and compression formats discard small pieces of digital information that represent the sound. As you might expect, this process degrades the sound quality. The amount of degradation is equivalent to how small you need to make the sound file to fit your bandwidth constraints. Some audio formats such as MP3 do a better job at compression than other formats such as AIFF or RealMedia's original audio compression scheme.

Embedding narration in a web page

There are several formats widely used to stream narration: RealAudio, Windows Media, QuickTime 4, MP3, and Flash. RealAudio is the most popular and well-tested system for streaming audio. If you are embedding audio on a large web site with hundreds or thousands of visitors per day and need technical support, use the RealAudio system with a dedicated RealServer. If you are more daring or have more technical skills, you can deploy an MP3 server. Most popular audio players and plug-ins such as RealAudio, Windows Media, and Flash play back MP3 files.

HTTP pseudo-streaming with RealAudio, Flash, or Shockwave is a viable alternative for those who do not have administrative access to a web server. It is best suited for web sites with low traffic volume or for cutting-edge sites that have an audience willing to download the plug-in or look past the occasional audio drop-out error message. The Shockwave audio player is customizable and easy to embed directly in a web page.

You'll find more information on RealAudio in Chapter 7 and on Shockwave and Flash in Chapter 10, or you can visit the following sites for additional information:

RealAudio: *http://www1.real.com/devzone/index.html*
Shockwave/Flash: *http://www.macromedia.com/shockwave/*

Using sound effects

Sound effects are generally short, interface-oriented audio clips triggered by user action. Button sounds make it easier for people to navigate your web site. An audio cue, in addition to a graphic button, adds another sensory dimension to your web page.

Sound effects can also be used as short audio clips synchronized with animation. An animated intro screen or home page with audio pulls people into your site. Sound effects are a great way to engage your audience and get them interested in your site's content.

Sound effects should be relatively short in length so they can download and play back quickly. Lengthier sounds take too long to download and should be incorporated into a site as a streaming narration or a music file. Figure 1-2 shows a typical button sound just over a second in length. Notice the quick fade-in and immediate rapid decay.

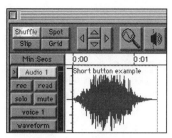

Figure 1-2. *A one-second button sound effect*

The color of sound

Walter Murch, the father of modern sound design and the creator of the soundtracks for such legendary films as *The Godfather* and *Apocalypse Now*, describes the basic components of sound design, the term he originated in the early 1970s.

"Sound is analogous to light and the color spectrum of a rainbow," says Murch. "At one end of a rainbow you have violet and at the other end you have red. At the violet end you have sounds that convey a high degree of information such as speech and dialog. At the opposite end you have infrared sound such as music, which has little code, language, or specific meaning, but tons of emotion and an unrivaled ability to communicate mood to the audience."

However, Walter points out that "in the real world, sounds rarely ever fall clearly into one category or the other. There are elements of language that work their way into music, and by the same token, there are elements of music that work their way into the cadence of the spoken word. In between the two is this rather vague middle area of pure sound: it's not dialogue or speech any more, nor is it really music. This middle area that comprises the vast majority of film sound is known as sound effects and foley." So when it comes to web audio, don't limit yourself to simple narration and background music. Get more creative and use sound effects to add another layer of richness to your interactive web content.

Figure 1-3 shows an example of a sound effect used for a Flash intro
screen. The sound is just over four seconds in length. Notice the
more gradual fade-in and fade-out. The sound file has two peaks in
volume that correspond to events in the animation. The volume
peaks of both the intro and button sounds have been normalized or
raised to reach just below the maximum volume level. By using the
full dynamic range, you get higher quality audio playback. For more
information about digital audio basics and enhancing your sound
files, read Chapter 2, *The Science of Sound and Digital Audio*, and
Chapter 4.

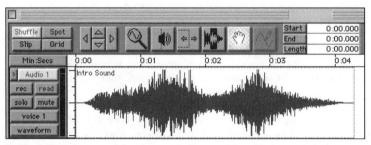

Figure 1-3. *A four-second intro sound effect used for an animated Flash site*

Designing music loops

Music on the web is found in three forms:

- Ambient sound loops via Flash, Shockwave, Beatnik, or MIDI

- Radio-style music broadcasting via RealAudio, Windows Media,
  or QuickTime 4

- Distribution and sales via downloadable formats such as MP3
  and Liquid Audio

For purposes of designing web audio in limited-bandwidth environments, this chapter focuses on creating great music loops. Since web
sound design relies on bandwidth-friendly techniques, short catchy
loops that do not become monotonous or get on your nerves are the
sounds you want to hear.

There are many techniques and tools for creating seamless loops. If
you create loops frequently, it is worth investing in the software.
Infinity Looping Tools for the Macintosh by Antares Systems auto-
mates many of the painstaking steps of building seamless loops in a
standard sound editor. Bias Peak is another audio editing application
that features many looping tools. If you are a Windows user, try using
the Sound Forge Acid looping tool or Cool Edit.

Sound effects libraries

The sounds depicted in Figure 1-2 and Figure 1-3 earlier in this chapter were taken from The Hollywood Edge "Premiere Edition" sound effects library (*http://www.hollywoodedge.com*). The web site for this book, *http://www.designingwebaudio.com*, contains 80 royalty-free sounds from The Hollywood Edge collection. You can purchase high-quality, royalty-free professional sound effects packages from $50 to $100 for a 90-minute CD or up to $1,000 for an entire collection. Professional effects packages are used by sound designers because their sound quality is high and because they contain many variations of similar effects, such as a storm sound effect with rain and one with rain and thunder.

For a low-cost alternative, you can download audio clips from a variety of web sites that provide free or cheap sound effects. A few are listed in the buyers guide in Appendix A, *Creating the Ultimate Web Sound Studio: Buyers Guide and Web Resources.* Keep in mind that you get what you pay for: cheap sound effects packages generally contain less variety and poorer-quality audio files with more background noise and other glitches than do high-end packages.

Background audio loops convey emotion and create mood, and they are most effective when they do not overpower the text and graphics on your web site.

A good loop sounds as if it were being randomly generated over time instead of repeating over and over. The trick to making a good background loop is to recreate the same auditory experience someone would have walking in the forest or along the ocean or listening to a music recording. This effect, also called *sonic realism,* is difficult to achieve in limited-bandwidth environments using two- to four-second loops. Sonic realism is much easier to achieve in a high-bandwidth environment with six- to thirteen-second loops. Three factors that help build this sense of realism are good mixing, optimum loop length, and seamless loops.

Sound loops versus repetitive sound effects

Sonic realism is achieved when there are no perceptible gaps or noticeable "pops" when the loop repeats or when the two endpoints meet. An ambient sound loop is different from a repetitive sound effect. A repetitive sound effect is a sound with fade-ins and fade-outs and gaps of silence between cycles or loops. A true sound loop is seamless and infinite with no recognizable start or endpoint

In some cases, it may be more appropriate to use repeating sound effects with long gaps of silence rather than ambient loops. This is due in part to the lack of scripting controls for elegant cross-fades between sound loops, and the danger of loops becoming too monotonous. For example, if someone clicks on a link to a section of your web site that has a different sound loop, the new loop abruptly cuts in and stops the previous sound. If you built your web pages entirely within the framework of a Shockwave movie, you could use Lingo to script cross-fades between loops. But if you embedded Shockwave in frames as we'll discuss later in this section, you cannot use Lingo for cross-fades. For these reasons, you may decide that in this rare case a repeating sound effect set to retrigger after a few seconds of silence creates a better effect than an ambient loop.

Good ambient loop mixing

One key to good ambient loop mixing is to avoid using distinctive sounds that overpower the other sounds in your mix. Include one sound element that continues through the entire loop. Build your audio loop in layers starting with a soft, background ambient music wash, a continuous noise such as chirping crickets, or an undulating synth drone. Then add subtle, varied sound effects to the loop such as a bird chirp, drops of water, long notes rising in pitch, or a short drumbeat.

Ornamental sounds should be used sparingly in your loop, and they should rest just above the continuous background sound or even faintly below the surface. It is best to make a sound almost imperceptible rather than overstate it by making it too loud. The idea with loops is to create a gentle continuous landscape that does not have jagged peaks or rugged valleys. Like a chef using spices, audio mixing is an art form that takes many years to master. The previous techniques are merely suggestions of approaches you can take to make a good ambient loop.

Optimum loop length

The key to a successful sound loop is to create the shortest loop possible that still sounds dynamic and random. If the loop is too short, you will recognize the start and endpoints, making the repetition more noticeable. Longer loops allow for greater intervals between distinctive noises, which creates the illusion of infinite sound. If you make the loop too long, however, it will require too much bandwidth.

In our experience, the optimum loop length is between 10 and 13 seconds, depending on the type of sound you are looping. That length is just long enough to create the impression that the loop is an infinite background sound, as shown in Figure 1-4.

For certain web applications or page-size constraints, you may have to compromise and make loops shorter than an optimal 13 seconds in length. In fact, if your target audience is using 33.6 Kbps modems,

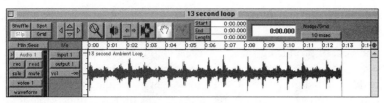

Figure 1-4. *Optimum loop length of 13 seconds*

you will be limited to two- to four-second sound loops. If you have to create shorter loops, keep the mix simple by using fewer ornamental sounds and more synthesizer drone sounds, or incorporate rhythm, a naturally repetitive sound texture.

By incorporating a percussion rhythm or short melody in your ambient loops, you can produce a two- to four-second loop that sounds intentionally repetitive or musical. If you use music or rhythm, make sure the loop lines up on the start and endpoints of one complete rhythmic pattern, as discussed in the "Building seamless music loops" section later in this chapter. It is easy to visually spot where loud percussion hits appear on your waveform-editing screen when you audition your rhythm track. Locate the first beat, such as from a snare or kick drum, and the point where it next repeats in the cycle, then select the area in between the two points to capture a seamless rhythm loop.

One of the best ways to embed a loop into your web page is to use an audio file with a transparent Shockwave movie. (Note that you can use Flash in the same manner.) Attach the Shockwave file to a frame. Place the content of your web pages within the frame. Now the loop will play back continuously across any pages placed within the frame.

The main advantage to embedding Shockwave in frames is that if some visitors do not have the plug-in, they won't receive an error message; the loop simply will not play. Shockwave lets you set many of the parameters directly into HTML pages, including the loop mode, which specifies that a browser keep looping the SWA sound file.

For an average web site with four main sections containing four subcategory pages each, create a frame for each main section. Embed the subcategory pages within a frame. By using four separate frames, you can play different ambient loops for each section. By using several loops, you avoid the monotony of having one sound playing throughout the entire site. To create silence and a break from the ambient loops in the rest of your site, do not place a loop on the home page. See Chapter 5 for a step-by-step guide to using Shockwave loops.

Sound loop tutorial: creating seamless loops with a sound editor

The goal of producing seamless loops is to cross-fade the overlapping endpoints of your audio file so they blend perfectly. Imagine bending a straight piece of metal into a circle, welding the ends together, and sanding down the rough edges until it is impossible to feel the two endpoints in the circle. That's what we're trying to do with a seamless loop.

Making a sound file loop is easy. Making the loop seamless is not. Here is a step-by-step walk-through of one of the more popular methods of creating loops in a standard multitrack sound editor:

1. To make an ambient loop, download the sample file from *http://www.designingwebaudio.com/samples/foo.wav*, shown in Figure 1-5. (If you are making a music loop or a loop that has a distinctive continuous rhythm, such as an undulating synth drone or drum beat, quickly review this section and then proceed to the "Building seamless music loops" section.)

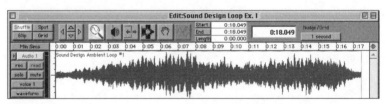

Figure 1-5. *The waveform of a mono sound file imported into a Pro Tools session*

2. Select approximately two seconds of the last portion of the audio clip as shown in Figure 1-6. After you have made your selection, leave the two-second portion highlighted.

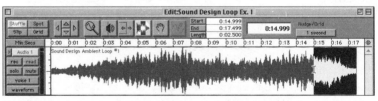

Figure 1-6. *A two-second selection at the end of the audio region*

3. Zoom in close. Hold the Shift key down and modify your selection so that the left end of the highlighted region starts at a zero point on the waveform, as shown in Figures 1-7 and 1-8. Then your highlighted selection on the right part of the audio region should simply go to the end of the sound file. Making your edit

point at the zero point is the best way to avoid pops and glitches at the beginning of your loop. This rule of thumb pertains to all digital audio editing. With stereo files, you may have to compromise when trying to locate a zero point on both tracks.

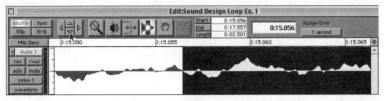

Figure 1-7. *A close-up of a proper edit selection*

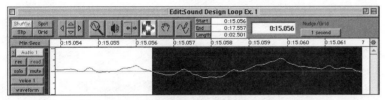

Figure 1-8. *A sample view of a selection made at the zero point of the waveform*

4. Once you have your selection, cut and paste it to a new track as shown in Figure 1-9. Make sure it is placed at the very beginning of the track.

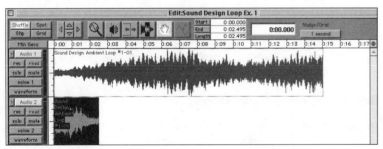

Figure 1-9. *The original audio file with the last two seconds cut and pasted into audio track 2*

5. Set the volume parameters of your cross-fade as shown in Figure 1-10. On the first track, set the fade-in diagonal volume points at 0% to 100% volume over the two-second overlapping portion of the audio clip. On the second track, set the volume points of the fade-out at 100% to 0% over the portion of the clip. Now select the top audio clip and listen in loop playback mode as shown in Figure 1-11. Often the first cross-fade you set will need minor adjustment. Play with the volume cross-fades until

you get a smooth transition with no dips or peaks in volume at the edit points. Note that a "linear" or standard "X" cross-fade will result in a dip in volume.

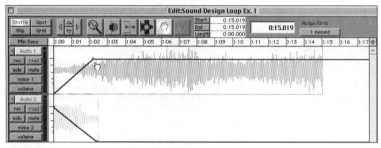

Figure 1-10. *The volume cross-fade settings for a seamless loop*

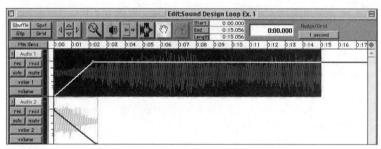

Figure 1-11. *A sample view of a selection made at the zero point of the waveform*

6. Once you have made minor adjustments to your loop, bounce the tracks to disk. Convert the file to your format of choice and you're ready to upload a professional loop to your web site. You can use this same technique to produce stereo audio loops.

Building seamless music loops

In many online projects, bandwidth constraints dictate minimal use of audio. Music or rhythm loops work great when bandwidth constraints limit you to short two- to four-second loops instead of the ideal loop length of about 13 seconds used in higher-bandwidth environments. Generally, it's very difficult to create good ambient background loops such as a soundscape of a forest, city, or peaceful synthesizer in two to four seconds. At that length, the audio tends to sound repetitive and monotonous. Music or ambient sounds with percussion, on the other hand, are naturally repetitive, so they often work well for short loops. Music styles that work particularly well are rap, techno, and "world beat." These styles are repetitive in nature, where the listener expects the music to "ride" on a rhythmic figure. Music that has a lot of melodic or harmonic rhythm (like many jazz or classical styles) does not loop as well because the listener expects the music to develop into other sounds.

If you have an audio clip that has a consistent rhythm such as rap, a percussive instrument, or a pulsing sound, you will need to take extra precaution to select the right edit point. Music loops or rhythmic loops are the most challenging to produce because the component of precise timing adds to the difficulty of making a good cross-fade.

A close look at the digital audio waveform can reveal the phrasing or timing of the music without your having to listen to it. You can often spot repetition in the waveform, which gives you the best visual indication of the start and endpoints of a music loop. Percussion is particularly apparent in a music waveform. For instance, you can see the amplitude from a sharp spike or snare drum, as shown in Figure 1-12. Using the snare drum as a landmark, follow these steps to select a musical measure:

1. Scan the audio waveform for a distinct pattern of peaks or spikes that correspond to percussive rhythm sounds in the audio file such as a snare drum or kick drum, as shown in Figure 1-12. Listen to the sound to determine if it hits on the same beat of each cycle or measure of music. The idea is to find a one- or two-measure unit of time that makes musical sense when repeated.

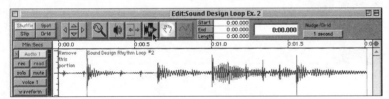

Figure 1-12. *A one-measure audio region of a music clip with distinct snare drum patterns*

2. Once you locate the repeating percussive sound in the waveform, make your short (one to two seconds) or approximately one-measure selection point at the precise start of the percussive sound, as shown in Figure 1-13.

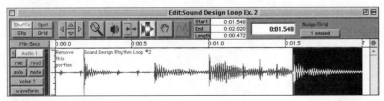

Figure 1-13. *A selected region of the second snare drum sound in the waveform*

CD sound versus web sound

Like web sound design, interactive CD-ROM sound design focuses on the use of sound loops and interactive sound effects triggered by scripts that react to user input. The major contrast between CD-ROM and web mediums is that the Web has unlimited storage capacity, but severely limited data-transfer speeds, whereas a CD-ROM has a comparatively high rate of data transfer but finite disk storage limitations.

3. Move your selection to track 2 as shown in Figure 1-14.

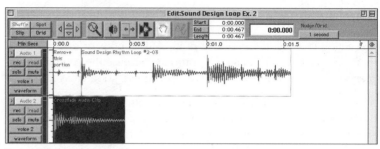

Figure 1-14. *The snare drum selection pasted into audio track 2*

4. Select the beginning portion of the audio clip on track 1 as shown in Figure 1-15. Select up to the percussive sound or peak in the waveform that you are using as your start point. In this example, it is the first snare drum hit.

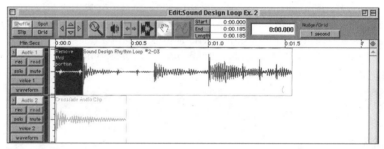

Figure 1-15. *A selection of the unwanted audio region to be removed*

5. Delete the portion of the waveform up to the point of the first percussive sound, as shown in Figure 1-16, so that both the percussive peaks on tracks 1 and 2 line up perfectly. At this point, the audio region on track 1 should be exactly one measure or cycle in length.

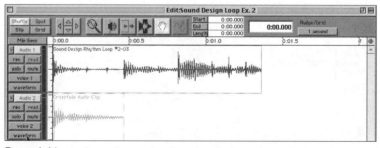

Figure 1-16. *Audio tracks 1 and 2 aligned perfectly; audio track is exactly one measure or rhythm cycle in length*

6. Set your cross-fade volume points as shown in Figure 1-17 and bounce the tracks to disk. Now you should have a perfect music loop!

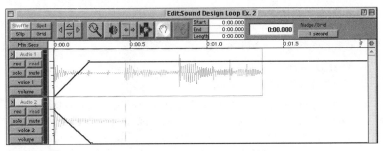

Figure 1-17. *Two audio tracks with appropriate cross-fade points*

Interactive sound effects and buttons

By nature, it is difficult to create short *and* interesting sounds, especially button sounds less than two seconds in length. With a two-second sound, there is not enough time for musical or rhythmic elements. The key to making a good short sound is to blend several layers of audio together to create a rich complex texture or mixture of sounds. The process of mixing and blending sounds together produces a rich sound that is more effective than using a single sound. Avoid using simple touch-tone beep sounds for rollover buttons.

Both of the sounds shown earlier in Figure 1-2 and Figure 1-3 were created by mixing three or more sounds together in a multitrack digital audio editing application. You can audition both of these sounds at *http://www.designingwebaudio.com*. The intro sound effect was created for a swirling water animation. That sound was created by blending various elements from a sound effects library: wind, flushing water, and a jet engine. The button sound was created by copying a segment of the original introductory audio clip. The point here is that you can often recycle portions of existing sounds to use as sound effects for other segments of your web site. To make your own button sounds using a multitrack digital editor, follow these steps:

1. Import several sounds that may sound interesting together, such as a piano note, a telephone beep, and a "synth" sound, as shown in Figure 1-18. Remember you are only going to use a brief portion of any given sound clip. Try using sounds that you might not ordinarily associate with a button noise, such as a train engine or industrial machinery. With button sounds, the emphasis is on trying to find compelling sound textures. The quick

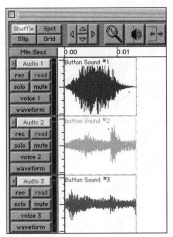

Figure 1-18. *A multitrack session in Pro Tools of a button sound effect comprised of three audio texture layers*

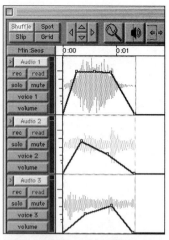

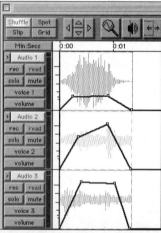

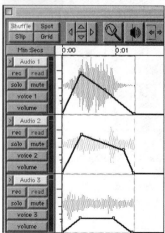

Figure 1-19. *Three audio sessions with different volume combinations*

fade-in and fade-out necessary in a button sound will render the other qualities of the sound unrecognizable.

2. Once you have imported several sounds, try alternating volume settings for each track to determine the best combination of sounds, as shown in Figure 1-19. Try making the piano sound the loudest and the telephone beep the softest. Then reverse the volume settings and listen to the difference.

3. After you have settled on a pleasing combination of sounds, "bounce" or mix-down the tracks to a mono file.

4. Now fine-tune the fade-in and fade-out of the mono button sound file. Experiment with subtle adjustments to the timing of the fade-in and the decay of the sound as shown in Figure 1-20. A button sound will have a more rapid fade-in and slightly longer decay than other sound effects. Bounce the sound to disk with the final volume and fade settings in place.

5. Now that you have a master button sound, you can create several variations as needed by shifting the pitch, as shown in Figure 1-21. First, from your master button audio file make several duplicate copies. Next, shift the pitch of each sound up or down three or five semitones. For example, pitch-shift one sound from C up to E or another from C down to A, as shown in Figure 1-22. Keep pitch-shifting the rest of the sounds until each one is of a unique pitch (this is how you create telephone beep sounds).

Make sure you have the time correction feature checked on to ensure that each button sound remains the same length. Although they may use different names for it, most digital editors have some form of time correction such as "maintain voice character" in SoundEdit 16. Pitch-shifting changes the length of the sound file. Specifying "time correction" (as in Pro Tools) preserves the file's original length.

Interactive sound design case study

Interactive CD-ROM is the closest medium that web audio developers can look to for guidance on creating sophisticated soundtracks. The basic principles for interactive CD-ROM design can be directly applied to the Web. Both mediums share similar technical limitations, bandwidth challenges, and logistical concerns.

There is much to learn by examining the mistakes and innovations made by those who pioneered interactive sound design in the CD-ROM medium. Here are some approaches to common problems.

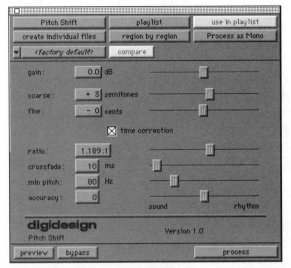

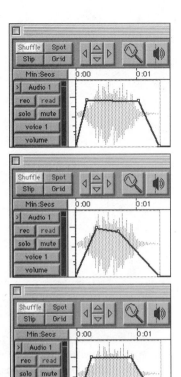

Figure 1-21. *The Pitch Shift window in Pro Tools set to +3 semitones or half-steps with time correction on*

Selecting sounds

Emphasizing lower frequencies over higher-pitched sounds greatly improves audio playback quality over the Web. If you know you are going to lose a lot of high-end frequencies through extreme compression for example, then avoid using high-pitched sounds at the outset.

Most high frequency sounds above 5,000 Hz and 10,000 Hz, such as whistles and shattering glass are lost when sampling down to 8-bit or when using extreme compression algorithms. For example, buzzing flies in a forest ambiance will lose its characteristic sound when reduced to 8-bit and will become random, indistinguishable noise. An effective strategy would be to add the lower frequency sound of owl hoots to your forest mix instead of high-frequency buzzing flies.

Timing loops

In late 1994, co-author Josh Beggs and audio engineer Reid Ridgway embarked on an eight-month soundtrack production for EMI Records. The project was to create a CD-ROM for the multiplatinum band Queensrÿche called the "The Promised Land"—an interactive rock-and-roll adventure game (see Figure 1-23) containing a separate fantasy world for each of the five band members. Each band member developed a unique theme, environment, and palette of sounds for his fantasy world. But due to technical constraints and limitations in CD-ROM storage capacity, the soundtrack had to be limited to an 8-bit, 22,050 Hz mono channel of audio.

Figure 1-20. *Three button sound fade-in and fade-out volume variations*

Figure 1-22. *The Pitch Shift window in SoundEdit 16 set to +4 half-steps with "maintain voice character" or "time correction" on*

As sound designers, the task was to create a rich and compelling interactive soundtrack despite the limited bandwidth and resources. Designing for an uncontrollable sequence of events was a recurring challenge. We discovered two ways to conquer this challenge:

- **Use repeating sound loops instead of a "play once" sound file.** One of the greatest challenges of integrating sound into the interactive medium is the inability to determine the length of time people will spend on any given page or screen. In the beginning of the Queensrÿche project, we set about creating the appropriate soundscapes for each of the five fantasy worlds that comprised the Promised Land disk. In the initial development phase of the sound design project, we created 35-second sound files to play across three or four screens. Each sound had fade-ins and fade-outs for smooth transitions from one audio file to the next, as shown in Figure 1-24.

Practicing good audio etiquette: multimedia rules of the road

Building a site with audio and animation can be a risky endeavor. If you implement full-scale audio, someone is likely to get an error message. Most of the time it will have nothing to do with your code. Often error messages appear because of a browser configuration mistake or a client-side anomaly beyond your control.

The following steps can help minimize the negative impact of audio:

- Inform your clients that using audio is a risk factor. Explain the drawbacks and benefits of a web soundtrack. Use audio with caution on web sites visited frequently for key information or used in the office during work hours. More conservative news and commerce sites should, at a minimum, incorporate button sounds for easier navigation and informative narration. Full-scale multimedia works best for entertainment and promotional web sites.

- If you are going to build a web site with a multimedia format such as Flash, Shockwave, or RealMedia, start with a home page that displays most of the important text and graphics in standard HTML format. For an example of this style, visit the Raspberry Media web site at *http://www.raspberrymultimedia.com*. If you construct most of the home page layout in HTML with your multimedia content playing in a smaller dedicated media window, you can avoid the undesirable situation of losing visitors who do not have the right plug-in or browser to view the home page. Embedding a smaller media window in your pages also reduces the file sizes of your animations and provides a sense of movement on the home page, as seen on the Raspberry Media web site.

- When possible, avoid music loops that repeat indefinitely. Make your loops fade out or stop after a reasonable number of cycles. Some sites tastefully include a "stop music" button on every web page that has an audio loop.

This approach was based on sound design techniques developed for linear media with predictable timelines such as film and television, but it proved to be inadequate for interactive media. If the user stayed on one screen or failed to pass through the next three screens before the sound ended, the audio would fade to silence, disrupting the ambience and realism the soundtrack was supposed to reinforce. Like many other pioneering interactive sound designers, we started to use loops or sound clips that seamlessly repeated infinitely to build a soundtrack that worked in an interactive environment. (Earlier in this chapter, we explored how to build good loops.)

AN INTERACTIVE CD-ROM ROCK AND ROLL ADVENTURE GAME

HYBRID 2-DISC SET

Figure 1-23. *The Queensrÿche Promised Land CD-ROM interactive adventure game*

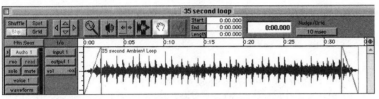

Figure 1-24. *A 35-second ambient sound with fade-ins and fade-outs*

- **Smooth the transitions between screens.** Smooth transitions are critical to good interactive sound design. In our initial approach, when the user moved from one screen to the next, the previous sound file ended abruptly, cutting to silence or to the next sound loop at full volume. Such abrupt transitions detracted from the effectiveness of the soundtrack. Remember that the idea was to create an ambient "soundscape" that made the user feel as if he or she were walking through that particular fantasy world environment. You may have encountered crude audio drop-outs on many web sites, where the sound abruptly stops when you click to another screen. It is not a pleasant experience.

To create smooth transitions between screens, we added "mouse-on" fade-out scripting controls. When the user clicked to move to the next scene, each sound loop would fade in, rising in volume over a period of a few seconds.

After creating a collection of loops for each world of the Promised Land, we embarked on the overall issue of where to distribute the loops. The interactive pathways or architecture of a CD-ROM look much like a web site. Both mediums generally consist of clusters or groups of screens linked to a start or index page that in turn is linked to another index page, as shown in Figure 1-25.

The challenge was to find a balance between diversity and consistency. We wanted to use several different sound files for each environment so that the sound experience for the user would change in different settings. We did not want one sound file to loop for several minutes or to play for only a few seconds. The goal was to distribute the audio loops evenly across one of the page groups or clusters, as illustrated in Figure 1-25.

The different cluster of pages in Figure 1-25 approximate a scene or landscape within the Queensrÿche CD-ROM. The index page represents the start point where visitors begin their journey on a pathway that leads in several directions, one into a dark forest, another down to an ocean lagoon, and two more that lead to secret doorways hidden in the nearby forest. Each cluster in the illustration represents the pages or screens associated with each separate pathway.

The most effective technique was to assign one sound loop to each group or cluster of pages. By scripting a sound file to play over several screens, we avoided the sound drop-outs associated with attaching an individual sound clip to each screen. The overall soundtrack was more effective in creating a mood or ambience when the sound was consistent or present as someone clicked through the multiple screens of a group.

The technique used for the Queensrÿche CD-ROM can be used in a web site built with frames. By placing the pages of a site within several frame sets, you can assign a looping audio file to play across several pages. For example, you could place five audio loops across a 30-page site by creating five unique frame sets with six pages each. One loop would play across all six pages within the frame set. If you build a Flash- or Shockwave-based web site using Shockwave's powerful Lingo script or Flash's limited set of command scripts, you will have even more control over how sound loops play back across pages.

Summary

Now that you've read this chapter, we hope you have developed an appreciation for the art of sound design as well as a framework for building effective web soundtracks. There are challenges to overcome specific to interactive media and limited Internet bandwidths, but the rewards are many. While we have laid down the structures and principles of good web sound design using narration, sound effects, and loops, it is important to remember that this new art form requires innovation, individual exploration, and problem solving. Unlike film and CD-ROM sound design, there are not as many established principles or methods for designing web audio. And there are

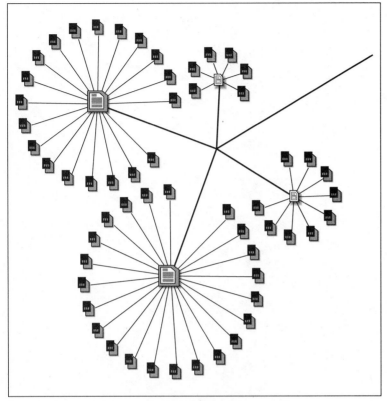

Figure 1-25. *A site architecture diagram of a web site or CD-ROM with pages clustered around a start or index page. In the Queensrÿche CD-ROM, audio clips were programmed to play across all pages in a cluster.*

a host of new technical challenges, namely the lack of sophisticated controls for audio playback and synchronization. Ultimately, we hope you find the challenge of designing web audio and contributing innovations to this new field an exciting adventure rather than a frustrating battle with bleeding-edge technology.

Now that you are excited about the possibilities of designing web audio, let's find out more about how sound actually works and how it gets converted into digital information in Chapter 2.

CHAPTER TWO

THE SCIENCE OF SOUND AND DIGITAL AUDIO

1968: Jimi Hendrix uses feedback to play "The Star Spangled Banner" at Woodstock, taking the electric guitar where it has never gone before.

1978: 100,000 people stand in awe and silence in the sweltering heat of Jamaica's national stadium, struck by the power and emotion of Bob Marley's "Redemption Song."

1998: The last note of the Bach Cello Suites reverberates throughout a state-of-the-art concert hall, and the audience stands in applause as Yo-Yo Ma takes a final bow with his 1712 Davidoff Stradivarius cello.

2000: Riding the wave of a new music revolution, an up-and-coming singer-songwriter without a record contract builds an enthusiastic fan base by publishing her music on MP3 sites.

These four moments in history demonstrate music's power to transform, excite, and entertain people. They illustrate a technical and artistic mastery of sound production and music-making by highly skilled artists. And they show the dedication of audiences around the world who travel great distances and ignore numerous technical challenges to hear their music.

Musicians spend years practicing the manipulation of sound. And they are always on the lookout for just the right instrument. Fans spend thousands of dollars on music collections, hi-fi stereo equipment, and concert tickets, all in pursuit of a good listening experience. So what does all this boil down to? The scientific phenomena of acoustics and sound wave production.

The difference between the sound an artist produces in a concert hall and the sound produced by the beginning student with a MIDI synthesizer player at home has everything to do with how the quality,

In this chapter
• The science of sound
• Digital audio demystified
• Summary

Psychophysical versus acoustic audio terms

Sound is often measured and described using two distinct reference points: the psychophysical perception of sound in the human ear and brain, and the scientific quantification of sound with acoustic measuring devices. Psychophysical terms such as loudness and pitch describe the human perception of the same acoustical phenomena as amplitude and frequency. For example, amplitude is the measurement of the range of air pressure quantified in decibels or dB. Loudness is the human perception of the range of air pressure in a waveform. Frequency is the measurement of the rate of repetition of a waveform. Pitch is the perception of how high or low a waveform sounds. Many audio equipment manuals and professionals use these terms interchangeably, which can create confusion for newcomers.

tone, richness, and substance of the sound waves reaches our ears. This chapter won't teach you how to become the next Hendrix, but it does examine the scientific phenomena of sound to help you design and produce better web audio.

The science of sound

Sound is the vibration of air molecules or variation in air pressure that can be sensed by the ear. The pattern and rate of audible vibrations give sound its unique quality. The range of auditory perception is approximately 20 cycles (or fluctuations) of air pressure per second to 20,000 cycles per second. Air pressure fluctuations outside of this range are not audible to the human ear and are called subsonic (less than 20 cycles per second) and ultrasonic (more than 20,000 cycles per second) vibrations.

Sound is generated by a friction-producing force such as a drum stick hitting a cymbal, a bow moving across a cello string, or a vibrating speaker cone that sets the surrounding air molecules into motion. From the point of impact or disturbance, sound waves or patterns of vibrating air molecules radiate outwards through the atmosphere to the ear like the ripples of water on a pond. Figure 2-1 shows a sound produced by a cello as it emanates from a speaker cone.

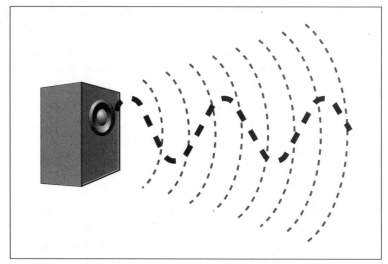

Figure 2-1. *A speaker cone produces sound waves by vibrating surrounding air molecules in fast, rhythmic bursts of energy*

As sound waves produced from a cello move rapidly outward through the atmosphere, they reflect off the various surfaces in the room and divide and multiply into thousands of reflections. Once these reflections reach the ear, they are converted into electrical nerve impulses and sent to the brain where they are stored and interpreted as a beautiful "cello" sound. Similarly, these air pressure fluctuations or reflections can be converted into electrical waves or signals with a microphone and sent to a recording device that stores a "waveform" pattern.

The unique pattern of air pressure variations or sound reflections produced by an instrument or a speaker cone are known as *waveforms*. Figure 2-2 illustrates three different sounds and their unique waveforms. In audio recording and web broadcasting, it is the ability to accurately capture and reproduce these waveforms that results in good sound quality. Improper recording and mastering techniques, poor equipment, and other mistakes may result in a blurred or distorted replication of the original waveform, resulting in poor sound quality.

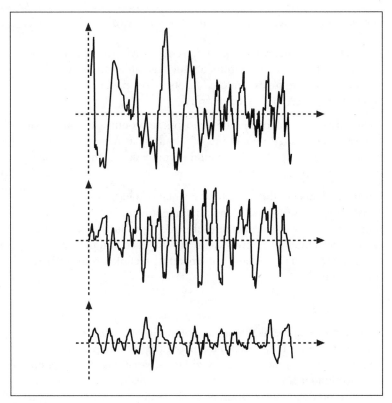

Figure 2-2. *Snapshots of three distinct waveforms, each displaying a unique pattern of air pressure variations or sound reflections*

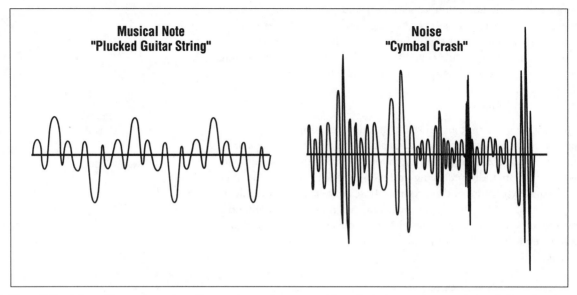

Figure 2-3. *A five-millisecond snapshot of harmonic waveforms created by a plucked guitar string and a cymbal crash*

Most musical sounds vibrate in orderly repetitive patterns (with the exception of percussive instruments such as rattles and shakers). In contrast, *noise* produces random, chaotic wave patterns. Figure 2-3 shows these two types of waveforms.

Each type of disturbance in the atmosphere produces a distinct pattern of vibrations. These patterns of vibrating air molecules give a sound its unique quality. The sound is composed of three elements: loudness, pitch, and timbre.

These elements are the three fundamental qualities of sound that scientists, audio professionals, and equipment manufacturers use to understand, measure, and control the audio production process. A clear understanding of how these terms are used will help you master proper recording, editing, and encoding techniques for web audio broadcasting.

Loudness

Loudness, or volume, is the perception of the strength or weakness of a sound wave resulting from the amount of pressure produced. Sound waves with more intensity or larger variations in air pressure produce louder sounds. Sound waves with smaller fluctuations in air pressure produce quieter sounds, as shown in Figure 2-4. Through the duration of the start and decay of most sounds and passages of music, these sound waves fluctuate at various intensities. This is known as the *dynamic range* of a sound or a passage of music. The dynamic range in an audio file refers to the difference or range in loudness to softness throughout the piece.

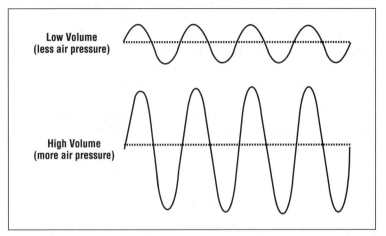

Figure 2-4. *An example of a "quieter" sound wave with less air pressure versus a "louder" sound wave with more air pressure*

Waveform intensity affects the blend of sounds in a mix, as shown in Figure 2-5. The louder a sound is, the more it will *mask* or dominate other sounds in a mix. Masking—the phenomena of louder sounds overpowering quieter sounds—is advantageous for an interview with someone at a noisy tradeshow but not for a voice-over with background music.

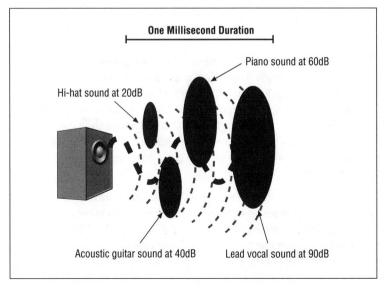

Figure 2-5. *The intensity of waveforms from multiple instruments affects the volume and the perception of a soundtrack creating a masking effect*

Loudness and amplitude

Loudness is not to be confused with *amplitude*. Loudness refers to the human perception of sound, while amplitude refers to quantifiable measurements of air pressure variations. Amplitude is the change in air pressure over time and is universally measured in decibels (dB).

Harmonics

A given note is comprised of a series of "pitches" that vibrate in harmony with its fundamental frequency or pitch. Musical tones contain many such pitches, known as *harmonics*. You can experience this phenomena both aurally and visually by listening to and watching a guitar string being plucked. The string will vibrate at a root, or *fundamental*, frequency, as well as at higher multiples of this frequency. These additional frequencies are the harmonics. For example, a cello note playing the pitch of middle C will predominantly resonate at 261 cycles per second, but it will also contain frequencies vibrating at 1,000, 2,000, and 4,000 cycles per second.

Pitch

Pitch is the psychoacoustic term for how high or low a sound is perceived by the human ear. Pitch is determined by a sound's *frequency*, or rate of repetition. Figure 2-6 shows a one-second duration waveform and the frequency rate for two different instruments. Middle C on the piano, for example, vibrates at 261 cycles per second. Frequency is measured in *hertz* or Hz (also known as cycles per second). The higher the frequency, the higher the pitch. The lower the frequency, the lower the pitch. On home stereo equipment, high-frequency sounds are referred to as treble, and low frequency sounds as bass. Figure 2-7 shows waveforms of relatively lower- and higher-frequency sounds.

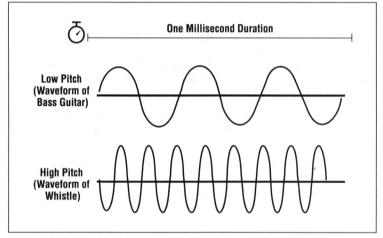

Figure 2-6. *Two different waveforms and their approximate frequency rate*

Notice that it requires more cycles in the same period of time to reproduce a high-pitch sound than it does to reproduce a low-pitch sound, as shown in Figure 2-7. Thus, high-pitch sounds such as a woman's voice or a buzzing fly require more digital information to accurately reproduce than do lower pitched sounds such as a man's voice or a bass guitar. This is why low-pitched sounds are less degraded by the process of converting a sound (encoding) to a low-quality format.

It is also important to note that most sounds are a mixture of waves at various frequencies. A cello note, for example, is composed of many frequencies across the *frequency spectrum*. The frequency spectrum is the complete range of frequencies we can hear, just as the color spectrum is the range of colors we can see. The term also is

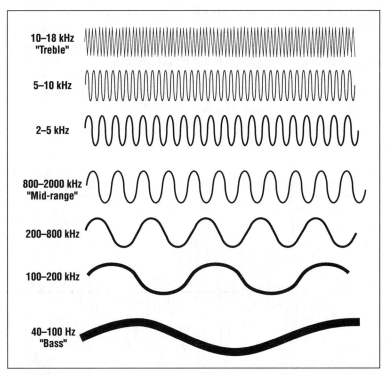

Figure 2-7. *Rapid vibrations of air molecules create a high-pitched sound (treble); a slower rate of vibration creates a low-pitched sound (bass).*

used relative to a particular sound, meaning the frequency spectrum is the range of frequencies present in that sound. A mid-range cello note, for instance, has a range of 500 Hz to 12,000 Hz.

The various frequencies that comprise a sound can be amplified or reduced with equalization (EQ) to change the sound's overall tone and character. Equalization for the Web is discussed in detail in Chapter 4, *Optimizing Your Sound Files.*

Timbre

Unlike loudness or amplitude, measured in dB, and pitch or frequency, measured in Hz, timbre is difficult to quantify. *Timbre* is loosely defined as the tone, color, or texture that enables the brain to distinguish one type of instrument sound from another. The term generally encompasses all the qualities of a sound besides loudness and pitch, such as "smooth," "rough," "hollow," "peaceful," "shrill," "warm," and so on. In simple terms, timbre is the sonic difference between a violin and a trumpet playing the same note at the same loudness or amplitude level.

Musical acoustics

For further study, read Donald E. Hall's *Musical Acoustics* (Wadsworth Publishing Co., 1980). This book gives one of the best in-depth explanations of the science of sound and human hearing.

You can also check out more information about sound and recording at the University of California, Santa Cruz Electronic Music Studios' web site, *http://www.arts.ucsc.edu/ems*.

Much of a sound's unique timbre is a result of its particular transient qualities. *Transients* are the attack and decay, or beginning and ending characteristics, of a sound, as shown in Figure 2-8. For example, the quiver of a violin bow as it strikes the strings or the brief squawk of a saxophone as the air begins to vibrate the reed are transients. Different instruments have unique transients that effect the way we hear a series of notes being played together.

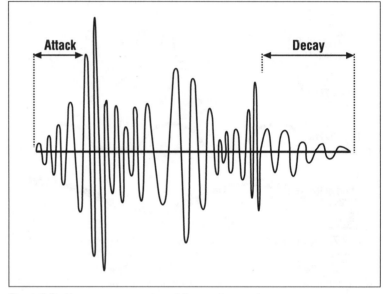

Figure 2-8. *Transients, or attack and decay, of a sound*

A sound's timbre is derived from two physical phenomena. The first is the acoustic properties of a particular instrument being played or an object being hit or vibrated. The second is the acoustics of the environment in which a sound is produced. A fine cello made with a resonant soundboard, the proper proportion of resin or lacquer coating, and good wood grain contains certain acoustic properties that imbue a sound with richness and purity. In the same way, you can hear the sound being imbued by the acoustics of the concert hall where Yo-Yo Ma is playing that cello.

Sound propagation and acoustics

Sound waves move like ripples of water after a pebble has been dropped on the smooth surface of a pond. As the ripples of water travel outward, they begin to reflect off the surrounding edges of the pond into ever smaller and more complex patterns. In the same manner, sound waves reflect and disperse off various surfaces in our environment such as the walls of a concert hall, as shown in Figure 2-9. But before these sound waves reach our ears, they've already traveled through the air, bouncing off any number of objects. We rarely ever hear the pure direct vibration of a sound wave before it is masked or altered by the coloration of thousands of small reflections.

In addition to being colored by reflections, sounds are also colored by the material and substances they travel through. For example, a voice projected through a wall sounds different than a voice projected directly into the ear. As sound travels through the dense materials of a wall, for example, the high frequency energy is absorbed into the wood leaving behind only the lower-frequency, muffled version of the sound. A voice spoken directly into the ear, on the other hand, can produce an unbearably loud sound. Without the impediment of a wall or other sound-absorbing materials, the energy of the higher frequencies of the voice travel straight to the eardrum.

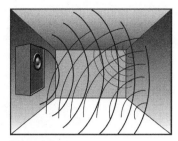

Figure 2-9. *Sound waves from a speaker reflecting off surfaces of a room*

Try this simple test. Take a metronome, ticking clock, or radio and set it down in the middle of a room. Listen to how the sound changes as you walk to different locations in the room. Try walking outside the room. Listen to the sound with the door open. Then close the door and listen again. Next, listen to the sound in different environments such as a tile bathroom, outdoors in the open air, or in a large stairwell. As you will observe, changing the environment creates subtle changes in tone quality, equalization, and timbre of a sound.

At first glance, this phenomena may seem rudimentary, but imagine if you had to recreate this effect artificially in the studio, as many sound designers do when producing a film soundtrack.

Reverberation and delay

When we speak inside a large cathedral or stairwell, our voices reflect back and forth off the surfaces of the walls for several seconds, creating a rich sound comprised of thousands of reflections, as shown in Figure 2-9. If a sound reflects off a wall that is close to our ears, we hear the reflections instantly as part of the richness of the original sound wave decay. Rapid reflections that strike our eardrum within 40 milliseconds of the original sound are called *reverberation*. If a sound bounces off a hard reflective surface that is far away, we hear the reflection as a second distinct sound echo or *delay*. Figure 2-10 illustrates the difference between a short reverb under 40 milliseconds in length versus a longer reverberation or delay.

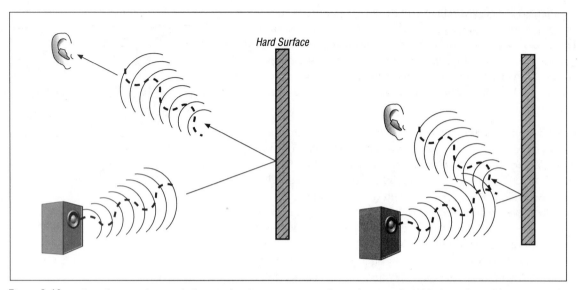

Figure 2-10. *Left: Reflections that reach the ear after 40ms are perceived as a distinct echo (delay). Right: Reflections that reach the ear within 40ms are perceived as richness and warmth (reverberation).*

These reflections blend with the initial direct sound source of a musical note or a voice to create an entirely different auditory experience than the original "dry" sound with no reflections added. The terms "wet" and "dry" are often used to describe sounds with or without reverberation and delay. *Wet* sounds have lots of reverberation and richness from the thousands of small reflections added to the original soundwave. The more reflections the more dense, or "wet," the sound becomes. A *dry* sound such as a musical note or a voice produced in a dense forest where sounds are absorbed into the random surfaces of trees and bushes contains little or no reverberation or delay.

Learning how to emulate the reverberation effects produced by the acoustics of real-world environments is crucial for good sound design. A sound designer should be able to artificially recreate any environment or perspective by applying the right effects to an audio clip. Just as imaging professionals use lighting tricks to enhance and manipulate an image, sound designers use effects such as reverb and equalization to enhance a sound or make a soundtrack more realistic. For example, if you are creating a button sound or narration for a web page that resembles a dark cavern, you will need to add the appropriate reverb and background ambiance for that environment.

Digital audio demystified

Sound is converted to digital information by means of a circuit that creates a set of numbers corresponding to the shape of an incoming electrical wave or current. Two sets of binary values represent digitized waveforms: sampling rate and bit-depth. A *sample* is the value and position assigned to a point of an electrical waveform. The number of samples taken per second is called the *sampling rate*. Bit-depth refers to the size of the binary numbers assigned to describe the dynamic value of each sample.

Sampling is the most important part of the digitizing process. A sample is simply a snapshot of a sound at a given point in time. The sampling rate is a measurement of how many snapshots are taken. To understand this, think about film. A movie camera takes 24 still photographs per second. When they are played back at a certain speed in the theater, the result is almost indistinguishable from reality. Each frame of film is a sample; 24 frames per second is the sampling rate. If you were to film at a lower sampling rate, there would be less information for each second of film. The result would be jerky motion. If you filmed at an even slower rate, the illusion of motion would disappear completely; the film would look like a sequence of still images (which it is).

Digital audio encoding standard

The sampling rate of 44,100 Hz was deemed sufficient for audio reproduction by the governing standards committee at the time audio CD technology was born. Many audio professionals argue that a higher sampling rate is required to accurately reproduce the full dynamic range and upper harmonics of sound and are actively pushing to develop standards that include a sampling rate of 88.4 kHz or 96 kHz.

Just as some audio professionals question the 44,100 Hz sampling rate standard, many have successfully pushed for audio systems with higher 20- and 24-bit encoding capabilities. The higher bit-depth audio systems reproduce more of the subtleties of softer sounds and long decays that are lost in 16-bit recordings.

Higher sampling rate and bit-depth encoding for basic studio recording and editing requires enormous storage space and computing speed in order to process and store the digitized audio. A stereo 16-bit, 44,100 Hz audio file requires the computing of 1,411,200 bits (1.4 Mbit) per second and 10 MB of storage space for every minute of recorded audio. A 20-bit, 96 kHz audio file needs more than twice that bandwidth and disk space and requires the computing of 3.8 Mbit per second.

Read Chapter 5, *Introduction to Streaming Media*, for more details about data compression for streaming web audio.

As with film, it takes a certain number of snapshots to realistically capture the reality of an analog sound. The magic number is generally agreed upon as 44,100 Hz. This number became the audio standard because it is the lowest rate that can accurately reproduce the highest frequencies of our audible hearing range. A 44,100 Hz sampling rate accurately reproduces frequencies up to and slightly beyond the 20,000 Hz hearing limit.

What happens when you sample at less than this rate? It's kind of like scanning a photograph at low resolutions. A 72 pixel-per-inch scan might be recognizable, but it will be of low-quality; you'll see the pixels, and the transitions between colors will be very choppy. If you scan even lower, say 10 ppi, the image will be unrecognizable, just a series of colored blocks. We can visualize digital audio the same way. If you place a grid over an analog waveform, you'll get better reproduction with a fine grid and worse reproduction with a coarse grid. Figure 2-11 illustrates this point.

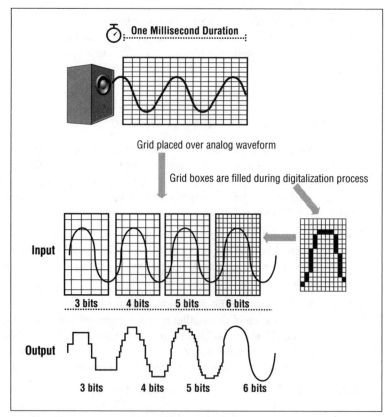

Figure 2-11. *Digital resolution can be visualized by overlaying a waveform on a grid. The finer the grid, the higher the resolution. The fineness of the grid is controllable by the sampling rate and bit-depth.*

Once we've sampled the sound at the optimal rate, we just need to store it as data. How much space do we take to store that data? For CD-quality sound, the answer is 16 bits. That's a measurement of bit-depth. Unfortunately, CD quality isn't practical for the Web, so we start throwing data out by reducing bit-depth. By the time we get to 8-bit sound, we've compromised quality quite a bit, but we've also arrived at some reasonable file sizes. Optimizing sound for the Web is a process of backing off from optimal sampling rates and bit-depths to arrive at something of acceptable quality and file size. Figure 2-12 shows the relationship between these two concepts.

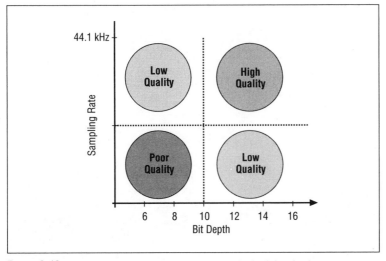

Figure 2-12. *It takes both a high sampling rate and a high bit-depth to get high-quality audio.*

Summary

We've covered the basics of sound and digital audio. You're now ready to learn how to capture high-quality source material and optimize it for web audio using the best software editing tools. Optimizing your audio with a sound editor, a conversion utility such as RealNetwork's RealProducer, or a batch-processing tool such as Wave's WaveConvert Pro can be tremendously difficult and frustrating. However, familiarity with basic audio terms gives you the knowledge base with which to tackle the information in the remaining chapters.

CHAPTER THREE

CAPTURING ORIGINAL SOURCE MATERIAL

The challenge to good recording is reproducing as accurately as possible a sound source without introducing system noise, distortion, or other unwanted artifacts. In theory, capturing sound is a relatively simple process: set up a microphone, run it through a microphone pre-amp or a mixing console, connect the output to a sound card or a digital tape machine, adjust the input level, and press record.

In the real world, however, good recording is complicated by elements such as wind, crowd noise, poor room reflections, sudden volume peaks, and the wide tonal range of musical instruments and voices. The tools for preventing or overcoming these obstacles are proper equipment and good recording techniques.

Whether you are adding rollover sound effects, background music loops, or narration to your site, the first step is to gather your source material. Music and sound effects can be collected easily from pre-recorded, royalty-free music or sound effects libraries. However, if you are recording voice-over narration, a live concert, or an on-location interview, you will have to record the sound yourself.

Selecting the right equipment

Using the appropriate equipment helps you produce high-quality audio. Resolution is the key difference between low-end and high-end audio gear. Professional-grade audio equipment captures higher fidelity sound and preserves the subtleties and nuances of the original source without adding unwanted system noise or distortion.

Applying solid recording techniques is more important than simply buying expensive equipment, however. Get the highest-quality gear your budget allows, then learn how each piece operates so you get

In this chapter

- Selecting the right equipment
- Recording techniques
- Summary

You get what you pay for

The dynamic range of audio equipment is the difference between the loudest sound the system can record before distortion and the softest signal recorded without being overcome by the *noise floor*, the level of ambient noise in the recording. This range is measured by the *signal-to-noise ratio*. The *signal* is the actual sound you're after; *noise* is any hiss or other artifact introduced by the amplifier, the microphone, or the other electrical components of the audio system. High-end equipment produces a +95dB or greater signal-to-noise ratio, which introduces less system noise to your audio. Cheaper equipment produces a +80dB or lower signal-to-noise ratio, which introduces more noise.

the best possible signal. In this section, we'll examine the following types of equipment:

- Microphones
- Microphone pre-amps
- Mixers
- Compressors and limiters
- Studio reference speakers
- DAT recorders
- Headphones
- Pop screens
- High-quality cables

If you are in the market for any of this equipment, consult Appendix A, *Creating the Ultimate Web Sound Studio: Buyers Guide and Web Resources*, for our recommendations.

Microphones

Selecting a microphone suitable for your recording situation is crucial to capturing a good signal—and one of the best ways to meet the recording challenges you will face out in the field where you can't control background noise. The two factors to consider when choosing a microphone are:

- Its transducer design, or the method of converting sound waves into electrical waveforms
- Its directionality, or pick-up pattern of surrounding sounds

Tranducer designs

A transducer is a device that changes information from one form to another. A microphone is a type of transducer device that converts sound waveforms into electrical waveforms, as shown in Figure 3-1. There are three main transducer designs for microphones:

- Dynamic microphones
- Condenser microphones
- Lavaliere clip-on microphones

Dynamic microphones

A dynamic microphone is recommended for live concerts and studio or radio voice-overs. A Beyer dynamic microphone is shown in Figure 3-2. Dynamic microphones are more suitable for live recordings because of their durability and reliability. Plus, they do not overload or distort as easily as condenser microphones. They also

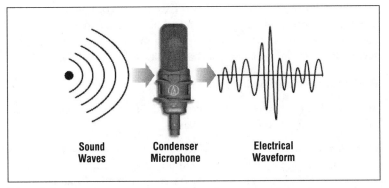

Figure 3-1. *Sound waves are converted into electrical waveforms via a transducer or microphone.*

tend to be less expensive than condensers, but generally do not deliver the even response across all frequencies needed in a studio recording. Unlike dynamic microphones, which amplify certain frequency ranges more than others, condenser microphones amplify all sounds across the frequency spectrum equally, thus producing a more accurate reproduction of the original sound source.

Condenser microphones

For capturing a more accurate, "flat" signal, use a condenser microphone. An Audio-Technica 4050 condenser mic is shown in Figure 3-3. Condenser microphones are better at reproducing the soft decays and subtle nuances of quieter sounds and are widely used in studio recordings where noise rejection and public address (PA) feedback are not a concern. They are most commonly used for recording acoustic instruments and voices. A good condenser microphone introduces less signal noise than a dynamic microphone and more accurately reproduces the complete frequency spectrum between 20 Hz and 20,000 Hz.

While we recommend a high-quality, all-purpose condenser microphone for most studio recordings, a large diaphragm condenser microphone can be too sensitive for extremely loud, continuous sounds like those from an electric guitar. A less sensitive dynamic microphone will pick up a smoother guitar sound without capturing every little high-end crackle.

Lavaliere clip-on microphones

Thumbnail-size lavaliere microphones are inconspicuous and portable, and can be easily placed close to the direct source of someone's voice. They are commonly used for video shoots and television talk shows. Using a lavaliere clip-on microphone and a hidden, portable DAT machine make the recording process less intrusive to the subject.

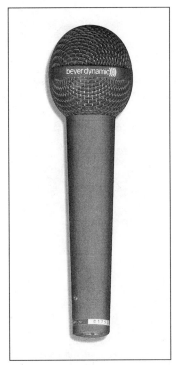

Figure 3-2. *The Beyer dynamic microphone*

Figure 3-3. *The Audio-Technica 4050 condenser microphone*

A lavaliere microphone does not work well for recording live concerts or for ambient field recording. Another disadvantage is that one mic can capture only one voice; capturing multiple voices requires several lavaliere microphones and an additional mixing board.

Directionality and pick-up patterns

All microphones employ one or more of the four directionality or pick-up patterns. The four patterns are:

Omnidirectional

Omnidirectional microphones capture sounds equally from all angles. They are commonly used for recording multiple instruments and voices.

Bidirectional

Bidirectional microphones capture sounds directly in front and in back of the capsule. A bidirectional mic is commonly used to record vocal duets or is placed above an acoustic instrument. Bidirectional microphones reject sounds from the sides, making them useful for situations where an unwanted source is present at 90 degrees, for example. They can also exhibit what is known as the *proximity effect*. Often employed by radio DJs and singers, this effect amplifies the bass frequencies of a voice as it gets closer to the microphone.

Cardioid

Cardioid microphones capture the sounds directly in front of the capsule, providing maximum noise rejection. Cardioid mics are used for live-concert vocal recording and amplification because the pick-up pattern does not capture loud, distortion-causing sounds such as those from a PA system. They also amplify the bass frequencies of a voice as it gets closer to the microphone, creating the proximity effect.

Shotgun

Shotgun microphones contain a recording capsule embedded in a long hollow tube. The capsule picks up a highly exaggerated hypercardioid pattern of sounds far in front and in back of the microphone. Shotgun mics are used for recording in an environment where a narrow pick-up range is needed, such as an interview conducted in a car.

Certain recording situations call for the use of different pick-up patterns. For example, using a cardioid microphone is more effective than an omnidirectional microphone when interviewing someone on a busy tradeshow floor. If, however, you wanted to capture the atmosphere and ambience of the tradeshow, the omnidirectional mic grabs all the surrounding sounds more evenly.

For an on-the-street interview, use a shotgun microphone that has a hypercardioid pick-up pattern. A shotgun mic allows for broader rejection of sounds outside its narrow pick-up range. A live vocal performance might call for a cardioid dynamic microphone with a limited pick-up range; this type of mic should eliminate feedback created when a microphone re-amplifies the amplified sounds coming from a PA system.

Figure 3-4 illustrates the area of maximum pick-up of the four most common patterns. Remember, all microphones pick up a small amount of sound outside of their respective pick-up patterns.

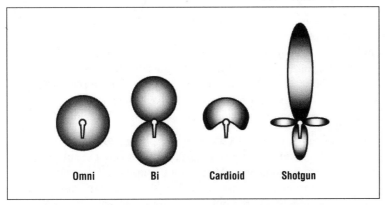

Omni   **Bi**   **Cardioid**   **Shotgun**

Figure 3-4. *The four major microphone pick-up patterns: (from left) omnidirectional, bidirectional, cardioid, and shotgun. These polar graphs represent the area and pick-up angle that each microphone captures.*

> ### Recording versus amplification
>
> It is not always necessary to record a performance with the same microphones used to amplify the performance to the audience. If you use separate microphones for recording, feedback becomes a non-issue and you are free to select from a wider range of more sensitive condenser microphones.

Frequency response

Very few microphones have a uniform frequency response. Most have bumps at various frequencies that add coloration to the sound. Dynamic cardioid microphones, often called "voice or PA microphones," typically have a boost in the 2 kHz to 5 kHz region, as this frequency range seems to make words easier to understand. Condenser microphones used for recording and music microphones are generally flatter, but have enough coloration to make the proper match of mic-to-instrument—a critical part of the recording art.

Some microphones have switches to change the frequency response. A common switch is to a low-frequency cut that reduces the proximity effect on a cardioid mic or low freqency rumble on a condenser mic.

When shopping for a microphone, look for a model that has a good high-frequency response and low noise. A high-quality mic should capture the entire frequency spectrum from 20 Hz to 20 kHz with a low 11dB of self noise. Inexpensive microphones generally only capture the frequencies between 50 Hz to 15 kHz and add a noticeable amount of noise to the audio signal. Microphones also come in high-impedance and low-impedance versions. Impedance is the amount of opposition to current flow. High-impedance types usually have single-conductor miniature phone plugs on an attached cable; low-impedance mics have three-prong "XLR" connectors. Good microphones are invariably low-impedance. A high-impedance mic can be used in a pinch, but it will hum if the cable is longer than two meters.

Microphone pre-amps

When recording, you want the loudest sound, or the highest amplitude point of a given passage of music or narration, to peak just under the maximum input level. By maximizing your input levels, you ensure that softer passages of music or quieter sounds stay well above the noise floor. Several factors determine your target input level: the loudness of the sound itself, the proximity of the microphone to the sound source, and the quality of your microphone pre-amp.

A good mic pre-amp boosts the weak output signal of a microphone without introducing signal noise, just as a telescope magnifies the image seen through its lens. Microphone output signals are inherently weak and must be amplified before entering your sound card or recorder. By amplifying the output signal to your sound card or tape recorder, you improve the quality of your recording.

Optimizing your hard drive for recording and editing

When recording or playing back audio, it is imperative that you use an optimized hard drive with a seek time fast enough to support audio data transfer rates. A seek time of 7.5 ms or better is ideal. Generally speaking, you should always work from your fastest, most reliable hard drive. Intensive editing and recording requires frequent disk optimization. Using a fragmented or slow hard drive may cause disk errors, skipping, or failure to play back or record audio tracks. Most drives purchased since 1996 are capable of writing and reading at a sustained rate of 180 KB per second or better, the necessary speed for recording and playing back CD-quality audio.

However, if your hard drive becomes fragmented, the sustained data rate may become too slow for audio playback. Sound files often are extremely large and need contiguous, uninterrupted hard disk space upon which to write large sound files. Using a separate, dedicated hard drive for audio recording and playback allows for easy optimization. If you only have one hard drive, you can avoid this problem by partitioning the disk. Remember: the faster and cleaner the drive, the more reliable the recording and playback of the sound.

Many sound cards have built-in mic pre-amp inputs for a microphone. You should avoid using these internal pre-amps whenever possible. Poor quality pre-amps add noise and low-level distortion to your recording, especially when capturing soft or quiet sounds. For a little extra investment, an external "outboard" mic pre-amp will noticeably increase the quality of your audio, especially if you are using an inexpensive sound card. Using a separate outboard mic pre-amp ensures that you are delivering a loud, or "hot," signal into your mixer or sound card. If you use the built-in pre-amp, make sure your microphone is properly placed—approximately six inches from the source—to get the hottest signal possible.

Mixers

Audio mixers blend or mix several discrete audio sources into a composite mono or stereo signal (hence the term "mixer). The mixer is the Grand Central Station of the sound studio. In addition to blending sounds together, mixing boards connect and route all the input and output signals from one component to another. Mixers save you the hassle of patching together different pieces of equipment for common, day-to-day studio tasks. They are often used for routing output signals from a DAT machine, CD player, or microphone into a sound card or recording device and then back out to a set of studio reference speakers.

Mixers generally contain built-in mic pre-amps and signal-processing capabilities such as equalization. For recording amplified or loud sounds, the built-in mixer mic pre-amps are ordinarily adequate. We recommend using a dedicated one- or two-channel outboard mic pre-amp for recording softer sounds, such as voice and acoustic instruments. High-quality mic pre-amp components are expensive; manufacturers of sub-$1,000 16- and 24-channel mixers therefore are less likely to use high-grade components.

The key specification of a mixing board is the signal-to-noise ratio, measured in dB. A good mixer with a +95dB signal-to-noise ratio or higher introduces less noise into the signal than will a low-end mixer. To confirm whether a mixer has low noise, plug in a pair of headphones or reference speakers and turn up all the faders on the board without turning on any sound. Then turn up the main output levels. If you hear excessive hiss and noise, the mixer has a poor signal-to-noise ratio. If you hear just a little hiss, or none at all, the mixer has a good signal-to-noise ratio. This is the primary difference between a $30,000 16-track mixer and a $1,500 16-track mixer.

Compressors/limiters

A compressor is used to even out and compress incoming audio signals that vary in dynamic range, such as a singer going from a soft whisper to a resounding scream. In the digital recording environment, a compressor improves sound quality and prevents distortion by reducing the amplitude or volume of incoming sounds that peak above the 0dB-distortion range. When loud sounds that would otherwise cause distortion are reduced in amplitude by the compressor, you can increase the input level of your microphone to get a hotter recording signal.

Old mics can still carry a note

What do Streisand and Van Halen have in common? Obviously it is not their style of music. But it is their choice of microphone. According to *The Wall Street Journal*, Barbra and Eddie both swear by mics made almost a half-century ago by the renowned electronics guru Georg Neumann. "The older, the better," according to Van Halen. When the band goes into a recording studio, they use a number of classic Neumann mics as well as vintage AKG Acoustics mics made in Vienna. Barbra won't record without a 1950s edition Neumann M49 because, according to the original "Babs," the mic "makes the sound feel warmer."

So why are these old mics finding new life in the new millennium? Film-score mixer Shawn Murphy, whose music credits include mega-hits *Star Wars* and *Saving Private Ryan*, says he prefers a Neumann M50 mic because "there just isn't anything manufactured today that does as good a job." And you won't find better harmony than in the words music producers use to describe these old mics—warm, alive, rhapsodic, and amazing, to name just a few.

While newer mics have a dedicated following, when most musicians rave, they rave about the old mic they have procured for their next recording session. And these vintage mics, which used to cost in the hundreds of dollars, are now going for many thousands. For example, the University of Southern California purchased a Neumann U67 for its audio lab at a cost of $3,500. This for a mic made in the early 1960s that when new, sold for less than $200. The AKG ELA M251, which cost less than $300 in 1960 now can fetch as much as $15,000. Typically, these vintage mics sell for much more than new high-end models, which cost between $3,000 and $5,000. This presents a dilemma for companies like Neumann and AKG—while it is complimentary to their consistent high-quality manufacturing, it is discomfiting to a business model when many customers prefer the old product to your new stuff.

So what is it about these old mics that has studio executives and musicians alike bucking the digital trend? The new models are just as well-designed as the older Neumanns and AKGs. In fact, newer mics are capable of giving off less signal noise and producing higher fidelity than their older counterparts. The answer may lie in the way the old mics were assembled, with simple electronic circuits built by hand—a manufacturing process that isn't suitable in today's competitive marketplace. But a better explanation may be the "coolness factor." As music producer Brendan O'Brien put it, "they look like what Frank Sinatra used."

So if you are charged with recording new material for your company's web site, and you've got the budget for it, take a new look at some old mics.

Studio reference speakers

High-quality studio reference speakers accurately reproduce a "flat," transparent representation of your audio without adding coloration, distortion, noise, or equalization.

Home stereo speakers, by contrast, are designed to boost the high and low audio frequencies to provide a richer, more pleasant sound. Reference speakers are designed to give you the most accurate sound, not the most pleasant.

Just as every computer monitor screen displays colors differently, every brand of studio reference speakers produces a slightly different sound. The most important thing is to use the same set of speakers every time you listen to your audio mixes. A favorite trick of savvy recording engineers is to play hit CDs on their reference speakers to hear how other mixes sound on their system.

DAT recorders

Digital audio tape (DAT) is the professional recording standard for digital stereo mix-downs and mastering. A two-track DAT cartridge looks and functions much like a miniaturized VHS tape. And a DAT cartridge is smaller and cheaper ($12) than the previous standard, analog tape reels ($40).

DAT machines come in two forms: the small portable recorders for outdoor field recording and the larger, rack-mount varieties for professional studio recording. High-end portable DAT players ($1,200 to $3,000) pack the same features as the studio rack-mounts, including XLR-balanced inputs and outputs (three-prong connectors versus mini-plugs or RCA jacks) for maximum recording quality and low signal noise. If your budget allows, avoid a DAT player with stereo mini plugs—spend the extra money and get the professional quality features.

Headphones

Several sets of high quality headphones that completely cover the ears are necessary for studio recording sessions and often for detailed sound editing. Studio reference headphones let you hear subtle details and noises that would be otherwise hard to detect, especially if your reference speakers are placed in an environment with excessive noise. Headphones also serve as a monitoring system during recording sessions where a live microphone is located near in the studio reference speakers. Do not use cheap headphones.

Figure 3-5. *Author speaking into condenser microphone with a pop screen attached to mic stand*

Pop screens

Pop screens are essential for recording voices in the studio. A pop screen is a circular hoop with a thin nylon covering that sits directly between the speaker's mouth and the microphone. Without it, your recording likely will include wind and breath noises, such as explosive "P" words. Figure 3-5 shows a typical pop screen setup. Most music stores carry them. In a pinch, you can get away with a home-made screen. Take some stocking hose and stretch it over a framing device, such as a bent metal clothes hanger or an embroidery hoop, and tape it to the mic stand with duct tape.

High-quality cables

Cables are the last item anyone wants to spend money on, but since they carry all your vital electrical signals, it is worth the extra expense to buy high-quality cables with reinforced connectors and proper shielding. Cheap, poor-quality cables produce noise and interference, and they frequently break.

Recording techniques

Capturing a signal to tape or disk clean of excessive reverberation or noise is critical. You can always add effects later to enhance or alter a sound, but it is difficult to remove distortion and noise from the original source. Compression in the encoding process also degrades your sound slightly. The higher the quality of the original source material, the higher the quality of the final output to the Web. In addition to selecting the right equipment, properly setting up your studio and reducing noise on location also results in a cleaner signal.

A studio environment is optimized for the best possible acoustics in music and voice recording. In a typical studio situation, you also work with well-rehearsed, professional voice or music talent and have access to a wide selection of high-quality microphones and effects processors.

In contrast, field recording requires capturing sounds in less than optimal conditions. Because most field recordings take place outdoors, it is difficult to prevent poor acoustics and the intrusion of extraneous noise. Furthermore, in a field-recording situation, your equipment is limited to a set of microphones and a small portable DAT machine, making it likely you will capture spontaneous, unrehearsed dialogue and sounds.

For both environments, there are recommended ways of dealing with unwanted sounds.

Watch the levels: analog versus digital distortion

In analog recording it was often advantageous to apply distortion—that is, push beyond the maximum recording level "into the red" by about 9dB. Such analog distortion enriches the sound by first raising, and then compressing the level of quieter sounds. Furthermore, analog "tube" distortion often produces the pleasing effect of adding harmonics or tones to a voice or an instrument track.

Digital encoding, on the other hand, cannot quantify signals above 0dB. Thus, digital distortion produces unpleasant noise and unwanted clicks and pops, known as artifacts.

If your digital audio signal is in the red, turn down the input gain levels until the green LED lights are bouncing up and down below the 0dB point. Set your reference levels by having the voice-over artist or musician briefly play the loudest passage of the piece and turn your input levels down accordingly. Better yet, insert a compressor in the signal chain between the mic pre-amp and the sound card to reduce volume peaks and keep the signal below 0dB at all times.

Studio recording

If you are recording voice or music talent on a regular basis, you will want to reconfigure an existing room to optimize the acoustics, or better yet, build a new room specifically designed for audio recording. A good sound studio should have optimal acoustics for music or voice (as described later in this section) and isolation from extraneous noises.

Ideally, your studio should isolate recording and engineering activities in separate rooms. This completely removes equipment noise from your recording environment. If you have only one room for recording, mixing, and monitoring your sound, implement some or all of these suggestions:

* Isolate and place noisy, fan-cooled hard drives or power amps into a padded box or a closet with enough air circulation around the components.

* Place the microphone as far away from the equipment as possible, and point it away from any noise sources.

* Cover the wall behind the voice talent with four-inch acoustical foam.

* Record at night, after office hours if your recording studio is in a busy office environment.

Proper room acoustics: capturing a "dry" signal

We perceive spatial distance audibly by the direction or angle of strong sound reflections. Minimizing reflections in your studio prevents these unwanted "directional" clues from being permanently imbued on your source recording. If you record a direct signal with as little reflection as possible, you can add artificial reverberation to recreate any acoustic environment. For voice-over work, recording a "dry" signal without reverberation provides the maximum flexibility to "sweeten" the sound with digital effects in the post-production process. If your source recording has highly distinctive characteristics, it is nearly impossible to remove those reflections in post-production.

To determine the characteristics of your room, try this simple test. Wait for a quiet moment and clap your hands loudly or yell. Listen to the amount of reverberation and reflections produced. If you hear an echo or large amounts of reverberation, consider using a different room entirely. If you hear a pitch or a ringing sound, a fair amount of acoustical treatment will be needed. An example of the use of acoustic foam is shown in Figure 3-6. If you hear only a slight echo or reverberation, which will be the case in most small, carpeted rooms in an office or home, you will need to make only a few minor adjustments to achieve good acoustics.

Figure 3-6. *A recording studio with a small strip of acoustic foam placed in the corner to dampen unwanted reflections*

Optimizing your recording environment

Isolating your studio from outside street noise is difficult. Anywhere air can pass into your studio—under doors, through cracks in window panes—noise will follow. You can reduce the intrusion of most high-pitched frequencies by placing rubber sealing strips along the sides of doors and windows and patching any other spots in your studio where air can pass through. Isolating your studio from bass frequencies is far more difficult. Unlike most high-frequency sounds, bass frequencies travel easily through walls.

True isolation from the sounds of passing cars or airplanes is achieved by constructing a room within a room where the walls of the outer room contain substantial mass, and the inside room is carefully isolated or physically disconnected from the walls of the outer room. In most cases, this process is far too expensive and laborious for small-scale audio production. If you are recording in an urban environment, select a room in the middle of a building or one with extra-thick walls.

The problems that arise from recording in small rooms are associated with unwanted reflections and echoes. Hard, flat surfaces, such as hardwood or tile flooring, bare sheetrock or cement walls, and glass windows are problematic because they reflect a slightly delayed copy of the original sound back to the microphone (in the form of an echo). This echo effect can be exacerbated if the sound is further reflected between parallel walls.

Placing thick acoustic foam on strategic spots on walls and ceilings is the easiest solution to reduce reflections. The usual strategy is to place foam opposite bare spots in a checkerboard pattern. The most common mistake is to use too much foam, which leads to unwanted bass build-up, since foam has little effect on low frequencies. If you cannot afford acoustic foam, you can improvise with additional wall hangings, rugs, bookshelves, and other furniture, as well as with pillows, blankets, or mattresses. These accessories help absorb the sound waves and create diffuse surfaces to reflect the audio away from the microphone.

Desktop audio recording

Managing your studio's acoustics, microphone placement, and recording talent are the more difficult aspects of studio recording. Actually getting the sound onto your desktop is easy. Most sound recording and editing applications use familiar tape deck controls,

Music recording

For recording music, you will want a "livelier" room with more reverb. A room with hardwood floors generally produces more pleasing acoustics than will a sound-deadening room with wall-to-wall carpet.

Recording voice-overs: tips from an expert

Reid Ridgway has been working with digital audio for 15 years. He is the owner and chief recording engineer for C.S. Audio Visual, a multimedia and recording studio in Santa Cruz, California. Ridgway's interactive sound design credits include MCA Records' *On the Road with B. B. King* CD-ROM for Mindscape, and Apple Computer's Twentieth Anniversary Mac welcome presentation. Reid also produces sound for television and film. See Figure 3-7.

Figure 3-7. *Reid Ridgway at the mixing controls of his Santa Cruz sound studio where the production of MCA Record's On the Road with B. B. King took place*

In addition to proper room acoustics and microphone selection, Ridgway says the key steps to capturing a good voice-over are microphone placement, talent selection, and coaching.

Microphone placement. Place the microphone approximately six to eight inches from the speaker's mouth. For a richer, deeper bass tone, place it a bit closer. Point the microphone slightly off-axis to the speaker's mouth to prevent air from blowing directly into the microphone's capsule. Place a pop screen between the speaker's mouth and the microphone to further reduce wind noises and unwanted P's and S's.

To determine optimal mic placement, ask the voice-over artist to speak at different distances and angles from the microphone. Listen to the sound change as the voice-over artist moves about and take note of the best distance or angle.

If you are using an inexpensive microphone, pay close attention to its placement. The pick-up characteristics of cheaper microphones vary widely. It is generally best to place a less-sensitive microphone as close as possible to a person's mouth to get a louder direct signal with less room noise.

→

Selecting a voice-over artist. Have three to four artists audition with a sample script in front of your client. Ideally, use a voice-over artist with theatrical experience and an even quality of voice who has some familiarity with microphone technique. If you can, hire the professional yourself instead of letting the client do it. Avoid getting stuck with a dry-sounding employee with little or no voice-over experience. A company representative may be handy at pointing out terms and jargon, but don't let them explore a new career in front of the microphone.

Coaching. Voice artists are essentially actors reading from scripts in a studio environment without an audience or the context of human interaction. You have to provide the context for the artist. If you allow them simply to read a script without feeling or inspiration, the results will be disappointing. Coaching is especially important if you are unable to get a professional voice-over artist.

such as play, record, pause, and stop. Macromedia SoundEdit 16's controls are shown in Figure 3-8. You'll also note a less familiar button—the loop control—activated; it continually repeats the selected audio.

The most important control in the recording process is the recording level. In SoundEdit 16, this control is located under Menu → Windows → Levels, and is shown in Figure 3-9. If your microphone is plugged into your computer and your sound card is properly configured, you will see green LED lights bounce up and down as the microphone picks up the signal. The green light represents the signal as it approaches 0dB; the red light indicates that the signal has gone over 0dB and is distorting your audio. Adjust the levels as you test the microphone placement until the signal stays completely in the green. We explore using SoundEdit 16 more in Chapter 4, *Optimizing Your Sound Files.*

Figure 3-8. *The controls window in SoundEdit 16 with (from left to right) record, stop, pause, play, and loop buttons*

Figure 3-9. *The Levels window in SoundEdit 16*

Field recording

Of course, not all the audio on your web site will be recorded in a studio environment. Capturing audio on location complicates matters considerably. Field recording requires the use of a lightweight, portable DAT machine with phantom power and high-quality built-in mic pre-amps. Microphone selection and placement are especially crucial

Figure 3-10. *Microphones placed in an x crossing position*

Figure 3-11. *Microphones placed in parallel, pointing slightly outward*

to capturing good sound on location. A few steps that also make for a positive experience include packing a foam microphone covering or windsock to protect against wind, carrying a backup microphone with an alternate pick-up pattern, or simply moving the microphone closer to the sound source. The following sections include some recommended methods for capturing sound in different scenarios.

Live concerts and events

There are two primary methods for recording the sound of live events and concerts: capturing the live stereo output of the public address mixing console or placing two condenser microphones in front of the stage or PA speakers. Capturing the mix from the PA console is more convenient, but using your own microphones generally results in a higher-quality recording.

All amplified events have some type of mixing console to blend the various microphones onstage into two left and right channels for output to the main speakers. A direct signal from the stage or main concert mixing board produces the cleanest recording without crowd noises and unwanted room reflections.

Connect one of the extra left and right output channels directly into your portable DAT machine. Check ahead of time that you have the proper adapter cables to connect your DAT to the mixing board outputs. Whenever possible, you should use XLR three-prong cables to connect to the back of the mixing board. If your portable DAT machine does not have XLR inputs, you will need an XLR-to-quarter-inch or stereo mini-cable adapter. (See Appendix A, *Creating the Ultimate Web Sound Studio: Buyers Guide and Web Resources*, for more on XLR and adapters.)

If you are at an event or concert without a PA system or you do not have access to the main mixing console, use a microphone plugged into a portable DAT to capture the sound source. Set up a six- to eight-foot tall microphone stand toward the middle or back of the concert hall at the center stage position. Attach two small diaphragm condenser microphones to the top of the stand and point them toward the stage. You can place the microphones in an "x" position, as shown in Figure 3-10, or parallel to each other and six feet apart, pointed slightly outward to the left and right sides of the stage, as shown in Figure 3-11.

On-location interviews and panel discussions

In-studio interviews are not always possible and, in some cases, not even preferred. Even if the acoustics and equipment selection are less than optimal, it is best to interview people in an environment in which they're comfortable. An on-location interview can be captured easily with a small portable DAT machine and a microphone. Set up your equipment efficiently and try to make the recording experience as transparent as possible. Often people are intimidated by speaking into a microphone or are uncomfortable just knowing every word is being captured on tape.

Depending on the level of extraneous noise in your immediate environment and the number of voices you are capturing, use one of these techniques to record interviews:

- A small lavaliere clip-on microphone attached to the interviewee's shirt and placed directly below his or her mouth is best for recording in noisy environments. An omnidirectional condenser microphone placed on a tabletop stand is best for capturing several voices in a quiet environment.

- A cardioid microphone placed on a tabletop stand works well for capturing a single voice in a quiet environment. (Place the microphone on a thick towel or foam pad to reduce thumps and eliminate the high-end coloration you often get from sound reflections off the tabletop.)

- Use a single omnidirectional microphone to record multiperson interviews and group discussions. You need to sit everyone at a round or square table equidistant from the microphone in order to capture all the voices at equal volume.

Capturing ambient sounds

To record ambient environmental sounds such as a city street with cars passing or a distant bird call in a forest, use an omnidirectional microphone with a wind protective foam covering (known as a windsock). A shotgun microphone works best for capturing the direct signal of a distant sound source.

The greatest challenge to ambient recording is capturing soft or distant sounds without increasing the level of system noise. Using high-quality, professional gear is the best way to ensure good ambient recording. If you are capturing the soft sounds of a distant bird call, for example, and use a consumer-grade portable DAT machine, you will instantly notice the presence of system noise in the form of a continuous "shhh." This is because boosting the input levels increases the system noise. Professional-grade DAT machines have higher quality mic pre-amps and do a better job of boosting the signal without introducing noise.

If you are using a consumer-grade DAT machine, avoid turning the input levels up too high. To capture a louder signal, position your microphone closer to the sound source instead.

Telephone interviews

The easiest way to capture a telephone interview is to use an inexpensive telephone recording box that sits between the wall outlet and your phone. Radio Shack's Telephone Recording Connector receives a standard RJ11 phone jack cord and contains a stereo mini output jack. To record the telephone interview, simply plug the stereo mini cable into a portable DAT machine.

Panel particulars

A single microphone will not work if your recording environment is too noisy or people are sitting side by side in a long row. For panel discussions, use a separate lavaliere or cardioid microphone for each person's voice. Run the microphones through a small eight- or twelve-channel mixer with built-in preamps. Mix the signals down to a stereo signal and run the output to a portable DAT machine.

Outdoor concert recording

One of the greatest technical challenges in field recording is avoiding wind noise, especially with extremely sensitive condenser microphones. John Neilson, live sound engineer and mixer for touring music acts such as Kenny Loggins and Peter, Paul, and Mary, offers several tips on the most effective techniques for reducing wind noise.

Placing a windsock over the microphone and making alterations to equalization settings are two effective steps to avoid wind. A windsock or foam covering diffuses the energy of incoming wind or bursts of air from certain vocal sounds (such as B's and P's) before they blow across and vibrate the microphone diaphragm. The downside is that windsocks reduce the energy of incoming high frequencies, requiring equalization adjustments to boost the 1,000 Hz-and-up treble range. Removing or "rolling off" the EQ below the 60 Hz to 80 Hz range will reduce most wind vibrations.

At an outdoor Kenny Loggins concert in Reno, Nevada, a windstorm unexpectedly blew in midway through the show. The stage crew had to quickly place windsocks over all the microphones and make EQ adjustments in the middle of a song to prevent wind sounds from drowning out the entire mix. Fortunately, Loggins prefers to use a less-sensitive dynamic cardioid microphone that does not pick up as much wind as a condenser microphone.

After placing a windsock over the mic, Neilson had Loggins sing closer to it so more of the direct signal would be captured through the foam material. Because the singer was closer to the microphone, Neilson turned down the bass to compensate for the proximity effect. To balance Loggins' vocals, Neilson made adjustments by ear, reducing the bass in the 120 Hz-and-under range, and boosting the overall higher frequencies above 1,000 Hz.

The sensitive small diaphragm condenser microphones used for the percussion instruments were more difficult to protect against the wind than the dynamic vocal microphones. The condenser mics were placed overhead several feet above the sound source, with the mixing board microphone pre-amps turned way up to capture the quiet sounds of the chimes and rattles on the percussion tree. This combination made the recording vulnerable to extraneous wind noise. After placing windsocks on the mics, Neilson had to make further equalization adjustments to avoid the wind noise. Starting in the 300 Hz-and-under range, the low-end frequencies were rolled off. The frequencies below 60 Hz and 80 Hz were cut out completely. But after rolling off the bass, the sound became thin. To compensate, Neilson was careful not to turn down too much bass and to boost the high-end frequencies above 1,000 Hz again.

At a Peter, Paul, and Mary concert inside the Santa Cruz Civic Auditorium, Neilson was faced with a different kind of "wind" problem. In this case, the singers preferred the sound of a more sensitive small diaphragm condenser microphone for their acoustic music. Despite being indoors, these sensitive mics needed windsocks to protect against the small amount of wind generated from singing B's and P's.

In this situation, the most effective method for avoiding air blowing against the sensitive condenser microphone diaphragms again was to use a windsock and roll off or remove all the frequencies below 60 Hz or 80 Hz. Rolling off the lows does not generally affect the vocal tone, since a human voice usually cannot drop below 60 Hz.

Summary

With audio, as with computers, the old adage "garbage in, garbage out" holds true. The final audio quality of any production absolutely relies on the quality of the original recordings. Ensuring you have the best quality source material is the first and most important step you can take to guarantee the quality of the final compressed sound you serve on your web site. All web audio encoders produce better files when clean source material is used to convert. Finally, remember that every extra hour spent optimizing your recording environment or adjusting the recording levels can save you at least three hours in the editing studio.

After reading this chapter, you should know what equipment you need and how to avoid the pitfalls of poor-quality source material. Now that you have your audio source material, let's take a look at how to optimize and prepare your sound files for the Web. Chapter 4 teaches you practical editing and mastering tricks to enhance poorly recorded sound files or to make a good recording sound even better.

CHAPTER FOUR

OPTIMIZING YOUR SOUND FILES

When you have captured your audio source material, there are three critical steps to take before you integrate audio into your web site:

- Perform basic sound editing to remove undesirable recording takes and unwanted artifacts, such as coughs or sneezes.

- Add digital effects enhancements, such as reverb, delay, and pitch-shifting to amplify your soundtrack.

- Apply web mastering techniques to optimize your sound files for web compression and delivery.

You can perform basic sound editing with any digital audio application that has routine cut, paste, and fade features. The sound-editing application we will refer to in this chapter is Macromedia's SoundEdit 16 (Macintosh and Windows). However, the concepts we discuss are the same for any basic sound editor, including CoolEdit (Windows), Sound Forge by Sonic Foundry (Windows), and Pro Tools by Avid (Macintosh and Windows NT).

Applying digital effects to your sound files is the most creative editing step, but it can also be the most confusing and troublesome. You can, for example, add too many effects and quickly lose track of what you've done to a file or how to backtrack to an earlier state. You can also add subtle effects such as reverb, delay, and equalization, or apply more drastic, sound-altering effects such as pitch-shifting, time expansion, and reverse. Learning which digital effects to use, and how and when to use them, takes practice and experimentation. In this chapter, you'll find guidelines to help fine-tune your application of digital effects.

In this chapter

- Basic sound editing

- Digital effects

- Web mastering: optimizing sound files for Internet broadcasting

- Summary

SoundEdit 16

Macromedia SoundEdit 16 is a common digital audio application used in the multimedia industry. It is often bundled with software packages such as Director Studio. SoundEdit 16 is a stereo two-track editor featuring standard audio effects such as normalization, EQ, reverb, and delay as well as cut and paste features. It also provides support for all major web audio formats. For the latest updates and plug-ins, visit *www.macromedia.com*. Note that audio applications such as SoundForge and CoolEdit perform the same functions as SoundEdit 16.

Web mastering is the final optimization process before you encode your sound files into a web format. Audio files need to be custom-tailored for their respective output mediums: radio, film, television, home stereos, and of course the Internet. In this chapter, we will also discuss the techniques used to prepare sound files for digital delivery, drawing from traditional CD mastering techniques such as normalization and equalization.

By removing unwanted artifacts and glitches, applying the appropriate effects, and properly mastering your sound files, you greatly enhance your web soundtrack or voice-over. This chapter familiarizes you with all three of these techniques which will help bring the overall quality of your sound files up to professional broadcast standards.

Basic sound editing

After capturing your raw source material, you'll probably have to remove unavoidable, extraneous noises such as pops or clicks, system noise, 60 Hz electrical hum, or throat-clearing noises and coughs.

Properly cleaning up a sound file can be a time-consuming process. To capture the cleanest signal possible, you should start with a recording that has good dynamic range, optimized levels, and little system noise. Remember, the higher the quality of the original recording, the better the final edited version will sound when compressed for web delivery. A few extra minutes of planning in the recording studio can save you hours later in the editing studio.

Choosing takes and removing artifacts

Recording multiple takes of the same sound passage isn't neurotic, it's wise. Once in the editing suite, select the take that sounds best, then edit or delete artifacts that may have occurred before, during, or after recording. For example, remove the throat-clearing and breathing sounds that occur before someone begins speaking and the miscellaneous studio noises, such as a microphone stand being adjusted, that occur right before a recording session.

You can do this easily by watching the waveform as you listen to the sound, highlighting the section where the noise occurs and then clicking the delete or silence command in your audio editor.

Avoiding gaps between edited sections

After you cut out the major artifacts and reassemble the best takes into a contiguous sound file or audio region, smooth out the silences or pauses, keeping a consistent room tone in between phrases and passages of music. Room tone is the natural ambient sound in any given environment, such as a subtle background wind outdoors or the distant hum of an indoor generator or fan.

Even the vibration of "silence" varies from room to room. All sound files also have an inherent noise floor or a certain amount of system noise. It is nearly impossible to capture an absolutely silent signal. Thus, if you simply delete an artifact, there will be a small gap of perceptible dead space with low-level system noise in between the "silent" passages. (This gap is especially noticeable with headphones or a high-fidelity sound system.) To compensate for this effect, record about 20 to 30 seconds of room tone or low-level system noise and paste this over any artifacts. This process eliminates the dead-air syndrome. A sound file that starts with a room tone recording is shown in Figure 4-1.

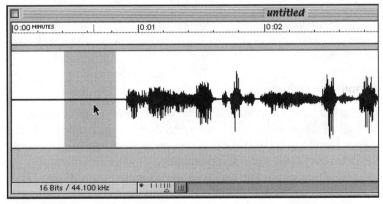

Figure 4-1. *A sound file with room tone in the beginning. Use this room tone to cover up any gaps that may appear in the editing process.*

Removing embedded artifacts

The final and most difficult step at this stage is to remove unwanted artifacts embedded within passages of music or voice-over phrases. Such artifacts must be carefully removed or reduced in volume without affecting the desired sound. In some cases, if the unwanted artifact occupies only a few milliseconds of time, you can simply delete that portion without detecting any major difference in the playback of the sound file. In most cases, however, you will have to settle for reducing the amplitude or volume of the spike or unwanted region to avoid a perceptible gap or glitch.

For longer playing artifacts, here are a few other techniques.

Deleting a spike

To remove a large spike from an audio waveform, use the zoom-in command until you locate and select the offending waveform. Audition the selection first to make certain that you have identified only the portion of sound you want to remove. Next, simply hit the delete key to remove the section. Figure 4-2 shows a sound file with a spike at the beginning and the same file with the spike removed.

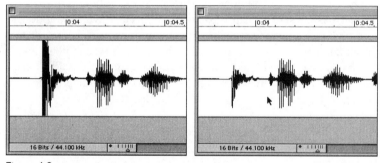

Figure 4-2. *A waveform spike in an audio file (left) and the fixed file with the spike deleted (right)*

Amplitude reduction

Cutting out an entire portion of audio often results in an unacceptable glitch when the two ends are spliced back together. If you have a loud waveform spike that cannot simply be removed from the middle of an important section, you will have to settle for volume, or amplitude, reduction. The idea is simply to reduce the volume of the specific selection in order to minimize the noise in relation to the rest of the sound clip.

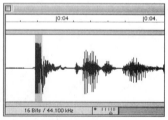

Figure 4-3. *The volume of the spike has been reduced without removing any data.*

First, select the artifact and try reducing its volume by −3dB to −9dB so that it stays just under the volume of your room tone. Select the section of noise from your waveform and choose the Amplify command. Enter a very low value like 5% or 10%. This reduces the selected waveform by a substantial amount. Compare the reduced spike in Figure 4-3 to the one in Figure 4-2. Avoid reducing the volume below the inherent room noise, however, as this will produce a noticeable gap or change in volume when the sound file is played back.

The best way to determine the right volume level is to watch the contour of the waveform in your editing window. Locate the spike in the waveform, then reduce it to the level of the surrounding room tone. Although this technique does not remove the glitch entirely, it makes it is less noticeable and in some cases almost imperceptible.

Equalization

Another commonly used method for removing artifacts while preserving the underlying sound file is equalization. Equalization is a more precise method for altering the gain or "volume" of a limited set of frequencies within an audio region. It is used as an alternative to globally reducing the volume of all the frequencies. For example, certain artifacts, such as wind noise or the sound of bumping a microphone stand, are diminished by reducing the frequencies below 60 Hz and 80 Hz. Reducing certain high frequencies is also useful for "de-essing," or removing over-pronounced "sss" sounds during a voice-over recording.

To boost or cut the frequency range of an unwanted artifact, audition the sound file in loop playback mode. Adjust the frequency slider that corresponds to the type of sound you are trying to alter (boost or cut), as shown in Figure 4-4.

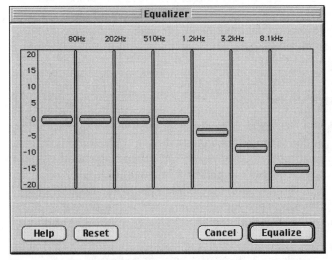

Figure 4-4. *The Equalization reduction process allows you to use the equalizer to cut or decrease frequencies of a particular sound. In this example, the frequencies are reduced in the 1.2, 3.2, and 8.1 kHz frequency range.*

Digital effects

Digital effects have evolved into highly sophisticated tools. Digital effects editing allows you to easily attach or apply many effects to an audio track, including reverberation or delay, preview it in real-time, make subtle adjustments to the effect, and then output or mix-down the track without permanently altering or changing the original sound file. Digital effects give sound designers more control and power to shape and craft sounds.

Before the advent of digital-editing applications and modern-day effects plug-ins, adding special effects to sound was cumbersome and time-consuming; effects were added by running the original "dry" audio signal through standalone effects boxes and then routing the processed or "wet" sound back to the tape recording device. The other alternative was to first record the original sound to a multitrack recording device and run it through an effects box during the mix-down (the process whereby all the tracks are blended to a stereo master tape). While this method preserved the original sound file, the creative constraints, real-time limitations of adjusting multiple effects devices, and time requirements involved in resetting and configuring the equipment were enormous. Now, however, experimenting with a whole range of digital effects is just a mouseclick away.

Professionals often refer to the process of adding effects to sound as "sweetening" the sound. When applying digital effects, use them sparingly and appropriately. You want to enhance your sound, not overwhelm it. A little bit of reverb or delay added to a sound file creates a nice sense of space and enhances the sound considerably. Too much reverb, on the other hand, can make the passage sound distant and unintelligible.

Destructive versus nondestructive editing

Destructive editing is the process of changing or altering an original master file. When a destructive edit is performed, the altered sound file is permanently rewritten to disk. In contrast, nondestructive editing never changes the original master file; it merely alters its playback. Nondestructive edits become permanent once the final mix is recorded to disk or if you save an alternative version of the sound file. But the original source files are always preserved as separate sound files. The only drawback is that you fill up more disk space since you are saving multiple, separate sound files. Of course, if you ever need to go back to the original and make different edits, you'll be glad you gave up the disk space.

Most multitrack recording and editing software includes both destructive and nondestructive editing capabilities. Many professional sound editors feature effects plug-ins that can be applied to a soundtrack for previewing and are written to disk only after you mix-down the multitrack session. Use nondestructive editing when you are deleting regions of a sound file you may want to save or when you are experimenting with different effects. Again, with nondestructive editing you can always go back to the original sound file and try a new edit or effect.

If you are in the final mastering stages of preparing your mono or stereo audio files for the Web or for CD reproduction, you may want to use destructive editing. Destructive editing is also an effective means of preserving disk space because you can delete large unwanted regions of an audio file. Destructive editing can also be used for rudimentary enhancements such as normalization and gain change or for permanently writing effects to disk when your software plug-in capabilities are limited (real-time effects previewing is RAM-intensive and requires lots of system resources).

This caveat applies to all digital effects. A good rule is to always use a little less effect than you think is necessary. In fact, when the effect starts to sound just about right, try reducing it by 50%.

Reverb

Reverberation is the natural return of sound reflecting off the surrounding environment, such as a wall or a hard reflective surface. The returned sound enters the ear just a fraction of a second after the initial sound. Reverb, in the form of hundreds and thousands of small reflections, adds a pleasant warmth and richness to a sound.

Reverberation is analogous to shading in graphic imaging and photography. Adding a drop shadow behind an object gives an image three-dimensional depth and richness. Similarly, adding reverb and delay effects to an audio file give it three-dimensional richness. Reverb and delay create a sense of physical space and simulate the direction and distance for a particular sound source.

Modern music, as well as film and television audio production, rely heavily on the use of artificial or synthesized reverb to simulate the effect of recording on an old-time sound stage with cathedral-like echoes and reverberation. Besides its use as a "sweetener," artificial reverb is used by sound designers to simulate the natural reverberation of different environments such as a hallway or an underground parking lot.

Generally, when you record a sound file, the recording is captured in a studio environment or a room with little to no reverb of its own. However, our ears are accustomed to hearing artificial reverb in film and television sounds. In such mediums, the effects are colored or enhanced to give the sound the appropriate ambience to match the environment on the screen. For example, a recording engineer might record an actor's voice-over in a studio for a scene filmed in a large stairwell. The sound designer then adds reverberation to the "dry" voice-over before the final soundtrack is mastered to film. Similarly, with web audio, to match the characteristics of real-world environments you may need to add reverb, echo, or other effects to your sound files.

Different software packages allow you to add effects in a variety of ways. For example, SoundEdit Pro has a preset list of effects, including reverb, delay, chorus, and equalization. Professional editing applications allow you to import third-party plug-ins and apply real-time nondestructive effects, such as preview, apply, and mix-down, without permanently altering the original sound file.

Keep the reverb consistent

If you use reverb to simulate the richness of a sound produced in a stairwell or an echo chamber, remember to apply the same type of reverb to all the sounds in your web soundtrack mix. This maintains consistency and realism in the soundtrack. Just as a skilled artist paints shadows that are consistent with the light source's angle, color, and intensity, the web sound designer should apply the same type of reverb to all the sounds in a particular web site environment.

Figure 4-5. *The SoundEdit 16 Reverb dialog*

To apply an effect using SoundEdit 16, import a sound file and select the region to be edited. Then choose Effects → Reverb. What you see is a dialog window with a slider control that allows you to choose the amount of reverb to add to the selection, as shown in Figure 4-5. Use the descriptive values, which run the spectrum from "Empty Room" to "Outer Space," to get an idea of how much reverb to add.

Delay

Delay is a useful effect for imitating real-world echos created when sound bounces off of a wall or a hard surface. Delay also is effective in adding an interesting twist to an ordinary sound or piece of music. In a music piece, delay applied to an instrument or vocal track adds rhythmic richness and depth. In fact, most pop tunes contain delay effects at some point, especially on the lead vocal tracks.

There are three parameters you need to adjust to apply delay:

- Volume of the delay over time
- Number of times the delay repeats
- Speed or tempo of the delay

When adjusting the volume of the delay, err on the subtle side by making the echoes much lower in volume than the original sound. The exception to this rule is when you're trying to simulate an echo-heavy environment like a canyon or an alleyway.

Adjusting the number of times an echo repeats is important for simulating real-world sound effects or to prevent a music mix from becoming too cluttered with repetitive delays. Generally, you want to set the delay parameter to repeat between two and three times before it fades to silence.

When adding delay to an instrument track in a piece of music, it is essential to calibrate or adjust the tempo of the delay to match the tempo of the music or beat.

To add delay to your sound using SoundEdit 16, simply choose Effects → Delay. The Delay dialog, shown in Figure 4-6, gives you two options. Apply the option that sounds best for your particular purpose. Click on the delay button to process the file. When finished, audition the sound and listen to the difference.

Pitch shift

The Pitch shift effect alters both the pitch and duration of a sound file by recalculating the length of the sound file, as shown in Figure 4-7. If you raise the pitch of a sound clip, it recalculates the length of the sound file, making the duration and disk size of the sound file smaller. To prevent a sound from changing in duration—such as

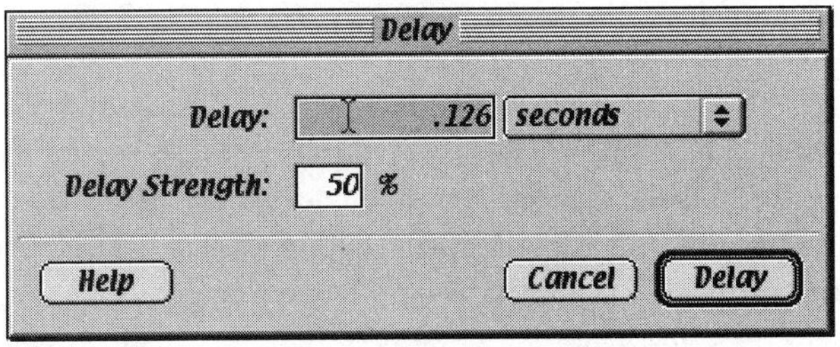

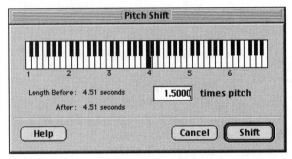

Figure 4-6. *The SoundEdit 16 Delay dialog*

when editing a sound clip for a music mix or a film mix where a particular sound is tied to an event—you can check the "time correction" or "preserve duration" button when pitch-shifting. Most professional editors such as Pro Tools and Sound Forge feature time-corrected pitch shift; SoundEdit 16 does not.

Figure 4-7. *Pitch shift condenses or speeds up the selected region to raise the pitch*

Pitch shift is a creative tool for altering or transforming a sound to create entirely new sounds; it is also a musical tool to lower or raise a passage of music to another key. Many recording engineers use pitch shift with precision to correct musical passages and vocal or instrument tracks that are slightly off pitch by a note or semi-tone.

By transforming a sound with pitch shift you can change the personality of your sound, making it deeper and more ominous, or higher, squeakier, and more comic. Brian Meyers, a former lead sound designer at Living Books in San Francisco, used pitch-shifting to get the professional sound he needed for a particular project. Meyers was working on a multimedia version of the Berenstain Bears books and was able to effectively use pitch shift to achieve authentic character voices. Instead of having the voice-over artists read in childlike voices, the producers recorded the actors' natural voices and performed pitch shift on the recordings to create appropriate voices for the baby bears. This case is a perfect example of using what is necessary and nothing more. In a world of digital effects where millions of possibilities exist, it is tempting to throw lots of effects into a project. "Less is more" is usually a good guideline.

Audition first and often

All digital processing lets you listen to a modified file and decide whether to keep the changes. It is a good idea to listen to each change before moving on. Audition an altered sound file right after it has been processed, and then choose undo and listen to the old version. Keep toggling between redo and undo to compare versions. If you have added too much reverb, or not enough, it is easy at this point to go back and reprocess the sound file.

Part of becoming a good sound "designer" is listening and learning which sounds are best in which applications. Practice often, until your ears are satisfied with the result. You cannot know which combinations will yield the sound you want until you try them out and listen to the differences firsthand. This is how the ear learns what sounds good and how you learn to recreate the sound the next time.

Closeup: The B.B. King Sessions

The world of recording and editing presents many unique challenges to sound designers. Many different techniques are used to produce some of the sounds you hear. Consider this question: What do you do when a client hands you a stack of audio tapes recorded over the past thirty years in different studios and in live concert venues and asks you to blend these various recordings to create a consistent feel as if they were recorded at the same place and time? Reid Ridgway, chief sound designer and recording engineer for C.S. Audio Visual (*http://www.csaudio.com*), conquered this challenge to produce a critically acclaimed soundtrack for MCA Records: *On the Road With B.B. King: An Interactive Autobiography with the King of the Blues.*

First off, you should know that designing sound for the Web is a lot like designing sound for CD-ROMs. In both mediums sound designers are often faced with the task of integrating mixed quality audio source material into a seamless, digital, highly compressed interactive soundtrack.

During the course of the B. B. King project, Reid was asked to blend a large archive of taped interviews into a seamless interactive audio biography. The project was a great challenge because of the wide range of recording quality between the different audio master tapes. Moreover, the final output stage required a reduction to an 8-bit 22 kHz mono audio format. A few of the taped interviews were in pristine condition but most were not. Most of the interviews were made in less than optimal recording environments, such as impromptu situations. Many were also recorded in an era when recording technology could not match today's sound reproduction. Adding to the challenge, many of the interviews were recorded outside with traffic noise and different equalization and room tone from one recording to the next. For example, Reid had to blend an outdoor interview of B.B. King with traffic and barking noises in the background with an interview recorded in a professional studio with high-quality microphones and sound deadening acoustic foam. The objective was to play the two interviews in consecutive order on the same screen of the CD-ROM and have them sound as if they were recorded in the same environment.

First, Reid tried to improve the quality of the outdoor recording by removing the tape hiss and background noises. However, he quickly realized he couldn't remove enough of the background noise.

After experimenting with several solutions, Reid decided the best option was to degrade the quality of the recording that was made in a professional studio to match the poorer quality recording captured outside. In this case, degrading the quality of one sound to match the other sound produced the best result. You will find that sometimes it's necessary to break the rules and use creative solutions to produce a consistent soundtrack with a unified sound from beginning to end.

Reid started degrading the studio recording by adding background noises of traffic and barking dogs acquired from The Hollywood Edge sound effects collection. Then he played the high-quality version through a speaker placed outside and re-recorded it so the EQ, would have the same characteristic as the outdoor interview. To further match the EQ he placed the mic about the same distance away from the loud speaker as the mic was from B.B. King during the outdoor interview.

$\rightarrow$

After achieving a consistent EQ sound using the outdoor speaker technique, Reid added some foley sound effects such as footsteps, door sounds, and an old plumbing clank and leak for ambiance. Also added were some of B.B. King's live recordings from the era. These where all blended to create a uniform background music to the final audio mix. In the particular scene Reid was working on, B.B. was talking about his experience at the Fillmore concert hall in San Francisco. Reid created a feel as if you were outside the concert hall. Then eventually as the graphics showed B.B. King entering the Fillmore, he switched over to the other recording to make any lingering differences in their sound characteristics less perceptible and the change more plausible.

To change the pitch of a sound in SoundEdit 16, select the region of the sound you want to alter, then select Effects → Pitch Shift. The Pitch Shift window displays a piano keyboard, the original time duration of the sound file, versus the previewed length of the sound file, and the multiple of the pitch shift. To preview and select the pitch shift of the sound region, click on any key of the piano then click the Shift button.

Bender

The bender effect allows you to adjust the pitch of a sound by an amount that can vary over the duration of the sound file. The result is a sound that seems to gradually raise or lower in pitch. Applying this effect also alters the length of the sound. If you want the entire sound file to uniformly shift pitches, it is better to use the pitch-shift effect. However, if you want the sound to alter pitch in a variety of ways over time, experiment with the bender effect.

With SoundEdit 16's bender effect, you can use a pitch adjustment line to represent how the pitch will be altered at each point in time along the waveform (as shown in Figure 4-8). The farther you move a handle away from the zero point, the greater the pitch changes. The scale that lies on the far left of the bender dialog box indicates the relative change in pitch. If you drag the handle in the positive direction, the pitch of the sound will be higher. Drag the handle in the negative direction, and the pitch will be lower. The range selections determine the amount of variation in the pitch shift. The options are 1 whole step, 1 octave, or 2 octaves.

Use the "1 whole step" option to create a vibrato effect, where the sound alters up and down a small amount between the original pitch. A step is the distance in pitch between successive notes of the diatonic scale, such as the distance between C and D. A half-step is the distance between a note and its sharp, such as the interval from C to C#. Generally, a half-step or whole step difference is a subtle shift in pitch as opposed to a one-octave (12-step) shift.

In Figure 4-9, the bender effect is used to alter the sound between +1/2 step and –1/2 step and create what is referred to as a "vibrato" effect. However, you could use "1 octave" or "2 octaves" to produce a more dynamic effect. Experiment with all three options as you search for the sound you want to achieve.

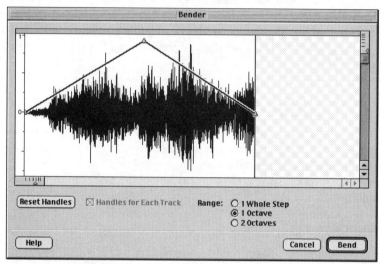

Figure 4-8. *The bender effect, often used for cartoon sounds, changes the pitch up then down 1 octave across the selected region.*

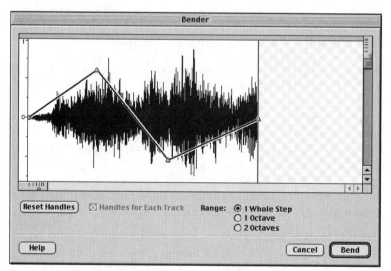

Figure 4-9. *Use the bender effect to create a vibrato effect by altering the pitch between +1/2 step and –1/2 step.*

Backwards

The backwards, or "reverse," effect is self-explanatory. This effect simply takes the selected waveform and flips it backwards so it plays in reverse, as shown in Figure 4-10. This effect is used by professional sound designers to add a special effect to a soundtrack or to generate new source material from existing sound files in their collection.

Although used infrequently, the backwards effect can result in some pretty wild and interesting sounds. You can use this effect to make voices sound like they are caught in an alternate reality or are in a dream state. You can also use short sound clips of speech or music that are one or two seconds in length and apply the backwards effect to create unusual, original sound effects.

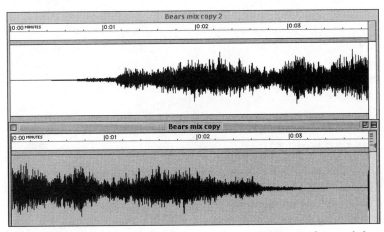

Figure 4-10. *The backwards effect simply creates a copy of the waveform and plays it backwards*

Web mastering: optimizing sound files for Internet broadcasting

Mastering refers to the process of preparing a group of sound files (i.e., music tracks of a CD) for final delivery in one uniform manner, medium, and level of quality. This means that each sound file has little unwanted noise and shares the same relative decibel (volume) levels and equalization characteristics with the rest of the audio files.

The practical reason for mastering groups of sound files is to prevent people from having to continually adjust the volume and equalization

Professional encoding services

Do you have a few more files to encode than your band's last live recording? Perhaps you've been asked to encode your company's entire archive of audio and video content. Don't worry, there are a few people in the industry you can turn to when you have to post hundreds or thousands of audio and video files. Loudeye is one of them.

Loudeye, formerly encoding.com, specializes in helping companies manage, encode, and stream large quantities of audio and video content (*http://www.loudeye.com*). Systems Engineer for Loudeye, Aaron Olson, contributed several web mastering tips for this chapter. So if you feel overwhelmed and need professional services, you have options!

settings of their sound system or computer each time a new song or sound passage is played. For example, it is generally undesirable to have one song where the bass guitar frequencies stand out in the mix and another song where the bass frequencies are relatively quiet. Nor would you want to have one voice-over track significantly louder than the following voice-over track. Mastering helps to balance each song and sound file so the mix or web soundtrack is consistent. Mastering also disguises the sonic variation between songs that may have been recorded in different environments or recording studios.

Mastering for the Web is the final optimization process before converting sound files to their respective web formats. The main web mastering tools you'll work with are normalization, compression, and equalization. Achieved with a sound editor, normalization helps guarantee that your files share the same relative loudness and optimal dynamic range for web conversion. Additional compression of the sound file with a compressor or peak limiter effect ensures the highest fidelity when converting to low-bandwidth formats with reduced bit-depths and sampling rates. Equalization (EQ) ensures the tonal consistency and quality between all the sound files you will incorporate into your web site.

Normalization: maximizing the dynamic range

If you are working with prerecorded material, the next step is to *normalize* your sound files before converting them to web formats. Normalization maximizes the bit-depth information available and provides consistent volume levels across all your web pages. It's important to maintain volume consistency among different sound clips; there's nothing quite as jarring as experiencing dramatic shifts in volume when clicking through a web site. Normalization corrects this problem by raising all sounds to one uniform standard amplification level.

Normalization raises the overall amplitude or loudness level of a sound file to the point where the loudest peak is just below clipping, while also boosting the entire signal evenly, including the noise, as shown in Figure 4-11.

Normalization makes maximum use of the dynamic range within the bit-depth of a digital audio signal, but it does not effect the dynamic range of the source audio. In other words, the dynamic range between softest and loudest material in the sound file is unaffected after normalizing, but the sound file is louder overall.

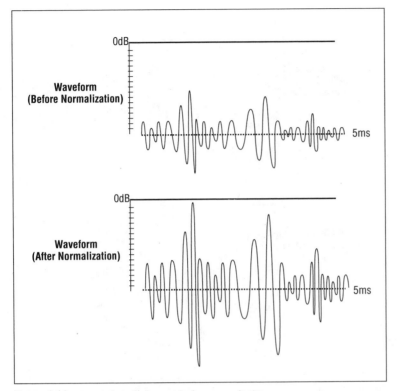

Figure 4-11. *A waveform before and after normalization*

Using a *compressor* or "look-ahead" *peak limiter* while normalizing your sound files produces better results than simple normalization alone, as shown in Figure 4-12. Compressors and peak limiters reduce the highest peaks or waveforms in your sound files, thereby allowing you to further boost the volume of softer sounds. Increasing the volume of the waveforms within a sound file allows you to maximize the dynamic range when converting to low bit-rate web codecs.

To normalize a file, SoundEdit 16 (or the editor you are using) examines the entire waveform, or a selection of the sound file, and finds the highest peak that any one sound makes in the given selection. The normalization dialog box, shown in Figure 4-13, then calculates the distance from that highest peak upwards towards the zero decibel (0dB) level. This distance is known as "headroom." The 0dB level is the highest level that sound can go in the digital world without "peaking the meters" and causing massive distortion in the sound. Remember not to confuse digital distortion with analog distortion.

Three reasons to normalize your sound files

- First, normalization maximizes the bit-depth information available by giving a sound a louder overall presence.

- Second, it provides volume consistency across multiple web pages or sound files.

- The third reason for normalization is to prevent distortion when encoding a stereo file into a single-channel mono file. If you are converting stereo files into low-bandwidth mono files, you should normalize to roughly 70% of the signal level of your input source. If you do not normalize a stereo file during or prior to its conversion to a mono file, you may experience digital distortion in your output file when the signals are combined and shoot above the maximum 0db level.

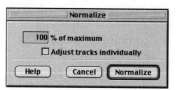

Figure 4-13. *In the Normalization window you can select the amount of normalization you want. Generally, 95% is a safe number for encoding to web formats.*

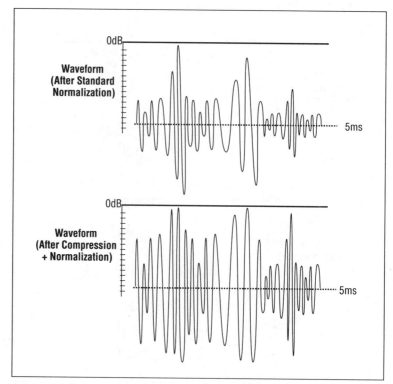

Figure 4-12. *A standard normalized waveform (top) and a compressed and normalized waveform (bottom)*

Analog distortion may sound good at times, producing interesting harmonics and tones such as those heard in classic rock-and-roll guitar solos. But digital distortion produces clicks and pops and nearly always sounds terrible.

When normalizing an audio file, SoundEdit 16 knows to avoid digital distortion and therefore will not make any sound greater than the 0dB cut-off point. Once it calculates the distance between the highest waveform peak and the 0dB cut-off point, SoundEdit 16 determines the number between the two and increases the rest of the sound file's waveforms by that amount. The overall effect increases all the levels equally without creating digital distortion at any point in the selection.

You can normalize an entire sound file or just a portion of it. To normalize part of a sound file, highlight only a specific region of the waveform. If no region is highlighted, SoundEdit 16 normalizes the entire file.

You can also set the amount of normalization you want based on a percentage of the maximum (100%). To be safe, you should try normalizing your files at 95% or –3dB below zero to allow for extra headroom, as shown in Figure 4-14. Flash and RealAudio, for example, have a tendency to distort certain sound files or frequencies that are normalized above 95%.

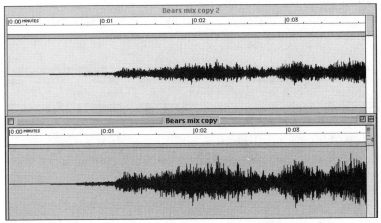

Figure 4-14. *The top audio file represents the audio waveform before normalization and the bottom waveform represents the audio file after normalization (set to 95% or –3dB below 0).*

Normalization is an important step to achieving high-quality web audio. By maximizing your dynamic range, your audio files will sound dramatically better when they are reduced to 8-bit sounds for the Web, especially for analog modem delivery. The dynamic range of lower bit-depth audio files is extremely limited, so softer sounds and quiet decays cannot be completely reproduced in an 8-bit sound clip. If you want the nuances of your sound design to be heard in low bit-depth audio, they cannot be subtle; faint decays and soft sounds simply will not come through.

Compression: reducing sound peaks and spikes

Using simple normalization alone to maximize the dynamic range has several limitations and drawbacks. Because the normalization process calculates only the available headroom, you are limited by the proximity of the loudest peak to the maximum 0dB cut-off point, as shown in Figure 4-15.

Generally, all sound files have a few short volume peaks or spikes, whether they are from a loud guitar solo section or a particular voice

Compressing film sound

When encoding for the web, audio that has either too strong or too weak a signal will have a negative impact on the output quality of the particular file. Some content, especially film content, uses extreme dynamic ranges to accentuate the emotion created by the content. Unfortunately, this dynamic causes negative results when encoded, causing previously unheard noise in the quiet parts and distortion in the loud parts. We suggest using some mild compression in order to help the encoder best deal with the source audio.

passage that is louder than adjacent sounds. Simple normalization is
not effective if there is already a peak just under the maximum 0dB
cut-off point. You can use a peak limiter or the amplify/gain process
in SoundEdit 16 to further maximize the fidelity of audio playback
over the web. A peak limiter is a dynamics processor that limits or
prevents signals from peaking above a specified amplitude level. The
average levels of your sound file can be raised several dB beyond the
regular normalization level by using a limiter to compress the highest volume peaks. Likewise, you can use an amplify/gain command
to reduce the level of a particular spike in your waveform.

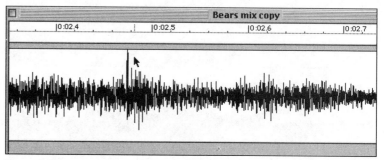

Figure 4-15. *A sound file with the amplitude peak going to the 0dB cut-off level*

By reducing these identified peaks, the entire level of the file can be
raised higher before reaching the 0dB cut-off, resulting in a higher
average signal level. You can achieve this function manually, by visually examining the sound file and locating and reducing individual
peaks using the amplify/gain command.

You can also use a peak limiter plug-in, such as Wave's L1 Maximizer, to reduce the amplitude peaks in your sound files. The L1
Maximizer works by compressing all sounds that peak above the
threshold setting of the dB level that you specify. The lower the
threshold point, the more the sound is compressed. Generally 3dB to
9dB of compression adds clarity and brilliance to the sound and produces an overall effect that is pleasing to the ears. However, be careful not to overcompress your sound files. Too much compression
(over 12dB) may make your sound files seem unnatural and "harsh"
to your listeners' ears.

Equalization: customizing your sound

Equalization is one of the most powerful tools you can use to enhance
audio quality. Through the process of equalization, you can increase
or amplify any specified range of frequencies within that spectrum.
Equalizing files destined for the Web can help compensate for lost or
reduced frequencies resulting from the drastic file-size reduction and

conversion process used to prepare sound files for analog modem delivery. For instance, sound files formatted for 28.8 or 56 Kbps modems lose most of their high-end frequencies. Most web formats reduce the sample rate, limiting the use of high frequencies.

Figure 4-16 illustrates an EQ boost in the low-end bass frequencies between 75 Hz and 110 Hz and the high-range vocal frequencies between 2,000 Hz and 7,000 Hz to add brightness to a mix and make the vocals more clear after web conversion.

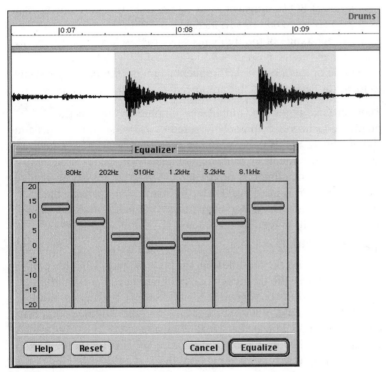

Figure 4-16. *Equalization boost of the 75–200 Hz and the 2,000–7,000 Hz ranges*

Often your final web audio sounds better if you eliminate high frequencies first. For instance, if you are reducing the sample rate to 22 Kbps, cut the frequencies over 10 Kbps. Frequencies above 10 Kbps create aliasing and other unwanted distortion artifacts when the conversion process tries to represent them and cannot.

There are two parameters you can specify to alter the equalization of a sound: the amplitude level and the bandwidth range of the frequencies. The amplitude level determines the loudness of a given range of frequencies. The bandwidth (usually from 200 to 500 Hz) determines the range of frequencies being amplified or reduced.

Three reasons to equalize your sound files

During the mastering process, equalization can enhance your audio and compensate for unbalanced sound levels in three different ways.

- First, equalization can be used to adjust the overall bass, midrange, or treble of a sound file.

- Second, it can be used to make the overall bass, midrange, and treble more uniform from song to song or from sound file to sound file.

- Third, it can be used to eliminate certain frequencies that cause distortion, or conversely to boost frequencies that get reduced when your audio file is encoded for the web.

Generally, you are never boosting or reducing one single frequency but instead a range of frequencies.

You may have used an equalizer on your home or professional sound systems. Equalizers generally have sliding levers, known as faders, that represent the different ranges of frequencies between 20 Hz (low) and 20,000 Hz (high)—the normal hearing range of a human. Home sound system EQs generally feature five to ten faders or bands of EQ starting at the 50 to 120 Hz range on up to the 8,000 Hz to 10,000 Hz range. A professional equalizer features 20 or more separate bands of EQ starting as low as 20 Hz to 60 Hz and going as high as 16,000 Hz to 20,000 Hz. To increase, or boost, the relative amplitude of each range of the frequency spectrum, select the corresponding fader and move it up until you are satisfied with the relative amplitude or loudness of that frequency range. Likewise, if you want to lower or cut sound in that frequency range, slide the fader down.

There are two types of EQ interfaces: graphic and parametric. A graphic equalizer is commonly featured on home sound systems and "boom" boxes and is the easiest and most popular form of equalization. A graphic equalizer contains multiple sliding levers or faders along a horizontal line that represents the different ranges of frequencies between 20 Hz and 20,000 Hz. To increase or decrease the amplitude of each frequency range, move the fader up or down in a +10dB or −10dB range for best results.

A graphic equalizer is the easiest EQ interface to use especially for beginners, but it's the least flexible for professionals. Unlike a parametric EQ where the frequency bandwidth of each knob can be adjusted, the faders on a graphic EQ affect a predetermined bandwidth. For example, a 300 Hz fader on a five-band home sound system EQ generally boosts the signal along a tapered arch starting at 200 Hz on the low end, 300 Hz at the top, and 400 Hz on the high end. This means that the fader is boosting a 200 Hz–wide range of frequencies. Professionals demand more accuracy for precision adjustments and thus tend to use parametric EQs instead.

Because it requires a fairly deep understanding of audio theory, a parametric equalizer is used primarily in professional applications. Unlike a graphic equalizer, a parametric equalizer allows you to specify the desired bandwidth range (50 Hz, 100 Hz, 500 Hz, etc.) and the exact frequency (256 Hz, 1,350 Hz, 4,560 Hz, etc.) of the EQ setting before boosting or reducing the amount of gain. Parametric equalizers feature several twisting knobs for adjusting bandwidth and gain instead of a horizontal row of faders. Certain applications require boosting or reducing a more narrow or more broad range of frequencies than a graphic equalizer allows for, making a parametric equalizer ideal in these cases.

Using EQ to enhance audio

During the mastering process, equalization can enhance your audio and compensate for unbalanced sound levels in two different ways. First, equalization can be used to adjust the overall bass, mid-range, or treble of a sound file. Second, it can be used to make the overall bass, mid-range, and treble more uniform from song to song or from sound file to sound file.

To apply EQ to a sound file, first listen to it to see if it contains one or more of the three most common EQ imbalances. The first is a "muddy" or muffled sound with too much bass or "low end" in the 100 to 800 Hz range. The second is an irritating or "honky" sound from too much mid-range frequencies in the 1,000 to 5,000 Hz range. The last is a dull sound from not enough bright, high-end frequencies in the 5,000 to 10,000 Hz range.

Use equalization to "fatten" your sound by boosting the low bass frequencies in the 40 to 200 Hz range, or conversely to clean up a "muddy" sound file by reducing the low frequencies in the 300 Hz range. Likewise, you can reduce the harsh or "honky" mid-range tones by reducing sound in the 1,000 to 5,000 Hz range. Lastly, you can increase the brilliance and clarity of a dull sound by boosting its high frequencies in the 5,000 to 10,000 Hz range, or to avoid unpleasant, sharp piercing sounds, reduce super-high frequencies above 8,000 Hz.

Removing sibilance

Before you've completed the equalization process, it's a good idea to remove some of the unneeded higher frequencies. For example, you may have noticed that your voice-over contains many "ssss" sounds and short P's and T's. This is referred to as *sibilance*. The occurrences of sibilance can be lessened by cutting the levels of the higher frequencies, as shown in Figure 4-17, or by using a De-esser effects plug-in.

Reducing sibilance with EQ by cutting a selected range of high frequencies should be a last resort effort. This technique decreases the selected range of high frequencies across the entire sound file producing a more dull sound. To avoid sibilance problems, deal with the issue during the recording process. Run your incoming signal through a De-esser digital processor or plug-in to remove sibilance before the audio is written to disk or work with your voice talent to produce less sibilance.

Cut the noise: Equalization for low bandwidth

The audio encoding process accentuates background noises that you may not have noticed in the original audio source. Generally, the two areas to focus on are the highest 1/4 and lowest 1/4 of your audio frequencies.

The higher frequencies (above 10,000Hz) tend to carry a lot of the background noise, such as hiss and scratchiness, in an audio file. Meanwhile, the lower audio frequencies (below 75Hz) tend to carry a lot of the rumble that can occur from background noises such as H/VAC systems, or the microphone rumble caused by wind.

To correct this problem, eliminate the low-end frequencies between 20 and 75Hz and the highest frequencies above 10,000Hz, using the equalization faders in your sound editor (i.e., high-pass low-pass filters).

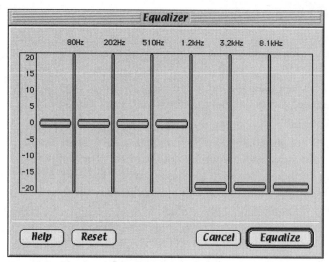

Figure 4-17. *The Equalizer window allows you to reduce or cut-off high-end frequencies with the 1.2, 3.2, and 8.1 kHz faders.*

Using low-pass and high-pass filters

You may find it useful to use the equalizer as a filter that removes all sound in frequencies above a certain point. This is referred to as a low-pass filter. This process allows all the frequencies lower than a number you specify to "pass" through, while any sound above the target frequency is "filtered" out. Use the low-pass filter to eliminate hiss entirely or to wholly remove sounds in the upper frequencies. You can create a low-pass filter by simply sliding the high-end frequency faders to the –20dB levels.

Alternatively, there may be situations where you need to use a high-pass filter. With a high-pass filter, you effectively remove everything below your specified cut-off frequency and allow anything higher to pass through. This is useful in removing lower bass sounds, such as the rumble of an automobile engine or the sound of a jet plane flying overhead.

To remove lower bass sounds, you can create a high-pass filter by taking the sliders below 510 Hz and moving them down to the –20dB level, as shown in Figure 4-18. Again, these are only starting points. You may wish to move some faders to –20db and keep some at –10dB, or whatever combination sounds right to you. As with any process, trial and error is how you find the sound you want. Try boosting or cutting frequencies in order to hear the difference each movement of the fader makes. Just remember to choose undo before you try a new equalization or effect, so that the previous change isn't added onto the new one you're trying out.

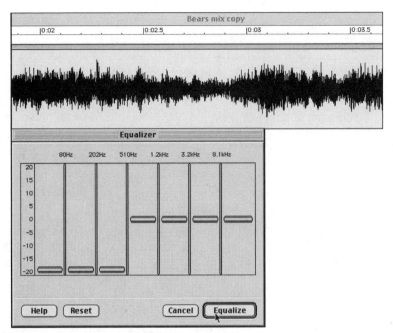

Figure 4-18. *The Equalizer window allows you to reduce or cut-off low-end frequencies with the 80, 202, and 510 Hz faders.*

Summary

In this chapter, you learned how to prepare, enhance, and master your sound files for optimal playback over the web. The first part of this book gave you the basics of sound design, recording, and editing. Now you are ready to start integrating audio into your web pages. The second part of this book explains the technologies that makes streaming audio work and covers the most popular formats used for web delivery.

Save time: Use all-in-one batch conversion tools

Batch conversion tools save time and prevent human error by automating the mastering and encoding process for multiple audio files. Two of the most popular tools for mastering and batch conversion are Wave Convert Pro and BarbaBatch. Both applications convert multiple audio files into various sample rates, word lengths, channels (stereo/mono), and file types (MP3, RealAudio, QuickTime, Shockwave, AIFF, SDII, and .WAV), while retaining optimal sound quality.

Wave Convert Pro from Waves runs on Macintosh and Windows 98, and can be purchased at *http://www.waves.com*).

BarbaBatch runs on Macintosh, and can be purchased at *http://www.macsourcery.com/web/BarbaBatch/barba-batch.html.*

CHAPTER FIVE

INTRODUCTION TO STREAMING MEDIA

I nternet streaming media changed the Web as we knew it—changed it from a static text- and graphics-based medium into a multimedia experience populated by sound and moving pictures. Now streaming media is poised to become the de facto global media broadcasting and distribution standard, incorporating all other media, including television, radio, and film. The low cost, convenience, worldwide reach, and technical simplicity of using one global communications standard makes web broadcasting irresistible to media publishers, broadcasters, corporations, and individuals. Businesses and individuals once denied access to such powerful means of communication are now using the Web to connect with people all over the world.

The remarkable technology that allows a web site visitor to click on a button and seconds later listen to a sporting event, tradeshow keynote, or CD-quality music is the result of a rather simple but powerful technical innovation—*streaming media*. Streaming works by first compressing a digital audio file and then breaking it into small packets, which are sent, one after another, over the Internet. When the packets reach their destination (the requesting user), they are decompressed and reassembled into a form that can be played by the user's system. To maintain the illusion of seamless play, the packets are "buffered" so a number of them are downloaded to the user's machine before playback. As those buffered or preloaded packets play, more packets are being downloaded and queued up for playback. However, when the stream of packets gets too slow (due to network congestion), the client audio player has nothing to play, and you get the all-too-familiar drop-out that every user has encountered.

In this chapter
• Streaming protocols
• Streaming media formats
• Selecting the right format
• Summary

Streaming protocols

The big breakthrough that enabled the streaming revolution was the adoption of a new Internet protocol called the User Datagram Protocol (UDP) and new encoding techniques that compressed audio files into extremely small packets of data. UDP made streaming media feasible by transmitting data more efficiently than previous protocols from the host server over the Internet to the client player or end listener. More recent protocols such as the RealTime Streaming Protocol (RTSP) are making the transmission of data even more efficient.

UDP and RTSP are ideal for audio broadcasting since they place a high priority on continuous streaming rather than on absolute document security. Unlike TCP and HTTP transmission, when a UDP audio packet drops out, the server keeps sending information, causing only a brief glitch instead of a huge gap of silence. TCP, on the other hand, keeps trying to resend the lost packet before sending anything further, causing greater delays and breakups in the audio broadcast.

Prior to UDP and RTSP transmission, data was sent over the Web primarily via TCP and HTTP. TCP transmission, in contrast to UDP and RTSP transmission, is designed to reliably transfer text documents, email, and HTML web pages over the Internet while enforcing maximum reliability and data integrity rather than timeliness. Since HTTP transmission is based on TCP, it is also not well-suited for transmitting multimedia presentations that rely on time-based operation or for large-scale broadcasting.

Later in the chapter, you will learn why protocols are important. Some streaming technologies such as RealAudio and Windows Media utilize dedicated servers that support superior UDP and RTSP transmission. Other formats such as Shockwave, Flash, MIDI, QuickTime, and Beatnik are primarily designed to stream from a standard HTTP web server. While these formats are cheaper and often easier to use since they do not require the installation of a new server, they are typically not used in professional broadcasting situations that require the delivery of hundreds or thousands of simultaneous streams.

HTTP streaming is thus referred to as pseudo-streaming, since technically it is possible to stream via HTTP. But it is much more likely to cause major packet drop-outs, and it cannot deliver nearly the same amount of streams as UDP and RTSP transmission. Herein lies the difference between most low-end solutions and more professional broadcasting solutions that require dedicated servers and extra bandwidth and server capacity.

Lossy compression

Regardless of the advances in UDP and RTSP transmission protocols, streaming media would not be possible without the rapid innovation in encoding algorithms or codecs that compress and decompress audio and video data. Uncompressed audio files are huge. One minute of playback of a CD-quality stereo audio file requires 10 MB of data, approximately enough disk space to capture a small library of books or a 200-page web site.

Standard modem speed connections—including cable modems and xDSL systems—do not have the capacity to deliver pure, uncompressed CD-quality 16-bit, 44.1 kHz audio. In order to stream across the limited bandwidth of the Web, audio has to be compressed and optimized with *codecs*, which are compression-decompression encoding algorithms. In general, compression schemes can be classified as "lossy" and "lossless."

Lossy compression schemes reduce file size by discarding some amount of data during the encoding process before it is sent over the Internet. Once received on the client side, the codec attempts to reconstruct the information that was lost or discarded. The benefit to this sort of compression lies in the smaller file size that results from discarding the "lost" information. The JPEG image format uses lossy compression to sample an image and discard unnecessary color information. Similarly, lossy audio compression discards frequencies on the high and low end of the spectrum and attempts to locate and remove unnecessary audio data. The technique is often referred to as "perceptual encoding" since the user is unlikely to notice the absence of this information. Lossy compression offers file savings on the order of 10:1.

Since small file size is so important on the Internet, practically all of the formats we're interested in employ lossy compression. Here's how it works. First, the client player decompresses the audio file as it downloads to your computer. Then it fills in the missing information according to the instructions set by the codec. To illustrate why lossy compression is so crucial, consider the phrase, "Now is the time for all good men to come to the aid of their country". One way to compress this would simply be to remove all the vowels and spaces: "Nwsthtmfrllgdmntcmtthdfthrcntry".

That cuts the message from 71 characters to 31, a 56% file savings, but of course our compressed message is unintelligible. Imagine that our codec, however, has appropriate rules for decompressing this message with minimal distortion. The conversion likely wouldn't be perfect, but it would be good enough to understand the message, something like, "Now's tha ti'm for oll gudm en to com to the aad of their country".

This is exactly what happens with lossy audio compression. The compressed file is unintelligible to the listener; the decompressed file is intelligible but of a lower quality than the original.

For example, a RealAudio speech file encoded from a standard AIFF or WAV file is generally one-tenth the size of the original file after encoding. To reduce that file's size, first you preserve the integrity of the 1,000 Hz to 4,000 Hz frequency spectrum of the human voice and then discard the frequencies above and below those ranges. By eliminating the unnecessary low- and high-end frequencies, the encoder is able to reduce the file size while maintaining speech intelligibility. It should be noted that speech tends to have aural characteristics (sound) that extend into the 7,000 Hz range. When the area between 4,000 Hz and 7,000 Hz is reduced or removed entirely, encoded speech will sound intelligible, but it may lose clarity and sound unnatural. Furthermore, since some voices and sounds often reach into even higher frequency ranges, lossy compression and encoding can result in dull, muted, or abrasive sounds.

Lossless compression

In contrast, *lossless compression* squeezes data into smaller packets of information without permanently discarding any of the data. Instead of permanently discarding information, lossless compression discards it temporarily but provides a "map" with which the codec can reconstruct the original file. Lossless compression results in superior audio quality, but lower compression rates.

In the lossy example, our codec had some general rules for reconstructing the message—basically to add vowels and spaces in order to form English words. It wasn't perfect because it didn't know which English words to choose, and it wasn't always sure where one word ended and the next began.

Lossless codecs, on the other hand, are perfect. To reconstruct our message perfectly, however, would mean having a much more sophisticated set of rules. A lossless text codec would have to reproduce not only words but sensible phrases. It would have to be able to break words correctly. And it would have to have a mastery of the English language's inconsistent spelling patterns. It would in fact be, as the computer scientists say, a nontrivial endeavor.

The same goes for lossless audio codecs. They are difficult to develop (and thus expensive to license), they require substantial computing power on the user's machine, and the file savings are not as great as with lossy compression. Sadly enough, it appears that for the current time, lossy compression is necessary for knocking large audio files down to Internet-appropriate size. The good news is that lossy compression schemes are becoming more advanced, and over time the differences will become less and less noticeable to the human ear.

Now that we have discussed lossy and lossless compression and the types of protocols that enable the efficient delivery of compact audio files across the Internet, let's review the audio formats available on the market. Most of these formats will be discussed in greater detail in the rest of the book.

Streaming media formats

There are currently more than a dozen formats for streaming audio over the Web, from widely used formats, such as RealNetworks' RealAudio, streaming MP3, Macromedia's Flash and Director Shockwave, Microsoft's Windows Media, and Apple's QuickTime, to more recent entries that synchronize sounds with events on a web page, such as RealMedia G2 with SMIL and Beatnik's Rich Music Format (RMF). Also included are a host of downloadable formats, including Liquid Audio, MP3, MIDI, WAV, and AU.

While the high quality of MP3 has sent shockwaves through the recording industry, streaming formats like RealAudio remain the dominant audio technology on the Web right now. Indeed MP3 is being folded into multimedia streaming formats like QuickTime and Windows Media.

Throughout this book, we take an in-depth look at many of the more prevalent streaming formats. However, in this chapter, we will review all the streaming formats on the Web, including Windows Media and QuickTime, which are not featured in later chapters.

RealMedia and RealAudio

RealMedia is the most widely adopted streaming media format on the Web. Its popularity is due in large part to the fact that it was the first streaming technology on the market. But it's popular also because of RealNetworks' laser focus on ease of use, deployment of a wide palette of developer tools, continuous support for the latest multimedia technologies, and support for both Windows and Unix platforms. RealMedia is the format of choice for professionals who want advanced controls for serving, tracking, and managing large numbers of audio streams. RealNetworks has been a trailblazer in making advanced server features, which were once accessible only to those with advanced programming skills, available to the public.

And RealMedia is likely to attract more fans as web developers begin to use the RealSystem G2 and SMIL to stream synchronized multimedia presentations over the Web. G2's major advance is the ability to simultaneously stream multiple media types as separate files instead of as one RealMedia-encoded file. This makes updating multimedia content easier, since you can simply upload one element of a presentation instead of re-encoding the whole media file.

Perhaps the most powerful feature of RealSystem G2 is RealNetworks' server architecture. Broadcasting audio with a dedicated RealServer provides the following advantages over HTTP pseudo-streaming from a standard web server:

Bandwidth negotiation
> Ensures that all users receive the appropriate encoded content for the best audio quality at their available bandwidth, from slower analog modems to faster cable or xDSL connections. RealSystem G2's new SureStream technology is even more efficient than bandwidth negotiation. SureStream can dynamically change data rates midstream to accommodate fluctuating bandwidth.

Robust RTSP transmission
> Detects and compensates for lost packets, maintaining smooth, continuous audio playback—something that HTTP streaming can't deliver.

Splitting
> Allows for splitting and routing the audio signal from one RealServer to other RealServers located at different points across the Internet.

Clustering
> Allows multiple RealServers to be clustered together so they work as a single, multiprocessor machine.

IP multicasting
> Allows all users of a network to listen to a single live stream, making efficient use of network resources. Multicasting avoids delivering numerous simultaneous point-to-point connections by broadcasting one stream to a certain point in the network where other users are requesting the same file. Multicasting is ideal for reducing server load and bandwidth congestion during live broadcasts.

While RealMedia's powerful server-side architecture supports and manages robust streaming to large audiences, this core strength results in limited interactivity. Like Windows Media and other server-side streaming technologies, RealMedia waits for a request from a listener's browser before it begins to stream media files. This helps RealMedia negotiate bandwidth congestion on the fly by sending an appropriate size stream that matches the listener's real bandwidth. But it also produces a significant time gap of a few seconds between the listener's request and the response from the server. This small time gap is inconsequential with long-playing video and audio files, but it prohibits the use of interactive sound effects such as button rollovers, sound transitions from one page to another, and loops that must respond instantaneously to a mouse click.

Thus, RealMedia is inappropriate for high impact presentations with interactive sound effects and loops. Despite significant advancements in RealSystem G2, RealAudio still trails Flash and Director Shockwave when it comes to smooth playback of high-impact interactive multimedia. High-powered interactive media requires a client-side solution such as Flash, Shockwave, or Beatnik.

Windows Media Technologies (Netshow)

Microsoft's Windows Media Technologies for NT/Windows 2000 includes a comprehensive suite of authoring tools and streaming services for delivering audio, video, animation, and other multimedia over the Internet. Windows Media comes with a complete set of tools for encoding and authoring streaming content including Windows Media T.A.G. Author, a utility for arranging media elements along a timeline. Windows Media presentations are played back with the Windows Media Player, which plays most local and streamed media file types including Advanced Streaming Format (Windows' native file format), MPEG, WAV, AVI, QuickTime, and RealAudio/RealVideo. Since Media Player is distributed with Windows, it has widespread distribution.

If you need a Windows NT 4.0–based solution, Windows Media Services offers several advantages:

- The Windows Media Server comes free with unlimited streams with Windows NT Server 4.0 and later.

- It allows for better playback over machines running Windows. To enable smooth multimedia playback over the Web and avoid the problematic issue of cumbersome plug-in downloads altogether, Microsoft is moving towards integrating Windows Media Player, along with Internet Explorer, directly into the Windows operating system.

- Windows Media Server integrates with Microsoft Site Server to enable pay-per-view and pay-per-minute billing capabilities, usage analysis reporting, and personalized ad insertion.

- Tools for tracking behavior are tightly integrated with the Windows NT Event Viewer and Performance Monitor, making it easy

for seasoned NT administrators to manage the Windows Media
Server.

- For multimedia content developers, Microsoft provides helpful
  authoring tools. Creating a slide show of images with synchronized audio can be accomplished by using the Windows Media
  T.A.G. Author.

Compared to RealMedia, however, Windows Media has some serious
drawbacks:

- It runs only on Windows NT/2000. Many developers have
  reported problems with the stability of Windows NT for mission-
  critical applications such as 24-hour live broadcasts. This can be
  a show-stopper for those who demand the stability of Unix or
  Linux servers. In contrast, RealNetworks supports NT as well as
  Linux, FreeBSD, Solaris, and IRIX.

- It does not support Macromedia Flash or the Synchronized Multimedia Integration Language (SMIL) standard, both of which are
  supported by RealNetworks.

There are also some key differences in the way Windows Media and
RealMedia encode and deliver multimedia content. With RealMedia,
you can create multimedia presentations by using the SMIL markup
language to connect various media elements together. These media
elements are encoded as separate files: RealAudio, RealVideo, Real-
Pix, RealText, QuickTime, MPEG, and so on. The RealServer, much
the same way a standard web page is served up and delivered, then
streams the presentation as separate media files held together by
SMIL.

"Since G2 developers are creating multimedia presentations rather
than simply encoding audio or video streams, the format has a new
level of complexity," says Leah Goldberg, G2 media producer for
CMPnet. "However, web developers have long been familiar with the
flexibility and convenience of this approach to media delivery. The
challenge with G2," Goldberg claims, "is working out the timing in
the component RealPix, RealText, and RealFlash files. Since the idea
is to synchronize all the different media elements together, working
out the sub-timing issues within each of the component files can be
quite complex."

In contrast, Windows Media wraps all media elements into one Active
Streaming File (ASF), Microsoft's proprietary streaming media format.
According to Microsoft, with ASF any object can be placed into an
ASF data stream, including audio and video, scripts, ActiveX con-
trols, and HTML documents with T.A.G. Author. This approach, simi-
lar to Flash and Shockwave movies, provides less flexibility in terms

of updating and serving content, but it offers more stable client-side playback of various media elements and tighter authoring controls. For more information about creating ASF content, visit the Microsoft web site. Microsoft provides free code to members of its Developer Network.

QuickTime

Apple Computer's QuickTime enables the delivery and playback of video, audio, animation, 3-D, and panoramic images for Macintosh and Windows. QuickTime is also the leading video production platform for both Windows and Macintosh. Most multimedia on computers begins with or involves QuickTime. Accordingly, the QuickTime technology is a natural for high-quality audio and video playback over the Web. Similar to Windows Media, QuickTime does not charge licensing fees for the number of simultaneous streams served. QuickTime can be streamed from the Mac OS X Server, the Darwin Streaming Media Server, and RealNetworks' RealServer 8.0.

The latest version, QuickTime 4, features many enhancements including:

* Smaller "component" codec architecture so that the initial download is as low as 1.7 MB. Additional codecs are transparently downloaded in the background when required for a specific media element on a page.

* Support for an increased number of formats, including MP3, Flash, MIDI, and almost every audio, video, animation, 3-D, and virtual reality format available.

* Improved codecs.

* True RTSP streaming when used in conjunction with the Mac OS X Server.

One of the keys to the success of the QuickTime technology and plug-in is that it can handle all types of media elements. For those of you trying to design for the greatest number of users and the least number of plug-ins, this can be a significant benefit.

In addition to playing MP3 content, QuickTime supports Timecode tracks as well as MIDI standards, including the Roland Sound Canvas and GS format extensions. QuickTime also supports key standards for web streaming, including HTTP, RTP, and RTSP. Plus, QuickTime supports every major file format for images, including JPEG, BMP, PICT, PNG, and GIF. QuickTime also features built-in support for digital video, including MiniDV, DVCPro, and DVCam camcorder formats, as well as support for AVI, AVR, MPEG-1, and OpenDML.

Finally, the newly designed interface is attractive and user friendly. In addition to the traditional controls you'd expect to find on a television—like volume controls and pause and play buttons—the Quick-Time Player gives you enhanced controls for online movie playback. The QuickTime Player's LCD section includes a time display, a time slider that shows you the length of the file being played, and a chapter marker. You can switch chapters on the fly even at the beginning of a video stream.

Flash and Director Shockwave

Macromedia Flash is the solution for full-scale, high-impact web multimedia with short sound effects and loops. Flash's bandwidth-friendly vector animation is ideally suited for web content delivery. Flash encodes embedded soundtracks in MP3 format that allows for better streaming and higher quality audio playback.

Flash is also tightly integrated with RealMedia. You can combine a Flash animation with a RealAudio soundtrack using the Real-Developer tools to encode a RealFlash presentation. RealFlash allows linear playback from within the RealMedia architecture taking advantage of RealMedia's advanced bandwidth negotiation for streaming audio and video and Flash's streamlined vector graphics for interactive animation.

Director Shockwave is the format of choice for building complex "CD-ROM-like" interactive web presentations and games that utilize Macromedia's powerful Lingo scripting language. Originally designed for full-scale development of interactive CD-ROM content, Director has been retooled to export highly advanced interactive Shockwave presentations for the Web.

Although Macromedia continues to integrate Flash's vector technology into Director and some of Director's advanced programming features into Flash, Director still stands apart in its support for the Lingo script. To preserve its highly compact plug-in file sizes and ease of use, Flash does not incorporate Lingo. Lingo is a powerful scripting language that enables developers to create and customize much more interesting interactive media such as complex strategy games, compelling music videos, and educational tools.

Beatnik's Rich Music Format (RMF)

Beatnik's Rich Music Format (RMF) is an HTML-based format that utilizes common scripting languages such as JavaScript to sync sophisticated interactive soundtracks that combine MIDI sounds and short audio samples to web content. Beatnik allows you to create full-scale, multilayered, interactive soundtracks and compositions that transform and change with user actions. Beatnik presentations sound excellent and download fast. And Beatnik can be incorporated into a web page along with other technologies such as commerce engines and backend databases.

Beatnik has a few distinct advantages over technologies such as Shockwave and Flash. For one, it uses MIDI, a highly compact language for scoring music, to play back audio from a dedicated synthesizer engine such as the Beatnik player. With the same file size (15 to 30 KB) as a two-second Flash audio loop, Beatnik can transmit a great-sounding MIDI score several minutes in length. But Beatnik is much more than MIDI—it also supports the delivery and playback of short customizable digital audio samples, making it far richer than MIDI playback alone.

The downside to Beatnik is that it has a steep learning curve and takes a considerable amount of time to debug to ensure smooth playback. Unlike Flash, Beatnik relies on the Beatnik plug-in, as well as a scripting language like JavaScript to control audio playback and synchronization. Beatnik will likely become more stable and reliable as the technology is refined and as more authoring tools such as Dreamweaver and NetObjects begin to include built-in JavaScript support.

MP3

MP3 has gained huge popularity as an encoding format because of its great sound quality. For radio-style broadcasts, professionals unanimously agree that it is the best-sounding format. MP3 is most commonly used for easily and efficiently uploading and downloading music files to the Web. MP3 is especially popular among downloadable music enthusiasts because it preserves audio quality while creating file sizes that are up to 12 times smaller than uncompressed WAV or AIFF audio files. MP3 is also quickly becoming the preferred format for streaming music as well, even though it is more complicated than setting up a RealMedia Server.

MP3 is derived from the group known as MPEG (Moving Pictures Experts Group). The members of MPEG are responsible for establishing standards for digital encoding of moving pictures and audio.

Unlike Liquid Audio, MP3 is not a proprietary end-to-end music delivery system. This distinction is important since companies concerned about copyright protection and secure delivery may decide to use the Liquid Music System for music distribution instead of merely posting MP3 files on a web page. On the other hand, the fact that MP3 is an accessible standard means it has the advantage of widespread industry support and compatibility with many applications and media players, including RealPlayer G2, Beatnik, Shockwave, QuickTime 4, and Windows Media.

Liquid Audio

Liquid Audio provides a complete end-to-end solution for secure music delivery over the Internet. Unlike Flash or RealAudio, Liquid Audio is less of a sound design format for adding audio to your web site than it is a professional utility for music sales and distribution. Accordingly, if you want to sell digitized music files over the web, Liquid Audio is the clear choice. You can purchase a starter package for less than $1,000. If you just want to broadcast audio so listeners can preview your music, you may wish to use a less expensive option such as RealAudio or MP3.

The Liquid Music System consists of four core products: Liquifier Pro, Liquid Server, Liquid Player, and Liquid Express. Every component of the Liquid Music System has been designed specifically for electronic music distribution. Here is what each component lets you do:

Liquifier Pro

Liquifier Pro is an encoder that allows you to prepare and publish CD-quality, copy-protected music for purchase and delivery via the Internet. The Liquifier Pro includes DSP functions such as sample-rate conversion, four-band parametric EQ, and dynamics processing, and it provides the capability to include lyrics, credits, and artwork—all in one audio file.

What distinguishes the Liquifier Pro from other encoders is its powerful watermarking and anti-piracy protections. Liquid Audio watermarking inaudibly embeds digital data, which identifies authentic copies of the music into the audio file. Liquid Audio employs multilayer security, which provides data on who owns the music and who bought the music.

Liquid Server

Liquid Server lets you publish and host Liquid Tracks. The Liquid Server also includes an SQL database and can even hook into larger, industry-standard SQL databases, such as those from Informix and Oracle. The flexible design of the server allows you to send dynamic product and promotional information such as sale prices, tour schedules, discounts, and coupons, along with the Liquid Track to be received by the Liquid Player.

Liquid Player

Liquid Player allows you to preview and purchase CD-quality Liquid Tracks on your Macintosh or Windows PC. The Liquid Player is software that lets you preview or purchase CD-quality music from the Internet. It also allows you to see album graphics, lyrics, liner notes, and promotions while listening, as well as easily record a standard "Red Book" audio CD that is playable on any home, car, or portable stereo system.

Liquid Express

> Liquid Express is a software package specifically designed for audio professionals in film, radio, television, music, and advertising that allows for the secure real-time preview, approval, delivery, and archiving of broadcast-quality audio.

Liquid Audio now also supports secure MP3 delivery through its watermarking and file security technology. This helps ensure that appropriate copyright and security information will adhere to MP3 files distributed over the Internet, providing the first step to some form of copyright standardization and unified structure to MP3 delivery.

MIDI

Although MIDI is not a streaming format, it downloads so quickly and is so widely used that we decided to include it in this list. If you are looking for an easy, low-cost solution for adding a little theme music or a button rollover sound to your web site, but you don't want the long waits associated with downloading digitized audio clips, MIDI may be a great option.

MIDI (Musical Instrument Digital Interface) is a super-compact musical language that transmits instructions such as pitch, volume, and note duration to MIDI-compatible sound cards and synthesizers. Since MIDI is a text-based musical scoring language, it downloads super-fast and is ideally suited for HTTP delivery.

The downside is that MIDI is not sound itself; rather, it is the coded representation or score of how the sound should be reproduced by the user's MIDI sound engine. Many browsers and computer systems feature different MIDI sound engines that greatly vary in quality and instrument playback style. This variation makes it difficult for developers to predict what an end user is going to hear.

Selecting the right format

Each format discussed in this chapter has advantages and disadvantages depending on the requirements of your project. There is no single format appropriate for every situation. To determine which format is best for you, first identify your needs, then select the format that best suits those needs. There are huge differences in server requirements for broadcasting CD-quality music to a limited audience versus wide-scale broadcasting to a large audience with diverse bandwidth capacity. Similarly, the differences between authoring and delivering interactive content such as a game or product demo versus encoding and broadcasting a video file are completely different.

RealAudio, MP3, and Flash are familiar names, but a host of alternative formats, including Windows Media, RMF, and Liquid Audio might better suit your needs. Let's take a look at the factors that will determine the most appropriate format for you.

Interactive sound design capabilities

Before you look at browser compatibility, cost, audio fidelity, and server performance, you will need to determine whether you need a format that supports interactive presentations or one that supports continuous playback of audio and video files. Several formats such as Flash, Shockwave, and Beatnik are designed for rich interactive media content such as games, educational material, product demos, and promotional pieces where instantaneous feedback via sound effects are essential.

In contrast, formats such as RealMedia, MP3, Windows Media, and QuickTime are primarily designed for continuous playback of audio and video files where server-side bandwidth negotiation and management are key. When they do support interactivity, it is usually in a more limited form such as slide shows and synchronized sound with video or text.

First, determine whether you want a format for delivering interactive content or simply a format for encoding and broadcasting audio and video files, then let the following criteria guide your final decision.

Browser compatibility

Let's face it, if people do not have the plug-in or technology to view or listen to your content, it is much harder to get your message across. This does not mean that you have to select a format that has 100% acceptance, but you will need to assess how tech-savvy your audience is and what format is going to be the most widespread among your target audience. If you are targeting a tech-savvy audience, they will be more likely to download the newest version of the plug-in if they do not have it installed. Do not count on a less technical audience to successfully download and install new technologies.

Cost for streaming audio

To add streaming to your web site, you may need to purchase one or more of the following:

- Encoding software to convert your raw media files into the appropriate format for web delivery
- Dedicated server software to stream your encoded media files

- Hardware to install your server on (this may include several systems for redundancy and scalability)

- Bandwidth to transmit data from your server over the Internet

The cost of streaming can range from free to hundreds of thousands of dollars depending on how many of the above items you will need to purchase. For example, if you are already running an NT server and have a dedicated T1 line, you can use Windows Media for no extra cost. Some vendors provide free introductory-level streaming solutions such as Real Networks. If you have administrative access privilege to your web server, you can install the free Basic RealServer G2. Alternatively, if you are a multimedia producer and own a copy of Macromedia Director or Flash, you can export Shockwave files and stream them from your regular web server for free.

On the other end of the spectrum, if you are a major Internet portal running a hot Sun machine with thousands of simultaneous listeners, you are going to need a healthy budget for equipment and bandwidth and, if you are using RealMedia, the appropriate number of streaming licenses. Keep in mind that you may not need to spend as much on streaming licenses as you may have thought. A 60-stream license can go a long way. If your average user listens to your audio for five minutes or less, you can deliver 17,280 streams per day with a 60-stream license.

Learning curve and documentation support

As is the case with limited budgets, everyone has a tolerance level for learning new technologies. Keep in mind that some formats provide much more documentation and software tools for getting started. RealMedia, for example, has outstanding documentation and software support, including sophisticated tools for automatic server configuration. In contrast, other formats such as MP3 and MIDI are not all-in-one proprietary streaming solutions but are merely standards for audio compression or musical notation and thus do not offer a single source for documentation and support.

Besides documentation and support, the real hurdle depends on the scale of your streaming needs. If you merely want to broadcast the annual company report to a few hundred nationwide sales representatives, streaming audio is a much simpler affair versus competing with Spinner.com to become the king of Internet radio. The difference in the infrastructure required for streaming to a few hundred listeners per day versus tens of thousands is night and day. If you are broadcasting to a huge audience with a scalable robust system, the learning curve is going to be much steeper than setting up a free Basic RealServer or throwing some audio files up on your HTTP web server. Large-scale professional broadcasting requires advanced configurations and logistics, such as multicasting with multiple servers and backup systems in place for redundancy.

Audio fidelity and compression

Audio fidelity for the end listener is determined by the quality and specific setting of the codec used for audio compression and decompression. Better compression algorithms, such as MP3, result in higher fidelity audio playback over the same bandwidth connection. Audio fidelity is also determined by the target file size and bandwidth settings you are using when encoding the sound file. A larger target file size requires less compression and audio degradation but more end-listener bandwidth capacity.

Server performance—the ability of the server to detect and send the appropriate stream to the end listener—is often just as important a factor in producing an overall quality listening experience as the codec.

Low bandwidth performance overall

Nobody likes to scrimp on quality or excitement, but if you have to tailor your media to fit the lowest common denominator of your audience, you will have to make some tough choices. Some formats, such as RealMedia, excel in bandwidth and browser compatibility. Other formats, such as Shockwave or Flash, work better in high-bandwidth 56 Kbps and DSL environments and provide little to no support for server-side bandwidth negotiation.

There are two factors to consider when selecting a format for low-bandwidth environments: the inherent ability of the format to provide compelling media with small file sizes, and the server-side technology to manage the delivery of media when constrained by low or fluctuating bandwidths.

Beatnik, for example, packs a huge punch of interactive excitement in an extremely compact file size because it utilizes MIDI. The use of bandwidth-friendly MIDI technology gives Beatnik an inherent advantage over Shockwave or RealMedia. On the other hand, RealMedia provides better server-side support for ensuring that files get delivered and do not drop out, regardless of the bandwidth of the end user.

Server performance and software quality

Thinking big? For those of you who need to stream audio and video content to thousands of simultaneous listeners on the scale of a CNN, NPR, or C|net, you will need a format that provides powerful server-side features and tools. And if you plan on broadcasting live events, you will need a real-time encoding and streaming system that runs on a dedicated web server.

RealMedia and Windows Media are the leading technologies for large-scale broadcasting, with SHOUTcast (MP3) and QuickTime close runners-up. The RealServer and Windows Media Server provide bandwidth negotiation that ensures smooth audio playback for the end listener and prevents annoying drop-outs when bandwidth fluctuates.

Beyond the actual server software you choose to install, whether it's RealMedia, Windows Media, SHOUTcast (MP3), or QuickTime, streaming to a large audience is just as much or more about the hardware and bandwidth as the format you choose. Large-scale broadcasting requires multiple systems, servers, and huge bandwidth connections. That's why many companies outsource their media broadcasting to companies like Broadcast.com or Network24.com. For a further analysis of the characteristics of each format, refer to Appendix B, *Audio Format Comparison*. It contains a chart that will help you select the appropriate format.

Summary

With so many technology options available for delivering media over the Web, it can be a challenging process to try to select the appropriate format for your multimedia web pages. This chapter attempts to point you in the right direction and provides you with a thumbnail view of the many options available.

It's time now to take an in-depth look at the most popular audio solutions available on the Web. We will begin with RealAudio.

CHAPTER SIX

ENCODING, SERVING, AND STREAMING SOUND WITH REALAUDIO

RealAudio is the premier platform for streaming audio and video on the Web. While MP3 and QuickTime may have higher quality audio and video compression, neither provides RealAudio's advanced server functionality, reliability, and administrative tools—features that are needed to carry out large-scale professional broadcasting. RealAudio not only provides a streaming media delivery format and media player, but its server technology optimizes audio playback over multiple modem connection speeds.

The RealMedia System works behind the scenes to deliver the best quality audio stream to both high- and low-bandwidth users. Interactive short-form audio formats such as Flash, Shockwave, and Beatnik are tailored for sound effects and loops and do not offer features for managing and controlling streams over various connection rates. Flash and Beatnik are also more likely to cause audio drop-outs and error messages when streaming long-form audio files.

Professional developers opt for RealAudio for a number of reasons, including:

- RealAudio provides the most reliable cross-platform server system for broadcasting audio and video to large audiences.

- The RealEncoder (renamed RealProducer in the G2 version) offers tools that make encoding an effortless task.

- RealAudio has the largest install base of viewers and listeners, with QuickTime a close second.

In this chapter, we introduce you to the basic components of the RealMedia System and then show you how to encode and stream RealAudio content. We also explore advanced real-world case studies to show you how the technology is used in professional applications.

In this chapter

- The RealMedia System

- Streaming RealAudio from a web server

- Professional webcasting

- Advanced RealAudio applications

- Live broadcasting with RealAudio

- Case study: N2K streams live Mötley Crüe concert

- Summary

RealAudio listening guides

To hear RealAudio broadcasts on the Web, check out the thousands of listings on *Broadcast.com* or RealNetwork's RealGuide at *http://www.real.com/ realguide/index.html*. The *Broadcast.com* and Real-Guide web sites offer some of the largest directories of RealAudio programming on the Net. Both sites feature business, news, sports, music, politics, and entertainment content. To list your site or event on Real-Guide, click on the Add Your Site/Event link at the bottom of the RealGuide home page. Fill out the event questionnaire and enter the URL for your RealAudio content, and a RealGuide reviewer will verify your URL and list your programming in the appropriate category.

The RealMedia System

The RealMedia System is comprised of three core components: RealEncoder, RealServer, and RealPlayer. In addition, RealNetworks provides a suite of RealMedia tools and utilities. This chapter focuses primarily on RealMedia 5.0 components and features. A large portion of your listening audience may not have the G2 plug-in yet. Thus, for many developers, RealAudio 5.0 is still the preferred format. Figure 6-1 illustrates the process of RealMedia creation and delivery including the interaction between server-side and client-side components.

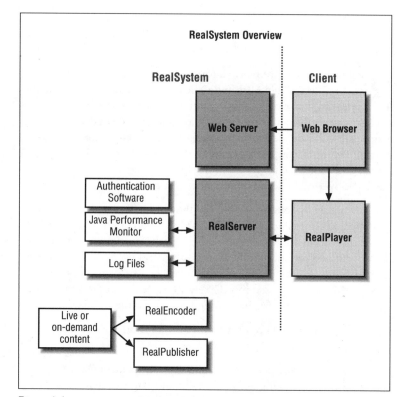

Figure 6-1. *An overview of the RealSystem 5.0*

In brief, when a listener clicks on a web page that contains a RealAudio link, the web server does not stream the audio file but instead prompts the web browser to start up the RealPlayer application. RealPlayer then requests the audio file from RealServer. RealServer in turn streams media content generated from RealEncoder and RealPublisher. Finally, RealServer keeps track of media usage via the Java performance monitor, log file records, and authentication software.

The RealAudio generation gap

This chapter documents basic RealAudio operations, as found in RealAudio 5.0, the last version of RealNetworks original streaming media platform. RealAudio 5.0 is still widely used for ensuring backwards compatibility with older RealPlayers. Most of the information in this chapter is still relevant to later versions. RealMedia version 6.0 and later represent RealNetworks second generation streaming media platform (G2) with enhanced encoding and playback performance and powerful new multimedia capabilities including support for SMIL. These multimedia features are covered in the next chapter.

RealMedia 7.0 features better server performance and integration of server-side advertisement management features that let RealNetworks customers stream and track their rich media advertising. RealMedia 8.0 represents a major quality breakthrough including the following:

- Significantly enhanced video quality (VHS quality at 300 to 500 kilobyte throughput)

- Server support for streaming QuickTime files from a RealServer

- Remote license management (for system administrators) that lets companies split one license across several machines/servers

- MP3 streaming directly from the RealServer without using third-party plug-ins

Figure 6-1 also helps to distinguish the process of RealMedia delivery with a dedicated RealServer as opposed to streaming audio from a standard web server.

RealEncoder and RealPublisher

RealNetworks offers two applications for encoding audio and video: RealEncoder and RealPublisher. The free RealEncoder, shown in Figure 6-2, enables you to encode audio or video files or a live input signal from an audio or video device into one or more RealMedia codecs. The RealPublisher offers the basic features of the free encoder plus advanced features such as wizards for creating HTML and built-in FTP support. The RealPublisher is especially useful for creating web pages that contain an embedded RealPlayer. The RealEncoder and RealPublisher both feature *static encoding* (for Macintosh and Windows) for pre-existing audio or video files and *live encoding* for broadcasting live events.

With the release of RealSystem G2, the RealEncoder and RealPublisher content creation tools have been renamed the RealProducer. The current version of RealAudio uses RealNetwork's new G2 compression technology. G2's new codecs offer tremendous improvement in sound quality over the RealAudio 1.0 and 2.0, which had been inferior to Shockwave's MPEG-based compression algorithms and Liquid Audio's Dolby compression technology.

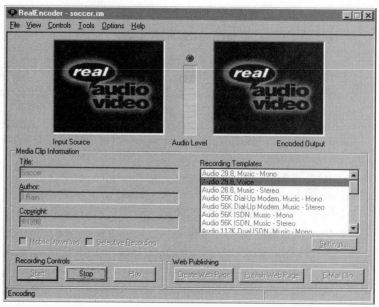

Figure 6-2. *The RealEncoder 5.0 lets you encode audio or video files or a live input signal.*

RealServer

RealServer works in conjunction with a standard web server to stream encoded audio and multimedia content over the Internet. RealServer is the key component that separates RealAudio from other formats that primarily rely upon HTTP or TCP streaming from a web server. A dedicated RealAudio server offers greater reliability than a standard web server and features more sophisticated streaming capabilities, such as robust UDP and RTSP transmission, bandwidth negotiation, live splitting, IP multicasting, and clustering. RealServer also allows for more control over the stream, such as the ability to seek forward without waiting for the content to download. Additionally, data is sent across the network in a more consistent, regulated rate as compared to a web server's tendency to deliver data in bursts. The Real-System also provides detailed usage logs and tracking analysis of hits and playback errors—essential tools for system administrators and web developers.

RealPlayer

The last piece of the puzzle is RealPlayer—the player or "decoder" (shown in Figure 6-3) that receives the incoming audio signal. The RealPlayer decodes incoming audio packets that have been compressed with the RealEncoder. The RealPlayer is free and features random access controls such as scroll, stop, start, and pause. The RealPlayer Plus lets you set custom presets or channels that point to your favorite RealAudio broadcasting sites and record RealAudio clips to your desktop. The G2 RealPlayer Plus includes a graphic equalizer video brightness, contrast, and tint controls (see Chapter 7, *Designing Multimedia Presentations with SMIL and RealSystem G2*, for more information about RealSystem G2).

Figure 6-3. *RealPlayer 5.0 decodes incoming audio packets that are compressed with the RealEncoder.*

RealAudio web resources

Visit the RealNetworks Developer Zone web site at *http://www.real.com/devzone/index.html*. The Devzone's documentation library allows you to access hundreds of pages of online manuals and content creation guides. You will also find an impressive amount of free information including an extensive index of downloadable PDF RealMedia guides, side-by-side comparisons of the latest codecs, software developer kits, and an open forum with answers provided by RealAudio technical experts.

The RealAudio forum is an especially useful resource for finding solutions to a broad range of common problems. You can also read through past issues of the bi-weekly "digested" RealAudio forum to look for previously posted workarounds and solutions. You can even look through a searchable archive built by the media experts at Stanford University's MedNET site (*http://mednet.stanford.edu/realforum.html*) that contains all the previously posted RealAudio forums.

RealNetworks also provides a comprehensive content creation and authoring products site (*http://www.real.com/products/index.html?src=eml,hardware,productsmain*) with more than 20 free and commercial media products for Macintosh, Windows, and Unix from RealNetworks and other industry-leading companies.

RealAudio utilities

RealNetworks provides several RealMedia tools and utilities for editing and synchronizing RealMedia files, such as RMEdit and RMMerge. These tools come pre-installed with the RealEncoder.

RealMedia tools allow you to alter file information such as title, author, and copyright information, and features such as selective record and mobile playback. The selective record feature allows listeners to save RealAudio clips to disk, whereas mobile playback allows listeners to save audio clips for playback over an alternative listening device. The RealMedia tools also enable you to listen to the contents of a RealAudio file and perform simple editing to an *.rm* file, such as pasting multiple clips into one clip or shortening the length of a clip. For more information about specific utilities and tools, visit RealNetwork's Devzone.

RealAudio 5.0 file types and metafiles

The RealSystem 5.0 uses several file types, each identified by a specific file extension:

RealMedia Clip (.rm)
> RealMedia Clips are audio or video encoded to RealAudio and RealVideo formats. The *.rm* files can contain multiple streams, including audio, video, image maps, and events. Note that previous versions of the RealAudio System used the *.ra* extension for RealAudio clips.

RealMedia metafile (.ram)
> The metafile located on your web server connects a web page to your RealAudio, RealVideo, or RealFlash clips. The metafile contains the URL of one or more clips located on the RealServer. This file launches the external player, which then requests the RealMedia (*.rm*) file referenced in the metafile.

RealPlayer Plug-in metafile (.rpm)
> The RealPlayer metafile is similar to the RealMedia metafile but it is used with the RealPlayer Plug-in when the player is embedded directly in a web page. Note that this metafile will not launch the external player.

RealAudio delivery

Figure 6-4 illustrates how a RealMedia clip is delivered to a listener. The numbers in Figure 6-4 correspond to the sequence of events that lead to the final delivery of a RealMedia clip:

1. The browser displays a web page containing a link to a Real-Audio metafile.

2. The user clicks on the link. The browser requests the metafile from the web server.

3. The web server delivers the RealAudio metafile to the browser. For files with a *.ram* file extension, the web server sets the MIME type of the file to *audio/x-pn-realaudio*. For files with a *.rpm* file extension (RealPlayer Plug-in), the web server sets the MIME type of the file to *audio/x-pn-realaudio-plugin*.

4. The browser looks up the MIME type of the RealAudio metafile. Based on the MIME type, the browser starts RealAudio Player as a helper application and passes it to the metafile.

5. RealAudio Player reads the first URL from the metafile and requests it from RealAudio Server.

6. RealAudio Server begins streaming the requested RealAudio clip to RealAudio Player.

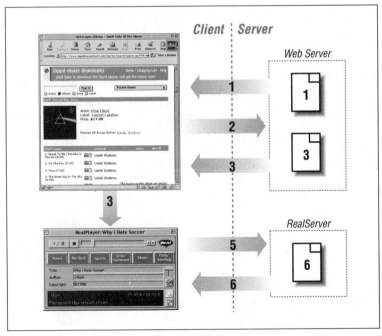

Figure 6-4. *Many steps are involved from your first click to the final delivery of the audio stream.*

Support for simultaneous streams

The number of streams supported by your web server or dedicated Real-Server is largely determined by your available bandwidth. Bandwidth usage of HTTP streaming is dependent on the combined bitrates of the content being streamed. Sixty simultaneous streams of 20 Kbps RealAudio clips would roughly consume the better part of a T1 line (1.2 MB out of 1.5 available).

Streaming RealAudio from a web server

If you are adding streaming media to your web site for the first time, you may wonder where to start. If you have your own web server, your first option is to download and install the free RealServer 5.0 or RealServer G2 basic servers from the RealNetworks web site. For the simplest and most cost-effective way to add streaming media to your web site without installing RealServer, HTTP pseudo-streaming from a standard web server is a good solution.

You can serve RealMedia content from your existing web site in the same manner that you serve JPEGs, GIFs, and HTML. However, remember that while an ordinary web server can deliver a RealAudio clip, it cannot fast forward the clip or compensate for network congestion. Computer networks are not built for real-time media delivery. To compensate, a dedicated streaming media system such as RealNetwork's Basic Server Plus employs many sophisticated techniques for delivering media efficiently and robustly.

Although streaming media from a web server is not as reliable as a dedicated RealServer, it is adequate for small-scale broadcasting to a handful of simultaneous listeners.

Pros and cons

There are advantages and disadvantages to streaming audio from a web server. HTTP pseudo-streaming, for example, is a good option for serving RealAudio and RealVideo files on the Web without the added management requirements and expense of server-side streaming software. And from the developer's point of view, there's no added work because RealAudio and RealVideo files require no special handling for HTTP serving.

One of the main disadvantages to HTTP pseudo-streaming is that it is not well-suited for high-volume sites serving numerous simultaneous streams. There are some important differences, however, between the capabilities of HTTP and those of specialized server software such as RealNetworks' RealServer 5.0. For example, you can't automatically detect the user's modem speed using HTTP. Instead, files optimized for each of the various connection speeds must be made available for users to select themselves. Also, the HTTP-based approach does not allow for live streaming audio or video presentations because complete files must be stored on the web server before they can be accessed.

Finally, HTTP does not perform well under heavy server loads. But for sites serving no more than a handful of simultaneous streams at any given time, this is a great way to add streaming audio and video features to your web site without incurring extra costs.

Requirements for HTTP streaming

The only requirement for HTTP streaming is a web server configured to recognize the *.ra*, *.ram*, *.rm*, and *.rpm* MIME types, which are standardized file classifications. You or your ISP will have to define the following MIME types for your web server:

audio/x-pn-realaudio
> Files with a *.ra*, *.ram*, or *.rm* file extension

audio/x-pn-realaudio-plugin
> Files with a *.rpm* file extension

Many servers already use the appropriate MIME types. If not, it's a relatively simple process to configure your host server for these types, and you can request that your service provider add this feature for you.

Let's take a quick look at how to broadcast RealAudio clips from a web server. Most popular web servers automatically support the *.ra* and *.ram* extensions. However, you may need to add the more recent *.rm* and *.rpm* file extensions since many web servers do not yet understand them. Note that many of the problems associated with embedding the player in web pages spawn from missing or incorrect MIME typing.

HTTP streaming tutorial

To prepare, upload, and broadcast your RealAudio content from a HTTP web server, perform the following steps:

1. Plug your audio source into the "line in" on your soundcard.

2. Start a basic sound recording and editing application such as SoundForge, CoolEdit, or SoundEdit 16. Open the record window and make sure you are getting an incoming signal (green LEDs should be flashing up and down). Even though it's possible to record directly into the RealEncoder 5.0, you get better results with a standalone recording application that has editing capabilities. To enhance your sound file, remove unwanted noises and silence at the beginning of a track, add fade-ins and fade-outs, and normalize the sound file before converting it to a RealAudio clip.

3. Bring up a volume control window and adjust the amplitude gain for optimum recording levels. Try a few short tests to make sure the input gain is not too low or too high. If the input gain is set

too high (if the meters peak into the red), you are likely to get distortion. If they are too low, you will get more system noise and dull-sounding files. When you are satisfied with the recording level settings, click Record.

4. Optimize and edit your file as mentioned in step 2 and save it as a WAV file. Refer to Chapter 4, *Optimizing Your Sound Files*, for more in-depth information about file optimization and editing techniques.

5. Start the RealEncoder 5.0 application and select File→New Session, as shown in Figure 6-5. An Advanced Mode dialog window will appear, asking you to specify input and output settings. Under input settings, you will need to specify whether you are encoding a live signal or a prerecorded sound file. For the output settings, you will need to specify the various codecs for different bandwidths that you want. If you are not sure which settings to choose, try the step-by-step Wizard Mode guide accessible from the dialog box.

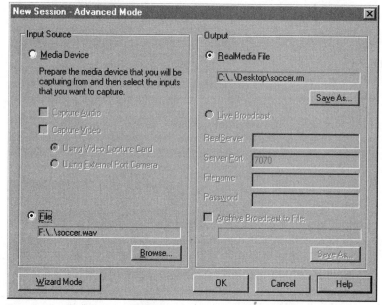

Figure 6-5. *In RealEncoder's Advanced Mode window, you specify whether you are encoding a live signal or a prerecorded sound file.*

6. Consider backwards compatibility. Even with the release of RealSystem G2, many listeners still use RealPlayer version 3.0 or lower. If a lot of your listeners are using older players, download a "legacy" 3.0 RealEncoder from the RealNetworks DevZone and

create an 8 Kbps encoded *.ra* file. Then create an additional
hyperlink on your web page to the alternative *.ra* file that's compatible with older RealPlayers.

You might also want to include a third link to·a high fidelity file
encoded with the new G2 RealProducer encoder for listeners
with high-speed connections.

Under Input Source, select File to import your audio file. If you
do not have a sound editor for recording, you can capture an
audio input signal directly into the RealEncoder 5.0 by selecting
Media Device and Capture Audio as shown in Figure 6-6.

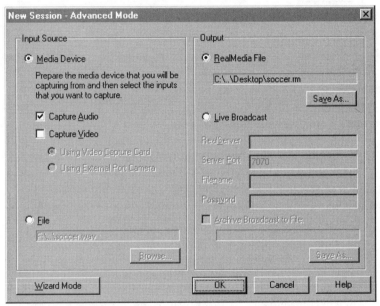

Figure 6-6. *Select Media Device and check Capture Audio to capture an audio
signal directly to RealEncoder.*

7. Under Output Source, select RealMedia File then hit OK. A dialog box will appear asking you to specify a codec, the Media
   Clip Information, and checkboxes for Mobile Download and
   Selective Recording as shown in Figure 6-7. Mobile Download
   enables users to download audio clips in a format suitable for
   playback over an alternative mobile playback device. Selective
   Recording allows users to record and download audio clips to
   their desktop.

8. After you have selected a good all-purpose codec such as Audio
   28.8 Voice, click on Start, and the RealEncoder will be converted
   your audio file into a RealMedia file named *yourfilename.rm*. At

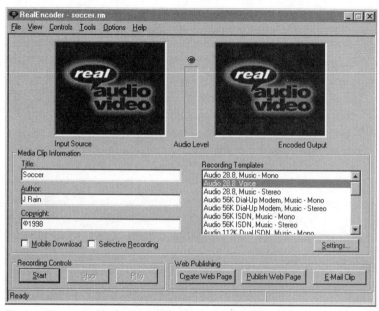

Figure 6-7. *The RealMedia Output dialog box*

this point, you should see the green LED lights. The LED amplitude meter should not trigger the red peak light indicator at the
top of the graph. If the signal peaks up in the red zone, go back
to the original file and use a sound editor to reduce the amplitude peak before encoding. When the encoder is finished converting your file, you'll see the message "Encoding Complete."

9. Use a text editor (such as Notepad or Simple Text) to create a
metafile (*yourfilename.ram*) containing a link to the RealAudio/
RealVideo file (*yourfilename.rm*). A metafile is a simple text document containing a URL that points to the RealMedia file. The
contents of the file will look like this:

```
http://www.hostname.com/yourfilename.rm
```

10. On your web page, create a hyperlink to the metafile. The code
should look like this:

```
<A HREF="yourfilename.ram">
```

If you want to use absolute paths, you must include both the
hostname and the complete path. For example:

```
<A HREF="http://www.hostname.com/yourfilename.ram">
```

11. Upload the both the *.ram* file and the *.rm* file, along with the
new HTML page, to the web server, and you should be up and
running with a sound-enhanced web site.

All things audio

Exactly on the hour, a lone SGI Challenge computer in the middle of Washington, D.C., opens its audio input port, receives a five-minute live news update, converts the audio signal to the appropriate format, sends the file to the RealServer, and then streams it across the globe without the touch of a human hand.

For National Public Radio's webmaster, Robert Holt, processing and encoding NPR's daily programming is one of the greatest challenges of broadcasting RealAudio content. Robert created a custom Unix script to automate the entire RealAudio conversion and streaming process for NPR's hourly news update.

At 55 minutes after the hour, NPR's SGI Indy machine runs a time query that syncs the machine's internal clock with NPR's master clock. Then, at exactly one minute past the hour, the SGI opens its built-in audio port and records a five-minute live feed from NPR's broadcast sound studio. At seven past the hour, the SGI computer converts the five-minute AIFF file to a WAV file. A script then commands the RealEncoder to encode the file and place a time and date stamp into the *.ra* file. Finally, the script copies the file through a firewall to NPR's RealServer, replacing the previous five-minute news update file.

NPR's system configuration is a dedicated audio server consisting of a RealServer 5.0 running on a Sun Sparc 20 and Netscape Enterprise web server software running on an SGI Origin 200 server. The system includes 128 MB of RAM to ensure enough memory for NPR's thousand-stream license, and a 10 GB hard drive to hold NPR's RealAudio content. NPR has a partial T3 connection (equivalent of five T1 lines) to the Internet.

Installing the system was a simple process for Robert: "For the most part, installing the RealServer is a just a matter of configuring your MIME types and going through the automatic installation process." And there was little trouble keeping the system running smoothly. In fact, the hardest part about maintaining the RealAudio System is not the server but the content. "It's easy to get the system up and working. The hard part is feeding the beast new content and retooling your audio files with the newest codecs."

Robert works as part of a three-person team, editing, encoding, and administering the delivery of over five hours of daily programming, in addition to the five-minute hourly news update. Since the installation of NPR's RealServer in 1995, Robert has edited, processed, and served many RealAudio files. Here are some of his tips for getting quality results from RealAudio:

* Use the highest-quality source audio files you can get. Internet compression algorithms, especially higher-bandwidth 40 and 80 Kbps codecs magnify mistakes or glitches in the original recording. NPR is fortunate enough to use source files that have been recorded in their custom $150,000 broadcast studio, with top-of-the-line Neumann condenser microphones. All the audio is recorded from the very beginning with the proper equalization and compression. Note that even if you do not have a deluxe studio, there are steps you can take to capture high-quality source material. See Chapter 3, *Capturing Original Source Material*, and Chapter 4 for more information.

$\rightarrow$

- Make sure you have plenty of disk space for all of your content. An hour of content encoded with the RealAudio 28.8 algorithm fills 8 MB. All your programming, especially if you keep archives on disk, can quickly add up to a huge amount of disk space.

- Make sure your connection to the Internet is stable and that you are using a high-quality Internet Service Provider. Call your ISP and check the data throughput with a program such as Net Medic.

- Make sure your ISP has enough bandwidth to deliver all your streams. One of the most common problems with the RealAudio System is not the system performance or the CPU speed, but inadequate bandwidth. Typically, bandwidth on the Internet router gets swallowed up first. There is not much you can do about that, but you can make sure your connection to the Internet is big enough to meet your needs.

- If you are broadcasting from your own in-house server, always watch system performance. Keep an eye on CPU usage and keep the load balanced between two servers. Always pay attention to memory and system speed.

Professional webcasting

While simple HTTP pseudo-streaming is adequate for small-scale broadcasting purposes, it is not a professional solution for large-scale broadcasting. If audio is a mission-critical component of your web site or simply needs to be 100% reliable, use a dedicated RealServer. This section provides a step-by-step guide on how to prepare and serve professional-quality RealAudio.

The first step to professional RealAudio broadcasting is to capture the highest-quality RealAudio source material. If you are using RealAudio in a professional situation, you need to maintain broadcast-quality production techniques.

To achieve the best fidelity:

- Start with a high-quality digital audio tape or CD when transferring audio to your computer.

- Set the input levels into your sound card as high as possible without distorting.

- Remove all unwanted noises and sound artifacts in your original source files with a sound editor.

- Make sure to start with a stereo 44.1 kHz 16-bit audio file when encoding to lower-bandwidth audio codecs.

To create the best quality RealAudio clips:

- Normalize your sound files to 95% of the maximum dB level.

- If your clips do not have enough bass or treble, try boosting the low-end or high-end frequencies in your sound file before encoding to a particular codec. For bass, use EQ to increase the low-end frequencies in the 100 to 200 Hz range. For treble, boost the high-end frequencies from 5,000 to 8,000 Hz. Remember, anything higher than 8,000 Hz will get cut when you compress the file using a low-bandwidth setting. For voice, the sweet spots to boost are 500 Hz and 3,500 Hz. Boosting the bass frequencies for voice below 250 Hz may have little effect or may cause distortion of the voice.

- If you are encoding for low-bandwidth codecs (14.4 and 28.8), use a low-pass equalization filter to cut frequencies above 10,000 Hz. (For a comprehensive overview on how to capture and edit high-quality audio, see Chapters 3 and 4.)

- Avoid flat or dull-sounding RealAudio clips by adjusting the amplitude of your signal with a sound editor instead of recording directly into the RealEncoder. Recording into a sound editor maximizes the available dynamic range.

- Prevent signal clipping by making sure that loud sounds in your original audio file signal do not exceed the acceptable amplitude levels. Clipping or "going in the red" can give rise to harmonic distortion in the form of clicks or crackling sounds on playback due to the introduction of odd harmonics. If your source file contains a clipped signal, your final RealAudio or RealVideo file will have high-frequency background noise or static. Lowering the input volume will help reduce clipping.

- Limit excessive low-frequency noise by eliminating any DC offset. (DC offset occurs during the analog to digital conversion process when the 0-point in the waveform isn't actually at 0 but offset either above or below. AnalogX (*http://www.analogx.com*) offers a Direct X plug-in that corrects DC offset errors. The AnalogX DC Offset plug-in is compatible with any Direct X application such as CoolEdit, Cakewalk, WaveLab, Paris, etc. DC offset is commonly produced in cheap PC sound cards. Several editing applications have built-in settings for fixing DC offset.

- Ensure proper grounding in audio equipment to prevent AC 60 Hz line noise. If AC line noise is present in your audio files, you can partially remove it with EQ by lowering the frequency range that contains the noise. You can also try using special noise reduction software to perform this task.

In low-bitrate encoding, every bit of bandwidth is important. Every bit wasted on noise reduces the number of bits allocated to the desired content, thus reducing the quality. Noise includes any audio information other than the desired content such as background noise, distortion, quantization noise.

Selecting the right RealAudio codecs

Once you have captured or imported a high-fidelity sound file into the RealEncoder, you need to select which codecs to use when exporting duplicates of the file. Choosing codecs can be a confusing process. With the release of RealSystem G2, there are six RealPlayers and dozens of RealAudio codecs in use. Compounding the problem, connection speeds vary greatly across the Internet.

Although RealSystem G2 simplifies the encoding process with its "encode once, stream anywhere" SureStream technology, it will take a considerable amount of time for the millions of people still using older players to upgrade to the new G2 player.

To make sure your audio is available to the widest possible audience, include several duplicate audio clips encoded at different bitrates. Generally, three or four codecs—such as 20 Kbps mono, 56 Kbps ISDN, and stereo ISDN—are adequate. *Bandwidth negotiation* is a RealServer feature that automatically detects the bandwidth of a listener and then streams the appropriate RealAudio clip. To use bandwidth negotiation, you need to select several RealAudio codecs.

To determine which codecs to use, remember that the cumulative bitrate of all files in your RealMedia presentation should equal no more than 75% of your target bandwidth. For example, if your target audience has standard 28.8 Kbps modems, your presentation bitrate should be 20 Kbps. Table 6-1 shows the optimum streaming rate for each target connection speed.

Table 6-1. *Suggested maximum bitrate for different connection speeds*

Target connection speed	Suggested maximum bitrate for streaming files
14.4 Kbps	10 Kbps
28.8 Kbps	20 Kbps
56 Kbps modem	34 Kbps
56 Kbps ISDN	45 Kbps
112 Kbps ISDN	80 Kbps

When choosing a RealAudio codec, keep in mind that different types of sound require higher-bandwidth codecs due to their frequency range. As discussed in Chapter 2, *The Science of Sound and Digital Audio*, higher-pitched sounds need a higher sampling rate to be accurately reproduced. Most popular music recordings have a frequency range between 60 Hz to 16,000 Hz, whereas speech primarily resides in the 200 Hz to 5,000 Hz frequency range. Thus, 28.8 Kbps RealAudio clips can reproduce frequencies only under 4,000 Hz to 5,500 Hz. Accordingly, a 28.8 codec can reproduce speech quite well but not music.

You will need a higher bitrate codec for high-quality music broadcasting than for simple speech. Table 6-2 shows the low- to medium-bandwidth encoding options and lists which codecs the various Real-Players support. Make sure that some of the codecs you use support older 2.0 player versions.

The table also lists each codec's frequency response. The higher the frequency response, the better the audio quality. Notice that the newest G2 codecs produce a much higher frequency response resulting in greatly improved music playback than older codecs. To view the full table, go to the RealAudio 5.0 Content Creation Guide.

Table 6-2. *RealAudio's bandwidth codec chart (from low to medium)*

Audio Codecs Supported	Players Supported	Frequency Response	Comments on Codecs
5 Kbps Voice	G2, 5	4 kHz	
6.5 Kbps Voice	G2, 5, 4	4 kHz	
8 Kbps Voice	G2, 5, 4, 3, 2,	4 kHz	Superceded by 8.5 Kbps Voice Codec
8 Kbps Music	G2, 6	4 kHz	Generation 2 Codec
8 Kbps Music	G2, 5, 4	4 kHz	
8.5 Kbps Voice	G2, 5, 4	4 kHz	DolbyNet Codec
11 Kbps Music	G2	5 kHz	Generation 2 Codec
12 Kbps Music	G2, 5, 4	4 kHz	DolbyNet Codec
15.2 Kbps Voice-Mono	G2, 5, 4, 3, 2	4 kHz	Superceded by 16 Kbps Voice Codec
16 Kbps Voice-Mono	G2, 5	8 kHz	Highest bitrate Codec for voice
16 Kbps Music-G2 Mono	G2	8 kHz	Generation 2 Codec
16 Kbps Music-G2 Low Resp.	G2, 5, 4	4 kHz	DolbyNet Codec
16 Kbps Music Mono Medium Resp.	G2, 5, 4	4.7 kHz	Suitable for Pop/Rock music DolbyNet Codec
16 Kbps Music Mono High Resp.	G2, 5, 4	5.5 kHz	Classical Music—DolbyNet Codec
20 Kbps Music-G2 Mono	G2	10 kHz	Generation 2 Codec
20 Kbps Music Stereo	G2, 5, 4, 3	4 kHz	DolbyNet Codec

Setting the proper timeout values

Before batch-encoding, make sure to change the default timeout value from 60 seconds to a greater value—such as 9,000 seconds—to ensure adequate time for encoding all your files.

Using the RealEncoder

There are several methods and tools for converting standard WAV, AIFF, or SND audio source files into the appropriate RealMedia *.ra* and *.rm* formats. The cheapest and simplest way to encode files is either to use the free RealEncoder available on the RealNetwork's web site or to export your files from an editing and recording application, such as CoolEdit, that supports *.ra* and *.rm* file extensions. The better alternative for *.ra* and *.rm* file conversion, if you can afford an extra few hundred bucks, is to use a batch conversion application such as Wave Convert Pro by Waves or BarbaBatch by Audio Ease. See Appendix A, *Creating the Ultimate Web Sound Studio: Buyers Guide and Web Resources*, for more information about these applications. These batch conversion tools feature superior processing and file optimization capabilities and will make mastering your source files into high-quality RealAudio clips a much easier process. Here is a description of the options in the RealEncoder 5.0:

File Information

In the Properties section of the RealEncoder window, you can enter title, author, and copyright information for your output file. This information is displayed in the player.

Mobile Playback

RealPublisher features a Mobile Playback option, which enables users to download your audio clips for playback at a later time or via an alternative playback device.

Selective Record

To let RealPlayer and RealPlayer Plus users save your RealVideo or RealAudio clips to disk, click Selective Record before you output the file. If you frequently use the same codecs or copyright settings, you can set your default settings in the RealEncoder 3.0 Preferences window.

Using Templates

RealEncoder and RealPublisher 5.0 come with predefined templates comprised of various codecs that enable you to encode your content specifically for your target audience. You can adjust these templates or define a new one to optimize the type of audio and video you are encoding. You can select one or more templates that best suit your needs.

To create a custom template, select Custom from within the Advanced window on the RealEncoder 5.0. If one of the predefined templates does not achieve the effect you are looking for, you can modify the parameters and save it as a new custom template. Make sure to save the template as a new file so you do not overwrite the predefined template.

Encoding RealAudio with a batch processor

Running files through the RealAudio encoding algorithm is a time-consuming process. If you have to process dozens or hundreds of sound files at a time, a batch processor application can save hours and days of work. Wave Convert Pro for Mac and PC and Barba-Batch for Mac are great batch conversion and mastering tools. Wave Convert Pro and BarbaBatch will import an entire folder of audio files, normalize them, perform EQ enhancements, and convert them to RealAudio clips on the fly.

Advanced users can use the command-line RealAudio utilities for batch processing of multiple files. Within the DOS command line, you can automatically encode several files sequentially by using the following syntax:

```
RVBatch RVEncode.exe options
```

Table 6-3 lists the command-line batch encoding options in the Rven-code directory.

Table 6-3. *Command-line batch encoding options*

Option	Description (default in parentheses)
/I	Use this option to specify an Input File.
/O	Use this option to specify an outfile or directory—Output File Name or Directory (*infile.rm* or *dir\YYYYMMDDHHMMSS.rm*).
/L	Use this option to specify Use Live Input.
/S	Use this option to specify server[:port]/file—Server Name, Port, and File (Port 7070).
/W	Use this option to specify password—Server Password.
/D	Use this option to specify *hhh:mm:ss*—Maximum Encoding Duration (continuous).
/A	Use this option to specify an Audio Codec (0).
/V	Use this option to specify a Video Codec (0).
/F	Use this option to specify a frame rate—Frame Rate (Optimal).
/B	Use this option to specify total Kbps for clip (100).
/N	Encoding Speed range 1 to 5, where 1 = normal, 5 = fastest (1).
/M	Optimal Framerate Bias, where 1 = sharpest image, 3 = smoothest motion (2).
/Q	Use this option to specify Quality, 1 to 100 (100).
/T	Use this option to specify a Clip Title.
/U	Use this option to specify a Clip Author.
/C	Use this option to specify a Clip Copyright.

Video capture cards

Looking for the best video capture card? The Osprey 100 ($199) for Windows NT is the most highly recommended one on the market. In fact, it is the card RealNetworks uses for all their live video capture needs. If you have a reasonably good sound card installed, the audio sync is as good or better than more expensive cards with on-board audio, according to Real-Network engineers. To capture video from a VHS tape, first capture the footage to an uncompressed AVI file, then compress it in non-real-time. (This takes large amounts of disk space, however.) You can find the Osprey 100 at *http://www.real.com/products/tools/*.

Most video capture cards have a 2 GB AVI file size limitation. Some video card manufacturers purport to have solutions to break this barrier. However, the SGI is the only platform that truly supports 2 GB+ video file formats. RealNetworks has an encoder for the SGI IRIX OS, which in conjunction with the video file format, offers the best solution for long format video clips.

Table 6-3. *Command-line batch encoding options (continued)*

Option	Description (default in parentheses)
/R	Use this option to enable Selective Record. Valid options are 0 Disabled and 1 Enabled (1).
/K	Use this option to enable Mobile Playback. Valid options are 0 Disabled and 1 Enabled (0).

Macintosh users can use AppleScript to batch-encode audio files. Table 6-4 describes the encoding parameters for Macintosh. These can also be obtained by opening the *RVBatch* Dictionary installed with the RealEncoder.

Table 6-4. *Macintosh encoding parameters*

Parameter	Description
encode	Use this option to specify an Input File.
output	Use this option to specify an FSSpec or full pathname of the output file.
audio	Enable audio encoding.
using audio codec	Audio codec name.
video	Enable video encoding.
using video codec	Video codec name.
at frame rate	Frame rate.
optimal bias	Determines the behavior of optimized encoding and can be one of the following options: sharpest image, normal, or smoothest motion.
cropping	Sets the cropping rectangle and follows this form: top, left, bottom, right.
at bitrate	Total bitrate.
at quality	Video quality setting (1–100).
encoding speed	Speed of encoding—the faster the speed, the less the quality of the encoding. Can be one of the following options: normal, medium, fast, faster, or fastest.
title	Title string.
author	Author string.
copyright	Copyright string.
Mobile Playback	Enable Mobile Playback.
Selective Record	Enable Selective Record.

Once you have encoded your source material using the appropriate RealAudio codecs, you are ready to stream your RealMedia files with the RealServer.

Preparing and encoding audio for RealVideo broadcasting

Audio quality is the biggest tradeoff when preparing content for low-bandwidth RealVideo. Because video is so data-heavy, only a small percentage of the bandwidth can be allocated to audio. For most RealVideo broadcasts, better picture quality takes priority over audio quality.

At Fox News, RealVideo clips generally contain shots of newscasters talking. Stationary video footage of "talking heads" are ideally suited for low-bandwidth RealVideo encoding. If there is little motion in the video feed, you can set the ratio settings in favor of video quality while still preserving speech intelligibility.

According to David Dadekian, technical director for Fox News, the RealVideo 20 Kbps stream allocates 6.5 Kbps to audio and 13.5 Kbps to video. The 50 Kbps Fox News stream allocates 8.5 Kbps to audio and 41.5 Kbps for the six frames per second video. Devoting a higher ratio of bandwidth to video preserves picture quality. Raising the audio portion of the audio-to-video data ratio degrades the respectable 176-by-144 pixel video quality.

For some content, increasing the ratio of video bandwidth will not help picture quality. High-motion video, such as sports footage with rapid action or music videos with dancing, are not suited for low-bandwidth codecs. For instance, video clips of regular season NBA basketball highlights encoded with the same settings used for Fox News footage resulted in indistinguishable blurry pictures. Reducing the frame rate of the basketball reel produced a higher-quality picture.

The best approach for encoding sporting events is to create a slide show with the video set to one image per second and the rest of the bandwidth allocated to audio. You do not get true video action, but at least you get high quality stills.

Encoding video content with music requires a higher ratio of bandwidth dedicated to audio. Music content is generally unacceptable at the audio rates of 6.5 Kbps and 8.5 Kbps used by Fox News. When David encodes RealVideo clips with music content for TV Guide Entertainment Network, he sets the audio at a minimum of 15 Kbps. For a 50 Kbps stream, he sets the audio at 32 Kbps and the video at 18 Kbps. Setting the bandwidth ratio at 32 Kbps/audio and 18 Kbps/video produces an engaging slideshow of one image per second with good music quality.

Broadcasting audio with the RealServer

To broadcast audio with the RealServer, you can either install your own RealServer or contract with an outside service provider to host your RealMedia content.

If audio is a small component of your web site, you probably want to consider installing a 25-stream Basic RealServer available for free at the RealNetworks web site. If you need more streams or advanced features, you will need to consider one of RealNetwork's commercial server options, which range from $695 to $30,000, depending on the range of simultaneous streams you need and extra features you want, such as live broadcasting, RealFlash broadcasting, and commerce functionality. Visit RealNetworks' Servers and Solutions page at *http://www.real.com/solutions/servers/index.html*.

If audio is an integral part of your web site and you broadcast to a large audience of more than 1,000 simultaneous listeners, consider using a third-party hosting service that guarantees superior reliability, fault tolerance, load balancing, and a number of simultaneous streams. For example, the RealNetworks Broadcast Network can support up to 50,000 simultaneous unicast streams. You can find a list of RealMedia-qualified ISPs at *http://www.real.com/solutions/partners/isp/index.html*.

RealServer installation

Installing and configuring a RealAudio Server is a four-step process that entails:

1. Downloading the appropriate platform-specific server package from RealNetworks
2. Running the automatic installation process
3. Launching the server
4. Testing the server to ensure audio playback

One of the strong points of the RealSystem is easy automatic installation for a variety of popular platforms including Unix, NT, Windows 98/2000, and Macintosh. Once you have purchased and downloaded the appropriate RealServer package, run the automatic installer application to configure the settings for your platform. The RealServer installer asks a series of simple questions regarding personal information, directory names, and default port setting options, then automatically installs itself on your system with the appropriate settings.

To install the RealServer on a Unix machine, create a separate directory to hold all of your RealAudio clips before launching the application. Do not place the RealServer under the root directory; instead create a separate directory with its own user ID to prevent access to your machine (Unix). Once you have placed the RealServer and all of its corresponding files into a separate directory, launch the server from the command line.

Make sure to type in a command in the boot script so that your machine will launch the RealServer whenever the computer is rebooted.

Finally, make sure you test your RealServer by connecting a web browser via HTTP to the RealAudio port 7070 (*http://yourservername:7070*). This port has a link to pre-installed stock audio samples for testing, so you don't have to encode your own test file. The RealServer diagnostic test detects that you are making an HTTP request rather than a standard RealAudio request and generates system reports on the fly. If you hear the audio playing back, you should be ready to stream RealAudio.

RealServer system requirements

To run your own RealServer, you need the following items. (For more detailed information, refer to the RealAudio Server documentation located at the RealNetwork's Developer Zone.)

- A computer running one of the supported operating systems: Macintosh System 8 or greater, Digital Unix v3.2, Microsoft Windows NT 4.0, Solaris 2.5, Linux 2.03, Sun OS 4.1.x, Silicon Graphics IRIX 6.2 and 6.3.

- Space on the computer's hard disk for the RealServer software and RealAudio clips. You need upwards of 1 GB or more of hard disk space if you are serving high-bandwidth streams with bandwidth negotiation. One 6- to 10-minute audio file encoded with a range of high- and low-bandwidth codecs for bandwidth negotiation requires 15 MB to 20 MB of disk space. If you have disk space constraints, stick with low-bandwidth codecs.

- A network connection with sufficient bandwidth to serve your users. For each listener connected to the Internet backbone, the RealServer requires at least 10 Kbps for 14.4 format and 20 Kbps for 28.8 format. A T3 line, for example, could stream 4,500 simultaneous streams. See Table 6-5 for the number of approximate streams for each bandwidth connection.

Table 6-5. *Number of streams at different connection speeds*

Network connection	Number of 14.4 Kbps streams	Number of 28.8 Kbps streams
ISDN (128 Kbps)	12	8
T1 (1.5 Mbps)	150	90
T3 (45 Mbps)	4,500	2,700

- A web server that supports configurable MIME types. RealServer works with the following web servers:

  Website for Windows NT
  Apache 1.1.1 and higher
  Mac HTTP
  HTTPD4Mac
  Netscape Netsite and Netscape Enterprise Server
  Microsoft Internet Information Server (IIS)

NCSA HTTPD (v 1.3, 1.4, 1.5)
CERN HTTPD (v3.0)
EMWAC HTTPS 0.96
Spinner 1.0b12–1.0b15 / Roxen 1.0
Webstar and Webstar PS

- Sufficient processor and memory capacity. RAM, not processor speed, is the gating factor for the computer running RealServer. A 90 MHz Pentium processor, with enough available bandwidth, can simultaneously deliver at least 500 28.8 streams. For example, Real Audio Server 3.0 requires 20 KB RAM for each simultaneous stream. A stream of 60 simultaneous audio files requires approximately 4 MB of available RAM. 1,000 streams requires 70 MB of RAM, and so on.

Using bandwidth negotiation

Once you have installed the RealServer or found an ISP running one, use bandwidth negotiation to manage the delivery of RealAudio content. Bandwidth negotiation checks the listeners' modem speed settings then sends the appropriate stream for their bandwidth. If you encode three or four versions of your audio clip, you can reach a wider audience by offering low-bandwidth users a smaller compressed RealAudio clip and high-bandwidth users a CD-quality clip. Note that when bandwidth negotiation checks the connection setting of the client player, the player reports the speed at which it has been set, not the speed of the actual network connection.

In most cases, bandwidth negotiation works fine. On occasion, however, the RealServer overestimates a RealPlayer's "real" connection speed. Many web developers run into problems because the default setting of the RealPlayer is 28.8. This setting may not be optimized for the user's available bandwidth. Frequently, RealPlayer bandwidth preferences are set too high for the actual available data throughput. If a user clicks on a link to a RealMedia clip that streams at too high a data rate for the user's real connection speed, a somewhat cryptic error message will appear indicating that the network connection or CPU speed is insufficient to view the content.

RealSystem G2's SureStream technology promises to alleviate this problem. The RealPlayer G2 "switches down" to a lower bandwidth without rebuffering the clip when a user's Internet connection degrades or when the user's bandwidth was misjudged. RealEncoder G2 with SureStream generates one master file that includes several different bandwidth settings. In the future, as older players get upgraded, the G2 Encoder will make it easier to reliably stream Real-Audio content.

If you are using RealServer 5.0, include a separate file for 28.8 Kbps modems, 56 Kbps modems, and ISDN connections along with one or two files for older players. For example, if you want to encode an important tradeshow presentation so people with 14.4, 28.8, and 56 Kbps modems can listen, encode the live audio to three different files or capture the audio to a *.wav* first and then encode it three times.

To stream a presentation using bandwidth negotiation, follow these steps:

1. Encode your audio content into at least three separate files:

   — 14.4: Encode one file at 5 Kbps, 6.5 Kbps or 8.5 Kbps

   — 28.8: Encode a higher-bitrate file with a maximum of 20 Kbps

   — 56: Encode a final audio clip with a 40+ Kbps stereo or mono codec

2. Create a generic directory (not a file) in the RealServer Content directory: *C:\real\server\content\tradeshow.ra.*

3. Place the files generated in step 1 into that directory. For example:

   C:\real\server\content\tradeshow.ra\tradeshow_14.ra
   C:\real\server\content\tradeshow.ra\tradeshow_28.ra
   C:\real\server\content\tradeshow.ra\tradeshow_56.ra

4. Change the filenames to the following (as listed in the Content Creation Guide):

   C:\real\server\content\tradeshow.ra\pnrv.18
   C:\real\server\content\tradeshow.ra\pnrv.36
   C:\real\server\content\tradeshow.ra\pnrv.43

5. On your web page, reference the files as *pnm://yourservername/ tradeshow.ra.*

Be sure to add RealAudio 2.0 codecs for people using 2.0 players. Use RealEncoder 3.0 to create RealPlayer 2.0 compatible codecs. Remember, you will have to manually name the files generated by the RealEncoder 3.0 and place them in the proper folder.

The RealSystem is a versatile tool that does much more than bandwidth negotiation. Let's take a look at some of the other advanced RealSystem features and encoding techniques.

Advanced RealAudio applications

Now that you are familiar with broadcasting prerecorded content, let's explore some of the advanced capabilities of the RealSystem,

Selecting the right TCP/IP port

If the RealServer is configured on the same machine and IP address as the web server, the web server's TCP port must be changed. The RealServer uses the standard TCP Port 80 for its "cloaking," so the web server has to be relocated to Port 81 or any other available TCP port. A single machine also could have two IP addresses with the web server bound to the first IP address and the RealServer bound to the second.

such as synchronizing media presentations, indexing regions of a large file, broadcasting through firewalls, archiving and delivering RealMedia content with a database, creating RealFlash content, and broadcasting over an Intranet.

Broadcasting through firewalls

When RealAudio first hit the market, many listeners behind corporate firewalls could not receive RealAudio content because all UDP traffic was blocked from their networks. RealAudio, similar to other streaming media formats, uses UDP for bandwidth efficiency. UDP is more efficient because it streams multimedia content without tediously checking for transmission errors. Therefore, in congested networks, UDP tends to step on TCP traffic. TCP, on the other hand, is designed to throttle back during congestion. Primarily for this reason, most firewalls block UDP traffic.

Thus, RealNetworks has incorporated TCP and HTTP streaming in RealSystem 5.0 for broadcasting through firewalls. TCP and HTTP are better than UDP for broadcasting through firewalls since TCP ports are generally open to allow FTP, HTTP, and Telnet traffic through, and HTTP ports are usually always open.

Make sure your RealServer is not set to multicast delivery only. Enable HTTP Cloaking in the RealServer config file (*rmserver.cfg*) located in the application root directory. Open the file and change the value with a text editor. HTTP Cloaking disguises a UDP stream with HTTP headers. With HTTP Cloaking enabled, a player will try to connect with UDP first, then TCP, and finally HTTP Cloaking if the first two methods fail to connect. For live events, RealNetworks uses the following protocols in the following order, which is also the order of decreasing efficiency:

1. Multicast IP

2. UDP

3. TCP

4. HTTP

The process works as follows:

1. First, the user, either via the plug-in or a *.ram* file, is directed to the RealServer via a TCP connection from within the firewall to the RealServer.

2. Next, the server, via a TCP connection, sends the stream information (header, if you will) to the player.

3. Third, the server sends the stream to the client via the most efficient mechanism, as noted above. If no data is received after a

specific amount of time, usually two seconds for the RealPlayer, the player notifies the server and the server streams the content via the next most efficient protocol. This continues until there is no connectivity even via HTTP. The player then gives an error message and stops trying.

If you need to stream audio from behind a firewall to the public Internet, you have two options:

- Place your server outside the firewall or configure the firewall to ignore traffic to and from your individual IP address.

- Configure the firewall to map a port or address through the firewall to your server's IP address. You can pass PNM traffic through a firewall using a proxy kit available at *http:// www.real.com/firewall/index.html*.

Broadcasting to a corporate LAN (Intranets)

For broadcasting audio over an Intranet instead of the public Internet, you need to take extra steps to prevent network congestion. Nick DelRegno, engineer for MCI Enterprise Information Systems, outlines the best method for broadcasting over an Intranet:

To broadcast RealAudio or RealVideo, configure the LAN/MAN/WAN for IP Multicast. By using IP Multicast for the live broadcasts, you can hit every employee with minimal impact on the network. With the advent of IP Multicast–aware Ethernet Switches, you can even control the impact of Multicast on your flat LAN segments.

MCI Enterprise Information Systems has had very good success with multicasting 20 Kbps to 300Kbp RealAudio and RealVideo streams across their network. The only problems encountered have been on busy LAN segments and on Token Ring LANs.

RealNetworks also supports unicast (UDP, TCP, and HTTP) streaming so that anyone on a non-multicast-enabled portion of the network, such as dialup, can access the content via a unicast connection. With the deployment of Resource Reservation protocols and IP Quality of Service, busy LANs should become less of an issue.

MCI Enterprise Information Systems has deployed several servers to handle the load, one with redundancy for live events and several others to replicate content and distribute the load for archived content. "We don't do any splitting because of the nature of our network; however, for LANs connected by thin pipes, this is a nice option. Our servers are located centrally within our Intranet so that the encoder can sit anywhere, even in very remote locations connected via ISDN dialup."

For security, Nick set up specific multicast address ranges, which get blocked at MCI's boundary routers. He also set relatively low TimeToLive (TTL) settings on MCI's multicasts. This helps prevent multicast leakage onto the public Internet, yet allows them to multicast globally.

Creating custom player controls

The RealSystem provides three basic playback choices:

- Bypass the player interface so that your audio content will begin playing immediately when a user enters a web page.

- Build the player interface directly into your web page.

- Use the standalone RealPlayer controls.

Embedding controls into your web page is a visually more attractive option than having another window pop up in front of your content. Individual interactive components, such as a play button or volume slider, can be placed anywhere on your web page, just as you would place an image using the <IMG> tag in HTML. Here is the HTML source for the embedded player controls used in Raspberry Media's Radio CounterCulture page (*http://www.counterculture.com*), as shown in Figure 6-8:

```
<OBJECT ID="RVOCX" CLASSID="CLSID:CFCDAA03-8BE4-11CF-B84B-
    0020AFBBCCFA" WIDTH="350" HEIGHT="100" BORDER="0"
    NAME="player">
<PARAM NAME="SRC" VALUE="/ram/radio/003-y2k.ram">
<PARAM NAME="CONTROLS" VALUE="All">
<PARAM NAME="CONSOLE" VALUE="cons">
<EMBED SRC="/ram/radio/003-y2k.ram"
    TYPE="audio/x-pn-realaudio-plugin" WIDTH="350" HEIGHT="100"
    CONTROLS="All" CONSOLE="cons" BORDER="0" NAME="player"></EMBED>
</OBJECT>
```

The drawback to using embedded controls is that the audio will stop playback when a user leaves the site. Many listeners prefer to listen to audio while they view other web sites. If you want to cater to the "listen while they surf" crowd, you will have to hide the player by embedding the player in a zero height or width frame or by simply not embedding the player in the web page. By hiding the player in a zero height or width frame, you can continue to play the content until the user manually enters a new URL or until a _top or _parent frame target is used.

Creating custom controls with JavaScript

With JavaScript, you can use custom graphics to build your own Real-Player console with unique start, stop, and play buttons. The following JavaScript example, by Nick DelRegno from MCI Enterprise Information Systems, is designed to create a RealMedia interface with customized GIF or JPEG start and stop video playback buttons. (Real-System G2 offers more customizable controls besides start, stop, and pause, such as volume control.)

Figure 6-8. *The Radio CounterCulture page with embedded RealPlayer controls*

Here is the JavaScript and appropriate embed tags necessary to create the customized RealPlayer console:

```
<head>
<script language=JavaScript>
function PlayClip(clipname)
{
        //alert(clipname);
        if (navigator.appName == "Netscape") {
                document.video.DoStop();
                document.video.SetSource(clipname);
                document.video.DoPlayPause();
        }
        else
        {
                video1.DoStop();
                video1.Source=clipname;
                video1.DoPlayPause();
        }
}
</script>
</head>

<OBJECT ID="video1"
CLASSID="clsid:CFCDAA03-8BE4-11cf-B84B-0020AFBBCCFA"
ALIGN="baseline" BORDER="0" WIDTH="240" HEIGHT="180">
```

```
<PARAM NAME="console" VALUE="Clip1">
<PARAM NAME="controls" VALUE="imagewindow">
<PARAM NAME="autostart" VALUE="false">
   <EMBED SRC="empty.rpm" ALIGN="baseline" BORDER="0"
WIDTH="240" HEIGHT="180" NAME="video" CONTROLS="imageWindow"
CONSOLE="Clip1" AUTOSTART="false">
</OBJECT>

<A IMG="image.gif" onMouseOver="PlayClip('pnm://server_name/
filename.rm')"><IMG SRC="imagelocation/start.gif" BORDER="0"
WIDTH="80" HEIGHT="40"></a>

<A onMouseOver="PlayClip('pnm://server_name/filename.rm')">
<IMG SRC="image_location/start.gif" BORDER="0" WIDTH="80"
HEIGHT="40">
</a>
<A onClick="PlayClip('pnm://server_name/filename.rm')">
<IMG SRC="image_location/start.gif" BORDER="0" WIDTH="80"
HEIGHT="40">
</A>
```

The "Stop, Load Clip, and Start Video" function that JavaScript placed within the header tag allows you to activate the playback of audio and video content based on a user action such as a mouseover or mouse-click. It can also be used with additional scripting to launch audio or video playback based on the time of day, day of the week, or season. You could also use a variation of the code to build a virtual radio or jukebox. It is best to define this function in the header tag.

For an explanation of the JavaScript code, read the descriptions in Table 6-6.

RealAudio playback with a transparent plug-in

It may be preferable to have automatic audio playback when a user clicks on a page without the RealPlayer coming to the foreground. For example, if you want to include an optional audio commentary to accompany a web tour, you can use hidden frames to embed a transparent RealAudio plug-in. This allows the audio to play back across several pages without bringing the player controls to the foreground. If you have a "hidden" frame page, create a link or a button that retrieves a web page into that hidden frame containing the RealAudio plug-in set to autoplay. The user can then navigate through several pages while the RealAudio cliptd is playing.

One of the last steps before you broadcast your audio is to determine how you want the Real-Player controls to appear on your web site. You can customize the RealPlayer with the ActiveX and Netscape plug-in controls via HTML or JavaScript. You can find a detailed list of player plug-in methods and properties in the DevZone, under Toolkits/SDKs.

Table 6-6. *JavaScript code descriptions*

Code	JavaScript Description
`function PlayClip(clipname)`	Defines the function used to initiate playback of the clip.
`if (navigator.appName == "Netscape") {`	Tests for Netscape compatibility (Netscape and IE properties are a bit different).
`document.video.DoStop();`	Stops current clip; does nothing if the current clip has already stopped.
`document.video.SetSource(clipname);`	Sets the source of the player to the value passed into `clipname` from the calling location `document.video`.
`document.video.DoPlayPause();`	Starts the video (since we stopped it before). If used elsewhere when the video is running, it pauses the video.
`}` `else`	Non-Netscape browser assumed to be IE (for Internet use, further testing may be required; for Intranet use, limited browser assumptions are valid).
`{` `video1.DoStop();`	Stops current clip; does nothing if the current clip has already stopped. Note slight difference from above.
`video1.Source=clipname;`	Sets the source of the player to the value passed into `clipname` from calling location.
`video1.DoPlayPause();`	Starts the video.

The object tag embedded within the body of the HTML page actually places the player on a web page:

```
<OBJECT ID="video1"
CLASSID="clsid:CFCDAA03-8BE4-11cf-B84B-0020AFBBCCFA"
ALIGN="baseline" BORDER="0" WIDTH="240" HEIGHT="180">
<PARAM NAME="console" VALUE="Clip1">
<PARAM NAME="controls" VALUE="imagewindow">
<PARAM NAME="autostart" VALUE="false">
    <EMBED SRC="empty.rpm" ALIGN="baseline" BORDER="0"
WIDTH="240" HEIGHT="180" NAME="video" CONTROLS="imageWindow"
CONSOLE="Clip1" AUTOSTART="false">
</OBJECT>
```

The image tag placed within the body of the HTML page acts like a normal hyperlink, except that when clicked the browser executes the JavaScript function instead of changing page location:

```
<A IMG="image.gif"
onMouseOver="PlayClip('pnm://server_name/filename.rm')">
<IMG SRC="imagelocation/start.gif" BORDER="0" width="80"
height="40"></A>
```

The mouseover tag can also be accomplished with an onMouseOver or onClick event handler. onMouseOver activates the player when the mouse is over the link or the link is clicked; however, it is not widely used this way. It is more often used with onClick. Here is the onMouseOver version:

```
<A onMouseOver="PlayClip('pnm://server_name/filename.rm')">
<IMG SRC="image_location/start.gif" BORDER="0" WIDTH="80"
HEIGHT="40">
</A>
<A onClick="PlayClip('pnm://server_name/filename.rm')">
<IMG SRC="image_location/start.gif" BORDER="0" WIDTH="80"
HEIGHT="40"></a>
```

A popular way to use a mouseover image to play the audio file is to use a picture of a CD player. Use an image map to define the areas containing the play button and the stop button. Use the JavaScript stop and start commands to activate those regions.

Note of caution

This script should work fine for Internet Explorer 3.x or higher and Netscape 4.x and higher. With older browser versions, you may see JavaScript errors and other anomalies, especially if you embed the player within a table.

Internet Explorer understands the <object> with the clsid as an ActiveX object. Since the second embed is within the <object> tag and has no bearing on the ActiveX object, IE ignores it. Netscape understands embed and not ActiveX objects. Netscape understands the <object> tag, but not the identifier, so it ignores it. Instead, Netscape uses the information within the <embed> tag.

Note that the embed text refers to an *empty.rpm* file. This is truly an empty file created with a simple text editor like Notepad. This is necessary because Netscape uses the MIME information associated with a file extension to determine which plug-in to load. ActiveX objects explicitly define which ActiveX control is to be used. Netscape must rely on the web server to send the MIME information. Since this embed tag is part of a dynamic page, which can load any number of source files, you do not want to explicitly define one source.

Therefore, the *empty.rpm* allows for the passing of the appropriate MIME information without passing any other information. If you want a default source, you can place a *pnm://servername/filename.rm* statement within the *.rpm* file just as you would with a *.ram* metafile.

Embedding custom player controls with RealPublisher

One of the easiest ways to embed custom player controls, such as play, stop, and pause buttons, into a web page is to use the RealPublisher to generate the necessary HTML. The publish function in the RealPublisher grabs the *.ram*, *.rm*, and HTML files, edits the links in the HTML and the *.ram* file, and sends them to their respective locations on your web server. Once you have generated the appropriate HTML with the RealPublisher, you can copy it to any other web authoring application such as Macromedia Dreamweaver. If you upload your new page from another editor, make sure to update the links to the audio files. When you have finished editing your web page, use the RealPublisher to upload the page to the server or to manually change the link names in the RealPublisher-generated HTML yourself.

To properly upload RealPublisher-generated player controls to your web server, use one of three methods:

- Create your HTML in the RealPublisher, and then publish it to the server.

- Create your HTML in the RealPublisher, copy and paste it into another HTML editor, and then use RealPublisher to upload the finished web page.

- Create your HTML in the RealPublisher, copy and paste the HTML into your HTML editor, and then manually edit the links in the RealPublisher-generated HTML to point to the server. Once you have manually changed the links, upload the page with your favorite HTML editor.

Playing clips with a hidden control or plug-in

If you want to play RealAudio or RealVideo clips without having a visible plug-in control, hide the control by embedding a plug-in in a page that has its size set to width=2 height=0, and no image will appear on your web page. You can control the plug-in with Java-Script. This example works in both Netscape and Internet Explorer:

```
<script Language=JavaScript>
function playSource()
{if (navigator.appName == "Netscape")
{document.javaPlug1.DoPlayPause();}
else
```

```
{RAOCX.DoPlayPause();}
}
</script
<A HREF="#" onClick="playSource()">
<IMG SRC="button.gif"></A>
<OBJECT ID="RAOCX" CLASSID="clsid:CFCDAA03-8BE4-11cf-B84B-
0020AFBBCCFA" WIDTH="2" HEIGHT="0">
<PARAM NAME="SRC" VALUE="pnm://audio.real.com/welcome.rm">
<PARAM NAME="CONTROLS" VALUE="PlayButton">
<embed src="start.rpm" WIDTH="2" HEIGHT="0"
CONTROLS="PlayButton" NAME="javaPlug1">
</OBJECT>
```

Indexing RealMedia clips: creating a table of contents

Use an index to make repeat listening of a longer-playing file easier or to point listeners to important content items within an audio clip. An index prevents you from having to break up a contiguous audio file into smaller parts. Short clips do not increase server performance. While short files would make playback more convenient for the listener who wants to jump from section to section, they are a hassle for those who want to listen to the whole program at once. An index is the perfect solution: it helps listeners get the specific information they want and simplifies encoding and cataloging for the developer. With an index, you can present one stream while giving users access to points within the stream.

For example, a one-hour music CD or instructional video could be indexed by utilizing the start and stop tags within a *.ram* or *.rpm* file. To create a *.ram* file for indexing a RealMedia clip, simply add the start and stop parameters to the URL in your metafile as shown below:

```
pnm://servername.com/yourfile.rm?start=2:23.4&end=2:59.2
```

Most of the time, these files are preset when the clips are published, but if you enter your start and stop information in a database, you can generate the *.ram* file on the fly. By doing this, you can place a table of contents on the page with each topic pointing to a *.ram* file with the appropriate start and stop information. This technique gives you the ability to use one file to provide full-length playback or random (shuffle) play.

Another common technique for indexing files is to use CGI or Java-Script to generate a metafile using a timestamp that you pass to it. The following example is a JavaScript function and the call to the function, provided by Steve McMillen, senior systems engineer for RealNetworks. This example starts a RealVideo or RealAudio clip at a specified time.

In the head part of your HTML document, insert the <script> tag with the following function:

```
<script language="JavaScript">
 function startClip(Clip,Start,End,Title,Author,Copyright) {
// uncomment next two lines or set server in HREF below
// server = 'pnm://yourRealServer.com/'
// Clip = server + Clip;
   if(Start == null) Start = '0';
   Clip = Clip + "?start=" + '"' + Start + '"';
   if(End != null) {
     Clip = Clip + "&end=" + '"' + End + '"';
   }
   if(Title != null) {
     Clip = Clip + "&title=" + '"' + Title + '"';
   }
   if(Author != null) {
     Clip = Clip + "&author=" + '"' + Author + '"';
   }
   if(Copyright != null) {
     Clip = Clip + "&copyright=" + '"' + Copyright + '"';
   }
// uncomment following line for testing:
// alert("URL: " + Clip);
   if (navigator.appName == "Netscape") {
     document.VideoObjName.DoStop();
     document.VideoObjName.SetSource(Clip);
     document.VideoObjName.DoPlayPause();
     } else {
     VideoObjName.DoStop();
     VideoObjName.Source= Clip;
     VideoObjName.DoPlayPause();
   }
 }
</script>
```

This function pastes together the necessary URL to play a clip, stops the previous clip (if any), sets the source of the plug-in to the new clip, and starts playing at the indicated start time. The server location is included in the call to the function. You can also hardcode the function itself at the indicated location within the function. The only required parameter is the clipname. Use 'null' (notice the single quotes) if there is no value for an argument. clipname includes the complete address and filename.

At the minimum, the plug-in should look something like this:

```
<embed name="VideoObjName" type="audio/x-pn-realaudio-plugin"
width="176" height="144" controls="ImageWindow">
```

This code will work in both IE 3.0 and greater and Netscape 2.0 and greater. It is strongly recommended that you not put the <embed> tag within a table for cross-platform compatibility.

When you link to the content, call the startClip function, as follows:

```
<br> <A HREF="JavaScript:startClip( 'pnm://your.realserver.com/
glasr56.rm', '00:00:27.0', '00:00:54.1', null, null, null)"> TimeN
</A>
```

Or you can use an image and call JavaScript using the onClick function, as follows:

```
<IMG SRC="button.jpg" onClick=startClip(video1.rm, 00:02:37.0,
    00:03:34.1, null, null, null)>
```

The downside to this solution is that you are hardcoding your times into the HTML.

Creating RealFlash content

RealFlash is a hybrid file format utilizing the bandwidth-friendly vector animation and image compression of Macromedia Flash with the reliability and superior streaming efficiency of RealNetwork's RealServer. Flash is better suited for short interactive event sounds or sound effects such as buttons and transitions that call for immediate playback. Flash does not reliably stream long-playing audio files or feature sophisticated server-side applications such as bandwidth negotiation, multicasting, or splitting. In contrast, RealMedia is suited for broadcasting long-playing media files over short interactive sounds. Thus the marriage of the two formats into RealFlash results in the ideal solution for interactive presentations with audio files of several minutes or longer in length.

To broadcast RealFlash, you need to purchase an extra license from RealNetworks. For specific pricing information, visit *http://www.real.com*. For more information about Flash, see Chapter 10, *MIDI: Quick and Easy Audio for the Web*.

For some of the most cutting edge RealFlash content, such as riding a motor scooter through Montmartre on a virtual web tour of Paris (shown in Figure 6-9), visit *shockwave.com*.

To create your own RealFlash content, build a multimedia presentation in Macromedia Flash, and then export the animation as a Shockwave movie file and the streaming audio portion as a separate AVI video file. Use the RealNetworks tools to convert the Flash video file into the RealAudio format. Your final RealFlash presentation will consist of two files:

Shockwave Flash file (.swf)
> Created with the Flash Authoring tool

RealAudio file (.rm)
> Created with RealEncoder or RealPublisher

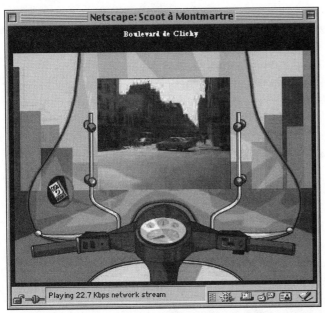

Figure 6-9. *The Club Internet RealFlash motor scooter tour of Montmartre in Paris with a RealVideo window embedded in a Flash animation screen*

If you are using RealSystem G2, read the RealFlash G2 section in Chapter 7.

To properly export your Flash animation file, follow these steps:

1. Open the Flash file in Macromedia Flash, and select File → Export Movie.

2. In the dialog box, choose *.swf* as the file type. Make sure to type the *.swf* extension at the end of the filename before clicking OK.

3. From the Export Shockwave Flash dialog box, set JPEG quality to 50 or less.

4. From the Audio Steam and Audio Event drop-down boxes, choose Disable to turn off the Flash Audio tracks.

5. Click OK to create the animation-only Shockwave file.

To create a RealAudio file, follow these steps:

1. With the same Flash file still open, select File → Export Movie.

2. In the dialog box, choose AVI as the file type. Make sure to use the *.avi* file extension in your filename.

3. In the Export Windows AVI dialog box, select dimension 32 × 32 regardless of the movie's true dimensions. Click OK to create the AVI file. This minimizes file size and creation time.

4. Open the RealEncoder or RealPublisher and choose File → Open Session.

5. On the Source panel, click File and add your AVI file to the list box. On the Destination panel, click RealMedia and specify an output filename with the *.rm* extension. Click OK.

6. In the Templates panel, click Advanced and deselect video. Then select an audio codec. This tells the encoder to save only the synchronized audio portion of the AVI file.

7. Enter a template name and click Save. Then click Close.

8. In the Templates panel, click Start to create your audio file, and you are ready to go with RealFlash.

Once you have created the *.swf* and *.rm* files necessary for a RealFlash presentation using the RealSystem 5.0, your web pages will need to link to the appropriate metafile, which in turn points to the DNS name or IP address of the computer on which your RealServer and RealMedia files are located.

For a RealFlash Animation metafile, you should combine the audio filename with the RealFlash filename by using the plus (+) sign, as follows:

```
pnm://www.server1.com/hello.rm+hello.swf
```

One of the challenges to creating RealFlash presentations is optimizing the bandwidth consumption of the separate audio and animation files. You can optimize your RealFlash media with the RealFlash Bandwidth Tuner. The Bandwidth Tuner is included in the RealFlash Content Creation Kit for Windows and is designed to graphically analyze and adjust the bandwidth consumption of a RealFlash presentation. The utility, *swftune*, optimizes or tunes "audioless" Shockwave Flash files and allows the user to compare and adjust bitrate and buffering time for an optimal balance.

To broadcast RealFlash, you need a RealServer to perform the synchronization of the RealAudio track (*.rm*) and the Flash animation (*.swf*). Additionally, the two datatypes are married together using a URL syntax not recognized by web browsers:

```
pnm://server.domain.com/realaudio.rm+realflash.swf
```

Creating synchronized RealAudio presentations with RealSystem 5.0

While synchronized media is easier to create and broadcast with the newer multimedia-enhanced RealSystem G2, many web producers still use RealSystem 5.0 due to pre-existing infrastructure constraints and the number of viewers with older RealAudio plug-ins. If you are not already using RealSystem 5.0 or are not tied to 5.0 for a compelling reason, we recommend you use G2's SMIL, RealPix, and RealText to create and broadcast synchronized media presentations.

If you are using RealSystem 5.0, there are two basic options for creating real-time multimedia presentations with fast forward, rewind, and pause controls:

- You can use the Cevents utility to create a binary event file for synchronizing web pages with audio. (RealAudio 3.0)

- You can create an output presentation file using the *RMMerge.exe* tool to synchronize RealAudio content. (RealAudio 4.0 and 5.0)

Next, we look at how David Dadekian from Internet News Services used RealAudio to produce a guided tour of the TV Guide Entertainment Network.

At an All-Star Game Fan Fest, News Corp. hosted a booth to educate people about its media presence on the Web. News Corp. developed a RealAudio-guided tour for large screen video display to promote their various web site properties such as TV Guide Entertainment Network. RealAudio, combined with the Cevents command-line tool included in the RealServer package, provided a simple solution.

By simply adding an extra Cevent text file containing all the URL links and their time specifications into the same directory as the *.ra* file, Dadekian quickly generated an audio-visual guided tour.

To create your own 12-page guided tour, follow these three steps:

1. Create a text file containing the written display time for each page in the tour. With a standard text editor, create an input file with a total of 12 lines of text specifying the display time for each URL in the tour. For example, the first line specifies the start time for the URL, *http://www.tvguide.com*, at 0 seconds and the end time at 30 seconds. The next line specifies a new URL at a start time of 31 seconds and an end time of 60 seconds, and so forth. Repeat this process for all 12 pages. See the *tvgentour.txt* example text file below.

   You can also add comment lines to the *.rae* (RealAudio Event) file by beginning them with the # symbol:

```
#u <starttime> <endtime> <URL>
#i <starttime> <endtime> <Title>
#a <starttime> <endtime> <Author>
#c <starttime> <endtime> <Copyright>
u 00:00:00.0 00:00:29.9 http://www.tvguide.com/index.sml
u 00:00:30.0 00:00:59.9 http://www.tvguide.com/tv/
u 00:01:00.0 00:01:29.9 http://www.tvguide.com/tv/listings/
u 00:01:30.0 00:01:59.9 http://www.tvguide.com/tv/listings/
    editions/ny/g10.sml
```

```
u 00:02:00.0 00:02:29.9 http://www.tvguide.com/tv/listings/
   editions/ny/quickpicks.sml
u 00:02:30.0 00:02:59.9 http://www.tvguide.com/tv/listings/
   editions/ny/search.sml
u 00:03:00.0 00:03:29.9 http://www.tvguide.com/tv/watch/
u 00:03:30.0 00:03:59.9 http://www.tvguide.com/tv/circuits/
u 00:04:00.0 00:04:29.9 http://www.tvguide.com/area52/
u 00:04:30.0 00:04:59.9 http://www.tvguide.com/soapdish/
u 00:05:00.0 00:05:29.9 http://www.tvguide.com/movies/
u 00:05:30.0 00:05:59.9 http://www.tvguide.com/movies/
   database/
```

This code launches a browser window external to the player.
While this code is suitable for using with the standalone Real-
Player, it won't work when the player is embedded in a web
page. This code causes the web browser to load the synchronized web page, changing away from the web page with the
embedded Player. If the player is embedded, embed the player
in one frame and leave a large secondary frame for the synchronized content. Point the events at the secondary frame by
appending &&secondary_frame_name&& to the front of the URL.

2. Convert the text file to a Cevent file. To create a RealAudio Event
   file, run the *cevent32.exe* program in the *raencode* directory from
   a DOS prompt (command line). For example:

   ```
   cevent32 tvgentour.txt tvgentour.rae
   ```

3. Upload your RealAudio (*.ra*) and RealAudio Event (*.rae*) files to
   the RealServer. For example, after creating the Cevent file,
   Dadekian uploaded a six-minute *.ra* file along with the *.rae* file
   to the same directory on the RealAudio Server. When a *.rae* file
   is placed within the same directory as the corresponding *.ra* file
   on the RealServer, the server default setting is automatically configured to recognize the *.rae* file (*pnmn://av.newscorp.com/
   tvtour.rae*).

When a user accesses the guided tour, the server goes to play the
tour.ra file but notices there is a *tour.rae* file in the same folder. As
the RealAudio Event file plays, it triggers the web browser to display
web pages at the proper times.

RealAudio 5.0 uses the RMMerge tool to generate timeline files. To
create a synchronized media presentation with RealAudio 5.0, follow
these two steps:

1. Using a text editor, create an input events file specifying the display time for each URL, title, author, or copyright.

2. After creating a text version of the input events file, generate an
   output presentation file. This is done with the *rmmerge.exe* tool

that comes with RealEncoder 5.0 and RealPublisher 5.0. For more information, see the RealAudio 5.0 Content Creation Guide at *http://www.realaudio.com*.

To find out more about synchronized presentations with SMIL, read Chapter 7.

Database management and tracking of RealAudio content

If you have hundreds or thousands of RealMedia files, archive management becomes a difficult issue. One method for archiving and managing RealAudio content is to store the *.ram* and *.rpm* text files in a database. Since *.ram* and *.rpm* files are text-based, they can be generated by Java servlets or CGI scripts.

A database can also be useful for implementing a variety of interesting applications besides simply organizing your content. For example, with Cold Fusion from Allaire you can select a particular *.ram* file in a tree and then execute it according to the day of the week or a particular category selection made by a user. Further, MCI's Nick DelRegno reports that their database is tied to their live scheduling system to dynamically return live events upon request and generate the appropriate *.ram* or *.rpm* file for the user.

Larry Bouthillier, head of multimedia production at Harvard Business School, recommends building a database of all the metadata of your content, including title, filename and path, servername, start time, end time, and so on. A Java servlet can then be used to piece together a *.ram* file-type string and return it to the browser with the appropriate MIME type header.

One good thing about having all the metadata in a database is that you can make a web form that enters new entries into the database. According to Bouthillier, "Creating a new video clip is as easy as filling in the filename, start and end times, and saving it to the database. You also have the beginnings of a primitive online video editing system."

For more on Java servlets, see *Java Servlet Programming* by Jason Hunter (O'Reilly, 1998).

Load balancing

If you need to deliver simultaneous streams to a large audience, consider clustering several servers together. In order to set up a cluster of RealServers to handle the load of RealPlayer file requests, you should use a Perl script to manage load balancing, according to Kim Ayers, software engineer for RealNetworks. The following Perl script, written by Rob Bowden, can be used to balance the load across multiple RealServers:

```perl
#!/usr/bin/perl
# usage:
http://www.webserver.com/cgi-bin/load?anything.rm
#@ip = ( 'server1', 'server2', 'server2', 'server2', 'server3' );
#$content = $ENV{'QUERY_STRING'};
srand($$ + time);
$count = int(rand($#ip + 1));
print "Content-type: audio/x-pn-realaudio\n\n";
print "pnm://$ip[$count]/$content\n";
```

To get the Perl script up and working, follow these steps:

1. Put the Perl script in the *cgi-bin* directory of a web server.

2. Make the content link point to this script with the argument being the requested content. For example:

   http://www.webserver.com/cgi-bin/load?anything.rm

   Note that the Perl script is called *load.pl* but the *.pl* suffix is not included because the RealNetwork's web server is configured to recognize Perl scripts in its *cgi-bin*. The argument following the "?" is the name of the content.

3. When the link is hit, the script returns text that combines a server chosen randomly from the list of servers specified in *load.pl* with the content name.

In the code above, the ip array contains five elements:

```
ip[1] = server1
ip[2] = server2
ip[3] = server2
ip[4] = server2
ip[5] = server3
```

Using this list, server1 will get 20% of the load, server2 will get 60%, and server3 will get 20%. By adding multiple entries, you can obtain any prescribed balance.

You can easily modify this Perl script to randomly select RealAudio clips. For example, if you want visitors to your site to be able to listen to a different audio file each time they visit a particular page, you could modify the Perl script to randomly call 1 of 10 files.

Another method of load balancing is the use of a hardware-based solution like the Local Director from Cisco. For example, MCI achieves load balancing by having several servers, whose content is fully replicated among them, sitting behind a Local Director router. Whenever a request hits the router, it routes the TCP connection to the machine with the lowest load. This hardware load balancing is completely transparent to the user and allows for greatly improved fault tolerance, reliability, and the ability to easily take systems out of service for maintenance by migrating traffic off of the server in question. In the wide area, MCI is using a similar system, aptly called Distributed Director, to route the request to the closest cluster.

Now that you have explored some of the advanced capabilities of the RealSystem, let's take a look at one of the more popular advanced applications: live broadcasting.

Live broadcasting with RealAudio

Live broadcasting of tradeshow events, radio shows, and music concerts, is one of RealAudio's most popular applications. Figure 6-10 shows the live encoding process.

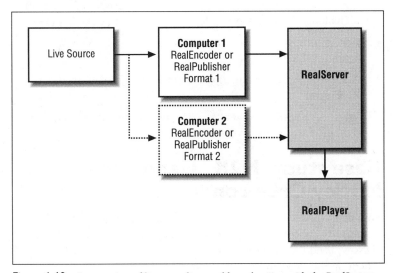

Figure 6-10. *An overview of live encoding and broadcasting with the RealSystem*

To deliver live content over the Web you will need the following resources:

- A live audio source
- A dedicated computer running the RealEncoder
- An additional computer running the RealServer
- A live broadcasting license from RealNetworks

Note that encoding a live broadcast for later playback or archival purposes does not require a special license.

To reach the widest possible audience, broadcast at least two audio streams encoded for high- and low-bandwidth connections. To broadcast several versions of the same audio feed, you will need to run a separate computer and RealEncoder for each codec. (Note that Linux and Solaris support encoding with multiple sound cards on one machine.) RealSystem 5.0 does not support bandwidth negotiation during live broadcasting. If you are using a Mac system to broadcast live audio, you need to use the 3.1 Mac RealEncoder or the Mac G2 encoder when it is released by RealNetworks (5.0 does not support live encoding).

There are several challenges to live broadcasting with the RealAudio System:

- Capturing a good source feed with the proper mix, volume, and EQ. Recording live events in less than optimal conditions, as opposed to recording in a controlled studio environment, can be a challenge. Read Chapter 3 for more in-depth live recording tips.

- Configuring your live encoder for remote management and optimum reliability.

- Achieving adequate data throughput from the RealEncoder to the RealServer.

- Ensuring adequate server capacity and bandwidth to meet the demand for popular live events.

Case study: N2K streams live Mötley Crüe concert

Now that you are familiar with some of the challenges of live broadcasting, let's take a look at how N2K Entertainment, now part of CDNow, used the RealAudio System to broadcast a Mötley Crüe concert at the Roseland in New York.

As manager of Online Technologies for N2K Entertainment, Tim Nielson is responsible for managing N2K's RealAudio live concert cybercasts and 24-hour RealAudio broadcasts of WBGO's Jazz Central Station in New Jersey and WQXR's Classical Insights in New York City. N2K Entertainment produces the popular Music Boulevard (see Figure 6-11) and Rocktropolis web sites and was one of the first companies to pioneer live webcasting and online music sales over the Internet.

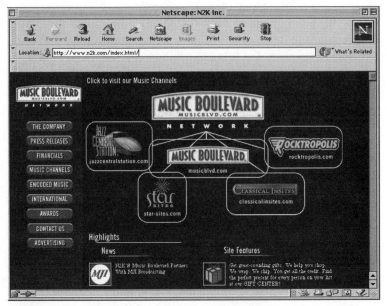

Figure 6-11. *The N2K home page at http://www.n2k.com*

Capturing high-quality live sound

The greatest challenge in broadcasting live events is supplying the RealEncoder with a high-quality source signal. Capturing a good audio feed is a difficult task, since the two easiest methods for recording live audio—getting a signal direct from the concert PA mixer or setting up a pair of microphones—have serious tradeoffs.

Recording a direct stereo signal from a monitor mixing board is problematic since every concert venue requires special equalization to prevent distortion and to custom-tailor the sound for the acoustics of the concert hall. This means that you will often get a mix that sounds great when it's played back in a particular concert hall but sounds terrible when played back anywhere else.

The other option, using a pair of microphones to capture a live event such as Mötley Crüe's show at the Roseland in New York, has other inherent problems. Sensitive stereo condenser microphones are not suited for events with loud crowd noises.

At events where there is excessive crowd noises, N2K prefers to capture the audio signal directly from the house-mixing console. For events with little or no crowd noises, such as a classical music concert, theater performance, or speech, N2K uses two overhead condenser microphones.

On the night of the Mötley Crüe concert, N2K was fortunate enough to have the best of both worlds—a clean, noise-free audio signal with optimum equalization settings. N2K captured the sound from a separate audio feed instead of using microphones or the house-mixing console.

By chance, another production company was on location to mix the Mötley Crüe concert for radio syndication. N2K was able to feed the live mix from the remote digital mixing studio parked outside the club through an 80-foot long XLR cable with a stereo mini jack converter connecting to a SoundBlaster Pro sound card running into the RealAudio Live Encoder.

Capturing live audio with the RealEncoder

From the SoundBlaster card, N2K routed the audio signal through two custom rack-mountable 200 MHz computers running Windows 95 into the Live Encoder. To get the maximum performance and reliability out of N2K's Live Encoders, Tim Nielson uses the cleanest machines with all other applications and extensions de-installed, except for the Live Encoder and the Operating System. Note that after using the SoundBlaster Pro, Tim Nielson recommends using a better sound card such as Digidesigns by AudioMedia III for better analog to digital conversion. Other developers report very little difference between the $20 audio boards and the $500 boards, as long as there is a clean input signal and proper grounding. While a less-expensive sound card may not be as noticeable with low-bandwidth encoded audio files, higher-bandwidth files will reveal the inferior signal-to-noise ratios inherent in poor-quality sound cards.

Make sure to watch the Volume Controls from the option menu to ensure that you have the optimum input levels set. While you encode RealAudio, you can monitor the audio input level to be sure you are encoding the optimal dynamic range. Green indicates a normal reading. Red warns that you are close to overloading the input. According to RealNetworks, the level meters in the RealEncoder are not accurate and are merely for gross amplitude level information. For best results, allow for plenty of headroom by staying in the yellow bar section of the input meters. The best sound quality will occur when the top bar is lit often but the clipping indicator never goes off, according to Tim Nielson.

After routing the audio signal to the two rack-mount computers, Tim Nielson set the correct format settings for the encoders, checked the Encoder preferences, and made sure he had a good connection to the RealServer. Taking advantage of RealAudio's bandwidth negotiation feature, he configured one Live Encoder to produce a 28.8 full response *concert.ra* file and the other Live Encoder to produce a 56K/ISDN stereo *concert.ra* file. Note that bandwidth negotiation works only if the files have the same name and are placed in the same directory.

Just as in a regular RealAudio broadcast of prerecorded audio material, you can configure the RealServer to deliver live streams encoded with different algorithms. By connecting multiple computers, each one running a Live Encoder configured to a different bandwidth format—such as RealAudio 2.0 at 14.4 and RealAudio 3.0 at 28.8—to one RealServer, you can deliver the format that targets your audience's bandwidth capabilities.

Archiving live broadcasts

The RealAudio system makes it extremely easy to record and archive live streams. This is a useful feature if you plan to make your live recordings available to users at a later time.

The RealServer can be configured to archive material in several ways: it can save a complete file of the event, make a new file based on elapsed time (such as every hour), or make a new file based on file size (such as every 5 MB). The RealServer automatically archives live audio streams that arrive at the server if the LiveFileTarget and Live-FilePassword settings are specified in the server's configuration file.

The encoder supports streaming to a disk as well as to a server, providing a local copy of the content. If capture is performed by the RealServer and there are any network drop-outs between the encoder and the server, the Server stores the errors. Capturing to disk at the encoder removes the network uncertainty from the equation.

If you need to archive particular hours of a 24-hour live broadcast, you can use a product called VCR 2.0 from Lariat Software, which can be found at *http://www.lariat.com*.

Using the time-out preferences to avoid crashes

After specifying the proper format options, Tim Nielson makes sure to change the default Time-Out Preference setting in the Live Encoder Preferences window. The Time-Out Preference displays an error message warning you that your audio content is no longer being streamed and that the connection between the encoder and server has been broken. Once a broken connection has been detected, the Live Encoder starts feeding the signal into a buffer until the connection is established again.

The Time-Out Preference determines how long the Encoder fills its buffer before displaying the error message. Tim Nielson recommends setting the Time-Out Preference to 600 seconds to allow enough time for the Encoder and Server to reconnect. If the specified time for the Time-Out Preference passes or the buffer fills up before the connection is repaired, the error message appears, requiring shutdown and restarting the Live Encoder. N2K generally specifies a large time-out value of 600 seconds to avoid shutdowns in the middle of the night when the staff is not around to restart the encoding machine. If N2K is streaming a live event where a technician is always at hand watching the machine, it is best to set a lower time value.

Once Tim Nielson specifies the appropriate Time-Out Preference, he routes the signal from the encoders at the Roseland in New York to N2K's RealServer in Wayne, Pennsylvania. The ideal option, even though it was not used during the Mötley Crüe concert, Tim Nielson explained, would have been to have a direct ISDN connection between the Live Encoders in New York and the RealServer in Wayne, Pennsylvania. A direct ISDN connection guarantees enough direct bandwidth between the encoder and server with the least amount of packet loss or hops from one IP point to the next. RealNetworks recommends a connection from the encoders to the servers that is twice as large as the aggregate bandwidth of the encoded streams. For example, for 20 Kbps and 45 Kbps streams, RealNetworks recommends a network connection no less than 130 Kbps. This allows for the variability in their encoding as well as network errors and protocol overhead.

Splitting a live broadcast for more efficient streaming

If you purchase an additional server license from RealNetworks, you can use live splitting to "split" the live audio stream from one RealServer to several other RealServers placed at different strategic points across the globe. Figure 6-12 illustrates how this works. By allowing users to connect to the closest RealServer, you ensure better quality and performance. For meeting the high demand of a large worldwide broadcast, combining splitting with clustering is highly recommended. Clustering lets you operate several computers as one RealServer. With a computer running RealServer and operating both as a cluster control server and a splitter, you can supply a large number of connections to a single live audio stream coming from the broadcast site.

For the Mötley Crüe concert, N2K split the concert feed from their master server in Pennsylvania to RealServers in New York, Palo Alto, and Vancouver. For security purposes, N2K does not stream files to the general public from their master server. The RealAudio master server in Pennsylvania is primarily used for splitting the audio stream to other RealServers placed in strategic locations. N2K's RealServer runs on an SGI system running IRIX.

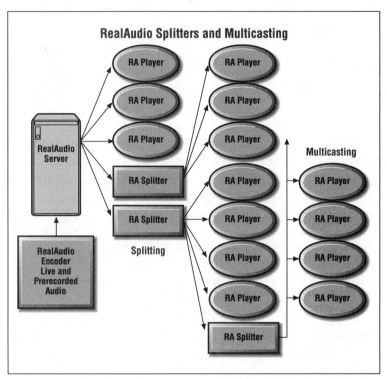

Figure 6-12. *Multicasting and splitting allow you to broadcast to a greater number of RealPlayers from one licensed RealServer by using the exponential power of multiple servers. This figure shows how 5 streams can quickly turn into 15 streams, with no extra load on the original server, by broadcasting a stream to another server (RA Splitter), which splits and sends the signal to more RealPlayers.*

Remote encoding and management

Although the two-hour Mötley Crüe broadcast did not require remote encoding, many situations, especially 24-hour live broadcasts, call for a remote management solution. The live RealEncoder for Unix and Windows includes a command-line interface that can be remotely managed. If you are running the RealSystem on Linux, Solaris, or

IRIX, you can remotely access the encoder through Telnet. On Windows, you need a third-party Telnet daemon, or you can set up an HTTP server and use CGI scripts via web pages to administer the encoder. In general, the Unix solution is easier, more reliable, and less limiting, according to RealNetwork engineers.

If it is mission-critical that your RealEncoder stays up 100% of the time and must be remotely managed, pay close attention to purchasing the right system. Most experienced RealMedia developers report that the RealEncoder running on Solaris or Silicon Graphics is more reliable and easier to manage than the Windows NT version. An SGI O2 or a Sun Ultra10 are great systems for keeping a 24×7 RealEncoder running and are similar in price to a fully loaded, dual-processor PC.

If you have to use Windows NT, split the video and audio inputs to a spare backup system. Set up a script that will monitor the stream of the first encoder and start the second encoder (via the command-line interface) if the first encoder goes down.

The RealNetworks Consulting Group has developed several tools for remote management. The Remote Encoder is a customized version of the RealPublisher 5.0 (NT only) that allows the user to remotely initialize, start, and stop an encoding session. The Monitor Encoder for Windows 95 and Windows NT detects dead silence in the audio stream. Once the silent period exceeds a certain threshold set by the system administrator (e.g., 10 seconds), it sends an email warning. The Monitor Encoder also has a second warning threshold that once exceeded, terminates the encoding session automatically.

If you are interested in one of these remote management tools, send email to *consulting@real.com*. The license for the Remote Encoder solution and Monitor Encoder are available on a per-site basis, according to RealNetworks.

Summary

Now that you have covered the basics of the RealMedia System, you're ready to explore the powerful new features in RealSystem G2 (RealAudio 6.0 and up). Read the next chapter for cutting-edge tips on creating and broadcasting multimedia content with SMIL and the RealSystem G2.

CHAPTER SEVEN

DESIGNING MULTIMEDIA PRESENTATIONS WITH SMIL AND REALSYSTEM G2

The RealSystem G2 is a completely re-engineered architecture of the RealMedia system and was built from the ground up to replace the entire line of RealAudio 5.0 encoding and streaming tools. RealNetwork's second-generation platform introduces enhanced streaming features and powerful new media capabilities that allow you to stream multiple media and datatypes, including separate audio, video, image, and text files, in a synchronized presentation. In addition, G2 offers many improvements in the efficiency and functionality of encoding and streaming media files.

RealSystem G2's SMIL-based multimedia may not have the interactive power and graphics sophistication of Flash or Shockwave presentations, but it has the advantage of a huge user base and the ease of creating multimedia with a simple markup language. By copying the SMIL tags in this chapter, you can get up and running with a fairly rich, albeit simple, multimedia presentation. In contrast, Flash packs more power and automatically takes care of complex timeline issues, but it requires learning a whole new proprietary authoring environment. Expect to see Flash used more widely for more complex high-impact presentations, such as movie and game trailers or product demos, and SMIL for more common everyday uses, such as audio slide shows, sound with scrolling text captions, and video news feeds.

The creation of streaming multimedia presentations is accomplished by using a combination of three new XML-compliant markup languages: the W3C's Synchronized Multimedia Integration Language (SMIL) and RealNetwork's RealPix and RealText. Since SMIL is an open standard, there are a wide range of applications that allow you to easily create synchronized multimedia content for RealSystem G2.

In this chapter

- SureStream
- SMIL
- RealPix
- RealText
- RealFlash
- Delivering backwards-compatible content
- Case study: TechWeb Today
- Summary

Applications that support SMIL authoring include:

Extend Media TAG

As the high-end solution of choice, TAG features all the bells and whistles for quickly producing complex SMIL presentations (*http://www.extend.com*).

Veon VeonStudio

While not as powerful as TAG, VeonStudio is a complete authoring environment for creating interactive broadband content with SMIL and is one of the easiest authoring tools on the market. VeonStudio is free. The VeonServer can be purchased for a small fee (*http://www.veon.com*).

RealNetworks RealProducer Pro

Falling between TAG and VeonStudio in horsepower, RealProducer Pro packs powerful tools for building SMIL presentations (*http://www.realnetworks.com*).

Sausage SMIL Composer SuperTool

SMIL Composer is a freeware authoring tool that allows you to easily add available media types, arrange their layout and sequence, and decide how they are played in your composition. Then, with one click, you can view your SMIL code or preview your composition in your RealSystem G2 Player. Unlike TAG, RealProducer Pro, and Veon, the SMIL Composer does not support the editing of RealPix or RealText files. The tool assumes you have RealPix and RealText files ready to go before you embed them in your SMIL presentation (*http://www.sausage.com*).

Allaire Homesite

This HTML editing application features a helpful SMIL tag pack for simple SMIL authoring (*http://www.allaire.com/products/homesite/*).

Macromedia Dreamweaver

The extensions in Dreamweaver support embedding SMIL-based RealPlayer objects into web pages. You can download the Dreamweaver extension free from RealMedia (*http://www.dreamweaver.com*).

RealNetworks RealSlideshow

This free SMIL authoring tool enables consumers to compose quick slideshows. The RealSlideshow Plus is inexpensive and packs more interesting features (*http://www.realnetworks.com*).

RealSystem G2 also supports an increased array of file types and formats via the RealTime Streaming Protocol (RTSP) such as JPEG, GIF, QuickTime, MPEG, MP3, MIDI, VIVO, VRML, AVI, WAV, AIF, AU, and Microsoft's ASF (Active Streaming Format). RealSystem G2 also supports other datatypes for specialty applications.

Additional key innovations in encoding and streaming include:

- **On-the-fly dynamic bandwidth allocation with SureStream.** This technology automatically adjusts data transmission rates to match fluctuations in bandwidth conditions. If a listener's bandwidth drops off suddenly, SureStream detects this change and sends a smaller stream to accommodate the lower bandwidth instead of continuing to try and shove an egg through the straw. SureStream alleviates the breaks and pops associated with bandwidth negotiation and rebuffering in RealSystem 5.0, which is a much needed improvement as 5.0 often overestimates the bandwidth throughput of a user's modem.

- **Vastly improved sound quality with an 80% increase in frequency response over the previous 20 KB 5.0 codecs.** The new G2 audio codecs are the first to be developed in-house by RealNetworks. They reproduce higher frequencies better than previous codecs and result in brighter, more realistic audio. The G2 codecs take advantage of new encoding technologies and vastly improved algorithms for compressing file sizes.

- **Simplified encoding process.** In RealSystem G2, one file serves up to six different connection rates. The default bitrate settings are for 28 Kbps, 56 Kbps, single ISDN, dual ISDN, xDSL, and T1. For the T1 setting, select whatever bitrate you want to encode to, with the maximum at 1.2 Mbps. RealSystem 5.0 requires encoding multiple files for bandwidth negotiation.

- **Faster encoding.** The G2 encoder offers audio encoding that is five times faster than with the previous RealEncoder 5.0.

SureStream

SureStream technology is a vastly improved method for streaming media. SureStream eliminates the breaks in media transmission due to changes in network conditions, such as a drop in throughput from 50 Kbps per second to 20 Kbps. In previous versions, the RealPlayer buffered a certain amount of data in the queue before it began to play. If the connection rate declined, the stream would still play. However, if it played the contents of the queue before the connection resumed, a break in the transmission would occur until more data was received.

G2's SureStream technology makes possible a dynamic bandwidth-detection relationship between the client and server throughout the serving process. When encoding a RealAudio or RealVideo file, the G2 encoder creates several embedded copies of the file at varying discrete data rates. The server then has the ability to dynamically switch streams based on the client's changing bandwidth conditions.

As illustrated in Figure 7-1, if a connection is initially established at 56 Kbps, and then drops to 48 Kbps, the server can detect this change and respond by altering the serving rate, at a preset increment, to accommodate the new connection speed. If the connection rate increases, it can adjust to that rate as well.

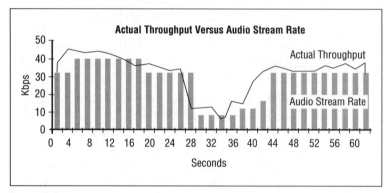

Figure 7-1. *Streaming rates are tied to actual connection speeds with SureStream.*

A RealAudio or RealVideo file encoded with G2 SureStream will be much larger than it would be if encoded with RealEncoder 5.0. The larger file size reflects the many embedded copies of the file that have been encoded at different bitrates. While G2 *.rm* files require somewhat larger storage space, they do not require extra bandwidth to stream because only one bitrate version of the file is streamed at any given time. The others simply remain on the server and are employed only if necessary, due to changes in network connections.

As a key broadcasting innovation, SureStream greatly simplifies the delivery of audio and video content to multiple bandwidth connection rates and ensures a high-quality viewing or listening experience free of drop-outs. SureStream will produce a quantum leap in streaming quality on the Web as more and more developers incorporate the G2 technology, especially those who found bandwidth negotiation with the previous RealMedia platform too complex to implement.

SMIL

A SMIL file takes the place of a RealSystem 5.0 *.ram* file and has three main purposes:

- It describes the overall layout of the presentation.
- It serves as the macro metafile for the presentation, sourcing media and data files, as well as other, more specific metafiles.
- It establishes the overall presentation timeline.

Because each element in a SMIL-based presentation can be encoded and transmitted separately with synchronization control, content creators can optimize their presentations by choosing the least bandwidth-intensive format necessary to transmit data. This reduces the bandwidth required to stream the whole package and makes it easier to edit the presentation later.

A powerful advantage to encoding pieces of the presentation in separate files and using SMIL to control their interaction is the increased ease and flexibility over editing presentations encoded together in a single file. For example, if you decide after finishing the presentation that you would like the audio portion of a presentation to begin five seconds after the rest of the presentation begins, you can use SMIL to set a start time for the audio track at five seconds, without having to edit the audio file itself.

SMIL syntax

In general, SMIL is a tag-based markup language similar to HTML. A few basic syntax rules to remember in SMIL are:

- All SMIL tags that do not have a corresponding closing tag are self-closing; they must end with a forward slash (/).

- All tag and attribute names must be lowercase, and attribute values must be enclosed within double quotation marks.

SMIL files begin with an opening `<smil>` tag and end with a closing `</smil>` tag. As in HTML, SMIL files have two primary sections—a header and a body. The SMIL header contains two basic elements— meta tags and layout tags. The body contains all the file source tags. In its most skeletal structure, a SMIL file looks like this:

```
<smil>
   <head>
      a series of <meta> tags
      <layout>
         <root-layout/>
         a series of <region/> tags
      </layout>
   </head>
   <body>
      a series of file source tags
   </body>
</smil>
```

The meta tags use name and content attributes to assign the author, title, and copyright information that is displayed in the "Clip Info" area of the RealPlayer:

```
<meta name="title" content="My RealPix Show"/>
<meta name="author" content="Jane Doe"/>
<meta name="copyright" content="© My Company, 1999"/>
```

The SMIL advantage

The W3C's Synchronized Multimedia Integration Language (SMIL) adds new punch to the previously limited multimedia capabilities in versions 5.0 and earlier.

Stretchable media windows

With the introduction of RealPlayer 7.0, the image window region or playback area of your RealMedia presentation can expand and stretch to any window size on the fly. If a viewer expands the media window, all the datatypes in the RealMedia presentation will now expand accordingly.

The layout of the presentation is described through a series of <region/> tags which appear between the <layout></layout> tags. First, the overall size of the presentation is set in the <root-layout/> tag. This is the size to which the display area of the RealPlayer will conform, before the presentation begins. It remains constant throughout the entire show. The region size can be set to any number and is similar to setting the parameters of a normal web page. Similar to designing content for the Web, you will need to consider that some people may view your content at 600×800 resolution.

The <root-layout/> tag is followed by a series of <region/> tags. Each region is given a unique name (id) and is defined by its height and width, as well as by the x and y coordinates of its upper-left corner. Layers may overlap, and the z-index attribute assigns the stacking order of the layers; the layers with higher z-indexes appear on top of the lower-numbered layers.

In Example 7-1, the total display area is 300×300 pixels, and there are four regions inside this area. None of the regions overlap, so they all share the same z-index. Some regions are named with the media type that is displayed in them, while other names are more content-oriented. You may assign any names you want to your regions, as long as each is unique within the file.

Example 7-1. *Basic layout of a SMIL display area*

```
<layout>
<root-layout width="300" height="300"/>
<region id="video" width="160" height="120" top="10" left="10"
    z-index="1"/>
<region id="text" width="110" height="120" top="10" left="180"
    z-index="1"/>
<region id="videocaption" width="160" height="140" top="150" left="10"
    z-index="1"/>
<region id="slideshow" width="110" height="140" top="150" left="180"
    z-index="1"/>
</layout>
```

The body of the SMIL file serves as a metafile for all the media and data files that comprise the presentation. Specific media or data files must be sourced into the regions that are named and described in the SMIL file's header. The following syntax is used:

```
<video src="myVideo.rm" region="video"/>
<text src="myText.rt" region="text"/>
<text src="myVideoCaption.rt" region="videocaption"/>
<img src="mySlideshow.rp" region="slideshow"/>
<audio src="myAudio.ra"/>
```

Notice that the audio file is not associated with a region. This is because, as the only nonvisual element of the presentation, it is not displayed in the player. The audio track will simply accompany all the visual elements. Figure 7-2 illustrates the basic layout of this presentation.

It's important to note that media files such as audio, video, and Flash are sourced directly in the SMIL file. However, a still graphic, such as a JPEG, is not sourced directly into the SMIL file. All <img> tags must source a RealPix file, and the JPEG graphics are, in turn, sourced in the RealPix file. Similarly, all text content must reside in a RealText file. <text> tags in the SMIL file simply source the *.rt* file, which in turn, contains the text itself.

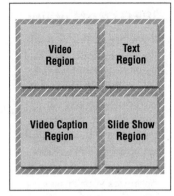

Figure 7-2. *An example of basic layout and data placement*

Establishing a timeline

The SMIL file also establishes the overall timeline and synchronization of a presentation. The <par> tag designates a group of files that will stream and play in parallel with each other or at the same time. The <seq> tag designates files that are played in sequence. More than one file may be placed in the same region, but not at the same time. <par> and <seq> tags may be nested inside each other as shown in Example 7-2.

Example 7-2. *Sample parallel and sequential playback*

```
<par>
    <text src="myText.rt" region="text"/>
    <text src="myVideoCaption.rt" region="videocaption"/>
    <img src="mySlideshow.rp" region="slideshow" begin="10s"/>
    <seq>
        <audio src="myAudio.ra"/>
        <video src="myVideo1.rm" region="video"/>
        <video src="myVideo2.rm" region="video" clip-begin="10s"
            clip-end="57.5s"/>
    </seq>
</par>
```

In Example 7-2, the RealPix file and two text files are all within the same <par> tags, so they will all begin at precisely the same millisecond. (RealPix is discussed later in the chapter.) Nested within the <par> tags are <seq> tags, which contain information about playing one audio file and two video files. Because the three files are within <seq> tags, they will play one after the other, in the order in which they are listed. Because they are nested within the <par> tags, the audio track (or perhaps a brief introduction) will play first, at the same time as the image and text files, which are also within the <par> tags. As soon as the audio file has played, the first video will begin, followed by the second video.

You will also notice some begin and end attributes in Example 7-2. The begin attribute enables you to stream two files simultaneously, but delay the start of one. The *mySlideshow.rp* file actually begins playing 10 seconds after the other files within the <par> tags.

The clip-begin and clip-end attributes apply only to media files with internal timelines. In Example 7-2, only the 47.5-second portion of the second video, between its 10-second and 57.5-second marks, will play.

For more information on SMIL, visit RealNetwork's RealSystem G2 Production Guide at *http://service.real.com/help/library/guides/ production/realpgd.htm.*

For more complete documentation on SMIL authoring, visit *http:// service.real.com/help/library/guides/production/htmfiles/smil.htm.*

RealPix

RealPix is the markup language that serves as a metafile for the static graphics used in G2 presentations. RealPix supports delivery of JPEGs and GIFs. While these graphic formats are themselves static images, you can nonetheless create compelling slideshows with motion and transition effects, all coded within RealPix.

RealPix also offers powerful timeline capabilities with millisecond control, allowing you to synchronize the appearance and behavior of images to other streaming media files, including audio tracks and videos.

RealPix syntax

RealPix files begin with the opening <imfl> tag and end with the closing </imfl> tag. All other RealPix tags are self-closing, and as with SMIL, they must end with a forward slash (/). All tag and attribute names must be lowercase, and attribute values must be enclosed within double quotation marks.

RealPix files have three basic components: the header, the image tags, and the effect tags.

All header information is contained within the <head/> tag. The associated attributes allow you to define title, author, and copyright as well as set necessary parameters such as the presentation dimensions, duration, time format, and streaming bitrate. For example:

```
<head
    name="My RealPix Show"
    author="Jane Doe"
    copyright="© My Company, 1999"
    timeformat="dd:hh:mm:ss.xyz"
    duration="24"
    background="#FFFFFF"
```

```
bitrate="20000"
width="200"
height="200"/>
```

The header is followed by a series of <image/> tags, each one providing the filename and location of an image to be used in the presentation and assigning it a unique numerical handle. Example 7-3 is a RealPix slideshow that uses three images. The first two images are located in the same directory as the *.rp* file, and the third is located one directory below the *.rp* file.

Example 7-3. *Image for RealPix slideshow*

```
<image handle="1" name="frog.jpg"/>
<image handle="2" name="cat.jpg"/>
<image handle="3" name="/images/dog.jpg"/>
```

Next, timing and behavior of the images are coded in a series of effect tags, which use the target attribute to refer to the appropriate image where the target value is the image's handle number. The five RealPix effect tags are <fadein/>, <fadeout/>, <crossfade/>, <wipe/>, and <viewchange/>.

The <fadein/> tag creates a transition from a background color to the new image. The <fadeout/> tag provides the opposite functionality, creating a transition from an existing image to a background color. The <crossfade/> tag creates a transition between an existing image to a new one. Figures 7-3 through 7-5 display examples of the <fadein/>, <fadeout/>, and <crossfade/> effects.

Figure 7-3. *An image appearing from a white background color, using the <fadein/> effect*

Figure 7-4. *An image disappearing to a black background color, using the <fadeout/> effect*

Figure 7-5. *One image transitioning to another, using the <crossfade/> effect*

Each effect tag also has a series of attributes that assign its timing and placement. The start attribute marks the time from the beginning of the presentation to when that effect should begin to take place. The duration attribute refers to the length of time it takes for that effect to complete, not the length of time that the image will display.

In Example 7-4, the background color described in the header first fills the presentation region. One second later, the first image begins to fade in. The fade-in takes two seconds to complete. Seven seconds later (at the 10-second mark of the overall show), the first image begins to crossfade into the second image. This transition takes three seconds to complete. Finally, 20 seconds after the show began, over a period of 4 seconds, the second image begins to fade out, to a solid bright red color.

Example 7-4. *Fadein, crossfade, and fadeout effects*

```
<fadein start="1" handle="1" duration="2"/>
<crossfade start="10" handle="2" duration="3"/>
<fadeout start="20" duration="4" color="#FF0000"/>
```

The <wipe/> tag creates a transition from one image to another, either by covering the displayed image or by pushing it out of the way with a sliding effect (see Figure 7-6). The required direction and type attributes assign the basic parameters.

Figure 7-6. *One image transitioning to another using the push type of <wipe> effect*

In Example 7-5, the first image begins to appear two seconds after the presentation begins. It moves into and fills the region, from left to right, for a duration of three seconds. At the 10-second mark, over a

3-second period of time, a second image begins to appear at the top of the region, and pushes the first image down and out of the region, until only the second image is visible.

Example 7-5. *Wipe effects*

```
<wipe target="1" type="normal" direction="right" duration="3"
    start="2"/>
<wipe target="2" type="push" direction="down" duration="3" start="10"/>
```

The <viewchange/> tag provides ways to zoom in on a portion of an image, pan back from it, make it appear larger or smaller, or move it from one area of the player window to another. These movements rely heavily on the source and destination placement and size attributes, which set the dimensions and the (x,y) coordinate of the upper-left corner of the image. The source and destination coordinate and size attributes may be used with all five effects but are most frequently used to assign <viewchange/> behavior. These attributes include:

srcx
> X coordinate of the source rectangle

srcy
> Y coordinate of the source rectangle

srcw
> Width of the source rectangle

srch
> Height of the source rectangle

dstx
> X coordinate of the destination rectangle

dsty
> Y coordinate of the destination rectangle

dstw
> Width of the destination rectangle

dsth
> Height of the destination rectangle

The <viewchange/> tag does not use the target attribute; it applies to the image with the most recent effect. In Example 7-6, an image fades into the presentation region, at a size of 120×120, with the top left corner of the image at the (40,40) coordinate of the overall region. At the four-second mark, the image begins to shrink to a quarter of its original size, having dimensions of 60×60. It simultaneously moves across the presentation region so that its upper-left corner is at the (20,100) coordinate of the overall region.

Example 7-6. *The viewchange command*

```
<fadein start="1" duration="2" target="1" dstx="40" dsty="40" dstw="120"
    dsth="120"/>
<viewchange start="4" duration="3" srcx="40" srcy="40" srcw="120"
    srch="120" dstx="20" dsty="100" dstw="60" dsth="60"/>
```

It is best to maintain the aspect ratio of an image when altering its size with <viewchange/>. In Example 7-6, the aspect ratio is maintained, and a graphic at its original size of 120×120 is reduced perfectly to 25% of its original size to 60×60. If, however, you try to reduce the image to 60×40, the image itself becomes distorted. RealPix shrinks the image to your designated size, but maintains the 60×60 aspect ratio area, and displays two black lines, each 10 pixels wide, on either side of the image. Figure 7-7 shows the <viewchange/> tag at work.

Figure 7-7. *A zoom effect created with the <viewchange/> tag*

Hyperlinking

RealPix supports hyperlinking to HTML pages, which display in a web browser window. This is accomplished through the use of the url attribute in an effect tag:

```
<fadein target="1" start="1" duration="3"
    url="http://www.mycompany.com"/>
```

In the initial releases of RealPix, a graphic could not be linked to another SMIL file to be played within the G2 player (6.0). RealPlayer 7.0 offers hyperlinking support between SMIL files in a RealPix presentation.

For complete RealPix documentation, visit RealNetwork's RealPix Authoring Guide at *http://service.real.com/help/library/guides/realpix/ realpix.htm*.

RealText

RealText is the markup language that defines how streaming text looks and operates within a G2 presentation. Because text files are typically small, streaming text consumes minimal bandwidth, usually less than 1 Kbps, and therefore has an almost negligible impact on the overall bitrate of a G2 show.

RealText syntax

Like SMIL and RealPix, standalone tags are self-closing—they must end with a forward slash (/). All tag and attribute names must be lowercase, and attribute values must be enclosed within double quotation marks.

RealText supports many standard HTML layout and appearance tags, including <br/> and <p> for line breaks and spacing, as well as <b> and <i> for bolding and italicizing. Coded characters such as   for nonbreaking space are supported as well. Many more advanced HTML features, such as tables and frames, are not supported. For a full list of supported tags and coded characters, refer to RealNetwork's RealText Authoring Guide at *http://service.real.com/help/library/guides/realtext/realtext.htm*. The SMIL 2 specification is expected to greatly enhance the functionality of the SMIL specification.

Window types

RealText files open and close with the <window> and </window> tags. The <window> tag must contain the type attribute, which designates the file as one of five preset types: generic, tickertape, marquee, scrollingnews, or teleprompter. Each type has preset parameters, as well as a number of attributes that can be applied to it, which define the appearance and functionality of the content. Within these parameters, you can define additional details such as font size and color:

- A generic window has no preset parameters, and you can use it to create any RealText display allowed by the markup. You can display and erase lines of text, scroll text through the window, set text to crawl from side to side, or create a simple, static text box.

- scrollingnews text is preset to scroll from the bottom of the window to the top, but it does not scroll from side to side. Scrolling occurs at a constant rate throughout the presentation.

- Text in a tickertape window crawls from right to left and can also loop back around to the right. It cannot scroll up or down. The <tu> and <tl> tags describe the appearance and behavior of the text that appears in the upper and lower rows of the window, in the style of a stock ticker.

- marquee text crawls from right to left and can loop, and it is centered vertically within the window.

- In a teleprompter window, text arriving at the bottom edge of the window causes the text above it to move up just enough to display the new line.

The <window> tag also describes the height and width of the file. It's important to note that the height and width of the window must be the same as the height and width of the corresponding region in the SMIL file where your RealText file is being placed. If the dimensions are not exactly the same, the text will be distorted in the display.

Example 7-7 is a simple RealText file, using a scrollingnews window type. The <center> and <font> tags function the same way as they do in HTML.

Example 7-7. *An example of a basic RealText file*

```
<window type="scrollingnews" height="40" width="200">
<center><font size="1" face="arial" color="#0000CC">
All text goes in here. All text will scroll from the bottom of the
window to the top, but not from side to side. Scrolling will occur
at a constant rate throughout the presentation. <b>This text will
be bold.</b>
</font></center>
</window>
```

RealText files can be more complex as well, with their own internal timelines. Example 7-8 contains the three captions that will appear beneath graphics consecutively in the same area, according to the indicated time settings.

Example 7-8. *An example of captioned graphics*

```
<window type="generic" width="200" height="20" duration="30">
<time begin="0.5" end="10"/>
<font face="arial" size="1">Graphic 1 caption</font>
<time begin="10.5" end="20"/>
<font face="arial" size="1">Graphic 2 caption</font>
<time begin="20.5" end="30"/>
<font face="arial" size="1">Graphic 3 caption</font>
</window>
```

Hyperlinking

RealText supports hyperlinking to both HTML files and other SMIL files. Any words in RealText can be hyperlinked with the use of the <a href=""></a> syntax, identical to HTML. The default target is a web browser, so to create a hyperlink to another SMIL file, use the tar-get=_player attribute.

For complete RealText documentation, visit RealNetwork's RealText Authoring Guide at *http://service.real.com/help/library/guides/realtext/realtext.htm.*

RealFlash

RealFlash provides the ability to stream vector animations made in Macromedia Flash and their associated sound files over the Internet and into the RealPlayer. RealServer is equipped to stream the Flash and audio clips to RealPlayer such that the animation and sound remain synchronized throughout the duration of the stream.

As a rule, RealFlash is best suited for streaming linear presentations that have continuous audio and images synchronized along a timeline. The streaming nature of RealFlash limits the complexity and interactivity that can otherwise be incorporated into non-streaming Flash. Branching and allowing for user-initiated events, such as clicking and rollovers midstream, are not recommended. Movie clips—series of animations independent of the timeline—should not be used either.

However, you can add interactivity by using the Shockwave commands play, stop, goto and play, and get URL, after a stream is complete. For example, you may want viewers to be able to click a graphic at the end of a RealFlash presentation that links them to a web page in a browser window. The Shockwave "get URL" command used with this graphic corresponds to an internal RealPlayer command that supports the link.

The nature of vector-based streaming animation is that it does not consume bandwidth at an even rate. At the start of a Flash presentation, images used in the animation are streamed, requiring the heaviest data transfer. After that, only "lightweight" instructions for manipulating the groups and symbols are transferred.

When creating your Flash files, it is recommended that you reduce the bandwidth spikes that correspond to the introduction of new scenes and objects and that may, in turn, cause buffering breaks. RealFlash provides two tools for accomplishing this: the RealFlash Bandwidth Tuner, and the RealFlash BitRate Calculation Spreadsheet, both available for free from RealNetworks.

Here are the basic steps to creating RealFlash:

1. Import your audio source (WAV or AIFF) into Flash and synchronize it with the animation timeline, thereby creating a soundtrack.

2. Export your Flash animation to a Shockwave Flash (*.swf*) file, creating a compressed version of the animation suitable for streaming. This disables the audio stream.

3. Export the Flash soundtrack and convert it to the RealAudio format, using the RealEncoder, choosing a codec that fits your clip's bandwidth and content requirements.

   When emphasizing complex animation, use low-bitrate codecs targeted for voice. When emphasizing music or narration, use higher-bitrate codecs.

Once you have created your RealFlash file, you can easily incorporate it into a G2 presentation by sourcing it into a SMIL file:

```
<animation region="flashregion" src="myFlash.swf"/>
```

To play the Flash animation and its associated audio track together in a G2 show, enclose them together in a set of <par> tags:

```
<par>
<animation region="flashregion" src="myFlash.swf"/>
<audio src="myFlashAudio.ra"/>
</par>
```

Additional information on RealFlash is available in RealNetwork's RealSystem G2 Production Guide at *http://service.real.com/help/library/guides/production/realpgd.htm.*

Delivering backwards-compatible content

RealSystem G2 incorporates a high degree of backwards compatibility. If you want to take full advantage of the new G2 and SureStream technologies, however, you will need to encode, serve, and play files using G2 software.

There is no need to change your existing 5.0 content for delivery in the G2 system. The G2 server and player can deliver 5.0 content, enabling you to include 5.0 files in SMIL presentations.

The new content you create in RealSystem G2 can also be played by people using a 5.0 player. The G2 SureStream encoder offers the ability to include a backwards-compatibility 5.0 codec. The G2 server can detect the player version and automatically provide the appropriate stream.

If you plan to deliver full SMIL presentations, you will need a G2 server, and these presentations can be viewed properly only in a G2 player. Likewise, the dynamic bandwidth detection abilities of SureStream function only within the G2 system.

If you are delivering SMIL presentations, you can still include RealSystem 5.0 files and have the server automatically provide the appropriate stream to the client. This can be accomplished two ways:

1. By embedding a single link in your web page to a *.ram* file, as you would in RealSystem 5.0. The syntax within your *.ram* file would be as follows:

```
rtsp://my-realserver.com/presentation.smi
-- stop -
pnm://my-realserver.com/video.rm
```

The G2 server will detect the player version, and stream either the SMIL file to G2 players or the single media file to 5.0 players.

2. By using RAMGEN. Rather than creating a metafile for every link to media content, you can use the /ramgen/ parameter and the altplay option in your URLs. This feature of the G2 server automatically generates *.ram* files on the fly if needed to serve 5.0 content. The following syntax is used:

```
http://my-realserver.com/ramgen/presentation.smi?altplay=video.rm
```

Case study: TechWeb Today

When RealNetworks introduced the preview version of its G2 player in June 1998, it offered its content partners (those that had a default button on the player itself) a few basic G2 templates to help create simple presentations. Many partners used those templates. However, to create TechWeb's daily streaming media show, *TechWeb Today*, the TechWeb team, including producer Leah Goldberg, decided to slave over the hot code and build a unique show from scratch. That way, they could explore and take advantage of the capabilities of this new streaming-multimedia platform.

In this section, we cover the steps Leah Goldberg used to build the *TechWeb Today* show featured in Figure 7-8, including code examples and helpful workarounds to common problems.

Figure 7-8. *A screenshot of the main channel of TechWeb Today within the customized G2 Player*

Deciding what to show

The first step to constructing a G2 presentation is to establish your content plan and graphic design. You have to determine what media and datatypes you plan to use. Will your show contain a video, or will you instead present your information in the form of a slideshow with an associated audio track? Will you stream information as text, or will you make and stream graphics that contain text?

The TechWeb production team decided to develop a segmented presentation to offer a more targeted user experience. Instead of a linear news program, the show is comprised of four five-minute distinct segments: an introductory segment and three topical sub-channels.

The introductory segment begins by announcing the day's programming on the sub-channels, then offers a three-minute video newscast. Viewers can click to visit any sub-channel during or at the end of the presentation. All three sub-channels have the same basic structure: while a video plays, text and explanatory graphics augment the video.

Once you have established your basic content plan and design, the next step is to roll up your sleeves and start coding to build the presentation piece by piece.

To do that, first design the overall layout of your presentation, including its size and the precise placement of each file being used. *TechWeb Today*'s introductory segment is composed of 14 distinct regions. Example 7-9 shows the code for the root layout and 4 of the 14 regions.

Example 7-9. *The code for TechWeb's root layout and four regions*

```
<root-layout width="421" height="323"/>
<region id="background" width="421" height="323" top="0" left="0"
    z-index="0"/>
<region id="date" width="180" height="14" left="30" top="74"
    z-index="1"/>
<region id="video" width="176" height="144" left="32" top="98"
    z-index="1" >
<region id="caption" width="176" height="60" left="34" top="255"
    z-index="1"/>
```

The background region in Example 7-9 is 421 pixels wide and 323 pixels high and begins in the upper-leftmost corner (0,0) of the overall layout. In fact, the overall size of the presentation is 421×323 pixels, so this region covers the entire area. Notice that the background has a z-index of 0, while the other three regions have z-indexes of 1. Therefore, the file that is eventually sourced into the background region will appear beneath all the regions with higher z-indexes, wherever they overlap.

The date region is 180 pixels wide by 14 pixels high, and its upper-left corner is at the coordinates (30,74). Similarly, the video region is 176×144 pixels, begins at (32,98), and is also placed over the background, where they overlap. Figure 7-9 shows four regions: the background region in gray and the date region that sits above the video region. The caption region sits below the video region.

In the body of the SMIL file, Leah Goldberg sourced the following files into the regions described in Figure 7-9:

```
<img src="background.rp" region="background"/>
<video src="newsVideo.rm" region="video"/>
<text src="date.rt" region="date"/>
<text src="captions.rt" region="caption"/>
```

Figure 7-9. *The four regions: background, date, video, and caption*

Synchronizing media types

The SMIL file also establishes the overall timeline and synchronization of a presentation. As described in the SMIL section earlier, the <par> tag designates a group of files that will stream and play in parallel with each other, or at the same time, and the <seq> tag designates files that will be played in sequence, or one after another.

In Example 7-10, the RealPix file and two text files are all within the same <par> tags, so they will all begin at precisely the same time. As soon as the video ends, a still image of *TechWeb Today*'s logo appears in the video space. Nested within the <par> tags are <seq> tags, which first source a video, and then a RealPix file, which sources the logo. Because the two files are within <seq> tags, they will play one after the other, in the order in which they are listed. Because they are nested within the <par> tags, the first one (the video) will begin at the same time as *background.rp* and the two text files, which are also within the <par> tags.

Example 7-10. *Code for the timeline*

```
<par>
     <img src="background.rp" region="background"/>
     <seq>
          <video src="newsVideo.rm" region="video"/>
          <img src="logo-end.rp" region="video"/>
     </seq>
     <text src="date.rt" region="date" begin="2s"/>
     <text src="br-captions.rt" region="caption" begin="2s"/>
</par>
```

You'll also notice some begin attributes in Example 7-10. This attribute enables you to stream two files simultaneously, but delay the start of one. The two text files will actually load two seconds after the other files within their <par> tag. This attribute was used so the background image has time to load before the overlaying text elements appear.

In *TechWeb Today*, the file *background.rp* controls the behavior and timing of four images: the background image and the three photos that represent each sub-channel.

Each image is first sourced and given a numeric handle:

```
<image handle="1" name="background.jpg"/>
<image handle="2" name="channel1.jpg"/>
<image handle="3" name="channel2.jpg"/>
<image handle="4" name="channel3.jpg"/>
```

Then timing and behavior of the images are coded in the effect tags.

For example, to get the background image (handle="1") to appear at the beginning of the show, Leah Goldberg used the <fadein/> tag to introduce the image. The fade-in effect starts precisely at the beginning of the show (start="0") and lasts one second (duration="1000").

Remember that the duration attribute refers to the duration of the effect, not the duration the image will display. The background graphic fades in over the course of one second, then stays in place for the show's duration. The line of code looks like this:

```
<fadein start="0" duration="1000" target="1"/>
```

Once the background has faded in, the first of the three channel photos appears in the same area where the video eventually appears. Unlike the background image, these are smaller images (176×131), and the idea was to get them to appear in a precise area of the display window, on top of the background image. Goldberg used the destination attributes to precisely place the upper-left corner of the photo at (32,105):

```
<fadein start="1000" duration="1000" target="2" dstx="32"
    dsty="105" dstw="176" dsth="131"/>
```

Next, the TechWeb team wanted the photo to become smaller and move to the right of the display window to take its place beneath the links that lead to its channel. They used the <viewchange/> tag to accomplish this effect. Again, they specified a start time and the duration of the viewchange effect.

For this effect, use both the source and destination attributes to specify the beginning and destination size and placement of the image. Between the 9- and 10-second marks, the photo will shrink from its original size of 176×131 to 55×40 (maintaining its aspect ratio). As it is shrinking, it also moves across the display window from having a top-left coordinate of (32,105) to (295,54):

```
<viewchange start="9000" duration="1000" srcx="32" srcy="105"
    srcw="176" srch="131" dstx="295" dsty="54" dstw="55"
    dsth="40"/>
```

Similar fade-ins and viewchanges are used in the rest of the file to describe the behavior of the next two channel photos.

As described earlier, any text used in a presentation must reside within a RealText file. The *date.rt* file in this case simply contains the date of the show. It appears in one location and never moves or changes:

```
<window type="generic" height="14" width="180">
<center><font size="1" face="arial" color="#993300">
Updated November 1, 4 p.m. PDT</font></center>
</window>
```

The file *captions.rt* contains the three captions that appear beneath each channel graphic consecutively in the same area, according to the following time settings:

```
<window type="generic" width="176" height="60">
<time begin="1.0" end="9.5"/>
<font face="arial" size="1">Channel 1 caption</font>
<time begin="10.0" end="19.5"/>
<font face="arial" size="1">Channel 2 caption</font>
<time begin="20.0" end="29.5"/>
<font face="arial" size="1">Channel 3 caption</font>
</window>
```

Problems and workarounds

As with all new technologies, there are lots of pesky little bugs and limitations that make coding for G2 that much more fun and challenging.

When *TechWeb Today*'s interface was first designed, the designers had intended that the channel photos would serve as clickable buttons that viewers could use to access the sub-channels. You will notice, however, that you must click on the text links and arrows that appear on the right side of the display window above the photos to view any of the sub-channels. If you try to click on the channel photos, either at their full or reduced size, you will not be linked to the sub-channel. The TechWeb team constructed the show this way because at present, a graphic can link to a web page that will load in a browser window, but a graphic cannot link to another SMIL file. Only text can link to other SMIL files.

Another frustration with coding for G2 is that a number of attributes and syntaxes are inconsistent across the three markup languages. For example, the syntax and default values for time are different in all three languages.

In SMIL, the attribute is begin, and time is denoted with a number followed by the abbreviations h (hours), min (minutes), s (seconds), or ms (milliseconds). Two-and-a-half seconds is written as begin="2.5s". Time can also be written according to the formula npt:hh:mm:ss.xy. Two-and-a-half seconds would be written as begin="npt:2.5". If you use that syntax, you must put npt: (normal play time) before the number.

In RealPix markup languageRealPix, by default, time is written simply as the number of milliseconds, and the attribute is start. Two-and-a-half seconds in RealPix is written as start="2500". However, you can specify a different time format in the header of the file, for example, timeformat="dd:hh:mm:ss.xyz". If you do this, all the time values in your RealPix file must follow that format, and two-and-a-half seconds is then written as start="2.5".

In RealText, time is denoted dd:hh:mm:ss.xyz, where dd is days and xyz is milliseconds. As in SMIL, the attribute is begin. Two-and-a-half seconds is written begin="2.5" (with no npt: prefix, and not followed by s).

Why are there differences in syntaxes and functionalities between RealText and RealPix? Part of the answer is that RealNetworks developed RealText in-house but outsourced the development of RealPix. Although all three languages work together to build a cohesive presentation in the same platform, producers need to remember three slightly different ways of coding the same thing.

Summary

Despite the frustrations, the quirks and problems encountered in G2 are not enough to overshadow the power and potential of this platform. The ability to stream multiple datatypes in a synchronized presentation over the Internet gives producers a materially new method of delivering content.

As the platform matures, its functionality will undoubtedly improve. We encourage anyone interested to jump in, but expect some head-scratching and hair-pulling along the way. However, with trial and error, you will likely emerge with a great new product.

Now that you have gotten your feet wet with the RealSystem G2 and RealMedia SMIL presentations, it's time to take a look at one of the Internet's other popular formats—MP3.

CHAPTER EIGHT

PLAYING, SERVING, AND STREAMING MP3

The MP3 revolution will not be televised. The MP3 revolution will not be sold in stores. The MP3 revolution will, however, be available online.

Whether MP3 is in fact a revolution remains to be seen. But it is no less than a grassroots phenomenon that is changing the way people listen to music, the way musicians build audiences, and the way record companies and promoters do business. So what is so exciting about MP3? Simple: the MP3 format provides relatively good audio quality in small file sizes, which means that music can be transmitted more easily over the Internet, and people can build file-based music collections without overstuffing their hard drives. It also means that artists have a new way to reach audiences without having to rely on the recording industry.

The MP3 format allows the person doing the encoding to establish his or her own quality-to-file-size ratio, so files can be very small with low fidelity, or comparatively large with high fidelity, or anywhere in between. These ratios usually are established by adjusting the sampling frequency and the number of bits per second (the bitrate) devoted to storing audio data. The de facto standard is considered 128 kilobits per second (Kbps), 44.1 kilohertz (kHz). At this quality level, a four-minute MP3 file weighs in at roughly 3.5 MB and sounds nearly as good as a compact disc. The same track in uncompressed WAV or AIFF format would be a whopping 40 MB. MP3 encoding can reduce the size of uncompressed audio by a factor of 10 or more while still retaining audio fidelity that approaches CD quality.

MP3 pros and cons

Naturally, there are both pros and cons to the MP3 format. Although it has garnered a huge following, the format does have disadvantages that should be considered by anyone preparing to test the waters of MP3 audio.

Advantages

- Relatively high fidelity
- Easy, inexpensive (generally free) encoding
- Simple distribution, via HTTP and FTP protocols, and via CD or other portable storage media
- Streaming implementation via server additions
- Availability of sample source code, which creates potential for lots of competition, players, and encoders for all platforms

Disadvantages

- Relatively large downloads for analog modem users
- Decoding device (MP3 player) required (though Windows and BeOS come with native MP3 codecs and players, and most Mac users have QuickTime, which can also handle MP3)
- Few security options available (although changes in this area are expected)
- Some downloaded files are of poor quality; poorly encoded files often exhibit a slight "hollowness" or "swishiness" and may contain skips or glitches

What is MP3?

The format known as MPEG-1, Layer III (or MP3 for short) was developed in the late 1980s and early 1990s and was finalized in November 1992 by the Motion Pictures Expert Group (MPEG) as part of the original MPEG-1 standard. The MPEG committee is a gathering of scientists and engineers who work under the auspices of the International Standards Organization (ISO) and the International Electro-Technical Commission (IEC). The members of the MPEG group are responsible for establishing standards for digital coding of moving pictures and audio. (See the sidebar "About the Motion Pictures Expert Group.")

MP3 is more than a simple compression scheme. Most people are familiar with file compressors such as zip. But if you've ever tried to zip up a WAV file, you've probably found that raw audio doesn't compress well at all. Compression shaves only a tiny percentage from the original file size. Instead, MP3 gets most of its compression from the science of *psychoacoustics*—the modeling of human auditory perception. The theory is that uncompressed audio streams carry a lot of data that isn't actually perceived by humans, for a variety of reasons. The logic follows: why store data that can't be perceived? MP3 encoders analyze audio streams and compare them to mathematical models of human psychoacoustics—a far more complex and mathematically intensive process than simple zip compression. The process is time- and processor-intensive (compared to zip, anyway), but it has the benefit of achieving more effective compression.

Of course, the act of discarding data results in an imperfect audio stream by definition. No MP3 file contains all the data found in the original uncompressed source stream. But in practice, MP3s can be created with high enough quality to render them indistinguishable from the source to even the most discerning listener. At mid-level bitrates (quality levels), MP3 streams can be indistinguishable from the source to the ears of most people. The trick is in finding the best possible balance or compromise between file size and quality.

About the Motion Pictures Expert Group

The Motion Pictures Expert Group (MPEG) was established in January 1988 with the mandate to develop standards for coded representation of moving pictures, audio, and their combination. It operates in the framework of the Joint ISO/IEC Technical Committee (JTC 1) on Information Technology. MPEG is the group that is responsible for defining the standard we call MP3, as well as numerous other standards.

Since its first meeting in May 1988 when 25 experts participated, MPEG has grown to an unusually large committee. Some 350 experts from 200 companies and organizations located in more than 20 countries typically take part in MPEG meetings. As a rule, MPEG meets three times a year.

A large part of the membership of the MPEG working group is composed of individuals operating in research and academia. Even though the MPEG environment looks rather informal, the group has to bear in mind standards that can be of high strategic relevance.

MPEG exists to produce standards. Published standards are the last stage of a long process that starts with the proposal of new work within a committee. The journey of the MPEG-1 Layer III standard that we know as MP3 may have begun in 1989 and become final in November 1992. However, the process of defining the MPEG family itself began long before that. The group is now focused on the finalization of MPEG-4, an architecture encompassing multichannel audio, video, multimedia, dimensional presentations, security mechanisms, and more.

MP3 technical details

As stated earlier, MP3 is a perceptual audio coding scheme. MP3 encoders analyze an audio signal and compare it to psychoacoustic models representing limitations in human auditory perception. They then encode as much useful information as possible given the restrictions set by the bitrate and sampling frequency established in the encoder application. A number of distinct steps comprise the encoding process, including:

Minimal audition threshold

There are many aspects of audio to which the human ear is insensitive. For starters, most audio streams cover a frequency range much broader than that which humans can hear. The human hearing range generally falls between 20 Hz and 20 kHz and is most sensitive between 2 kHz to 4 kHz. As people grow older, their auditory acuity is diminished—many people cannot hear tones higher than 16 kHz. MP3 encoders can immediately discard frequencies above or below this range. The minimal audition threshold represents the level at which the human ear will perceive sound. It is not necessary to code frequencies under or over this threshold, because they won't be perceived.

Masking effects

When two or more sounds are played simultaneously and one sound is louder than the other, the louder sound hides or "masks" the softer one (this concept is also discussed in Chapter 2, *The Science of Sound and Digital Audio*). If you record both sounds, the softer sound is still present in the recorded spectrum. However, since the softer sound is masked and therefore imperceptible, that sound can be safely removed from the recording. Similarly, if two tones are close together on the frequency spectrum, they may appear indistinct from one another. However, if the two tones are sufficiently distinct, they will be independently perceptible and must both be encoded. File size is cut dramatically when undetectable (or barely detectable) sounds are removed from the recording, preserving disk space.

These two effects are called "auditory masking" and "temporal masking" and may best be understood by analogy. If you watch a flying bird, its outline may be distinct against the sky. But if the bird passes in front of the sun, the sun's brightness completely overpowers the bird's outline. As the bird moves toward the other edge of the sun, it becomes visible again. The same principle applies with masking effects in MP3 encoding.

Reservoir of bytes

MP3 files are stored as a series of "frames," which can be thought of much like the frames that make up a movie. Each frame carries only a fraction of a second's worth of audio data and is preceded by a header section describing the bitrate, encoding method, and other metadata pertaining to the frame to come. In some cases, a portion of the audio stream may be adequately encoded with room leftover in its frame. The reservoir of bytes lets the MP3 encoder "borrow" space from unfilled frames to store data of adjacent frames that need additional space. The reservoir of bytes is a sort of space-lending concept that helps to ensure a consistent flow of data and quality rate.

Joint stereo

While not an essential part of the MP3 encoding process, joint stereo is an option in most encoders and is typically enabled by default. When joint stereo is enabled, stereo sound is represented using a mixture of true stereo and monophonic sound, along with some spatializing information. Joint stereo is useful because very low and very high frequencies cannot be located in space by humans with the same precision as normal frequencies. The MP3 format exploits this fact by encoding very low and very high frequencies in mono, thereby saving storage space in the resultant file. To save additional storage space, try encoding in mono. To make sure you trap all possible spatial data, encode in stereo mode. Most users find that joint stereo is adequate for most purposes.

Huffman encoding

As mentioned earlier, compressing a WAV file with zip doesn't shave much off the file size, which is why psychoacoustics are employed. However, the MP3 encoding process actually does employ the classic Huffman encoding algorithm. After all psychoacoustic methods have been applied, the Huffman encoding pass seeks out and compresses any remaining redundancies in the bit pattern. It's as though zip-type encoding were being run internally on the psychoacoustically encoded data. While psychoacoustic coding is great at dealing with polyphonous sections, it's not as efficient when dealing with highly repetitive, or "pure" sections. The Huffman pass, on the other hand, is great at handling redundancies, for the same reason a text file filled with a million zeros will compress to almost nothing.

The Huffman encoding "pass" is very rapid and allows a savings of 20% in file size, on average. The Huffman pass therefore makes a perfect complement to perceptual coding techniques.

A plethora of players

While we cover only a few players in this chapter, there are literally hundreds of MP3 players on the market for virtually every operating system. Some are free; some require a small fee; some are basic and lightweight; others are full-featured and sometimes even bloated. Some work from the command line, while others in a normal window, and still others operate within funky, irregularly shaped interfaces. Check the software libraries for a list of MP3 players for your operating system.

Note that when AOL purchased Nullsoft in late 1999, they made Winamp freeware. Traditional audio players have acquired MP3 playback capabilities as well. MP3 playback capabilities have been added to Liquid Audio's LiquidPlayer (see the "Liquid Audio: building a viable e-music system" sidebar later in this chapter), RealAudio's RealPlayer (and their popular RealJukebox), Apple's QuickTime, and Microsoft Media players.

Winamp tip

To minimize the amount of real estate Winamp takes on your desktop, double-click in the title bar of any of the Winamp modules. They'll immediately roll up into a thin, horizontal strip showing just enough controls to operate the player. This is known as the "Window Shade" mode.

Playing MP3 files

Later in this chapter, we will discuss how to encode, upload, and broadcast MP3 files, but first let's take a look at two of the most common playback software applications: Nullsoft's Winamp* for Windows and SoundJam for Mac OS. Both are downloadable shareware or freeware applications with a familiar, CD player-like interface, and graphic equalizers. The Winamp interface is shown in Figure 8-1.

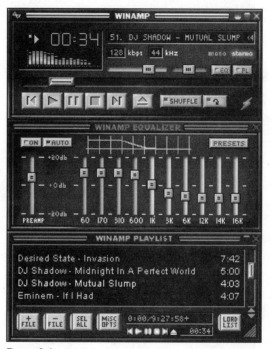

Figure 8-1. *The Winamp interface is similar to standard CD player interfaces.*

First, you need to download the Winamp (*http://www.winamp.com*) or the SoundJam player (*http://www.soundjam.com*) and one or more MP3 files from the Internet (see the "MP3 resources" section later in this chapter for a listing of good MP3 sites). Thus playing your files will be as easy as pulling down File→Open in Word or dragging a file onto an application window.

Winamp consists of four separate modules: the player interface, a graphic equalizer, the playlist window, and a mini-browser. The first time you start Winamp, all four windows are grouped in a neat square, but you can grab any module and position it anywhere on

---

* Nullsoft is now owned by AOL.

your screen. You can also close or minimize the modules with the standard top-right-corner controls. To play back an MP3 file, just drag it from the desktop or Explorer into the Winamp window, or tap the L key to access a Windows file panel. You can also click the Open button on the Winamp interface. Alternatively, drag any folder containing MP3 files onto Winamp to play all the files in that folder sequentially. That's all well and good, but to start having real fun, you need to start working with the playlist window.

Playlists

One of the most powerful aspects of maintaining a file-based digital music collection is that you can mix and match tracks at will. If you've ever made custom cassette tapes, you know how time-consuming it can be. But because playlists simply reference the locations of arbitrary tracks scattered around on your machine (or on the Internet), you can create custom "sets" within your collection quickly and easily.

The easiest way to create a playlist in Winamp is to drag and drop your MP3 files onto the Winamp icon or into the open playlist window. There is no limit to the number of MP3 files you can add, and you may even drag and drop entire folders.

Another alternative is to simply press the L key on your keyboard, which brings up a Windows file panel (you can also load in a whole directory, including subdirectories, or a URL from the Internet—right-click on the Add button to access these options). Repeat this step as often as you like, and reorder your playlist in whatever manner you choose—either by selecting and dragging entries up or down in the list or by selecting Sort with a right-click on the Misc button (you can then sort by title, filename, or path, or reverse or randomize the list). Figure 8-2 shows a Winamp playlist containing several songs. Be sure to experiment with each of the buttons at the bottom of the playlist window; these allow you to add, remove, sort, and organize your playlist in various ways. Try right-clicking the buttons for additional options.

Figure 8-2. *The Winamp playlist has multiple songs in its queue, ready to play in the order in which they appear in the playlist.*

When you're finished arranging your playlist, save it by selecting Save Playlist (Ctrl-S) from the List Opts button. If you want to replay that particular playlist at another time, just choose Open Playlist (Ctrl-O) from the List Opts button, or double-click or drag a playlist file onto the player or into the list window.

If you want to save your current playlist to an HTML document for future reference or to show other people what you're listening to, right-click the Misc button and select Misc → Generate HTML Playlist. A non-linked playlist will be launched in your preferred browser. To save the list, just pull down File → Save in your browser.

If you accepted all of the default options during Winamp installation, you can also right-click on MP3 files on the desktop or in Explorer and choose "Enqueue in Winamp." This adds the selected track or tracks to the end of the current playlist.

Basic MP3 player controls

Now that you have your files queued up, you're ready to play some music. Most MP3 players feature a standard set of CD-like controls for start, stop, rewind, fast forward, and so on. Figure 8-3 shows Winamp's set of controls. Right-clicking Winamp's control buttons reveals additional controls. For example, right-click on the fast forward or rewind button, and you can move to the next or previous track, advance or rewind the track five seconds, or jump to the beginning or end of the playlist. In the main interface, you'll find displays and controls for total elapsed time, basic spectral analysis, bitrate, stereo balance, volume, and repeat modes.

Figure 8-3. *Use Winamp's basic controls to play, pause, stop, and shuffle your MP3 files.*

Using the equalizer

The graphic equalizer is similar to other graphic equalizers you may have used. Each slider represents a frequency range, from 60 Hz (bass) on the left to 16 kHz (treble) on the right. The slider's values can be set to –20 dB at the bottom to +20 dB at the top. The best

WinAmp Easter Eggs

Like most heavily evolved software, Winamp has a few "Easter Eggs" tucked away—nonobvious "features" that one might only stumble upon by accident . . . or if one read about them in a book. Try these:

1. Right-click in Winamp's interface and choose "NullSoft WinAmp . . . " to bring up the About panel.

2. Click the Winamp tab to see the animated Winamp character.

3. With that animation running, hold down Ctrl+Alt+Shift and click on the copyright notice at the bottom of the panel. The character will be overlayed with a bitmap of Winamp's original developer, Justin Frankel.

Older versions of Winamp had additional Easter Eggs, though these seem to have disappeared after NullSoft was acquired by AOL.

way to understand the equalizer may be to think of the bass and treble controls on your home stereo—these sliders operate similarly but slice up the frequency spectrum into much finer cross-sections.

Since MP3 encoders effectively remove most of the original digital audio information, many MP3 files may exhibit a "hollow" or "swishy" sound. It is true that equalizers can help to boost or cut levels to defeat some of the hollow sound and to allow for a more personalized listening environment. However, the real purpose of equalization is to compensate for less than optimal speaker placement, room dynamics, speakers, and frequency response from any of your equipment, or in some cases, poor original recordings. Equalization cannot be used to entirely defeat the swishy or warbly effect found in poorly encoded MP3s.

Always take care when playing with equalizers. Many novices immediately pump up the bass and high frequencies to get a brighter, punchier sound. This, however, seldom accomplishes much beyond creating a sound that's untrue to the original source. The goal of equalization, and the goal of any audiophile, is to achieve fidelity, or truthfulness in sound. Just as a brighter light is not necessarily a better light, a brighter sound is not necessarily better sound. Approach equalizers with care, and make small adjustments. Live with your changes for a while and listen to them carefully. Audiophiles rarely use equalizers except to compensate for awkward room dynamics or poor speakers and speaker placement. A popular equalization pattern is shown in Figure 8-4 where both the bass and the treble tones are boosted slightly to create a more full range of sound for an MP3 file. This curve is sometimes referred to as the "Fletcher-Munsen" curve and is similar to what you get when you press the Loudness button on your home stereo. The effect is to enhance frequencies that aren't easily heard at low volumes. If you're listening to your MP3s at normal or loud volumes, you won't need this curve. In any case, experiment with the equalizer controls, and you'll quickly find your own preferred settings for different types of music. The equalization curves you're happy with can be saved for future use by clicking the Presets button and selecting Save.

Winamp comes bundled with several preset equalization patterns, from Classical to Techno. Click on the Preset button at the top right and choose Load → Preset from the pop-up menu.

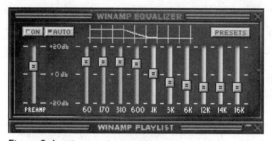

Figure 8-4. *This graphic equalizer pattern balances the bass and treble frequencies slightly to create the illusion of a fuller sound to MP3 files.*

Skins

Most MP3 players, including Winamp, allow the user to make cosmetic and functional enhancements by way of third-party plug-ins and "skins." *Skins* are the equivalent of wallpaper on your PC; they are bitmaps cut to the dimensions of each component of the MP3 player. Taken together, these custom bitmaps exactly fit the dimensions of the player, hence the name "skin." Designing skins for Winamp and other players is something of a cottage industry with thousands of skins available from various web sites. Check out *http://www.winamp.com/skins* for starters. Figure 8-5 shows four examples of skins.

While most popular MP3 players have their own skin format, the Winamp skin format is by far the most popular. Winamp skins can be used by non-Winamp players and are not restricted to Windows users. Popular MP3 players for BeOS, Mac OS, and Linux can use Winamp skins as well.

To use alternative skins, download them into the Skins subdirectory of the Winamp installation directory. To access the skin chooser, right-click any blank area of the Winamp interface and then choose

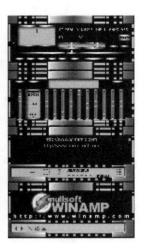

Figure 8-5. *Skins featuring Star Wars, Titanic, X-Files, and Star Trek's Enterprise are just some of the endless patterns that you can create for your MP3 player.*

Skins → Skin Browser, or tap Alt-S. You can even choose to have Winamp select a random skin at startup. If you're using an older version of Winamp, you need to unzip your skins in the Skins directory. Later versions will unzip skins on the fly, saving you the extra step.

If you use multiple operating systems that can mount Windows partitions, or multiple players that utilize Winamp skins, you may want to store the skins in a universal directory such as *c:\data\skins*, rather than keeping them under Winamp's roof.

Skin-making tutorial

Making your own skins to use with Winamp or other compatible MP3 players can be fun and easy. Before you begin, there are two things you need:

- A graphics and imaging application such as Photoshop or Paint Shop Pro.

- Winamp's skin template. You can download the template after you join their skin developers group at *http://www.winamp.com/ authentication/join.jhtml*. If you'd rather not join, you can use any existing skin just as easily.

Now follow these basic steps:

1. Download and unzip the Skin Template zip file into a new directory located in your Winamp Skins directory. For example, you can call it *Winamp/Skins/MySkins*.

2. After you have installed the Base Skin, take a look at the files in that directory. There should be a number of cursor (*.cur*) files,

several bitmap (*.bmp*) files, and a few text (*.txt*) files. It's important to note that all of these files are optional—Winamp uses the built-in default files if it finds any pieces of the skin collection missing.

The filenames for the cursor files are fairly self-explanatory. For example, *EQTitle.cur* is the cursor for the equalizer's title bar. Likewise, *normal.cur* is the default cursor used in Winamp's main window. The Playlist Editor WindowShade sizing area is referred to as *PWSSize.cur.* If you have questions about which file is which, try making changes to see where the change takes effect. You will need a third-party utility such as Microangelo (*http://www.impactsoft.com*) to create custom cursors.

The process of editing the bitmap files can be a bit more complicated. As with the cursor files, the bitmap files are named according to their functions and have the *.bmp* extension. The file *pledit.bmp* alters the look of the Playlist Editor. The file *eqmain.bmp* changes the look of the graphic equalizer, and all the other *.bmp* files change the look of individual controls of the main controls.

3. To create your skin, open and edit each *.bmp* file in your graphics editor; be sure to use the same filenames. To be safe, you should save your new skin files to a separate directory—always keep the same filenames.

4. After you've made changes to the different bitmap files, you'll want to see the changes you've made in action. To do this, either restart Winamp or hit the F5 key to refresh.

5. You can change other aspects of Winamp via the three *.txt* files included in the Skin template archive. Again, after making changes to these files, be sure to restart Winamp or hit F5 to reload the skin.

The *pledit.txt* file changes the font and color of the playlist text. The format is:

```
[Text]
Normal=#00FF00
Current=#FFFFFF
NormalBG=#000000
SelectedBG=#000080
Font=Arial
```

After the [Text] line, the first line specifies the text color (in hexadecimal values) for unselected entries; the second line specifies the text color for selected entries; the third and fourth lines specify the background colors for unselected and selected entries, respectively. The fifth line, obviously, specifies the font.

The *viscolor.txt* file has 24 lines, with each line consisting of an RGB triplet and a comment. For example, a line in the file could look like this:

```
32,37,21, // comment
```

These 24 lines define the colors used in Winamp's built-in visualizer. The default *viscolor.txt* is well commented, and will tell you which lines change which colors.

region.txt is for specifying transparent regions in your skin, which lets you create nonrectangular shapes or cut-outs in Winamp's main and EQ windows. Careful editing of this file will let you include the parts you wish to show, and make the rest transparent. Remember, if you have trouble with this or other files, you may simply delete them and the default Winamp settings will be used.

6. When you're finished creating your skins, zip them up and upload them to an Internet skins archive so others can enjoy your creations as well.

Netscape, MP3, and the Mac

While downloading MP3 files on the Macintosh, older versions of Netscape Navigator (4.0 and earlier) may display a "Q" or QuickTime logo and fail to play the MP3 file. This is a problem with Netscape's default preference settings, which may incorrectly try to play MP3 files using QuickTime (older versions of QuickTime, version 3 and earlier, do not support MP3 files). If this happens, you should immediately cancel downloading and follow these steps:

1. Change your preferences by opening Netscape Navigator and selecting Edit → Preferences. Click on Navigator and then Applications. This is where you configure Navigator's helper applications.

2. Scroll down until you see "audio/mpeg," and double-click on it.

3. Select the Choose button and locate the MP3 player you want Netscape to launch (after an MP3 file is downloaded). If there is a plug-in already selected, choose the Edit button and then click the Application radio button. Then click the Choose button next to the Application button and locate your MP3 player.

4. Click OK out of all dialog boxes.

5. Scroll through the description list again and repeat steps 2 through 4 for the MPEG audio, *audio/x-mpeg,* or *audio/x-mp3* descriptions if they exist in the list (note that *audio/x-mpeg* is the correct MIME type for MP3). Other MIME types are technically illegal—but don't remove them or you may leave your browser incompatible with some MP3 sites.

Now each time an MP3 file is downloaded, Navigator will play it using the MP3 player or plug-in you selected.

Plug-ins

While skins let you customize the appearance of your MP3 player, you can improve or extend the functionality of your player by adding modules to the plug-ins subdirectory. While most MP3 players support plug-ins, not all of them do.

There is a seemingly infinite variety of third-party plug-ins available, but they all fall into a few overarching categories:

- Input plug-ins allow your player both to play audio file formats that are not built into the player itself and to accept signals from external devices such as keyboards or stereo components.

- Output plug-ins allow your MP3 player to export signals to other audio file formats.

- DSP/Effects plug-ins let you apply any number of audio special effects, such as distortion, echo, reverb, and more.

- Visualization plug-ins, which are perhaps the most popular of the lot, let you "see" your music in displays far more sophisticated and psychedelic than the simple visualizers built into most MP3 players.

In addition, some plug-ins let you do things that aren't easily categorized, such as handling incoming signals from universal remote control units. Visualization plug-ins cover the gamut from 3-D graphics, to spectral analysis, to other exciting visual arrays, some of which are shown in Figure 8-6. If your platform is Be, check out the BeOS skin as shown in Figure 8-7.

Other plug-ins include audio processors, audio input and output modules, and general plug-ins that allow such functions as infrared remote control of your player. One such plug-in even allows control of MP3 playback over a local area network (LAN). Interest in MP3 plug-in development shows no signs of slowing down, which should lead to more and more sophisticated plug-ins and supported devices over time.

Making MP3 files

There are three steps to creating MP3 files for Internet distribution:

1. Your first step will often be to save your audio stream into AIFF or WAV format. This typically starts with a compact disc, in which case the raw bits on the CD need to be turned into a computer-recognizable audio format. The process of extracting audio CD data is called *ripping*. However, you can also encode live audio

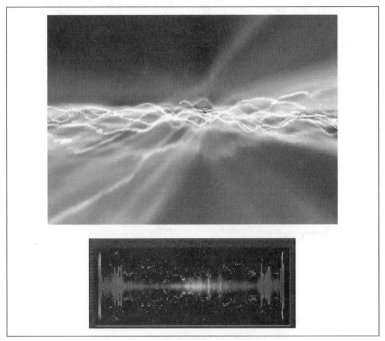

Figure 8-6. *A visualization plug-in based on the popular Geiss screensaver module*

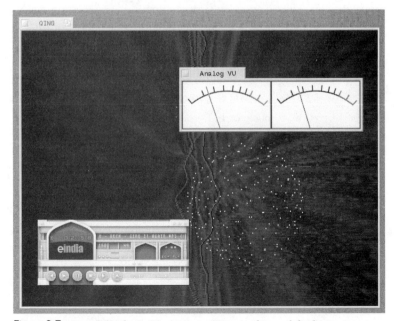

Figure 8-7. *SoundPlay for BeOS wearing a Winamp skin and displaying two visualization plug-ins (QING and VU Meter)*

streams to a raw format, which is typically not ripping but rather recording.

2. The next step is to encode your raw audio stream into the MP3 format. Fortunately, most modern encoding tools handle ripping and encoding all in one step, even if they work in two steps behind the scenes.

3. Optionally, and assuming the user holds the legal copyright to the music in question, you may want to upload your MP3 files to the Internet.

To work with and create MP3 audio, you need:

- An MP3 ripping/encoding tool

- An MP3 player so you can audition your MP3s for quality control before adding them to your permanent archive

- A digital audio file, compact disc, or live audio stream to encode

You'll find an abundance of free MP3 players and encoders online (see "MP3 resources" later in this chapter for more information).

Encoding MP3 files

Since most encoding is done directly from compact discs, we'll look at that process most closely, but keep in mind that most of these steps apply equally to audio streams coming from pre-existing WAV or AIFF audio files and to live streams. The single most important thing you'll need to keep in mind when encoding is the quality level, or bitrate. Here's a general guideline; a more complete quality comparison chart is shown in Table 8-1 later in this chapter:

- 64 Kbps and below: voice, lectures, streaming over modems

- 96 Kbps: low-fi music or hi-fi voice (such as newscasts)

- 128 Kbps: music files destined for Internet distribution

- 160 Kpbs or 192 Kbps: music files destined for your personal collection

- 256 Kbps or 320 Kbps: files for the most demanding audiophiles—virtually perfect quality, but much larger files

These bitrates all use the CD-quality 44.1 kHz sample rate, except the 64 Kbps settings and below, which use lesser rates of 22 kHz and 11 kHz, respectively, to achieve adequate compression for the lower bitrates.

In addition, you'll need to decide whether you want to create CBR or VBR files. CBR is constant bitrate and generates files in which every frame has the same bitrate, regardless of the complexity of the passage. Use the list above to determine a CBR setting. VBR means variable bitrate and generates files in which the bitrate is different for each frame. In VBR mode, the bitrate is adjusted dynamically, on the fly, to accommodate the simplicity or complexity of the passage in question. In VBR mode, quality thresholds are set by adjusting a slider from low quality to high quality (much as you would when saving a JPEG image, adjusting the quality level at output time). In VBR mode, a setting of 60% to 80% creates files that sound roughly equivalent to 128 Kbps to 160 Kbps CBR files.

CBR encoding is recommended for general purposes; in our opinion, VBR doesn't actually win you that much, and CBR files are more broadly compatible with a wide range of players and are less prone to glitches and errors. Some encoders create VBR files with track length written to incorrect portions of the file, which really messes up some non-mainstream players and players on other operating systems.

Working with the CDDB

If you've ever played a CD through your computer, you know that you are presented with only Track 1, Track 2, Track 3, and so on, in the information window and not with the names of the actual songs. Many people don't realize that artist, album, and track names are not on the disc itself. This is where the CDDB (compact disc database) servers come in to play. On the Internet is a collection of servers that provide access to an extremely large database of CD titles. If you run a CDDB-savvy CD or MP3 player or encoder, you have access to the CD database. When you insert a CD, it is identified by a special "hash" number, and a few seconds later, the CDDB returns artist, album, and track names, giving you much more useful information to work with. The main database is at *www.cddb.com*, though there are many mirrors and competing CD database servers out there.

> **VBR files**
>
> Some older MP3 players may not be capable of playing VBR files or may yield inaccurate time/ progress indicators. However, most modern players handle VBR files just fine.

Why is it called "ripping?"

The practice of extracting music from an audio CD to a digital audio file on your hard drive is called "ripping." Why? Because audio CDs don't use a filesystem corresponding to that of any particular operating system. Your OS's file manager can't see the tracks as it sees normal files on a data CD, so you either need to trick your operating system into seeing the tracks' file "handles" as actual WAV or AIFF files, or use a special utility to read the raw data from the audio CD and turn it into a WAV or AIFF file. Because special techniques or tools are required and you're not doing a straight file copy, another name for the process was required. No one seems to know where the term "ripping" originated, but it sounds intuitive and has been floating around in the computer vernacular for many years. Don't worry—ripping is a very simple process, and many tools completely hide the process for you, so you may not need to think about it at all.

Copyright issues

You should be aware that copyright issues are involved when using other people's music. You may legally encode CD tracks of music you have already purchased for your own use. However, you may not post or trade them over the Internet unless you hold the copyright. The Recording Industry Association of America (RIAA) is deeply involved in protecting artists and their copyrighted work from unauthorized distribution on the Internet. You should always be aware of who holds the copyright to a piece of music you intend to distribute. Furthermore, you must receive permission from the copyright holder to post any copyrighted work for distribution (and it's highly unlikely that any label will grant you this permission). For more information about the legalities of MP3, see the section "Legalities of MP3" later in this chapter.

You'll find CDDB lookups so powerful that you probably won't want to use an encoder without this feature. All the encoders featured in this chapter contain CDDB. By using a CDDB-savvy encoder, you can have meaningful ID3 tags (covered later in this chapter) inserted into your MP3 files automatically, rather than having to enter them by hand.

Getting started

For the purposes of this chapter, we will encode an MP3 file using two encoders: Xing AudioCatalyst and MusicMatch Jukebox. Xing has long been a pioneer in MPEG encoding, and its encoding algorithms are reliable and popular. In fact, MusicMatch also used Xing's codec in Jukebox until late 1999, when they switched to a slightly faster and better quality codec from Fraunhofer and Thomson. Xing's Audio-Catalyst also features faster-than-real-time encoding on modern machines, which is essential if you need to encode live streams. The downside is that you have to pay for the quality and extended features, but the price is modest. However, you can download a trial version of AudioCatalyst at *http://www.xingtech.com*, so you can try before you buy.

The second encoder we will use is MusicMatch Jukebox, a shareware encoder available at *http://www.musicmatch.com*. While early versions of MusicMatch were limited in encoding quality until you paid for the upgrade, MusicMatch changed their policy in early 2000; you can now download the free version and get full CD-quality encoding. MusicMatch Jukebox is an all-in-one ripping/encoding/playback/database application, and offers very good encoding capabilities. New users may find MusicMatch a little easier to use than AudioCatalyst, while more practiced users often gravitate toward AudioCatalyst.

Using Xing AudioCatalyst

Encoding tracks from CD with the Xing AudioCatalyst is a straightforward and relatively easy process. The interface is easy to follow, with the features you will use most often arranged in the main window, as shown in Figure 8-8.

Selecting tracks

When you launch AudioCatalyst, the first step is to select the audio file or files you wish to encode. You can encode files from a hard disk or a CD. If you select Add from CD, a prompt will ask you to select the file or files to add. If you want all the files on a CD, just

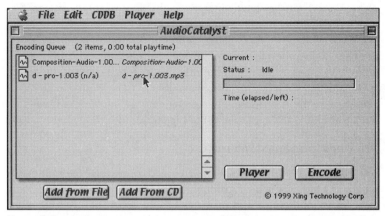

Figure 8-8. *The most important features in the AudioCatalyst interface, Add from File, Add from CD, Player, and Encode, are all located in the main window.*

click Add All. The Add All feature lets you batch-process several tracks or files at once, a handy time-saving feature.

Choosing your encoding options

The next step is to select your encoding options by choosing File → Preferences, as shown in Figure 8-9. The most important option in this dialog box is the bitrate setting—use the guidelines presented earlier to choose CBR or VBR and a quality threshold. You may also want to take a look at the stereo/joint stereo/mono options, as described earlier in this chapter. Again, we recommend joint stereo for most purposes.

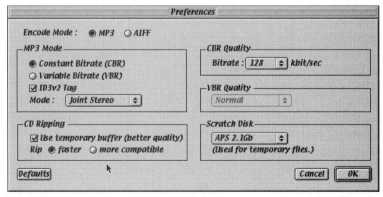

Figure 8-9. *AudioCatalyst's Preferences dialog, showing the preferred, default settings: constant bitrate, joint stereo, 128 Kbps.*

These default settings have emerged as the general standard with which the majority of MP3 files on the Internet are encoded, though 128 Kbps won't give you fidelity high enough to satisfy demanding listeners. Remember, the size of an MP3 file encoded at 128 Kbps is around 11 times smaller than the original, uncompressed audio file, and maintains a sound quality comparable to CDs. We recommend 160 Kbps for most purposes. Just remember: the higher the bitrate, the better the audio quality and the bigger the file.

128 Kbps Internet standard

The MP3 quality standard that has emerged for general Internet distribution is 128 Kbps, which maintains near-CD quality sound at a 44.1 kHz sampling rate and provides a fairly good quality-to-file-size ratio for Internet delivery. You can use the next higher encoding levels (160 Kbps or 192 Kbps) for your personal collection or the next lower (112 Kbps) if you need lower file sizes. Anything higher than 192 Kbps is overkill for most purposes, and anything lower than 112 Kbps loses the benefit of high fidelity sound. For perspective, consider that one minute of stereo 16-bit, 44.1 kHz CD-quality digital audio is roughly 10 MB, whereas the 128 Kbps encoded MP3 version will occupy less than 1 MB. At this rate, the average 4 1/2 minute song uses less than 4 MB, instead of the over 45 MB needed for the standard, uncompressed 44.1 kHz WAV or AIFF file. At the reduced file size of 128 Kbps, 44.1 kHz MP3 encoding, distributing near CD-quality music over the Internet is attainable and sensible, even when delivered at analog modem speeds. Table 8-1 details the relationship between bitrate, file size, and quality.

Table 8-1. *Results of encoding at different bitrates*

Bitrate (Kilobits per Second)	Size of Song	Quality
1,411	41.3 MB	CD
192	5.6 MB	Very close to CD quality, indistinguishable for all but the most demanding audiophiles
160	4.7 MB	High quality
128	3.8 MB	Approaches CD quality
112	3.3 MB	Below CD quality
96	2.8 MB	Well below CD quality MP3; "swishiness" almost always present
64	1.9 MB	Acceptable for voice, but not music; very noticeable quality artifacts
32	0.9 MB	Tinny, AM radio quality, lots of artifacts
16	0.5 MB	Shortwave radio quality—pretty much unusable

Working with ID3 tags

Storing additional information such as title, artist, album, year, comments, and so on, is performed by creating or editing ID3 tags. *ID3 tags* are bits of information stored within the MP3 file itself and are accessible and editable using most of MP3 players. A good MP3 encoding tool will also offer to store ID3 data within the files it creates as it's running. In other words, ID3 data can be created along with the file, or added or changed later through an MP3 player or with a third-party utility. To have AudioCatalyst store ID3 data, select a file or CD track within the main window and choose Track Information in the edit menu to display the window shown in Figure 8-10. Be sure to check the box next to ID3 in the Preferences window.

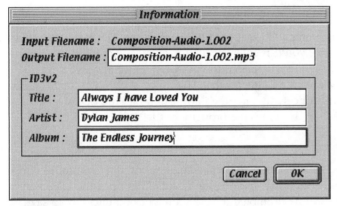

Figure 8-10. *Use the Track Information window to include output filename, title, artist, and album.*

Notes on numbering

If you're encoding your own albums, it's a good idea to include track numbers from the CD in the filenames themselves. Without them, the files will appear in the encoding output directory in alphabetical order, rather than in album order. But an album is a complete entity, not just a pile of singles. Artists put a great deal of effort into determining the ideal order in which tracks should be heard. If you choose to respect this prerogative of the artist, have your encoder prepend track numbers to the filenames so they appear in Explorer/Finder/Tracker in the proper order. When you drag the folder onto your MP3 player, you'll hear the album as it was meant to be heard, not willy-nilly. And remember: if there are more than nine tracks on the album, you'll need to make sure the encoder uses "01" rather than simply "1." Otherwise, your computer will order track 10 before track 1, and so on. To control this behavior in AudioCatalyst, look for the Track Number checkbox in the Naming section of AudioCatalyst's Settings panel.

Trial download

Trial versions of Audio-Catalyst are available for download from Xing's web site at *http://www. xingtech.com*.

CDDB database support

AudioCatalyst includes CDDB support, as described earlier, so you can get meaningful artist, album, and track data for your CDs automatically, and also have appropriate ID3 tag data inserted in your files.

To have AudioCatalyst automatically add the track information for your CDs, select Fetch Track Information from the CDDB menu. AudioCatalyst will then make the connection to the CDDB servers (via your standard Internet connection) and download the relevant information behind the scenes. If you're already online, this happens seamlessly. If you are not yet connected, AudioCatalyst makes the connection for you. Within 2 to 30 seconds (depending on the speed of your connection), your CD track names and play times are updated and can be included with the MP3 files you want to encode.

If you encounter a CD that can't be found in the CDDB (though this is quite rare), you can enter the album, artist, and track names manually and have them uploaded to the CDDB. Once approved by human editors, the listing for that CD will be accessible to others. Be advised that once you enter the information into the CDDB database, the entry becomes the property of CDDB.

Encode

Once you have selected your encoding options, the next step is to rip and encode the file by clicking the Encode button on the main window. You will be prompted to select a folder or a directory to save the encoded files to. AudioCatalyst will encode the file as quickly as it can, limited only by the speed of your computer's processor and by how quickly audio data can be extracted from the CD-ROM drive. Since MP3-encoding is processor-intensive, you should use at least a Pentium running at 75 MHz or better, but using a Pentium II running at 200 MHz or better is ideal and will shorten the time it takes your files to be encoded. AudioCatalyst is currently one of the fastest encoders on the market (but not *the* fastest as of this writing—that award currently goes to the commercial Fraunhofer codec, now used in MusicMatch Jukebox). This feature, along with batch and real-time encoding, can make the money spent on the application worth the investment in time saved.

Play

After the encoding is complete, you'll find a new file with an *.mp3* extension in the output directory. You can now listen to your MP3 file by clicking the Play button, which launches your MP3 player. Before you select Play for the first time, you must tell AudioCatalyst which player to use; set this setting with the SetPlayer option under the Player menu, as shown in Figure 8-11.

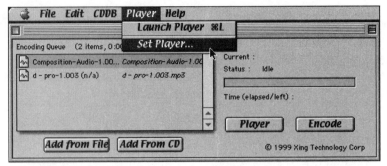

Figure 8-11. *Before you can play your new MP3 files, you must click on SetPlayer and select the player you want Audio Catalyst to launch.*

Using MusicMatch Jukebox

Using MusicMatch Jukebox is similar to using AudioCatalyst, though the interface differs somewhat. MusicMatch is an all-in-one tool that combines all the features you need to create and database your MP3 files. MusicMatch Jukebox also includes a built-in player, whereas AudioCatalyst requires you to install a separate player.

To encode to MP3 from MusicMatch, place an audio CD into your computer's CD drive and launch MusicMatch Jukebox. Click the button that says Recorder and the encoding recorder window will appear as shown in Figure 8-12. The tracks on the CD will be listed with track numbers.

Figure 8-12. *Click Recorder in the MusicMatch Jukebox interface to enter the encoding section of Jukebox.*

Selecting tracks

The next step is to select the tracks you wish to encode by clicking the checkbox next to each desired track. You may also select other audio files from your hard drive. When you have finished selecting your tracks, click the Start button found in the upper-right side of the window.

Recorder or encoder?

Though MusicMatch uses the term "recorder," this isn't technically correct. The signal you are working with, whether it comes from CD, a file, or a live stream, has already been recorded. The application really should call this feature "encoder," because that's what it is and does. MusicMatch probably calls it "recorder" just to make things easy for new users, but we feel MusicMatch is doing a disservice to the community by confusing—not clarifying—the difference.

Blame it on the Rio—and other MP3 hardware

Diamond's Rio player is a compact, portable music player capable of playing MP3 music files downloaded from the Internet or created from a CD or other digital audio source. This type of device signals a new era in personal music listening.

The player is about the size of a deck of cards and roughly the same weight. Even better, it has no moving parts so it won't skip, which is an important feature for people who use portable devices while driving or exercising. Because the device is energy-efficient, a single AA battery will power the Rio for up to 12 hours.

The low-end version of the Rio comes with 32 MB of rewriteable, built-in flash memory that holds about 30 to 35 minutes of 128 Kbps MP3 audio. External flash memory cards can increase playing time and are available where you purchase the Rio.

User accounts of the Rio in action are largely positive. Like the Sony Walkman of old, the Rio seems to be defining a lifestyle. With music moving from disc to chip, the Rio was the first of many players ushering in the new era of file-based music consumption. Samsung, Sony, Fisher, and Sanyo have introduced MP3 players similar to the Rio, as well as a new line-up of other personal home and car audio players.

Another product of interest is called the Personal Jukebox PJB-100 from HanGo, a Korean manufacturer. This product holds over 1,000 hours of music on a 4.5 GB internal hard drive. The beauty of this product is that it not only can it store so much music (roughly 3.2 days of continuous, non-repeating music, assuming 128 Kbps files), but it also includes other handy features. It features a built-in organizer, which is ID3-ready, allowing easy access and categorization of your music titles from *www.cddb.com* databases, including song title, artist, album, and other information. HanGo's Personal Jukebox, like similar products, includes its own ripping/encoding utility.

Yet another product, the Yamakawa AVPhile 715 player, has taken the concept one step further and included the ability to play back multiple formats of audio and video. Besides playback of MP3 files, this unit will play back DVD, CD, VCD (MPEG-1 video), and SVCD (MPEG-1 supervideo) files. This type of player paves the way for a centralized player that is connected to the Internet and will play all types of media in your home (or anywhere else for that matter).

Beyond these new products, larger companies such as Sony, Sanyo, and Fisher have released next-generation portable and home players. These devices play both MP3 and other, more secure file formats and are destined to be compliant with SDMI (Secure Digital Music Initiative), which will give music retailers a modicum of security against piracy. One such device is the sleek and slender Sony Music Clip. It can hold 64 MB of MP3s (actually, the unit converts your MP3s into the less common but more efficient ATRAC format) and has a futuristic look, like a small microphone or fountain pen. However these product lines continue, the direction has been established. Future MP3 hardware devices will be smaller, play longer, and hold more music than previous generations of this new technology.

Specify encoding quality

As with AudioCatalyst, the default values for MusicMatch are 128bit, 44.1 kHz and are the Internet standard for bitrate and quality. However, if your needs differ and you want to increase the quality or decrease the file size, you can alter the bitrate and sample rate accordingly. Again, for personal collections we recommend 160 Kbps or 192 Kbps, 44.1 kHz. For Internet distribution, choose 128 Kbps.

Encode

Click the Start button, sit back, and wait for a few minutes while the track is encoded to MP3. When MusicMatch is finished encoding, you will find the new MP3 files named as the originals, with the *.mp3* extension added to each newly encoded file. Your files will appear in your MusicMatch database automatically. You'll find the actual files in a subdirectory of the MusicMatch installation directory. It's poor computing practice to store data files alongside application files, so we strongly recommend choosing a more neutral location for MP3 output, such as *c:\data\mp3*. You can change the output directory via Options → Recorder → Songs Directory.

Play

You may now play your MP3 files. This feature can also be performed within MusicMatch Jukebox. Simply click the Database button found at the bottom of the Recorder window. This will open the Database window. In the upper-left corner, you will see a field that says Add Songs From and prompts you with three choices: CD, Disk, and HTTP://WWW. Click the Disk button. Open the appropriate directory. In this case, the default directory should be *C:\Program Files\Brava\MusicMatch Jukebox\Music*. Highlight the tracks you want to add to the database; if you want to add more than one track, hold down the Shift or Ctrl key while you select tracks. The database differs from the playlist in that it holds a listing of all available MP3 files, while the playlist holds only the tracks ready to go in the play queue.

When you have highlighted all the tracks you want to add to the database, click OK. The database window will come up again with the list of the tracks you selected. Simply double-click the tracks to add them to the current playlist. When you've finished adding MP3 files to the database, you can hear any of them by clicking the Play button.

CDDB database support

Also included in MusicMatch is CDDB support, as described earlier in this chapter. This option allows you connect to the online CD database at *www.cddb.com*, as shown in Figure 8-13, to automatically include artist, album, and track information with your encoded files. This feature is a great time-saver because it relieves you from having to locate and enter the appropriate track information for each track on a given CD.

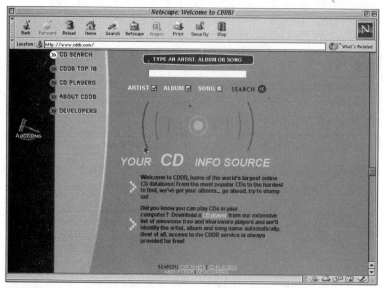

Figure 8-13. *The CDDB web site features track information for a variety of CDs from around the world.*

Creating a buzz: posting MP3 files to the Internet

Before we begin, here's an observation: very few MP3 files on the Internet have a right to be there. Original compositions and music or audio streams to which the person doing the posting holds the copyright are the only files that can be legally shared with others. Nevertheless, some readers of this book are musical artists looking to use the Internet as a distribution mechanism. It is also possible that you're creating an "Internet radio station" that will allow others to listen to your music without downloading it. This section is for those readers. It is not intended for people who simply want to encode their compact discs to MP3 and share their files with the world. Doing so is illegal and unethical (why would you want to rip off the artists you respect and like?), and we do not condone the practice (See the "Copyright issues" sidebar earlier in this chapter.)

After you have successfully encoded and auditioned your MP3 files and are pleased with the quality, the next step is to make them available to other Internet users. Unlike other complex streaming formats that require specific posting methods and server configurations, such as RealAudio, Flash, or Liquid Audio, posting MP3 files is easy. Simply post the MP3 files just as you would any basic file, taking into account any legal or copyright issues, of course. A simple HREF tag is all you need to allow users to download MP3 files:

```
<A HREF="music.mp3">Download!</A>
```

There may be one more step to consider—web servers need to be configured for each new file type, so they can send proper header data to visiting browsers (which, in turn, use the data to launch appropriate helper applications or to know how to display the page). There's a good chance your web server (or your ISP's web server) is already set up with the proper MIME types. If the download doesn't behave as you expect it to, ask your system administrator to add the MIME types:

```
audio/x-mpeg     .mpeg, .mpg, .mp3
audio/x-mpegurl  .m3u
```

Note that other MIME types also are commonly used for MP3 files, but they are technically illegal. Make sure you're using *audio/x-mpeg* and not *audio/mpeg*. The server software may need to be restarted for the new MIME types to take effect. Consult your server software's documentation to see how to map MIME types to filename extensions if you're not sure how all of this works. There are dozens of servers for many different operating systems, and it would be impossible to give you blanket guidelines on MIME configuration here.

Creating your own MP3 site

Because it is so easy to post MP3 files and serve them to the Internet public, you may think that there is nothing else to do. However, there are a couple of considerations to take into account before building your MP3 site.

First of all, if you plan on hosting your own MP3 site, you may want to set up your own FTP server because of the increased control and security features it affords over HTTP. With an FTP server, you can limit the permissions and access that a user has to your database of MP3 files. For instance, you may wish to allow users to download only a certain number of files. Likewise, you may opt to use the strategy that many others have employed, which involves allowing so many downloads for every upload. The usual ratio is somewhere around three downloads allowed for every valid upload received. In this way, the size and depth of a site like this will continue to grow without the site creator being the sole entity responsible for adding new music. In this way, the site will become self-perpetuating by its very nature. Note, however, that while you control the files you contribute to the site and can make sure they're legal, it becomes quite difficult to check for and enforce the copyright legality of files contributed by others.

The main difference between hosting a web site and an FTP server is that an FTP server offers specific features to control access and upload/download permissions. There is a lot of information out there on setting up FTP server software. You'll find listings of other popular FTP sites at *http://www.mp3.lycos.com* and *http://www.2look4.com*. Another helpful web site, complete with FTP software and configuring information, can be found at *http://www.jgaa.com*.

Popular web and FTP server software for various operating systems are listed in Table 8-2 (search your favorite software library for these if they aren't included with your OS). Far more options are available than are listed here—these are just some starting points.

Table 8-2. *FTP and HTTP server software for different platforms*

Platform	FTP servers	HTTP servers
Windows 95/98	War	OmniHTTPd
Windows NT4/2000	IIS	IIS
Mac OS	WebStar	WebStar
BeOS	built-in, Solo, campus	PoorMan, Apache
Linux	built-in	Apache

Once you have your MP3 files and/or FTP site ready for prime time, you can advertise and make them available to the world via some of the popular MP3 repositories. If you don't have the resources to host your own files and would like an excellent listing, register your original works with MP3.com. MP3 search engines such as Lycos (*http://mp3.lycos.com*) or 2look4 (*http://www.2look4.com*) are also excellent resources, featuring numerous MP3 files and FTP site listings. 2look4 even allows you to add your FTP site to its archive of MP3 sites. MP3now (*http://www.mp3now.com*) has a listing of the top 20 MP3 download sites. However, these sites list legal as well as illegal sites, and the success rate of finding MP3 files may be adversely affected since pirated illegal sites have a short lifespan. If you are looking for a more traditional record company persona, Emusic (formerly Good Noise), the Internet record company at *http://www.emusic.com*, may suit your needs. Emusic is one of the first online sites to offer MP3 files for purchase.

If you choose to create your own MP3 web site in order to promote your band's work, you may want to consider an alternative to normal MP3 downloads. Imagine, for instance, a web site for a garage band. If they simply post full-length, full-quality, 4.5 MB files of all their songs, they may not have many listeners. Who wants to download 4.5 megs of an unknown quantity? One alternative is to provide streaming files—possibly RealAudio, Flash/Shockwave, or streaming MP3s—so that users can start hearing the music as soon as the download begins. If they like what they hear, they can choose to download the full files. Another possibility is to put up samples of each track, say 20 seconds long, that will provide a high-quality sound bite of the band's music. Even though these MP3 files are small in comparison to the original files, they still require downloading time. For fast quality, simplicity, and quick access, consider streaming your MP3 files, a technology we'll cover in the next section.

Start your own MP3 radio station

SHOUTcast is the most popular software used for streaming MP3 to the world. (MP3 streams are not saved on the user's hard drive but are listened to as they're downloaded.) SHOUTcast comes from Nullsoft, creators of the Winamp MP3 player. Much as HTML editors made it possible for anyone to publish text and graphics on the Web, the SHOUTcast application and server (shown in Figure 8-14) makes it possible for the masses to broadcast audio over the Internet with a minimum amount of hardware and knowledge (although a good bit of bandwidth definitely helps).

> ### Icecast
>
> An open source, free alternative to SHOUTcast also exists called Icecast (*http://www.icecast.org*). Icecast was created in 1999 by two coders, Jack Moffitt and Barath Raghavan, to provide an open source audio streaming server that anyone could modify, use, and tinker with. It was further developed under the GNU General Public License by many people scattered around the globe. The upside is if you are a programmer you can use it free of charge and alter it in any way. The downside is that Icecast is a little more difficult to configure and set up, though you may find the payoff is worth the effort.

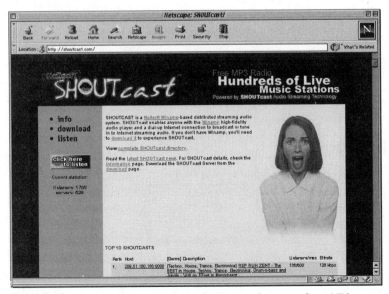

Figure 8-14. *The SHOUTcast DSP plug-in for Winamp lets you redirect MP3 streams to server software for Internet distribution.*

SHOUTcast streaming technology is a distributed architecture that lets people stream to the world, even over analog modem connections. However, keep in mind that a modem connection alone won't let you support many simultaneous listeners—to do that, you'll need to redirect your stream to a high-bandwidth server. SHOUTcast's unusual architecture lets you stream your MP3 files to a SHOUTcast server (which may be running on your machine or on someone else's machine, with permission) using your Winamp player and the SHOUTcast DSP plug-in. The SHOUTcast server (which requires a higher-speed connection) is available for Windows 95/98/NT and many Unix variants, including Linux.

Using SHOUTcast is much like using other streaming/distribution software, particularly those that use reflectors, such as CUSeeMe (a video conferencing application from White Pine Software). The idea is that you can distribute one stream to many users at once. This model is much like a typical radio distribution, where one broadcast goes out to many, who simply use a player to "tune" in the desired frequency. The distribution model for SHOUTcast streaming is as follows and is illustrated in Figure 8-15.

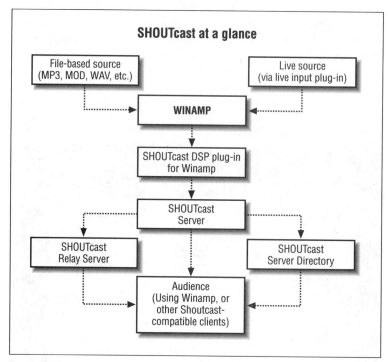

Figure 8-15. *Model of the SHOUTcast Internet distribution*

To listen to a SHOUTcast server stream, just open Winamp (or any other stream-capable MP3 player) and bring up the Open Location dialog box. Enter the URL of the server you want to listen to and hit Enter. For a list of SHOUTcast servers, visit *http://www.shoutcast.com*. Other streams can be found at *http://www.icecast.org* or *http://www.live365.com*. Once you've got a directory listing, try searching for a band or genre name and clicking the link to the stream you want to hear. Your preferred MP3 player will be launched and will start playing your stream automatically.

SHOUTcast is free for download for general non-profit use. For commercial use of SHOUTcast beyond the 14-day trial period, a one-time licensing fee of $299 will apply. Using SHOUTcast requires a bit of preparation and configuration, but it can be a lot of fun.

Running your own station

In a nutshell, here's what you do to set up your radio station:

1. Install the SHOUTcast DSP plug-in for WinAmp.

2. Configure the SHOUTcast server software.

3. Using the Winamp player, simply choose the files you want to stream (you can also stream live content via the Live Input plug-in), and press Play on the Winamp interface.

The SHOUTcast DSP plug-in re-encodes the playing audio at the desired transmission bitrate and then transmits that audio to a SHOUTcast server, running either on your own machine or on another machine with a faster connection. Metadata relating to your transmission, including IP address, URL, genre, station name, etc., will be transmitted to SHOUTcast's central server, shown in Figure 8-16, so other listeners can find you. Your connection between the player and the server must remain open until the transmission has been completed.

The Nullsoft SHOUTcast server runs as an application on supported operating systems such as Windows 95, 98, and NT, FreeBSD, and so on. The SHOUTcast server will accept connections via the SHOUTcast DSP plug-in in order to have a source stream to broadcast. You must keep the connection open, as the server streams what you are actively sending it via the Winamp plug-in. Once a stream has begun, the SHOUTcast server accepts only connections from other copies of Winamp in order to broadcast that source stream to each listener. In effect, you've just set up a microbroadcast system that allows people to broadcast audio content in any of the formats that Winamp supports. Through the use of specialized SHOUTcast broadcasting plug-ins, audio from a microphone as well as any device attached to the

Variable quality

MP3 streams dished up by streaming servers may be heavily downsampled by the person running the station in order to get their music through the skinny pipes of the Plain Old Telephone Service (POTS). In addition, many files are broadcast at very low bitrates, and lower sample rates, or in mono rather than stereo. In any case, don't expect streaming MP3 to sound as good as downloaded MP3. The Internet is too slow for most people, so it's just not possible. Many people feel MP3 sounds better at very low transmission rates than do competing formats like RealAudio, but you'll have to judge for yourself.

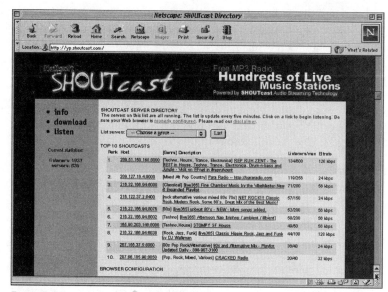

Figure 8-16. *The radio directory at http://www.shoutcast.com, which includes a listing of online radio broadcasts*

line-in port on the broadcaster's soundcard can be streamed via the SHOUTcast server. The SHOUTcast server is the key to connecting many people to one another via Winamp.

Installing the SHOUTcast DSP plug-in

The Nullsoft SHOUTcast DSP plug-in is a direct sound plug-in that enables Winamp to interface with the SHOUTcast server software. This plug-in is available only on the x86/Win32 platform, so if you are running any version of Windows 95/98 or Windows NT 4.x (Intel platform), you can stream to any number of SHOUTcast servers. The SHOUTcast server, unlike the interface plug-in, is far less platform-dependent and has builds for many operating systems. To communicate with any of those servers, regardless of platform, all you need is this plug-in with a copy of Nullsoft Winamp 2.2x.

After downloading the plug-in from *http://www.shoutcast.com*, install it as described in the "Plug-ins" section of this chapter. Start Winamp and tap Ctrl-P to bring up the Winamp preferences. Select the DSP/Effect subcategory under the Plug-Ins tree. If you see the SHOUTcast Source for Winamp written in the right pane, then you have successfully installed the plug-in.

Installing an appropriate MP3 codec

The DSP plug-in depends on the presence of an MP3 codec on the system running the source streamer. Because NullSoft can't provide this codec without paying huge amounts of money to Fraunhofer, they assume that the user already has an appropriate MPEG codec installed. Fortunately, users can freely download the codec from Microsoft or purchase a higher quality codec from a third party. To see if you have the codec installed on your system, launch the Windows Control Panel and navigate to Multimedia → Devices. Look under the Audio Compression Codecs section for an entry labeled "Fraunhofer IIS MPEG Layer-3 Codec." If you're using a recent version of Windows, or if you've installed the latest version of the Windows Media Player, you probably have this already. If you don't, you can install the codec that comes with the Microsoft NetShow tools package. You'll find a link to the latest version of this package at *http://www.shoutcast.com/download/broadcast.phtml#miscdownload.*

Note, however, that the Microsoft-provided Fraunhofer codec is limited to streams of 56 Kbps. While this should be plenty of resolution for almost all MP3 broadcast implementations, those with special high-bandwidth needs may install a high-end codec available from *http://www.opticom.de.*

Installing the SHOUTcast server software

Once you've selected the SHOUTcast DSP plug-in in Winamp's plug-in preferences panel, everything played in Winamp will be sent to the SHOUTcast server as well as to your own speakers. The server, however, will not redistribute music to the masses until it's been launched and enabled. Launch the SHOUTcast server (probably at *c:\program files\shoutcast\sc_serv.exe*), and you'll see a panel with a simple reporting window, which will show you what the server is up to at any given moment.

The default configuration of the server should be fine for starters, so you can now test the system. Make sure something is playing in Winamp, and then go to another machine, launch a broadcast-capable MP3 player, and enter the IP address of the host machine along with the port number. On a common "Class C" network, you might enter something like:

    http://192.168.0.3:8000

If you have a real IP address, you might enter something like:

    http://202.14.123.33:8000

After a brief delay, downsampled music playing through Winamp on the remote machine should start to play on the client.

Additional server options

Beyond the defaults, the server software offers a ton of additional options. All configuration of the SHOUTcast server is (as of this

Linux/Unix help

Most of these instructions assume you're working in Windows, but the SHOUTcast server is available for Linux and other Unix-like platforms. Configuration instructions are virtually identical for both operating systems. Linux users need to change permissions on the server binary with *chmod u+x* and to make sure the *config* file is readable by the user who is running the server. If the user is not root, he or she will not be able to use port addresses lower than 1024. Also, only the server component is available to Linux users, not the Winamp source stream plug-in. If you use Unix or Linux substitute *sc_serv.conf* wherever *sc_serv.ini* appears in this chapter.

writing) accomplished by editing the text file *sc_serv.ini*, which you'll find in the SHOUTcast installation directory. The file can also be accessed via the server's Edit Config pull-down menu. The *config* file is very heavily commented (commented lines begin with a semicolon) and should be relatively self-explanatory. Since *sc_serv.ini* is read into the server's memory when it's launched, you must kill and restart the SHOUTcast server after making any configuration changes. Note that many of the options in the *config* file are simple on/off switches, where 1 represents on and 0 represents off.

Configuring and starting the system

Select that entry, and a dialog will appear. To configure settings relating to your SHOUTcast stream, click the Set button to establish your stream settings.

The default configuration assumes that the SHOUTcast server is running on the same computer as Winamp. To change the configuration so that Winamp streams audio to a different server, click Set and enter the IP address of the machine that will be running the server software (which is probably you for now, but may be another machine later on). Next, enter the port number for the server in the Port field (the default is probably fine). If the server has a password set to prevent unauthorized streaming, enter it here. If you wish to have the server listed in the online SHOUTcast directory, make sure there's a check next to the Public Server option. Once you've entered everything correctly, click OK and then Connect. If all has been done correctly, it will display a little message that states "Source stream connected" in the bottom of the SHOUTcast Source window. You may now minimize that window and begin to play audio files within Winamp to have it streamed to your audience.

Now all that remains is to tell your audience how to tune in. Tell them to open Winamp, press Ctrl-L or go to the Open Location option in the Winamp main menu, type in `http://` followed by the IP number of the SHOUTcast server, followed by a colon and the port number you were also given. For example, a complete URL might look like this:

```
http://128.54.104.34:8080
```

Winamp should automatically connect and begin streaming audio their way. For more information, please refer to the SHOUTcast documentation.

An easier way?

If you'd like to run a streaming server without having to jump through so many hoops, and you are willing to experiment with an easy-to-use, free operating system designed for these kinds of things, download BeOS for free from *free.be.com*. Once installed and configured to your liking, download the audio player SoundPlay from *http://www.bebits.com*. Enable SoundPlay's HTTP plug-in, then open any web browser and enter the machine's IP address on port 80. For example, if your machine's IP address is 125.34.88.201, enter `http:// 125.34.88.201:80`. You'll see a page with Play and Stream buttons for each file in the current playlist. Users can stream files or playlists directly from your machine with no further configuration required.

Complying with copyright laws

Musical compositions and sound recordings are creative works that are protected by the copyright laws of the United States (title 17, U.S. Code) and other countries. Under U.S. law, the owner of a copyright has the exclusive right to (and to authorize others to) reproduce the work, use parts of the work in a new creation, distribute the work in whole or in part, and publicly display or perform the work (including on web pages and through webcasting). With few exceptions, it is illegal to reproduce, distribute, or broadcast a sound recording without the permission of the copyright owner. It is your responsibility to comply with the copyright laws when you become a webcaster or offer files for download.

There have been recent amendments to the copyright law regarding webcasting of sound recordings. These new provisions allow webcasting under the terms of a statutory license, as a way to help web-casters get permission without having to go to each sound recording's owner. The statutory license, however, has strict requirements that you must follow. Some of these requirements include the payment of license fees, limitations on the number of songs from the same album or artist that may be played in a three-hour period (called the sound recording performance complement), a prohibition on publishing advance playlists, and a requirement to identify the song, artist, and album on the website. There are other requirements as well. The Recording Industry Association of America provides quite a bit of information on copyright law as it applies to webcasting, and both ASCAP and BMI have created license agreements that they are willing to grant to webcasters that they believe conform to the provisions of the new copyright rules for webcasting.

For additional information on the statutory license and other aspects of webcasting, visit the following sites:

- The Recording Industry Association of America at *http:// www.riaa.com/weblic/weblic.htm*

- ASCAP at *http://www.ascap.com/weblicense/webintro.html*

- BMI at *http://www.bmi.com/iama/webcaster/index.asp*

If you are uncertain about what you can and cannot do, we suggest you check with the copyright owner or the owner's representatives (or the organizations above), or consult a lawyer.

Basic rules of the road

If you choose to transmit information and music via the Internet in this radio-like fashion, remember to observe basic laws of decency, and use common sense. Just because anyone can gain access to the technology does not mean everyone has a license to abuse the privilege. Be smart and present material that the Internet community can use and enjoy.

Legalities of MP3

Many questions have arisen concerning the legality of MP3 files on the Internet. There have been a number of court rulings, and there are many cases still pending on this issue. No doubt, this issue is at the heart of what will emerge as one of the most contested issues surrounding the Internet.

In many ways, MP3 will serve as a testing ground for how the United States courts and other legal entities of the world will respond to and shape their decisions concerning the future of Internet distribution. For now, the outcome is still unclear. However, certain aspects of this contested debate have begun to take shape.

Is MP3 legal?

The first question that must be addressed is one that many are still unsure of: "Is MP3 legal?" The answer to that question is a resounding "yes." MP3 is simply a file format, and the legality of a file format is not in question. MP3 files can be used either legally or illegally. The question is simply one of copyright infringement issues. MP3 merely magnifies the issues because it makes copyright infringement so easy, and because the stakes are so high.

Copyright infringement is a civil offense, punishable by fine. Distributing music to which you do not own the copyright is copyright infringement. Moreover, it's a criminal offense to copy music illegally and redistribute it for financial gain. You can be imprisoned for this sort of offense.

The bottom line is as follows: if you don't own the copyright to a piece of music or you are unsure of who does, you had better check it out, get proper legal advice, and be certain that you are not violating any laws that could serve to cause you legal problems down the road. And what about downloading files that other people have posted illegally? Simple: if you know the files are pirated before you download them, you're stealing. It's not likely you'll get caught, and it's more important for labels to find distributors than downloaders. But it doesn't make it legal or right.

It is, however, completely legal to make MP3 copies from a CD for personal use—you have the right to time-shift, space-shift, and media-shift playback of music you own (for the same reason it's legal to tape an LP so you can listen to it in the car). You purchase this right when you purchase the record/tape/CD. You should always check with the latest legal rulings regarding copying issues and MP3, and when in doubt, seek the advice of a legal professional. However, it is definitely illegal to encode MP3 files from a CD and trade them with others over the Internet unless you have the express permission of the copyright holder. Keep in mind that piracy laws precede MP3 by decades, and copyright laws are written right into the Constitution of the U.S. Most of the legal "questions" in MP3 land are not new—just more prevalent.

The Recording Industry Association of America (RIAA) is an association designed to protect the major record labels and their artists. It has made its position very clear. Fearing a loss of control of distribution, as well as the economic loss associated with sales of their artists' music, the RIAA has waged an all-out legal war concerning the MP3 distribution issue.

The actions of the RIAA have ranged from systematic, court-assisted shutdowns of web sites that illegally post copyrighted MP3 files, to the attack of the owners and creators of MP3 web sites and equipment manufacturers. For example, the RIAA once filed suit against Diamond over their Rio player, claiming that it encouraged piracy. The RIAA lost that battle, because the courts found that the Rio is not a recording device but merely a storage unit. And because Diamond was careful to build the unit so that files could be put in but not taken out again, it was nearly impossible to use the device for swapping files. In fact, this decision has shaped the whole arena of MP3 hardware, none of which makes it easy to transfer files from playback devices to other devices. However, the advent of flash memory cards has again introduced gray areas into the conversation, since people can easily swap memory cards. Still, the devices qualify as storage units and not recording units.

The RIAA, in conjunction with other groups, has proposed the Secure Digital Music Initiative (SDMI)—a grand plan to make all kinds of digital audio and video secure for Internet delivery. Likewise, companies such as Liquid Audio offer solutions for digital watermarking that can authenticate MP3 files in order to determine whether the file was obtained legally or not (see the sidebar "Liquid Audio: building a viable e-music system" in this chapter for information).

Diamond Multimedia, Xing Technologies, MP3.com, and a host of other MP3-related companies hold a number of disagreements with the RIAA. While all of them agree with the RIAA that artists and labels have a right to find means to protect copyrights and revenue streams, they disagree about how the SDMI should be implemented—parts of the SDMI proposal carry with it a "presumption of guilt," which assumes that all MP3 use is illegal and that most users are probably pirates. If SDMI passes in the form the RIAA has proposed, unsigned artists may find it difficult to use the MP3 format for unfettered distribution. While the RIAA assumes that unrestricted MP3 distribution is always the problem, that's exactly what many unsigned artists like about MP3—its ability to get music distributed far and wide, quickly. The trick will be in striking a balance between the needs of the industry and the rights of unsigned artists and the general public.

Legal MP3 files: headline artists sign up for MP3

Many artists, including Willie Nelson, Dionne Warwick, and the Beastie Boys, as well as record labels such as Hollywood Records and Emusic (which runs an online record company shown in Figure 8-17), have all signed up to distribute legal MP3 files—or at least excerpts—over the Internet. Furthermore, the growth rate of MP3 downloads and other market research reports support the view that MP3 distribution is growing into a viable medium. This points to a large and legal market emerging around the MP3 format. Legal MP3 files, freely available over the Internet, are no longer the sole domain of independent artists. This creates a strong sense of validation for the MP3 format being used by mainstream musicians in a legal way.

Figure 8-17. *Emusic (http://www.emusic.com) is the first Internet record company to offer MP3 files for sale by major recording artists.*

Further legitimizing MP3 as a commercial format was the announcement of MP3 files for sale. Emusic (*http://www.emusic.com*), and
Rykodisc (*http://www.rykodisc.com*), publishers of well-known musical artists, are teaming up to offer MP3 files available for legal download at a cost of 99 cents per track to customers over the Internet.
This is considered a major first step, and it is virtually assured that
other major record labels will follow suit. Ultimately, traditional music
distribution (which includes stores, truck drivers, warehouses, and
other middlemen) could be severely threatened. This is undoubtedly
bad news for music retailers, but certainly good news for online
consumers.

Ongoing legal battles

Despite its ongoing legal actions, as of this writing, the RIAA has
been largely unsuccessful in stopping the overall trafficking of online
MP3 files. It seems that new MP3 sites appear daily, and despite the
numerous legal actions and injunctions, there may be no way to permanently stop the underground distribution of MP3 files over the
Internet. However, there is no doubt that the legal battles will continue for a while. And these battles will most likely take several forms
and issues. Needless to say, the trend in the Internet industry, along
with the current climate associated with the freedom of the Internet,
seems to point to the validation of MP3 and similar digital distribution methods. The dam is beginning to break, and when it does, neither the RIAA nor anyone else is going to be able to stop the flood.

MP3 resources

Here is a list of some of the many online resources for MP3:

MP3 for Beginners
http://www.mp3.com/dummies.html
> This is MP3.com's beginners guide to using and creating MP3
> files, including encoding and playback. It offers information about
> where to find MP3 files, as well as players and encoders for a
> variety of computer platforms. Also featured is the latest in news,
> press releases, and headlines referring to all MP3-related issues.

Winamp home page
http://www.winamp.com
> This is the web site for one of the most popular MP3 players for
> the Windows platform. The site includes plug-in and skin files
> for customizing of your player.

SoundJam home page
http://www.soundjam.com
> This is the web site for the most popular MP3 player for the Mac-
> intosh platform.

The Grateful Dead on MP3

One enlightened take on MP3 comes from the Grateful Dead. The band has always allowed and encouraged fans to exchange tapes of its live shows with one another, but has frowned on people taking advantage of their "open source" attitude for commercial gain. Similarly, the band permits free dissemination of MP3 files and streams of their concerts, but forbids taking commercial advantage of the music—even indirect commercial advantage, such as selling ads on a site that offers audio files of Dead shows. Note that the Dead's liberal attitude toward MP3 distribution applies only to recordings of live shows, not to studio records (the rights to which are controlled by labels, not by the band). The Dave Matthews Band and Phish, among others, have taken a similar stance on free dissemination of live material.

Macast home page
http://www.macast.com

This is the web site for the second most popular MP3 player for the Macintosh platform.

SHOUTcast
http://www.shoutcast.com

SHOUTcast is a streaming audio system for Windows and Unix platforms. SHOUTcast allows anyone with Nullsoft's Winamp audio player and an Internet connection to broadcast audio via the Internet. The site features information on configuring and running your own Internet radio station using SHOUTcast.

Moving Pictures Experts Group (MPEG)
http://www.cselt.stet.it/mpeg

This is the official site of the MPEG group, which drafts the standards for MPEG. The site provides information about the MPEG specifications as well as the latest in standardization for MPEG.

Xing Technology web site
http://www.xingtech.com

This site is home to Xing Technology with information about Xing's commercially available MPEG products, which are among the best. Products include the XingMP3 Encoder, all-in-one AudioCatalyst, and the Streamworks MPEG audio server.

MusicMatch web site
http://www.musicmatch.com

This site is home to MusicMatch Jukebox, with information about the all-in-one product that allows ripping, encoding, databasing, and playback of MP3 files, all free of charge.

Diamond Multimedia
http://www.diamondmm.com

This site has information about the Diamond Rio MP3 player and much more on MP3. See also Diamond's *http://www.rioport.com* for access to lots of legal MP3 files.

Lycos MP3 search
http://MP3.lycos.com

Lycos created an MP3 database that lists millions of MP3-formatted songs available for downloading from thousands of web sites.

2look4
http://www.2look4.com

2look4 is an MP3 search engine with many features and additional information listings of MP3 FTP servers.

Emusic

http://www.emusic.com

> Emusic is known as the Internet record company. This site features tons of music, commercially available as well as free for download. It also features artist profiles.

Yepp Player

http://www.yepp.co.kr

> The Yepp player is Samsung's answer to the Rio portable player for MP3 files.

Microsoft Media Player

http://microsoft.com/windows/mediaplayer/download/Macintosh.asp

> The Microsoft media player supports MP3 playback, with certain caveats. Please read the latest information.

QuickTime Player

http://www.apple.com/quicktime

> The QuickTime player supports MP3 playback as well as a host of other formats.

Summary

In this chapter, we examined one of the hottest issues and formats on the Internet today—music creation and distribution using MP3 audio. MP3 is a file format that can produce near-CD-quality sound at a fraction of the file space consumed by uncompressed audio. To listen to MP3 files, you need an MP3-compatible player. We worked with Winamp, a popular shareware player, and learned how to use and customize it to meet our needs. To create MP3 files, you need to encode digital audio files (such as that found on an audio CD or in WAV or AIFF files) using an MP3 encoder. We worked with different MP3 encoders, including a commercial encoder from Xing and a shareware encoder from MusicMatch, and got a birds-eye view of issues surrounding HTTP and FTP MP3 distribution. We also looked at using MP3 files and the SHOUTcast software from Nullsoft to create an online radio station and stream MP3 files over the Internet. Finally, we examined the emerging legal issues associated with MP3 and defined more clearly the nature of the legal and illegal uses of MP3 files over the Internet. Though MP3 is still in its infancy, it is one of the most significant technologies to date associated with audio and music distribution.

Now that we have a taste for online distribution, let's examine a more refined (and proprietary) approach using Flash and Shockwave.

Liquid Audio: building a viable e-music system

MP3 has altered forever the way that music is distributed. Unsigned bands are building fan bases, music lovers are illegally sharing copied files with Napster, and hardware companies are promising Internet-connected, MP3-playing car radios. All of this raises serious concerns, however, for both record labels and their artists. The rock group Metallica proclaimed that the online community was ripping them off and filed suit against Napster, stating that users were robbing the band of royalties.

Suits like Metallica's indicate how untenable is the situation with MP3 for the music establishment. It is not an exaggeration to say that the MP3 revolution yanked the industry into the online content business against their will; now that the music is out there, the industry is desperate for a safe and secure transaction and distribution system. Many of the elements of a viable music transaction system—encryption, copyright protection, digital watermarking, e-commerce functionality, and of course CD-quality audio—have already been developed by a company called Liquid Audio. While Liquid has inked many marketing deals and is involved with the key standards committees, only time can say whether their technologies will be the platform for a transaction-based music system.

Also available in the Liquid Audio technology is the marriage of the new file formats and the next generation of portable listening devices, such as the Rio, Yepp, and the Sony Memory Stick players. Because of important technology deals and licensing arrangements, these new devices will all be able to play and store Liquid Audio files. And beyond online downloading, Liquid Audio is appearing in "pay by the song" kiosks in major record stores and other traditional retailers across the nation and the world. The case for Liquid Audio is that they have created a technology that will attempt to cash in on the future of digital downloads, from whichever distribution method and in whatever file format the user chooses.

The Genuine Music Mark

Liquid Audio was developed by veterans of the music industry and professional recording engineers as a solution designed specifically for the music industry. Their vision was to create the music distribution system of the future. With Liquid's technology embedded not only in the Liquid Player but also in new versions of the Winamp MP3 player and the RealPlayer software, consumers can buy music online in digital form and download that music to their computer, home entertainment system, or portable playback device, or burn it to a custom CD.

The heart of the system is that attached to each file will be a marker carrying authentication information. In an effort to establish its Genuine Music Mark (GMM) as an industry standard, Liquid Audio has formed the Genuine Music Coalition (GMC) with Diamond Multimedia Systems, Emusic Corp., and Nullsoft Inc. (acquired by AOL), three of the main players in the emerging MP3 market. With GMM, the coalition is offering intellectual property owners a way to protect themselves against copyright infringement by adding audible authentication of origin and ownership information into the MP3 format.

→

GMM works with Liquid Audio System's proprietary watermark and is embedded into the code of the MP3 file itself, guaranteeing that wherever the MP3 file travels, the GMM follows. It will not prevent Internet piracy of MP3 files, but will help ensure that proper identification and copyright information are "married" to the music file. It also protects consumers by letting them know whether the MP3 file they have downloaded is legal. This method of marking MP3 files helps increase musicians' and labels' confidence in distributing their music over the web in the MP3 format. Liquid Audio charges for the use of the watermark, making copyright protection for audio on the Internet available to any MP3 content owners who are members of the GMC.

Liquid is also involved with the Recording Industry Association of America's efforts to come up with a secure download system, the Secure Digital Mark Initiative. SDMI is supported by Liquid Audio as well as a growing group of Internet technology and software companies associated with digital music downloads. The future direction and outcome of the RIAA's initiatives, however, remains unclear.

The Liquid Audio system

In contrast to MP3, Liquid Audio provides an end-to-end solution for editing, mastering, purchasing, distributing, and playing high-quality audio over the Internet. Unlike RealAudio, Flash, and MP3, the Liquid Audio system is geared for commerce and the controlled distribution of high-quality digital downloads. It is designed to track sales, keep licensing and copyright information in place, and provide advanced security features, including digital watermarking and encryption. Perhaps the key element in the Liquid Audio package is its flexibility, which allows musicians to easily set conditions for how the file can be used. One label may choose to give away a song with no limitations; another may want a file to be disabled 60 days after album release or 30 days after download.

Another key part of the system is the many marketing deals Liquid has made with portals like Yahoo! (*http://digital.yahoo.com*), music sites like Direct Audio (*http://www.directaudio.com*), independent labels like Atomic Pop (*http://www.atomicpop.com*), and hundreds of radio stations. For a complete list of Liquid Music Network affiliates, go to *http://www.liquidaudio.com/music/index.html*.

The Liquid Player, shown in Figure 8-18, is similar to other players but has a few more features up its sleeve. In addition to playing music, the Liquid Player displays cover art, lyrics, credits, and copyright information. The Liquid Player also allows direct links to purchase the music being played. For instance, if you download a track from Amazon.com, clicking on the Buy CD button takes you to the Amazon page for that album. The software plays Liquid Audio, MP3, CD-quality Dolby Digital AC-3, or AAC encoded audio files.

The Liquid Player is the main user interface to the world of listeners and customers who download Liquid Audio content. It provides all the features you would expect in a music player, including extensive playback control, ability to view graphic images, and artist information. It also provides some features you wouldn't expect, such as copyright information, watermarking, the option to purchase the music online, and even a "Burn CD" command that allows you to create your own custom CD of Liquid Audio tracks.

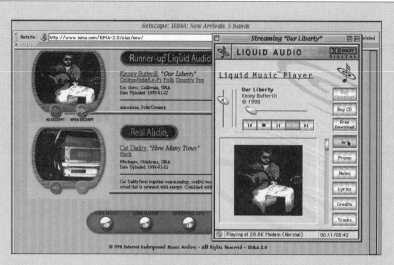

Figure 8-18. The free Liquid Player for Windows makes it easy to download CD-quality encoded audio files.

The Liquid Player lets users preview, purchase, download, play back, and record music on a custom CD, all from within one player. Other players require multiple, often external applications to accomplish these same tasks. In Figure 8-18, you'll see the usual audio controls like play, stop, fast forward, and rewind, a draggable progress bar, volume control and song title and copyright information.

The Liquid Player can also display album art and other promotional material, and link to other sites, including e-commerce sites and the artist's or label's site.

One of the most popular and exclusive features of the Liquid Player is the ability to burn downloaded music to an audio CD. This feature allows customers to make the CDs they really want instead of having to spend $20 on a CD to get two or three tracks. In addition, users may be more willing to pay for music if they can easily carry it away from their computer.

Liquifier encoding tool

To encode music for the Liquid format, use the Liquifier encoding tool, which provides a mastering-like environment for recording, editing, and encoding Liquid Audio content. The Liquifier also features basic waveform editing, excellent sample rate and format conversion, and smooth "single-click" uploading to a web site or a database. In addition, a comprehensive preview function allows you to easily audition your Liquid Audio clips at different bandwidth settings before encoding the files. The Liquifier also lets you combine audio with other media elements and text such as lyrics, band biographies, copyright information, credits, and CD artwork.

$\rightarrow$

Liquid Server

The secure Liquid Server provides a solution for online electronic sales, asset management, royalty tracking and reporting, and copyright protection. It allows the preview and delivery of high-quality, scalable audio over IP networks. The server can be licensed to provide a range of simultaneous audio streams for auditioning, as well as file transfers for purchasing encoded audio clips from either Unix- or NT-based platforms. However, the most heavily utilized method has been simply to use Liquid Audio or other large online distributors, such as Yahoo!, to access Liquid Server. That way all the maintenance, upkeep, e-commerce collection, and music distribution is handled for you.

Liquifier Pro

The Liquifier Pro is a mastering and encoding application from Liquid Audio. Liquifier Pro has everything you need to prepare and publish CD-quality music for secure, electronic distribution. It encodes the audio for optimum performance over a wide variety of connection speeds. It also enables lyrics, liner notes, and graphics to be combined with the music into a single file that is then published to the Liquid Music Network Server. Content submitted to the Liquid Music Network (LMN) is then automatically distributed to over 700 web sites. In addition, Liquifier Pro is the only Internet mastering tool with both Dolby Digital and AAC encoding. Liquifier Pro 5.0 also authors MP3 files.

Liquid in Winamp and RealPlayer

While Liquid's hold on the online music market is far from a lock as of this writing, their technologies do seem to be poised to provide much-needed structure and accountability. For example, in an effort to make the content on the Liquid Music Network more broadly accessible, Liquid Audio has made deals with AOL and Real Networks to allow the playback, purchase, and distribution of Liquid Audio–encoded files through these popular browsers. These appear to be the key deals that will make Liquid's technologies the platform on which a market for downloadable music can be built.

CHAPTER NINE

INTERACTIVE SOUND DESIGN WITH FLASH AND SHOCKWAVE

Two of the most popular tools for delivering interactive multimedia on the Web are Macromedia Flash and Shockwave. Both technologies offer superior control over multimedia creation and playback across various browsers and platforms. If you are developing interactive content with motion graphics and sound, using Flash *and* Shockwave should be your first choice.

While RealAudio was instrumental in bringing the radio broadcasting experience to the Web, Macromedia's influence on interactive media began with the launch of Shockwave in 1995, a technology that converted Macromedia Director presentations into a compressed format for web delivery. About a year after Shockwave's release, Macromedia acquired the technology that has become Flash, which uses efficient vector graphics and compressed audio to create web multimedia. While the two tools have some similar capabilities, they're aimed at different types of projects. Shockwave takes advantage of Director's scripting language, Lingo, to create complex presentations and games. Flash, on the other hand, is handy for simple button rollovers, presentations with basic branching logic, and situations where download speed is critical. Both formats provide the software components and authoring capabilities necessary to build advanced interactive soundtracks and customized media.

Flash and Shockwave allow you to create an immersive multimedia experience on your web site. Despite the introduction of RealSystem G2 and SMIL, we found that Flash and Shockwave formats still provide more creative, high-impact multimedia works.

In this chapter

- Flash and Shockwave basics
- Introduction to Flash
- Introduction to Shockwave
- Summary

Flash and Shockwave

Originally developed by FutureWave Software as the FutureSplash Animator, Flash utilizes vector-based technology to deliver interactive real-time animation and sound over standard modem speeds. And with the addition of ActionScript in Flash 4, Flash pieces can offer more advanced interactivity.

Shockwave for Director is a software component that enables compatible browsers such as Netscape Navigator and Microsoft Internet Explorer 2 and up to play Director movies over the Web. Shockwave is designed to work with standard HTTP servers and is ideal for streaming short- to medium-length audio clips and for scripting more advanced multimedia presentations and games with Lingo.

Flash and Shockwave basics

At the core of Shockwave and Flash multimedia lies a sophisticated authoring environment that exports various media elements into one compressed binary movie file. Using a standalone authoring environment to produce a self-contained media file has many advantages over text-based markup language media formats such as SMIL and Java. For example, the synchronization and playback of complex Shockwave and Flash presentations is more reliable than SMIL-based media. More important, the overall level of interaction between media elements is much more advanced in Flash and Shockwave than in text-based formats.

Although Shockwave was heavily promoted, it is not as ubiquitous on web sites as RealAudio or Flash because of its large plug-in size and higher bandwidth requirements. What Shockwave does best is create rich CD-ROM-like interactive multimedia. However, the result is often a download that is too slow over 56 Kbps modem connections. While Shockwave is a great multimedia-authoring environment, its bandwidth-hungry video and audio are best experienced with the throughput of xDSL or at least a T1 line. However, if you are careful with preloading and streaming, you can successfully create interesting Shockwave media suitable for modem users. The Enigma III Shockwave mixer, discussed later in this chapter, provides a good example of how you can create engaging Shockwave media over limited bandwidths.

Flash has gained a broad following, with its stripped-down and simplified authoring environment, small plug-in sizes, and low-bandwidth-friendly vector animation. Flash-based multimedia web sites are great for product or service demos, educational tutorials, targeted branding campaigns, and promotions that call for a high-impact, media-rich viewing experience. Flash also works well embedded as a small animation window in a standard text and graphics-based HTML page.

If a user does not have the Flash plug-in, you can use Macromedia's Aftershock utility to easily generate the HTML and JavaScript to automatically replace the Flash movie window with a static GIF image (see Figure 9-1). The Aftershock utility is a key breakthrough for web developers because it addresses their trepidation over implementing plug-in-dependent media on a high-traffic web site. The Aftershock utility also works with Shockwave. Aftershock is a free utility available on the Macromedia web site at *http://www.macromedia.com.*

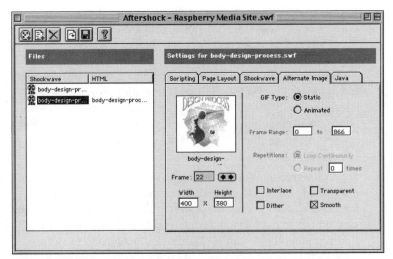

Figure 9-1. *The Macromedia Aftershock utility*

Flash and Shockwave are designed to be served from a standard HTTP web server like the rest of your web site content. On the upside, Flash and Shockwave content is easy to broadcast because you do not need to install special server software; the downside is that you do not have the benefits that dedicated server software provides, such as managing the delivery of streams to various target bandwidths. Depending on server configuration, bandwidth throughput, and router capacity, a standard HTTP server with a high-end system can broadcast up to 100 or more simultaneous Shockwave or Flash streams. However, with average bandwidth throughput, that same server cannot deliver more than a dozen streams. You can get around this problem by using QuickTime 4 to broadcast your Flash content or by porting your Flash movies into RealFlash and using the RealServer.

Drawbacks to Flash and Shockwave

Shockwave and Flash are not for everyone. Despite their exceptional interactive controls and authoring environments, there are a few drawbacks and limitations to using either technology:

- **Creating multimedia.** A proprietary authoring environment such as Flash or Shockwave requires web developers to learn an entirely new application as opposed to simply adding a few HTML or SMIL tags. For most developers, this trade-off is well worth it because they can create Flash and Shockwave presentations that look exactly the same on various browsers and platforms, and a standalone authoring application is infinitely more powerful for creating complex interactive presentations.

- **Replacing or revising content**. If developers want to revise content encapsulated within a binary movie using Flash or Shockwave, they must re-export and then upload the entire movie. While it is easier to upload a new audio or graphic file and change a few tags, both Flash and Shockwave support linking to external audio files as a workaround. For an example, check out the SWA CD player application at Macromedia's site (*http://www.macromedia.com/shockwave*). It can read an external text file to get the song list for a jukebox-style Shockwave movie.

- **Scalable server solution for managing streams**. Macromedia does not provide server-side management tools or dedicated servers for large-scale Flash and Shockwave streaming. Macromedia does support streaming for long-form audio files (audio clips more than a minute long) with RealAudio. Flash animation can be turned into a RealFlash presentation with a synchronized RealAudio clip. Recent versions of Director include a RealAudio Extra that allows you to add RealAudio to Shockwave presentations.

- **Server-side controls**. Shockwave and Flash do not have the server-side controls for random access to different parts of an audio file. If a user connection breaks halfway through an hour-long presentation, there is no way to resume playback at the point where the audio dropped out. The RealAudio Player, by contrast, offers random access to any portion of an audio file by sending a request back to the RealAudio Server.

- **Live encoding**. Shockwave and Flash do not support live encoding and broadcasting. If you want to stream live content, use RealAudio. Flash and Shockwave's inability to broadcast live events is not a problem, however, since interactive content is not usually a live endeavor.

Introduction to Flash

Macromedia Flash utilizes vector-based technology to deliver interactive real-time animation and sound over slow modem connections. Unlike Director, Flash was developed specifically for the Web. Mathematical algorithms enable Flash to stream high-resolution vector-based graphics instantaneously. Figure 9-2 shows vector artwork in the main Flash authoring window combined with bitmap images.

Flash's primary advantage over Shockwave is that its extremely small vector animations download quickly and play at real-time speeds, allowing more bandwidth to be allocated to audio content. For this reason, Flash is generally regarded as one of the few interactive

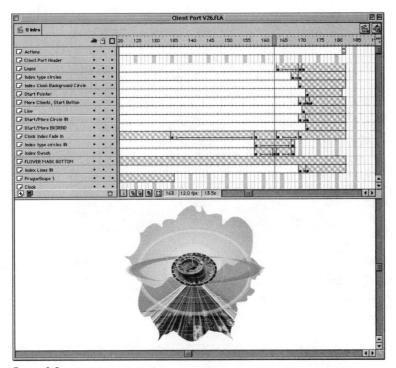

Figure 9-2. *Flash 4 scene window*

multimedia formats that really works over limited bandwidths. Flash
has expanded its user base even more since Macromedia declared the
Flash file format an open Internet standard. In 2000, Adobe will
release a product, LiveMotion, which writes Flash files as well as
many other files.

The Flash plug-in is also much smaller than the Director Shockwave
plug-in. Director Shockwave has the additional overhead of the Lingo
interpreter and streaming decoder. Macromedia was determined to
retain the Flash plug-in's optimal 150 KB file size. So despite the fact
that Lingo and SWA decompression capabilities would enhance Flash,
Macromedia did not incorporate them into Flash. Instead, Flash 4
now supports MP3 encoding for better audio quality and Action-
Script to give developers greater control and customization of their
Flash content.

While not as powerful as Director for creating advanced games and
more complex CD-ROM-like interactive applications, Flash's simplified authoring environment with predefined actions and JavaScript
support is ideal for most interactive web presentations with animation, button sounds, ambient loops, and streaming audio.

RealFlash

By using Flash in conjunction with RealNetwork's RealSystem 5.0 and up, you can create hybrid RealFlash presentations that are interactive and dependable (see Figure 9-3). Flash 4's bandwidth-friendly vector animation and image compression combined with the server reliability and superior streaming efficiency of RealAudio make RealFlash a real boon for web developers. For more information, read the section, "Creating RealFlash content" in Chapter 6. Note that you can also get the benefits of robust broadcasting using Flash with Qdesign music tracks in QuickTime 4.

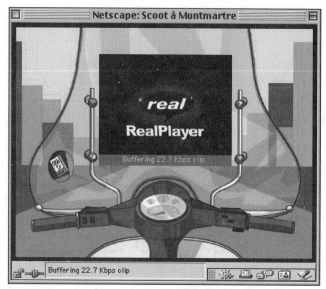

Figure 9-3. *A RealFlash presentation with vector line art and an embedded RealVideo window*

Flash audio: event-driven sound versus streaming sound

Flash allows you to integrate two basic types of audio: short event-driven *sound files* for button rollovers, loops, and transition effects; and long-playing *streamed sound files* for synchronizing speech and music to animation sequences.

Event-driven sound effects are embedded within a single keyframe of a Flash movie timeline and must be entirely downloaded before they can play back. Event-driven sounds are ideal for button sounds and loops that need to play instantly in response to a user action such as a mouse rollover or a particular animation event. An event-driven sound begins playback when a movie's timeline reaches a particular keyframe.

Once an event sound is triggered, it plays back autonomously from other elements in a Flash movie. Aside from the initial startpoint, event sounds cannot be continuously synchronized along a timeline to specific points in an animation sequence. Flash playback rates are largely determined by a computer's processor speed; thus, it is difficult to predict how an event-driven sound longer than 10 seconds will synchronize with specific animation sequences. To avoid synchronization problems and lengthy download times, use short event-driven sounds no greater than five seconds in length.

Unlike event sounds, streaming sounds are divided into smaller segments or packets of data and attached to each frame's image data. When playing back a synchronized streaming audio clip, Flash places a higher priority on keeping the sound in sync with specified keyframes rather than on preserving the overall frame rate. If there is not enough bandwidth to stream both the audio and the graphic data, Flash drops out image data or animation frames to keep in sync with the audio.

While both event-driven and streaming sounds allow you to specify the exact keyframe at which the audio file will start playing, only streamed audio lets you synchronize continuous speech, sound, or music to specific visual cues or events in an animation sequence. If you are creating a music-intensive Flash movie that needs to synchronize with motion graphics, use streaming audio. However, keep in mind that streaming audio tends to produce jerky animation and lost frames—which makes the use of event sounds a more favorable alternative for designers.

Flash allows you to control the following sound parameters:

- **In and out points**. One of the most useful features in Flash is the ability to define smaller sound clips by selecting in and out points from larger event sounds embedded in a Flash movie. You can drastically reduce your Flash download times by reusing sound data or applying different effects such as volume envelopes and looping to portions of the same sound clip. For example, you can use in and out points to make several short button sounds from a longer ambient loop file. Note that you cannot use this feature with streaming sounds.

- **Volume settings**. Flash allows you to set the volume level of an audio clip. Use volume settings to create fade-ins and fade-outs or as a sound design effect to manipulate softer sounds and louder sounds.

- **Stereo panning effects**. Flash allows you to set the stereo playback parameters of an audio clip. Using a short event sound that pans from left to right as it plays back can create interesting button and motion effects.

- **Looping effects**. With event sounds, you can build compelling loops by changing the envelopes over the course of the loop, looping segments defined by the start/stop handles, and layering multiple effects in the timeline.

Production tip

For reliable and quick delivery of embedded event sounds, combine all your separate sound clips into one contiguous audio file. Then set *in* and *out* times on your audio master file where each sound starts and ends.

Flash audio tutorial

We're not going to teach Flash here. What we're interested in is adding audio to a Flash presentation.

Case study: Bullfrog Production's multimedia web site

The Bullfrog web site (*http://www.bullfrog.ea.com*), shown in Figure 9-4, is a good example of a soundtrack that enhances the viewing experience, makes navigation fun, and draws in users.

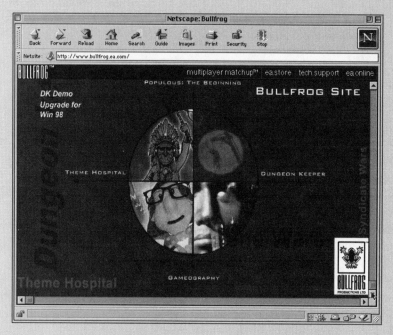

Figure 9-4. *The Bullfrog web site*

The web site was designed by Insomnious (*http://www.insomnious.com*). The site's sound design employs well-crafted, short event sounds that synchronize well with onscreen animations and button rollovers. The short intro event sound downloads quickly and sets the tone for the rest of the site. And richly textured rollover button sounds provide a satisfying auditory stimulus to the navigation experience.

If you continue to navigate the Bullfrog site, you will encounter a streaming soundtrack for the trailer preview of the game, "Populous: The Beginning" (*http://www.bullfrog.ea.com/populous3/trailer/trailer.htm*). Despite the trailer's simplicity, this is another good example of how a soundtrack synchronized with a few still images in a low-bandwidth environment can draw in an audience.

Adding an event sound

To add audio to your Flash presentation, follow these steps:

1. Under File, import an AIFF or a WAV file. The file will appear in the sound library window, as shown in Figure 9-5. Make sure to import a 22 kHz 16-bit source audio file for best results, especially if you want to take advantage of Flash's new MP3 support. If the audio file is set to a different sampling rate and bit-depth, change it to 22 kHz 16-bit before importing it into Flash.

2. Select Insert → Layer to add a new layer for your audio track. Figure 9-6 shows the main authoring window as seen in Flash 4 on a Mac. Here we have created a new layer called Sound Effects. We want this sound to start at the 5-second mark. So we select that frame on the timeline and choose Insert → Keyframe. Keyframes mark where a transition begins or ends in a scene or where some object, such as a sound file, starts to play.

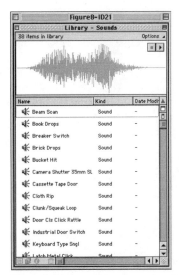

Figure 9-5. *Sound library window*

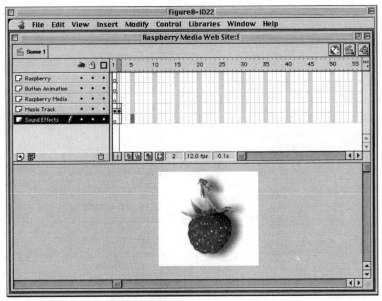

Figure 9-6. *The main authoring window*

3. Double-click on the desired keyframe to call up the Frame Properties dialog box, as shown in Figure 9-7. The Frame Properties window will default to the sound tab when you click on a frame layer with sound. Then choose the name of the sound file you want to associate with the keyframe. Note that the Frame Properties window features a pull-down of all the imported audio files in your sound library.

4. In the Sound window, make sure to select the appropriate options in the Effect, Sync, and Loops fields and then hit OK. Under Effect, you can select from a menu of predefined effects such as fade-ins and fade-outs and panning from right to left, as shown in Figure 9-8. For more accurate results, we recommend you apply custom effects manually with the volume and panning controls instead of using the predefined effects.

5. Under the Sync menu, make sure to select Event (for embedded short sounds) or Stream (for longer-playing streaming synchronized sounds). Here we chose Event, as shown in Figure 9-9.

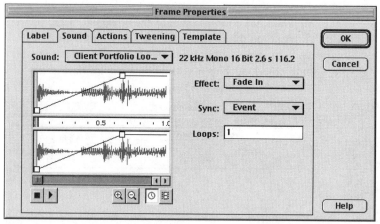

Figure 9-7. *The Sound tab within the Frame Properties window*

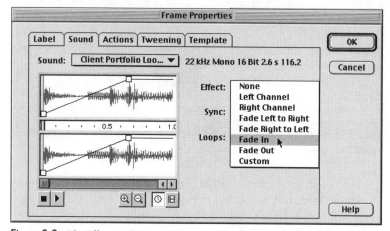

Figure 9-8. *The Effects pull-down menu*

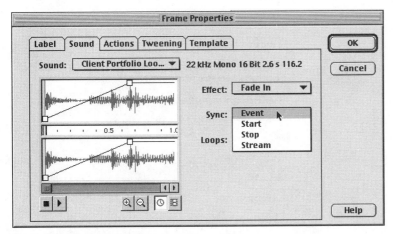

Figure 9-9. *The Sync pull-down menu*

6. In the Loop field, you can specify how many times you want the sound to repeat. The loop option is useful for creating ambient loops. Make sure to specify a large enough number to keep the loop playing for the duration of the scene. With embedded sounds, you cannot sync the exact end time of the loop with a particular animation frame in the movie.

Publishing and file size optimization

Once you have finished building your Flash scenes with all the animation and audio layers in place and properly synced together, you will want to optimize each sound to achieve the smallest file size possible. There are two ways to optimize the file size of your Flash movie: you can set the overall compression rate and encoding format for the audio stream (streamed sounds) and audio event (event-driven sounds), or you can specify individual compression rates for each sound in a Flash scene.

To specify separate audio compression rates, select a sound in the sound library window and go to the pull-down menu on the top right of the library window and click Properties. The Sound Properties window will then appear, as shown in Figure 9-10. The Sound Properties menu allows you to select the compression type, bitrate, and encoding speed for the selected sound.

By experimenting with different settings, you can optimize the compression rates for each sound. Some sounds work just fine at super-low bitrates such as 8 Kbps and 16 Kbps, while others (such as speech) might require a higher bitrate of 24 Kbps to pass your acceptable audio quality threshold. With a convenient Test button,

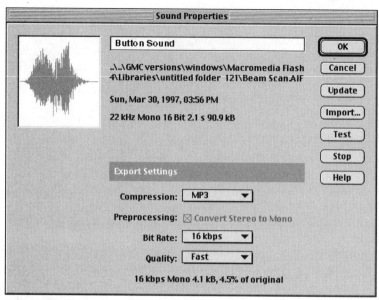

Figure 9-10. *The Sound Properties dialog box*

the Sound Properties window makes it easy to preview the result of any given bitrate and compression type. If you have a Flash scene with eight audio files, you can set five of them at a bitrate of 16 Kbps and the other three at a rate of 32 Kbps.

Optimizing separate sound files will come in handy when you run your scenes through the Flash Bandwidth Profiler to check frame by frame for data spikes that shoot above your specified stream rate. The Bandwidth Profiler enables you to manage your Flash streams by locating data spikes and moving content to different frames in order to spread out the bandwidth load. For example, if a certain frame peaks above your specified 28 Kbps stream rate, you can set some of the objects to preload in the beginning of the Flash movie, preventing glitches in playback. To use the Bandwidth Profiler, click the Test Movie menu option. Figure 9-11 shows a short intro scene from a Flash site in the Bandwidth Profiler window.

If you don't want to bother specifying a customized compression setting for each sound or if you want to override the settings, you can simply specify a universal compression type and bitrate for all sounds in the Publish Settings window when you go to export your Flash content, as shown in Figure 9-12. In the Publish Settings window, first select the "Override sound settings" checkbox, then specify the global sound settings for all event sounds and streamed sounds.

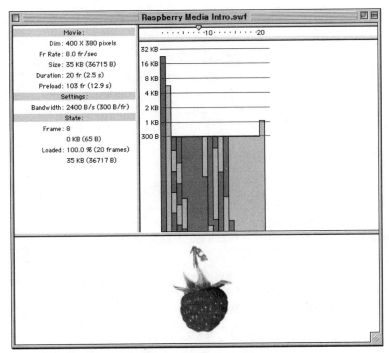

Figure 9-11. *The Bandwidth Profiler window*

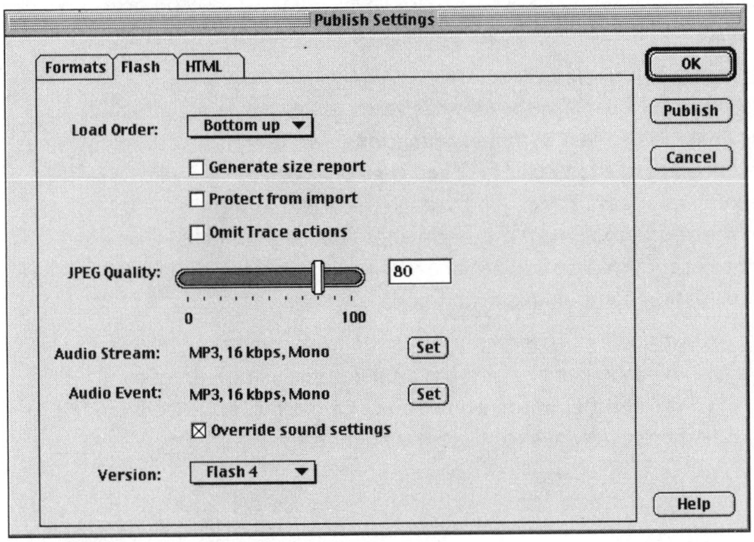

Figure 9-12. *The Publish Settings window*

Flash case study

Let's take a look at Raspberry Media's promotional Flash multimedia site, shown in Figure 9-13, at *http://www.raspberrymultimedia.com*. Raspberry Media, a web design firm founded by co-author Josh Beggs, redesigned its text- and graphics-based web site into a media-rich site with audio and animation. The plan was to develop a multimedia version of their existing sites so they could show clients the difference firsthand and give them a glimpse of what they could expect from a site enhanced with Flash.

Building a soundtrack in Flash

If you use Flash, you know that its compact vector graphics allow plenty of room for audio. According to Raspberry Creative Director Ethan Allen, it was important to incorporate audio into Raspberry's Flash site. "If we had to do all the tweening and overlay effects with bitmap images, like we did in the old days of Shockwave, there would be no bandwidth left over to include a soundtrack."

Even though Flash vector animation is extremely compact, it's still a tight fit to include additional audio information at 28.8 Kbps bandwidths. "When we first started designing the site, we were excited about implementing a diverse soundtrack with multiple tracks of sound firing off in sync with the animations. But when we started beta-testing the Flash site with three or five event-driven sounds for a particular animation sequence, we ran into major bandwidth congestion problems. With so many embedded event sounds, the Flash site would not buffer properly due to too much data throughput at a given frame on the movie timeline. We had to simplify most of the soundtrack to only include one music loop per animation sequence. Now that Flash supports MP3 compression, resulting in much smaller file sizes for event sounds, we plan on redoing the site to incorporate more sound effects."

With Flash movies you have to make a choice early in the site design to use either less audio and more intensive visual effects or more audio and less complex animations. "As is typical with many multimedia productions, we started producing the visuals first and then started adding audio later when the animations were nearly complete," says Ethan. "In hindsight, this was a mistake. We should have started thinking about the soundtrack from the beginning. Then we could have simplified the animations in certain spots to accommodate additional event sounds in the timeline. It is much more difficult to change the animation components at the end.

"Ultimately, we made the choice to go with only one or two event sounds per animation sequence. Every main section of the Flash site has an accompanying one-bar ambient music loop. In cases where we had enough bandwidth we added another short event sound to the movie. Since we were using so few sounds we had to find creative ways to make the soundtrack interesting."

$\rightarrow$

The key to keeping your Flash movie size small is to recycle or reuse sounds. As mentioned earlier, Flash allows you to set in and out points in the keyframe where the event sound is located. With a two- or three-second sound, you can use in and out points to create multiple button sounds from one event sound.

According to Ethan, what worked best with the Raspberry multimedia site was to use two event-driven sounds, a repeating music loop for background ambiance, and a short sound effect for buttons and transitions. "In several of the Flash movies, we tried to reuse portions of the music loop to add spice and variation to the animation sequence. This approach did not work because the reused sound effect was hard to distinguish from the original music loop. Reusing a louder portion such as a drum hit did not work either since it randomly came in over the music loop and sounded like a mistake."

Ultimately, the best approach was to incorporate a separate sound effect to overlay the music loop. Using two distinct sound files gave us the best result and the most flexibility, says Ethan. "With an additional sound effect we were able to add more variation to the soundtrack and accentuate the visual effects."

Figure 9-13. *The home page of the Raspberry Media Flash site*

Introduction to Shockwave

Shockwave for Director is a software component that enables compatible browsers such as Netscape Navigator and Microsoft Internet Explorer 2.0 and higher to play multimedia Director movies over the Web. Shockwave is designed to work with standard HTTP servers and is ideal for streaming short- to medium-length audio files and advanced multimedia presentations and games.

Shockwave movies are built within Director using the Score window, where all media elements are placed as cast members on channels or tracks along a timeline, as shown in Figure 9-14. Director is a powerful tool for orchestrating multiple media types such as video, animation, and sound into complex interactive presentations.

Director uses Lingo script to create sophisticated interactive games and presentations. Originally it was designed to provide CD-ROM developers with an advanced cross-platform authoring solution for building multimedia presentations. Shockwave uses Director's Lingo scripting to directly interact with the operating system and multimedia functionality of a PC. Lingo enables the development of complex interactive soundtracks with audio fade-ins and fade-outs and panning effects tied to specific user actions. For example, with Lingo you can specify elegant cross-fades of separate audio clips when a user transitions from one scene or web page to another, instead of abruptly cutting off a sound.

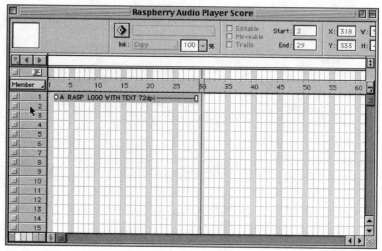

Figure 9-14. *The Score window used for orchestrating interactive events in Director*

The drawback to broadcasting Shockwave-based presentations is that they tend to be too large and cumbersome for 28.8 Kbps modems. As Internet bandwidth increases with xDSL and cable, Shockwave will play a more prominent role in web multimedia.

The Enigma audio mixer

Three monks stand in a darkened room. A distant rhythm begins to pulse in a repeating pattern. The beat gets louder and louder until one of the monks raises his head and begins to sing a mystical-sounding Gregorian chant before being joined by the other two monks. Their voices, along with the pulsing background rhythm create a rich-sounding music mix that seems familiar. Then, with the click of a button, two of the monks lower their voices in silence. The third monk sings for several seconds before fading into silence like the others.

The chanting combined with the pulsing rhythm loop sounds like a tune the popular music group Enigma might have created. In fact, as Josh Feldman, Creative Director at Prophet Communications, a division of Frog Design (*www.frogdesign.com*), pointed out, that was the purpose of the Enigma III Shockwave audio mixer he and Thor Muller created for Virgin Records.

Prophet Communications worked with Virgin Records to develop an online interactive experience to promote Enigma's album. The Shockwave audio mixer let visitors to the Enigma web site (*www.enigma.com*) create their own music mix using an assembly of instruments and voices. The mixer contains four music loops represented by the image of three monks and a drum set, as shown in Figure 9-15. When a user clicks on one of the objects, an audio loop begins to play.

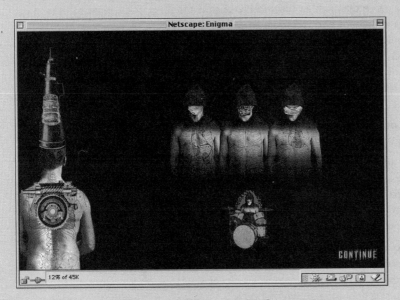

Figure 9-15. *The Enigma Shockwave Mixer by Prophet Communications*

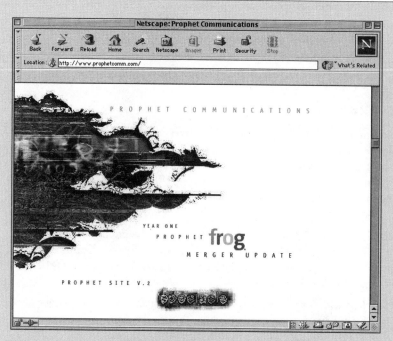

Figure 9-16. *The Prophet Communications home page at http://www.prophetcomm.com*

What made this mixer so successful was Prophet Communications' elegant use of simple Lingo scripts to make the mixer more than just an assemblage of simultaneous loops. Lingo scripts were used judiciously to add fade-ins and fade-outs to the monk's voices. Instead of an abrupt sound interrupting the audio mix, each new sound transitioned smoothly into the full audio mix, the same as it would in a live performance or recording. The use of fade-ins and fade-outs for all the sounds in the mix made for a good soundtrack that enhanced the entertainment experience and ambiance of the web site. Here are Prophet's top five tips for using audio with Shockwave:

- Leave four seconds of audio at the end of your Shockwave File. Shockwave will sometimes cut off the last three or four seconds of a streaming audio file, so it is always a good idea to put some blank space at the end of the sound file.

- Never use streaming audio when you need immediate user feedback. Streaming audio is great for reducing file size and playing long audio files, but remember that the streaming audio file has to preload for three to five seconds to play well. If you assign a streaming audio sound to a button, a user with a 28.8 Kbps modem connection who clicks the button will not hear the sound until almost five seconds later.

- Use Lingo variables to add richness to your interactive content. When a user clicks on a button or triggers an audio loop, a Lingo script can randomly select from many different *.swa* files residing on the server. Using variables is a clever way to add more content to your web site without requiring additional download time.

→

To configure random controls in Lingo, set the URL of member *"shockaudio"* = *"sounds/"* & *random(4)* & *"song.swa"*. Then set the preLoadTime of member "shockaudio" to 5 Play. This will randomly pick from four files called *1song.swa*, *2song.swa*, *3song.swa*, and *4song.swa* located in a folder within your master movie directory folder that contains all the media elements for your Shockwave presentation. The folder that contains your *.swa* audio files can be named any name you choose as long as you use the same name within your Lingo script. The folder then gets uploaded to a web server along with the master movie folder. Note that the above script was written for Director 5. If you're using Director 6 or higher you may have to change the way the streaming audio file is called up.

- When embedding a movie that contains no images and only plays a sound file, make the dimension of the movie 1 pixel by 2 pixels instead of 1×1. In older browsers, the 1×1 pixel movies often fill the whole screen instead of staying at their dimension. This error has been fixed in newer browsers. But to be safe, embed them as 1×2 pixels.

- Do not set levels to 100% when normalizing your audio files. Normalize to 85% or 95% to avoid distortion. 100% normalized audio files imported into Shockwave are likely to cause distortion when played back through cheap amps in PC sound cards. This also applies to audio files converted to RealAudio or QuickTime.

Make sure to visit Prophet's Spectacle.com web site (Figure 9-16) to see their showcase of innovative Shockwave and Flash entertainment content (*www.prophetcomm.com*).

Using Shockwave "internal" sounds: embedded cast members versus streamed SWA sounds

You can incorporate two basic forms of audio into Shockwave movies: embedded internal sounds (such as buttons, loops, and short transition sounds) and streamed audio with Director's Shockwave Audio (SWA). SWA is a variant of MPEG 3–based compression that adds support for storing cue point data in the audio file. Director allows you to attach cue points along an audio file that trigger events such as the start of a video clip or animation sequence. You can also use third-party solutions for playing audio through Shockwave, including RealAudio with the RealMedia Xtra, RMF files with the Beatnik Xtra, QuickTime audio, and even audio embedded into Flash movies.

Short button sound effects and loops are incorporated into Shockwave as embedded audio cast members, similar to event-driven sounds in Flash. Embedded audio clips play instantaneously when triggered by a user action. They also allow for greater Lingo scripting control than does streamed sound. Any short sound that is directly linked to the action of a user and requires instant playback should be placed in your Shockwave movie as an embedded audio file. Note, however, that despite Shockwave compression ratios of 44:1, embedded sounds still add tremendous size to your Director files, so use them sparingly.

With Director 6 and later, embedded audio can be delivered as a streaming cast member. This means you can orchestrate the download of different cast members so that content appears quickly while cast members from later scenes download in the background. Plan your streaming Shockwave movie carefully so any cast member that Lingo calls up will have previously downloaded into the cast member library. Director 7 also adds support for imported SWA cast members. In previous versions, SWA compression was applied to all audio cast members when the file was "burned" into a Shockwave (*.dcr*) file, and only one compression ratio could be applied to all the audio cast members. *.dcr* is the file type extension for movies exported from Director.

In Director 7, you can create SWA cast members at rates as low as 8 Kbps using audio-editing tools like Sound Forge, SoundEdit 16, or Peak, and then import the compressed cast members into Director. As of Director 7.0.2 and higher, you can import MP3 files in addition to SWA files.

Streaming sounds need at least a three-to-five-second buffer time before playback and are thus mainly used for longer-playing audio files. The preload buffer time required for smooth playback of streaming audio prevents this type of audio from being used for button sounds or loops.

Creating transparent Shockwave loops

One of the quickest ways to incorporate Shockwave audio into your web pages is to use a 1 × 2-pixel Shockwave movie to play audio loops or short greetings. To add a compelling soundtrack, use a transparent Shockwave movie with invisible frames to make one audio loop play across several web pages. By using transparent frames, you can use different ambient loops thematically throughout your web site.

Using different loops for various groups of web pages is a great technique for adding variety to a web site and a way to avoid the risk of annoying people with loops that stop playing when they click from one web page to another.

To get started, open the folder *bgkdloop*, found in the Shockwave or Director directories. It contains:

bgkdloop.dcr

> An almost invisible Shockwave movie.

bgkdloop.dir

> The source movie that produced *bgkdloop.dcr* (courtesy of Macromedia).

bgkdloop.htm

> An HTML template page that displays no interface or user controls. The default page simply autostreams a sound when the page containing the movie is loaded into your browser.

Drag the file *bgkdloop.htm* onto your browser icon, preferably Netscape or Explorer 3.0 or higher. After the page loads, it goes black and your SWA file begins to stream automatically. When you play the file back, you may see a tiny dot in the top-left corner of your browser window; this is the 1×2-pixel frame of the Shockwave movie.

The web page with the Shockwave movie should contain the following object tag:

```
<OBJECT CLASSID="clsid:166B1BCA-3F9C-11CF-8075-444553540000"
CODEBASE="http://active.macromedia.com/director/cabs/
sw.cab#version=6,0,0,0"
WIDTH="1"
HEIGHT="2"
NAME="Intro">
<PARAM NAME="SRC" VALUE="./allsongs.dcr">
<EMBED WIDTH="1" HEIGHT="2" SRC="allsongs.dcr" sw1="off"
swURL="intro.swa" swTEXT="" swPreLoadTime="5" sw2="1" sw3="0">
</OBJECT>
```

If the sound is playing properly, start adding pictures and text to your web page.

Shockwave streaming audio

There have been several major innovations in the latest versions of Shockwave. Shockwave movies exported from Director 5 and earlier versions had the capacity to stream only audio. Graphics and animations had to download in their entirety before they could play back. Thus, if you were streaming a music video, the graphic content would have to download first before the music video began to play. An average 250 KB Shockwave movie exported from Director 5 or lower produced extremely long wait times, causing many people to leave a page before the movie downloaded.

The release of Director 6 marked a major breakthrough. With Director 6 and later, individual cast members are broken into separate packets of data and streamed in the background while a *.swa* audio file plays. This means that a Shockwave streaming audio file can begin to play almost immediately with its accompanying visual content. This feature allows you to create longer, more complex movies and interactive entertainment.

Director 6 and 7 also have the capability to read markers on your audio file set in Sound Edit16. With this feature, it is possible to sync your streaming audio with the appearance of a designated graphic or animated cast member.

Exporting Shockwave audio files

Use Macromedia's SoundEdit 16 to create Shockwave audio (SWA) files using the SWA Export Xtra. You can also convert WAV audio files to SWA files in Director for Windows. When you create an audio file with the SWA Export Xtra, the new file is compressed using MPEG Layer 3 compression. To use the SWA Export Xtra, follow these steps:

1. In SoundEdit 16 version 2.0 or higher, open the audio file you want to export.

2. Choose Shockwave for Audio Settings in the Xtras dialog menu to configure the compression options. Figure 9-17 shows the Shockwave Xtras window with the bitrate set to 24 Kbps.

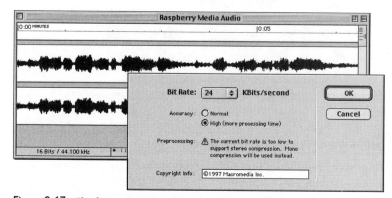

Figure 9-17. *Shockwave Xtras window*

3. Select the bitrate (Kbps) you want from the bitrate drop-down menu. Note that 24 Kbps tends to dropout over 28.8 modem connections. 16 Kbps is the preferred setting for low-bandwidth applications. Use Table 9-1 as a guide for setting the appropriate Kbps rate.

Table 9-1. *Shockwave streaming audio bandwidth settings*

Bitrate	Target audience connection	Sample rate
16 Kbps	28 Kbps modem connections	16 kHz
24 Kbps	56 Kbps modem connections	16 kHz
32 Kbps–56 Kbps	ISDN lines	22.050 kHz
64 Kbps–128 Kbps	T1 delivery	44.100 kHz

4. Check the Convert Stereo to Mono checkbox if you are converting a stereo file to mono. The SWA Export Xtra automatically converts a file to mono if you choose a bitrate of 32 Kbps or less.

5. Choose the appropriate Accuracy and Preprocessing settings. Accuracy refers to how much analysis is performed on the original file before creating the SWA output. High Accuracy offers better results but takes a lot more processing time than the default Normal setting. At the lowest bitrates, the difference is not significant. The Preprocessing checkbox gives the option of converting stereo files to mono as part of the SWA encoding process. At settings of 32 Kbps or lower, stereo files are automatically converted to mono (as shown in Figure 9-17). Choose OK to close the Shockwave for Audio Settings dialog box.

6. Choose File → Export to open the Export dialog box.

7. Choose SWA File from the Export Type pop-up menu. Name the file, then choose Save. The file is exported using the settings you specified in the Shockwave for Audio Settings dialog box. All files exported as SWA files use the same default setting until the parameters are changed again.

Optimizing your Shockwave audio files

The following tips help ensure the highest quality Shockwave audio:

- Work with 16-bit 22.050 or 44.100 kHz files (22.050 kHz is recommended).

- When using pre-existing 8-bit or 11 kHz files, re-sample them to 16-bit 22.050 kHz and leave them at this resolution when exporting to SWA format.

- To improve the quality of SWA files encoded at modem speeds (16 Kbps and 24 Kbps), filtering of frequencies in the range of 4 kHz to 8 kHz can reduce crunch and distortion on certain 22.050 kHz files.

Auditioning your Shockwave audio files

Use the Raspberry Player located at *http://www. designingwebaudio.com/ shockwave* to audition your *.swa* files. Move your *.swa* file into the *rasplayr* folder on your local hard drive and rename it *rasplayr.swa*. You can also use an alias of your *.swa* file as long as the alias is named *rasplayr.swa* and is placed in the *rasplayr* folder. You can place only one file at a time named *rasplayr.swa* in the *rasplayr* folder. Drop *rasplayr.htm* onto the Netscape icon (or click Netscape's Reload button), and click Play. You should now hear your *.swa* file playing from your hard drive.

- Stereo source files should share common information on both channels. If the two channels carry unrelated information, there will be an uneven quality level between them.

- As a last step before converting to an SWA file, normalize the audio file to 95%. Giving the file at least 5% extra headroom prevents distortion.

Quick and easy audio streaming with Shockwave

You can quickly get up and running with Shockwave by using the royalty-free Raspberry Media Player, shown in Figure 9-18, available at *http://www.designingwebaudio.com*. The Raspberry Media Player provides volume controls, stop, play, and pause buttons, a song selection menu, a status bar, and a blank area for placing your personal logo or custom graphics. With Director 5 or later, simply replace the Raspberry Media logo with your own logo, or replace all the graphics in the Cast Members window to create a new audio player interface, and export your own custom Shockwave player.

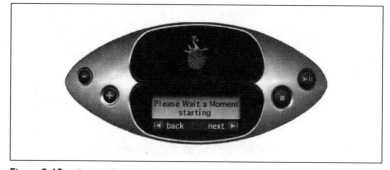

Figure 9-18. *The Raspberry Media Shockwave Audio Player*

To stream your Shockwave audio, customize the Raspberry Media Player and post it on your server with the following files placed in the same folder:

custom.dcr
> The movie that contains the interface

custom.htm
> The HTML document that calls *rasplayr.dcr* and tells the movie how to display itself and how to play the SWA file

custom.txt
> The text file with the list of songs and their corresponding URLs

custom.swa
> Your SWA files

When a user opens an HTML page with a Shockwave movie in their browser, it tells the browser to go to the URL specified by the EMBED tag in *custom.htm* and downloads the specified movie (*custom.dcr*). To use the Raspberry Player to stream your SWA files, you need to modify the following HTML EMBED attributes:

```
<EMBED WIDTH="368" HEIGHT="171"
SRC="http://www.raspberrymedia.com/audio/rasplayr.dcr"
swURL="http://www.raspberrymedia.com/audio/audio_samples/"
swList="sound_sca.swa,sound_eff.swa,world_bea.swa,
blues.swa,trance.swa,acoustic.swa,rock.swa,reggae.swa"
swTEXT="Sound Scape,Sound Effects,WorldBeat,Blues,Trance,Accoustic,
Rock,Reggae" swPreLoadTime=5 animate = "NO">
```

To modify the EMBED tags to play your audio files, open a copy of *rasplayr.htm* in a text editor and change the following EMBED tags:

SRC=*URL*

> SRC specifies the URL of the Shockwave movie. Put the complete URL between the straight quotation marks.

swURL=*URL*

> swURL specifies the URL of the SWA file. Put the appropriate URL between the quotation marks.

swList=*list*

> swList points to the SWA files listed in the player menu. List the names of all of your SWA files between the quotation marks.

swTEXT=*list*

> swTEXT appears in the selection window of the audio player. Name your SWA files and place them between the quotation marks.

swPreLoadTime=*integer*

> This is where you set the amount of preload buffer time in seconds. More preload time produces a greater delay between clicking Play and hearing your SWA file. Generally a four- to five-second preload time helps ensure continuous playback without drop-outs.

As the SWA file streams from the server to your computer, it fills the buffer. As the SWA file plays, it empties the buffer. If these two rates are the same, playback will not be interrupted. If the Internet is slow, the buffer may not be filled as quickly as it is emptied. This can result in playback stopping for a moment as the buffer waits to be filled up again.

Summary

Now that you have learned how to integrate compelling audio and multimedia into your web site with Flash and Shockwave, let's take a look at MIDI, a highly efficient format for delivering music over the Web.

CHAPTER TEN

MIDI: QUICK AND EASY AUDIO FOR THE WEB

One of the quickest and easiest means by which to add sound to a web site is to use MIDI (Musical Instrument Digital Interface). MIDI allows for universal, cross-platform communication between computers and composers. It lets you easily integrate sound into your site by utilizing the same principles musicians and producers have used for nearly two decades. What makes MIDI a popular format for web audio is its simple learning curve, its inexpensive price tag, and its conservative use of bandwidth.

MIDI developed out of the need for a standard. In the late 1960s and early 1970s, electronic instrument makers began to create the world's first commercial synthesizers. Companies created systems that could communicate only with their own synthesizers. These machines were made popular by such music pioneers as Keith Emerson, Joe Zawinul, Walter and Wendy Carlos, and most notably, Herbie Hancock.

In the early 1980s, synthesizers started becoming more mainstream and computer software was developed to communicate with the electronic instruments. With the introduction of each new synthesizer, manufacturers were forced to write complex customized code to interface with each new product line. Due to the inherent inefficiencies in developing new software each time a new synthesizer was developed, the larger electronic instrument companies like Roland, Sequential Circuits, and Yamaha decided to create a universal standard that all electronic instruments and computers could understand.

During a 1982 conference, a group of music industry heavyhitters gathered to discuss a common protocol. In 1983, the MIDI standard was born with the introduction of the first MIDI keyboards by Roland and Sequential Circuits. Soon after, virtually every synthesizer manufacturer in the world was producing MIDI-compatible hardware.

In this chapter

- MIDI: A universal approach
- Adding MIDI to your web pages
- Creating your own MIDI files
- Summary

MIDI: A universal approach

MIDI and MIDI-hybrid formats such as Beatnik or QuickTime Music Tracks are perhaps the best audio formats on the market for incorporating sound into limited-bandwidth environments. MIDI communicates between devices via a text-based code system or score. Much like the player piano of old, where hole-punch sheet music was fed into the piano, MIDI pianos and synthesizers can play back music translated into the MIDI format. When a user comes across a web page featuring MIDI, the embedded MIDI file or score is downloaded to the computer and played back via the user's MIDI-compatible soundcard or synthesis engine.

On most home computer systems, MIDI is played back with Apple's QuickTime plug-in or Microsoft's Windows Media system. These plug-ins feature a MIDI sound engine or a software-based synthesis module that replicates a set of common instrument sounds. Increasingly, popular web browsers such as Internet Explorer and Navigator 4.0 and later are starting to include built-in sophisticated MIDI sound engines.

Advantages to using the MIDI format

The main advantage to using MIDI on your web site is that MIDI file sizes are relatively tiny (usually between 2 KB and 25 KB) in comparison to other digital audio formats. Traditional digital audio files are measured in megabytes. Another advantage is that MIDI is a universal language, compatible with almost all browsers and computers across the Internet. In other words, you do not need a special plug-in, other than what is pre-installed in your web browser, to listen to MIDI files. This is important because many users are not comfortable with or do not want to download an extra plug-in to listen to other formats.

MIDI also happens to be ideally suited to the low-bandwidth web medium. MIDI playback has several key advantages over other web audio formats:

- Near universal playback.

- Availability of a copious amount of MIDI files featuring all types of music.

- Easy integration into existing HTML pages using a standard text editor.

- Availability of mature authoring tools, such as Performer, Vision, and Cakewalk, and a large base of knowledgeable users on the Internet and in the music industry.

- The smallest file size per minute of any audio format. (An entire minute of MIDI results in a mere 10 KB to 20 KB file, compared to a one-minute 500 KB MP3 file or a 120 KB 28.8 Kbps Real-Audio file.)

Despite its limited range, MIDI is so ideally suited for the Web that it's surprising that it's not used more often. However, MIDI is constrained in part by computers with cheap sound cards and by inferior software synthesis engines that cause more elaborate MIDI compositions to sound less than perfect. The MIDI file is simply a set of instructions about how a given synthesizer or sound engine should play back the particular MIDI file. All the texture and richness comes from the synthesis engine itself. For this reason, many people mistakenly assume that MIDI is to blame for the poor sound quality, when it is often the sound engine that is the culprit. When played back on a decent sound engine (software sound engines such as QuickTime are making nice advancements in quality), MIDI can sound very good, often making it difficult to tell whether the source was live or MIDI-produced.

However, cheap MIDI engines are not the only offender. Using poorly composed MIDI files or using unedited files grabbed from web sites also creates problems. With a little work, MIDI files can be made to sound good, even when played through a lower-quality MIDI sound engine.

If you follow good sound design techniques, you will find many uses for MIDI. And if you are already familiar with a MIDI editor, you will not have to face the steep learning curve involved with RealAudio, Flash, or Shockwave integration. MIDI is a good sound design alternative for creating mood and ambiance on your site. You don't always have to use the most sophisticated multimedia formats in order to add sound. If you just want to add a little intro theme music to your welcome page or a few button rollover sounds to your navigation bar, RealAudio and Flash may be overkill. Ask yourself if your site needs custom-built interactive Flash or Shockwave soundtracks or digitized audio broadcasts with RealAudio. If the answer is no, consider using MIDI.

So what's the catch? Despite some of MIDI's advantages, it has some drawbacks and limitations. For example, MIDI uses an entirely different method of producing sound than do traditional digital audio technologies. And because MIDI is basically a language for communicating music notation and not a storage format for digitized audio, there is no way to broadcast voices or prerecorded sounds with MIDI. Essentially, MIDI is limited to jingles, instrumental tunes, and ambient synthesizer background sounds.

Another disadvantage to MIDI is that each user's MIDI sound engine or hardware/software setup may contain a different set of musical instrument sounds. If you compose a piece of music in MIDI and use a great synth sound you have spent months customizing, chances are it is not going to sound the same played back over the SoundBlaster card or other MIDI sound engine loaded on your user's machine.

While initiatives such as General MIDI have helped to standardize MIDI playback, there is still considerable variance in playback from one device to another. General MIDI is a standard that specifies a common bank or a set of 128 musical instrument sounds that all MIDI devices share in common to ensure uniform playback. For example, with General MIDI, you can be assured program number 4 will be a honky tonk piano sound on any General MIDI device, instead of a flute or drum sound.

What a difference a good MIDI sound engine makes

To demonstrate the audible difference between various MIDI sound engines, compare the two MIDI examples at *http://www.designingwebaudio.com*.

Example MIDI #1 is a recorded excerpt of a MIDI file playing Beethoven's 5th Symphony. The file was played through the QuickTime music instruments and the result recorded in 44.1 kHz audio. As you listen to the sound, you may notice how the QuickTime MIDI sound engine produces every note of Beethoven's 5th, without missing a beat. You may also notice that the sound quality is pretty good for a computer and a software synthesizer. However, the deep, rich tones of the symphony are missing from this file. One reason why software-based synthesizers (like those developed for QuickTime) cannot reproduce the finer nuances of elaborate compositions is the current processor speed and power of PCs. As faster processors are developed, sound quality is expected to improve.

Now listen to the second example, MIDI #2. We used the same MIDI file, but switched the MIDI-compatible sound engine. We ran the MIDI file through an Alesis Quadrasynth Plus (a hardware-based keyboard/sound module) and recorded the outcome. As you listen to this recording, the difference is noticeable. You may even think the recording was made with real instruments. The reason Quadrasynth Plus has better sound is simple: the sounds are actually sampled from symphonic instruments and stored on ROM chips, then placed into the synthesizer's hardware architecture.

QuickTime also uses samples and wavetables via the Roland Sound set. However, a dedicated external synthesizer like the Quadrasynth Plus has more memory and dedicated ROM for samples and therefore yields better sound. Most hardware synthesizers sound better than most software synthesizers because they have dedicated DSPs (Digital Signal Processors) and because they're built specifically for music applications. A DSP is a dedicated microprocessor used to process sound by any number of ways the user requests. In the MIDI #2 file, the DSPs are working to create the sound. In other cases, the DSPs can be used to alter a sound by adding effects such as reverb or delay. The advantage of a DSP is that it can be programmed to perform almost any function.

But General MIDI is not a cure-all; it merely specifies that your instrument settings should be the same from one General MIDI device to another. General MIDI cannot tell each synthesizer or sound engine how to reproduce a particular bamboo flute, grand piano, or a more difficult sound, such as an angelic synth chorus sound. Each manufacturer's MIDI-compatible device uses a slightly different technique to reproduce sound. This means you cannot guarantee exactly how your MIDI music score will sound when played back through a user's particular set of instrument sounds, especially if you are using a subjective description, such as "tubular bells" or "Indian flute."

To avoid this problem, make sure your MIDI files are built around common instrument sounds that are easy to reproduce and fairly consistent from one device to the next, such as bass, organ, harmonica, and piano. Avoid using sounds that are difficult to reproduce, even instrument sounds such as guitar, saxophone, and most horn instruments, which all do synthesize well on expensive synthesizers. Later in this chapter, we show you how a new specification called DownLoadable Sounds (DLS), which offers more predictable playback with higher-quality synthesis, is helping create better standards, so you don't have to be as vigilant about your instrument selections. (See the sidebar "DLS: The future of MIDI" later in this chapter.)

The quality of MIDI playback is expected to improve in the near future as synthesis engines improve with faster chips and more extensive software. In 1999, we saw the advancement of some software synthesis engines, such as the new Unity DS-1 software sampler from BitHeadz. There are also several promising initiatives, including DLS, which is spearheaded by the MIDI Manufacturer's Association and companies such as Apple Computer and Microsoft. The music equipment industry is also seeking to improve the quality of MIDI playback via more powerful synthesis engines and standardization among sound cards.

Adding MIDI to your web pages

Making MIDI files can be fun and easy; placing them on your web page can be even easier. Simply enter this line of code in your HTML:

```
<BGSOUND SRC="Yoursound.mid">
```

Note that this example is for Explorer. If Navigator has trouble with the BGSOUND tag, try the following example in addition to the BGSOUND:

```
<EMBED SRC="Yoursound.mid" HIDDEN="true">
```

This code causes a MIDI file to begin playback whenever the page is loaded into the user's browser. Furthermore, you can set basic parameters such as looping, volume, and so forth, by simply adding them to the tag. Here is the most basic way to add MIDI sound to your web page:

```
<EMBED SRC="Yoursound.mid" HIDDEN="true"
loop="yes"
volume="10"
autostart="true">
```

This example HTML code will instruct a web page to play *Yoursound.mid*. The file will loop, the volume will be at the max limit of 10, the autostart function will be in effect, and the file will begin playback automatically

If you want to have MIDI sound available on your web page via a hyperlink, but do not want the file to begin playback automatically, simply add an HREF tag to the MIDI file, and it will be available for download whenever the user clicks on the link:

```
<A HREF="Yoursound.mid">
```

Making a MIDI jukebox

Many web designers have taken advantage of the short download times and cross-platform performance of MIDI and have created a variety of tools and tricks that you can use on your own web pages. One basic example of how to use MIDI on your site is the MIDI jukebox.

A MIDI jukebox functions as a typical jukebox functions in that a user selects a requested song by clicking a button. Once the button is clicked, the MIDI file is downloaded to the user's browser (both IE and Netscape have included MIDI-compatible plug-ins with releases 4.0 and later). It then begins playing almost immediately via any MIDI-compatible plug-in or external system (in actuality, the MIDI plug-in only pipes the MIDI data to the appropriate playback device, such as the Netscape MIDI window or QuickTime player). There's no waiting for long download times, just fast and easy music. A typical jukebox, as shown in Figure 10-1, can be used to provide examples of your music or simply to entertain visitors to your site.

To fill your MIDI jukebox with popular MIDI files, visit one of the many online MIDI archives. You also can easily create your own MIDI files with a MIDI sequencing application. We've used different applications, but one we have used extensively is Vision by Opcode Systems. Vision provides an ideal creative environment, syncs up easily to QuickTime and other standard digital audio file types, and is relatively inexpensive and easy to use. We have included a 30-day trial version of Vision at *http://www.designingwebaudio.com*. We recommend that you take advantage of the application and its tutorial sections. To find out where to find MIDI file libraries, check the

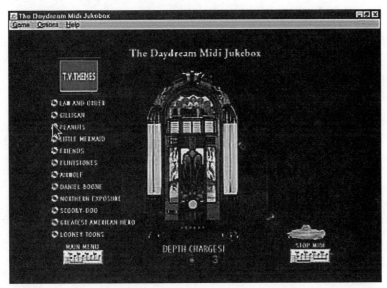

Figure 10-1. *A typical MIDI jukebox*

Opcode site at *http://www.opcode.com* or try any of the following sites:

- Harmony Central (*http://www.harmony-central.com*)

- The MIDI file and CD Music Finder located at the MIDI Manufacturers Association home page (*http://www.MIDI.org*)

- Laura's MIDI heaven (*http://www.laurasmidiheaven.com*)

Jukebox code: a step-by-step guide

To use the jukebox on your web site, customize the HTML code in Example 10-1 to your specifications.

Example 10-1. *HTML code for creating a jukebox*

```
<TABLE>
<TR>
<TD ALIGN="CENTER" VALIGN="MIDDLE">
<H2><FONT FACE="Arial, Helvetica, sans-serif">
    <A HREF="MIDI-Jukebox.com">MIDI-Jukebox.com</A>
<BR>
MIDI JukeBox</FONT></H2>
<BR>
<IMG SRC="http://www.yoursite.com/images/yourimage.gif" WIDTH="32"
    HEIGHT="32">
</TD>
<TR>
<TD ALIGN="CENTER" VALIGN="TOP">
<A HREF="http://www.yoursite.com/yourMIDIdirectory/yourMIDI.mid">
<FONT SIZE="1" FACE="Arial, Helvetica, sans-serif">Yoursong.mid</FONT>
```

Example 10-1. *HTML code for creating a jukebox (continued)*

```
<FONT FACE="Arial, Helvetica, sans-serif" size="1">
<BR>
Your Song</FONT></A>
</TABLE>
```

Example 10-1 includes an image tag for displaying a graphic or GIF animation. Remove the image tag if you do not want a graphic displayed on your web page. The table format in Example 10-1 tends to work best, but you can experiment with different graphic layout ideas. Simply repeat these steps for as many MIDI files as you want in your jukebox.

Add a bit of spice to your site

Another excellent way to implement MIDI on your site is to use small MIDI event sounds that start and stop within a few seconds. We have included a group of small MIDI files created by DigArtz, called "PageTunes" at *http://www.designingwebaudio.com*. These are short, extremely small (2 KB to 4 KB) MIDI files that are designed specifically for web-based interaction. For example, if users request a certain page, they will be greeted with a short MIDI file to let them know they have arrived. Along with PageTunes, we have included a set of Holiday PageTunes, and a set of special SoundFX PageTunes. Again, you may add any PageTunes or other short MIDI files to your site by using the basic EMBED HTML tag, as long as you give proper credit to DigArtz for their use.

Playing a different tune

When using sound on your web site, keep in mind that once a user becomes familiar with the sound, he or she may get bored quickly. Accordingly, it is wise to frequently change or alter the sound on your site to avoid repetition. You can do this by using a simple script that rotates the MIDI file (or *.au*, *.wav*, or other file type) each time a user enters your site or with a script that changes the tune on the hour, and so on.

Here is an example of a script that changes the MIDI file based on the time of day. The code is simple—just copy and paste it directly into your HTML code, then add your own MIDI files. Again, you can find MIDI files by visiting any number of MIDI archives on the Web, including those listed earlier in this chapter.

```
<SCRIPT>
<!--
var numMIDI = 12
```

```
day = new Date( )
seed = day.getTime( )
ran = parseInt((((seed - (parseInt(seed/1000,10) * 1000))/10)/
100*numMIDI + 1,10)
if (ran == (1))
MIDI=("web001.mid")
if (ran == (2))
MIDI=("web002.mid")
if (ran == (3))
MIDI=("web003.mid")
if (ran == (4))
MIDI=("web004.mid")
if (ran == (5))
MIDI=("web005.mid")
if (ran == (6))
MIDI=("web006.mid")
if (ran == (7))
MIDI=("web007.mid")
if (ran == (8))
MIDI=("web008.mid")
if (ran == (9))
MIDI=("web009.mid")
if (ran == (10))
MIDI=("web010.mid")
if (ran == (11))
MIDI=("web011.mid")
if (ran == (12))
MIDI=("web012.mid")

document.write('<EMBED SRC="http://yoursite.com/MIDI/' + MIDI + '"
WIDTH=0 HEIGHT=0 AUTOSTART=TRUE>')
document.write('<BGSOUND SRC="http://yoursite.com/MIDI/' + MIDI +
'" AUTOSTART=TRUE>')
// -->
</SCRIPT>
```

Creating your own MIDI files

Although it's easy to select your favorite MIDI files from the Internet
and post them on your site without the use of a MIDI editor or a
sequencer, there are situations where editing is needed. Downloaded
MIDI files often are too large (50 KB to 90 KB or more) or are
crammed with too many instrument sounds, making the music sound
cluttered on poorer-quality computer systems. For example, you may
download a file that tries to replicate an exact MIDI version of a
Top 40 hit down to the ear-numbing MIDI guitar riff. MIDI files also
are uploaded to the Internet by music aficionados who include every
note and subtle phrase of a piece. This is overkill if you just want
30 seconds of classical music on your welcome page. Such MIDI
files are candidates for a MIDI editor.

MIDI editors

A MIDI editor allows you to remove unnecessary sections or notes and tone down certain instrument sounds. MIDI editors also let you build your own MIDI file from scratch with your own musical ideas or with sections borrowed from another MIDI file. The first step is to select a MIDI file via the Web or from other music-related sources, and build from there.

Once you have selected a MIDI file, you can alter the sound to fit your needs or tastes. Most MIDI files are called standard MIDI files, or SMFs. SMFs come in two basic formats: single-track (type 0) and multitrack (type 1). In a single-track SMF, all the musical parts are merged into one track. In a multitrack file, each part or instrument sound is assigned to a separate track. Multitrack is the more common MIDI file and is preferable to work with because it is easier to edit the music when the instrument notes are on separate tracks.

MIDI editors are often referred to as sequencers and are similar to working with word processors. The difference is you are working with musical notes instead of text characters. If you work in time-based animation or with video programs, your skill sets transfer well to MIDI sequencers because MIDI sequencers are time-based and have similar functions.

Editing a pre-existing MIDI file

A MIDI editor has certain functions you can apply to alter an existing MIDI file or to create one of your own, including removing instruments, pitch shifting, changing notes, inserting regions, and creating your own tunes.

Precise note editing

If you are using Vision to edit a MIDI file and want to be sure you have adequate space to make a move and drag with precision, zoom in on the window, using the + magnifying glass button at the bottom right of the Sequence window. This is especially helpful when the note movement is small. If you want to make movements that are specific to a note duration (1 whole note, 1/2 note, 1/4 note, and so on), use the Grid function, located at the top right of the Sequence window, just to the left of the Exact button. By clicking this button and choosing a note value in the Note Value pop-up window next to the Grid button, you will be assured that any note movements or note selections will be constrained to this grid value. Similarly, you may make exact movements by clicking the Exact button. Now, every time you make a note movement or selection, a dialog box will appear asking you for the exact numeric coordinates of the move or selection you desire.

Removing instruments

Most MIDI files you download from the Web have several separate music tracks. They may have a drum track, a bass track, a piano track, and several other instruments, including strings, horns, and guitar, as well as special sounds or sound effects programmed as part of the file. If you want to use only the piano or the drum track, you extract only the parts you need and remove the others.

First, select the track by clicking on the track name, and then choose the Copy command from the Edit menu. If you want to change the assignment of a particular track to any of the 16 General MIDI instruments using a MIDI editor, click and hold on the Instruments column of the desired track, as shown in Figure 10-2. This changes the output channel of that track at playback. Each channel has an instrument assigned to it. If you want to allow the information on track 1 (where the instrument is piano, for example) to play through track 10 (where the drums are assigned), you make that alteration here.

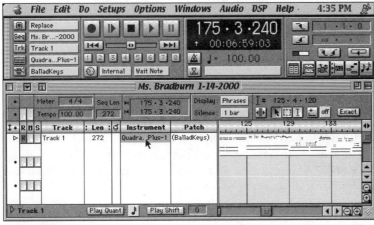

Figure 10-2. *To change a track so it is played by another channel/instrument, use a MIDI editor and then click and hold on the "Instrument" column.*

Pitch-shifting

If the MIDI file you downloaded is in the wrong musical key, you can change to the appropriate key and shift the overall pitch up or down using a MIDI editor or sequencer. You could also select one particular sound such as a high-pitched flute and lower it an octave, or choose any note and change its pitch to alter the melody or harmony of the music.

Changing notes

You may want to change specific notes. It is possible to change the note's duration, pitch, velocity (e.g., how hard the key of the piano is struck), vibrato, pan, volume, or a whole host of other controller functions that control the way each note is recorded and played back with MIDI. Each one of these controllers can add a certain amount of expression to a MIDI file that gives it more "live" characteristics.

Inserting regions

You may want to add a new section of your own, such as an intro or an ending to a pre-existing MIDI file. Or you may want to create a longer bridge in the middle of the track. With a MIDI editor, you can copy, paste, and insert entirely new sections of music anywhere in the MIDI file that you want.

Creating your own tunes

Finally, you may want to create your very own jingle or tune to accompany your web page. Making your own tunes with a sequencer is much like sitting in front of the word processor and writing a story. You start by typing in or playing different "notes," and when you have a section you like, you go back over and edit your work and prepare it to be played for others. Remember to test any piece of music with friends or colleagues first before placing it up on the Web.

MIDI file editing tutorial

We used Vision from Opcode Systems (*http://www.opcode.com*) for this tutorial. Make certain you take the time to properly install and set up Vision. The instructions for the 30-day trial package are available at *http://www.designingwebaudio.com*.

We will walk through the steps involved in enhancing or altering a MIDI file using Vision. Vision is a cross-platform sequencer. Other sequencers, such as Cakewalk and Performer, can also achieve the same results since each sequencer has the same basic functions. Vision offers an easy-to-use interface and many extended features, such as digital audio recording and editing, audio-to-MIDI functions, and several effects and capabilities helpful to desktop musicians and composers.

Initial steps

To work with a MIDI file in Vision, import your file into Vision by choosing File → Open. If the MIDI file is a multitrack (type 1) file, it will show up in the sequencer as several tracks, instead of all

instruments in one track, which would be the case with single-track
(type 0) files. We used Beethoven's 5th Symphony for our sample
MIDI file. From within your sequencer, choose File → Open and
select CD-ROM → Beethoven's 5th.

Extracting parts

We decided to use just the piano part, so the first step is to extract
that part from the MIDI file:

1. **Select notes.** Select all of the notes in the piano track by clicking
   on the bullet to the far left of the music track and name; the
   bullet will turn to a triangle and the track will highlight. Once
   the track becomes highlighted, as shown in Figure 10-3, the
   entire track is selected. This should give you a selection of all
   of the track data as well as individual notes and their duration,
   attack velocities, and so on, for the piano track.

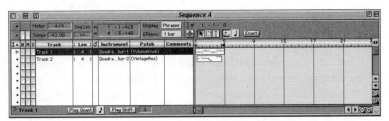

Figure 10-3. *By selecting the bullet to the far left of a track name, you effectively
select all data in that track.*

2. **Copy selected notes.** Just as in a word processing document, you
   want to copy this section of the MIDI data by selecting Edit →
   Copy.

3. **Create a new file.** Now create a new file by selecting File → New.

4. **Select a new track.** When the new file appears on your desktop,
   select the first track by double-clicking next to the title in the
   track 1 (generally "untitled") or within the first measure of the
   sequence where notes already exist.

5. **Paste the selection.** Now paste the data into the new MIDI file by
   selecting Edit → Paste. You now have a file with just the piano
   track from the original file.

6. Repeat this process for each part you want to extract from the
   original MIDI.

You can use these same steps to extract particular sections, measures, or notes from a MIDI file. Simply click or shift-click on the
part you select, then copy and paste into a new file. Much like a text

editor, you may cut, copy, paste, and edit MIDI notes and events to suit your needs. Think of a MIDI file as a template. Simply use the pieces you want, discard the rest, and build your personalized file from the pre-existing template.

Transposing pitch

To alter a particular instrument track or musical phrase that is too high or low in pitch, use the transpose command. For example, you may want to fix a bass guitar sound that is too low in pitch, or lower a flute that sounds too high. *Transpose* is the term used by musicians to change an entire section of music by a fixed amount, such as a half note (one semitone), a whole note (two semitones), or an entire octave (12 semitones). To use the transpose command, follow these steps:

1. **Select parts.** First select the part(s) or track(s) that you want to transpose by clicking or shift-clicking on the part(s) or track(s).

2. **Transpose.** Select Do → Transpose. When the Transpose window appears, the defaults will be "up," "0 semitones," and "0 octaves," as shown in Figure 10-4. To transpose the selection up a half note, enter "1 semitone" or "1 half step." To transpose the selection up an octave, choose "1 octave." In this case, try "up," "0 semitones," and "1 octave." This moves your entire selection up one octave. Now click the Transpose button.

3. **Audition the result.** When ready, audition your results. You should find that the notes are the same, only one octave (8 whole notes or 12 semitones) higher. If you are unhappy with the result, simply select Edit → Undo and start over.

You can use this method to change any section of a MIDI file, from one note to the entire track. You can change the selection from one semitone to several octaves.

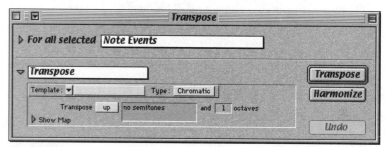

Figure 10-4. *Select Transpose up, no semitones, and one octave to transpose the entire selection up one octave*

Changing notes

You may want to do more than just change the pitch of a note. For example, you may also want to change a note's duration, velocity, or vibrato—the functions that control the way each note sounds, and give the notes a "human" feel. Using a sequencer, it is easy to select and change any one note or selection of notes:

1. **Alter the pitch higher or lower.** To change the pitch of one particular note, just click on the center of the note, and drag the note up or down, thus changing its pitch, as shown in Figure 10-5.

2. **Alter the time placement.** Similarly, click and drag the far left of the note to move the note forward or backward in time. For example, if the note currently began at beat 3 of measure 4, and you want to move it so that the beginning was at beat 4 of measure 4, click the left-hand side of the note and drag the note until it aligned with beat 4.

3. **Alter the note length.** Finally, if you want to lengthen or shorten the note's duration, click to the far right of the note and drag to the right to lengthen and to the left to shorten the duration of the note.

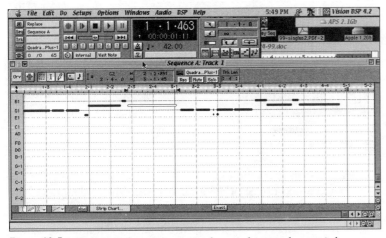

Figure 10-5. *Clicking and moving a particular note lets you change pitch, move the note forward or backward in time, and make the note longer or shorter.*

Using the strip chart

You may want to add vibrato or pitch bend to a group of notes to imitate a more "life-like" sound. To alter key velocity or pitch bend values of a MIDI note, selection, or file, use the strip chart. The strip chart is a chart that contains other MIDI information, besides note value, pitch, duration, and so on, and is found in the main Edit window. To use the strip chart:

1. **Access the strip chart.** To access the strip chart, first double-click the colored notation box that contains the sequence you want to change in the main Edit window (for example, the colored box on the righthand side of the piano track). Similarly, to open the track for editing, you may double-click the bullet to the far left of the track. A window will appear, with the title "Sequences—Your file." At the bottom left, there will be a small box that says "Strip chart," as shown in Figure 10-6.

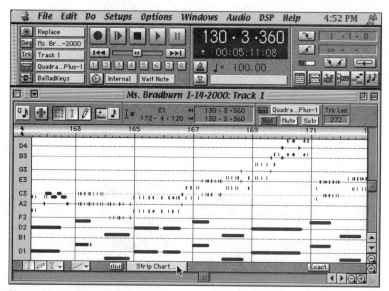

Figure 10-6. *By clicking and holding the strip chart column, you can effectively select the desired controller in which you want to add or alter information.*

2. **Select a strip chart controller.** Click and hold the strip chart button and a pop-up list of the available controllers will appear.

   By clicking and holding on the box that displays the controller value (the default is No strip chart), you may select any of the controller values associated with that MIDI file. Examples of a controller include velocity, pan, pitch bend, breath control, sustain, after touch, and so on. Each one of these controller names has a particular function, and you may want to experiment with them. However, for this tutorial, we need be concerned with only a few. For our purposes, we want to alter the pitch bend controller, so select pitch bend from the Strip Chart window. Now, in the box just to the left of the controller box, click and hold and then select Free from the pop-up options.

3. **Draw pitch bend values.** Now click on the pencil icon located two boxes to the left, so you can use the cursor as a pencil to draw in pitch bend changes.

   To create a realistic vibrato effect, zoom in until you are looking at the notes you want to alter, then draw a line up and down in short patterns as shown in Figure 10-7, just barely crossing over the center line each time.

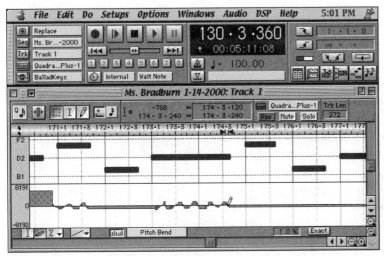

Figure 10-7. *Using the pencil tool, you can draw any controller information in the strip chart. In this case, we have attempted to simulate a vibrato sound by drawing small up and down pitch bend movements.*

4. **Audition the changes.** After drawing pitch bend values for a few notes, select the notes in the main sequence window. Make this selection by clicking and dragging over the notes you altered (you must drag over the beginning of each note you want to select). Audition them by pressing play on the main controller (the play button to the right of the controller palette, instead of the "play from beginning" button on the left of the controller palette). If you have made changes in the strip chart that you want to erase, drag over the changes and hit Delete.

The process of adding, editing, or deleting any other controller information is the same. Simply select the controller you want to alter in the strip chart and then perform your edits. Saving your file will automatically incorporate those changes into the file the next time you play the file.

Achieving consistent MIDI playback on the Web

Jeff Essex of Audiosyncrasy (*http://www.audiosync.com*) has spent the past eight years in the trenches of multimedia sound design, juggling MIDI and audio to create award-winning projects for clients that include Disney Online, Nickelodeon Online, Red Sky Interactive, and many others. Below are some of his tips for creating MIDI for the Web. (Portions of this section are derived from Jeff Essex's articles originally written for the Apple Worldwide Developer Relations Group).

MIDI is great for its small file sizes, but getting consistent playback, considering the different sound cards and unique user sound systems, is practically impossible. Here are some of the strategies used by professionals to get the best results.

Initializing

A MIDI file usually plays multiple instruments at the same time. Each is on a discrete channel, somewhat like a multitrack tape recorder. Each of these channels must be initialized with the proper settings for instrument assignment (program changes), volume level (controller #7), placement in the stereo field (pan, or controller #10), and effects level (reverb depth, controller #91). These instructions must be placed before any music note data, so that setup is complete before the music starts.

If your music has to loop, see the "Looping" section below for initialization ideas. If your music is a linear one-shot piece, insert a blank measure before the music and place these commands in the blank measure. Change either the tempo or the meter of the initialization measure to reduce the length of silence before the music starts. For example, set the first measure to a tempo of 500, then reset the tempo to the desired setting in the second measure where the notes start. Or set the first measure to a meter of 1/4, so it's only one measure, then change the tempo to 4/4 (or your desired meter) on the second measure.

Looping

You never know how long the viewer will remain on a particular page, so most of the music Jeff created has to loop seamlessly. But achieving a seamless loop while also initializing the data is quite a trick. If Jeff tells the synth to play the first note while also telling it "change from a piano sound to a guitar sound," there may be a glitch in the rhythm of the piece while the command is executed. Jeff offers three solutions to this problem:

1. Start with just drums or piano.

   The drum sound is always the same, and piano is the default sound that's played if no program change is sent. You can sneak the initialization info for the other instruments in while the piano or drums are playing.

2. Start with any one instrument by itself.

→

For example, one piece starts with a harp. The program data is placed just after the first note, so the first time users hear it, they'll hear one note of piano before the rest of the harp notes. But on successive passes through the loop, the harp will play the first note, since its instrument assignment was set on the first run through the loop.

3. Start with one tiny section of silence.

   This process is a bit more complex and requires taking advantage of some musical math. Say a piece is in 4/4 time. It's often possible to go to the last measure of the piece and see if there's a tiny bit of silence at the end (for example, a 16th note rest). We can define the last measure as 16/16 instead of 4/4, then take the silence during the last 16th note rest and stick it at the beginning of the piece. We end up with a piece that starts with one measure in 1/16, then lots of 4/4, and a last measure of 15/16. Now there's a 1/16 measure of silence at the beginning where we can initialize the file.

Volume levels

There's a wide variety in velocity response between various synthesizers. Try "normalizing" your key velocities to get more consistent results. Jeff scales the velocities so that they fall between the range of 60–127. Also, set channel volume levels to a maximum of 100. It's quite possible that distortion will occur if you have several channels playing notes struck at velocities of 127, while the channel volume is also set to 127.

Reducing data

Sure, MIDI files are small, but you can make them gigantic if you're not careful. You may want to strip out after-touch data, and thin the data on continuous controllers like pitch bend and mod wheel. If you're tweaking the bender or mod wheel prior to playing a note (like bending down before the note is struck, then bending back up to normal), strip out all the pitch bend data except for the last one that sets the actual value before the note event.

Testing

Know the enemy. Jeff authors on a Mac with a Roland Sound Canvas, the "Rosetta Stone" of General MIDI composition. If you're serious about web MIDI, try to get a real sound canvas. But after a piece is finished, check it on a PC through a Creative Labs SoundBlaster AWE32, a basic SoundBlaster 16 with FM synthesis, and on a Mac through the QuickTime Musical Instruments. Most of Jeff's pieces go through several revisions to balance the instrument levels between the different players.

Pray for deliverance

DLS, Beatnik, QuickTime, and DirectMusic are putting the responsibility for synthesizer performance back into the composer's hands. Let's hope these technologies are broadly adopted in the new millennium.

Making your MIDI music from scratch

You may want to compose and record your own MIDI music file. With almost 1,000 separate MIDI recording tracks and all the editing features you need to fine-tune every little note, you could become the next Mozart or at least the next Britney Spears. The Vision sequencer offers MIDI as well as digital audio recording, editing, and effects processing for adding audio tracks to your MIDI tracks. But since you cannot upload a MIDI file with digitized audio, we will not discuss the range of audio recording options. For more information about a digital audio editor, read Chapter 4, *Optimizing Your Sound Files*.

Creating your own MIDI file

Creating your own file from scratch is a bit complicated. Here's how to do it in Vision:

1. **Open a new sequence/MIDI file**. To create your own MIDI file, first choose File → New. A window entitled "Sequence A" will appear and automatically be record-enabled (the red *R* will be highlighted at the far left of the track as shown in Figure 10-8). You are ready to go.

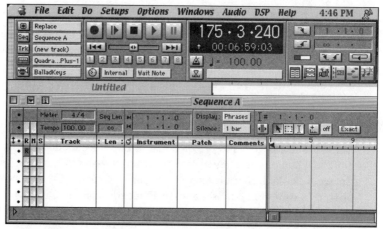

Figure 10-8. *Choosing File → New creates an untitled sequence window that is record enabled and ready for your new composition.*

2. **Connect your MIDI keyboard**. If you have a MIDI keyboard or other controller like a wind or guitar controller, you may connect it to Vision via a MIDI interface. Refer to the Vision documentation or your MIDI sequencer for the exact specification for setting up your MIDI controller and the accompanying studio

setup. For the setup, all you need is a MIDI interface, a MIDI keyboard, and a few connections within a secondary program such as Open Music System. (OMS is supplied by Opcode with the Vision package and is also available for download at *http://www.opcode.com.*). Once you have your MIDI keyboard or controller connected and transmitting MIDI information to your sequencer, you are ready to record.

Expert MIDI files: Twiddly Bits

One promising product for creating music with MIDI is called Twiddly Bits, from Keyfax Software (*http://www.keyfax.com*). Twiddly Bits are collections of MIDI samples recorded by world-class musicians and stored as MIDI files onto floppy disks. The musicians recorded licks, runs, motifs, and patterns that are typical of a particular instrument or style of music. You can load these files into your sequencer and have access to MIDI parts that can be pasted in any file or pattern. Because the music was recorded by world-class musicians (Bill Bruford of King Crimson, Steve Hackett of Genesis, John Bundrick of The Who, and Bob Marley, to name a few), the MIDI files sound almost authentic, with good feel and playability.

You can choose from a variety of styles in the Keyfax collection, including drums and percussion, MIDI breakbeats, guitar grooves, jazz piano, bass and drums, country, funk, world series Brazilian beats, Bill Bruford drums, and a host of others. The "Twids" come in standard MIDI files (SMFs) and can be played on Macs or PCs. We have included a group of 10 Twiddly Bits at *http://www.designingwebaudio.com* for you to use and experiment with. After you have opened a Twiddly Bit in Vision, press Play and audition them. Then choose places where you can use them in your own compositions or in other existing MIDI files. Try one of the following tips and tricks offered by Twiddly Bits creator Julian Colbeck:

- If your sequencer can play in reverse, you can create different patterns such as changing an "up" guitar strum into a "down" strum.

- Most of the Twids are designed to be looped in two-, four-, or eight-bar patterns. If you want to play four bars and have the fourth bar change chords, simply copy four bars, then transpose the fourth bar. For example, transposing +5 half steps or semitones will change a C minor chord into an F minor chord. Experiment with different patterns and transpositions.

- Try playing back the track at half-speed or double-speed to get an interesting variation. This is good for ringing the changes on a strumming pattern.

- You don't have to choose between a Twid part and something you have played yourself. You can mix and match. Do this by loading both parts next to one another on two separate tracks. Then mute the Twid part and as you play your part, unmute the Twid part at varying places until you find a good balance between the two. To complete the exercise, snip out the section of your part where you want the Twid and then merge the two. Think of it as sewing a patch onto your favorite pair of jeans.

3. **Record your MIDI file**. Click the Record button and begin playing notes on the keyboard. The default recording function in Vision is "Wait for Note," which means that Vision holds in record mode until you press your first key, at which time it will begin recording and capture all key, velocity, and controller data you send to it during the recording.

4. **Select your tempo**. The recording follows at the tempo specified in the tempo box, as shown in Figure 10-9. This value may be changed by clicking in the box and entering a new tempo. You may either enter the tempo manually using the numeric keys on your keyboard, or, if you hold the pointer inside the tempo box, it turns into an up or down arrow. Clicking the mouse button will move the tempo accordingly, in the direction of the arrow.

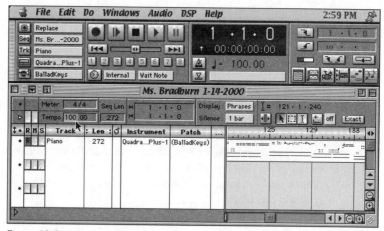

Figure 10-9. *You may change the tempo of your MIDI file by clicking in the tempo box and entering the desired tempo or speed of your file.*

5. **Choose a click track**. You can request Vision play a click track while you are recording to indicate the beat value and relative speed. This allows you to keep proper time during your recording. The option "Click in Record" is enabled by default and may be toggled by choosing Options → Click in Record. Also in the Options menu, you may select Click in Play, which causes the click track to play during playback as well. If you want to change the notes of the click track, select Options → Metronome Sound and change the values of the notes in the boxes provided, as shown in Figure 10-10.

6. **Click the Record and Play buttons**. To record your MIDI music, first click Record, then Play (or hit the spacebar) to begin recording. Now listen to the metronome count off and begin playing

Figure 10-10. *Choose your own metronome sounds by selecting an instrument (generally Instrument 10 for drums) and then two notes to represent the accented and unaccented beats.*

notes when you are ready. Play as much as you want, as there are no time limits and disk space is not a factor with MIDI files. You have approximately 100 hours of recording before you begin to run out of disk space on the average hard drive.

7. **Click the Stop button.** When you are finished, click the stop button or hit the spacebar. Your newly created MIDI file will now appear in the "Sequence A" window.

8. **Audition your recording.** You may hit the Play from Beginning button (the play button to the left of the stop button on the control palette, shown in Figure 10-11) to audition your recording. When you are finished auditioning, you may want to make some changes. To do the entire recording over again, select Undo.

9. **Minor edits.** If you want to fix a few notes that may have incorrect pitches or may fall at incorrect times, simply use your mouse to make these edits. Do this by double-clicking the part of the window where the MIDI notes appear or the left-most edge of the track, where the track selection bullet exists (the bullet will appear as a triangle if the track is currently selected). A new window will appear, in which you may edit and change the MIDI information, as described earlier in this chapter in the "Using the strip chart." You can change notes by clicking on them and then altering them to your specifications. Again, if you want to change the duration of a note, click the right side of the note and drag. If you want to change the pitch, click the center and drag the note up or down. If you want to change the space in time that the note occupies, click the far left side of the note and drag the note to the new desired location.

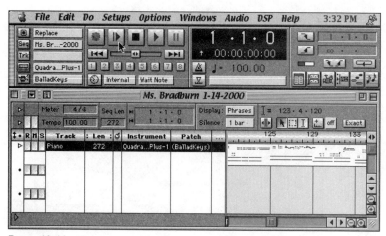

Figure 10-11. *There are two Play buttons on the control palette. The Play button to the left of the Stop button is called the Play from Beginning button, and it commences playback from the start of the piece. The Play button to the right of the Stop button continues playback from the point of the time marker.*

Adding notes without using a keyboard

Finally, you may want to add notes to your MIDI file without entering them via the keyboard, or even create an entire file without using a keyboard at all. You can accomplish this in two ways: by cutting and pasting or by drawing a note.

First, you could copy and paste notes from another file. Simply select a note or group of notes by clicking and dragging over the desired selection area. Then choose Edit → Copy, from one file, perhaps a previously existing file of a piece of music you like. Now, use the cursor to select an insert point of where you want the new notes to enter. Then choose Edit → Paste, and the new notes will become part of the new track.

Figure 10-12 shows a MIDI file before and after an edit insertion of notes. You may even choose to copy notes from other MIDI files such as the Twiddly Bits files. These files, described in the sidebar "Expert MIDI files: Twiddly Bits," are collections of professionally recorded MIDI files that are made to be copied and pasted into your own MIDI files. This sort of resource can add extra complexity and depth to your existing MIDI files.

The second way to add notes without using a keyboard or other controller is simply to draw them into the file. Heres how to draw new notes into the file:

1. **Select the file track that you want to draw the notes into.** Double-click the bullet to the far left of the track name to open the edit window for that track as shown in Figure 10-13.

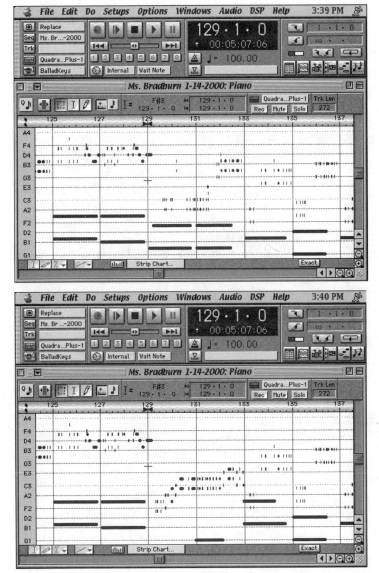

Figure 10-12. *A MIDI file before pasting in new notes (top), and after pasting in new notes (bottom)*

2. **Select the pencil tool.** After the file is open, click on the pencil tool located at the top left of the Edit window. With the pencil tool selected, begin clicking anywhere in the Edit window. Anywhere you click, a new note will appear, as shown in Figure 10-14. The note will have a specific value and have the pitch associated with the exact place you clicked in the window. To see which pitch it corresponds to, look at the list at the far right of the window. You will see note names and numbers,

indicting the octave of that note. C3 corresponds to middle C on the piano or keyboard. The default duration of the note is set to 1/4 note. You can also change this by clicking the pencil tool again, until the Settings window appears. When it does, you may click and hold on the icon of the 1/4 note; simply select the note value you desire, ranging from a dotted whole note to a triplet 32nd note.

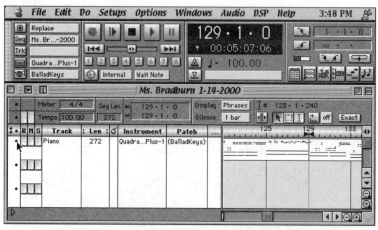

Figure 10-13. *To open a track for editing, double-click the small bullet to the far left of the Track name.*

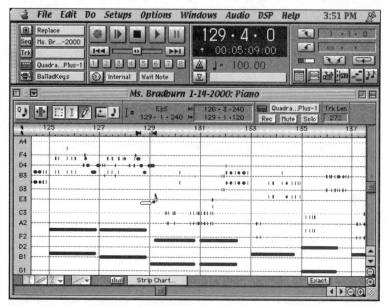

Figure 10-14. *After you select the pencil tool, the cursor turns into a note. A new note appears anywhere you click in the Edit window.*

3. **Draw more notes.** After you draw your first note, start drawing away until you have a section that you are relatively pleased with.

4. **Audition the new notes.** Select the newly drawn notes and choose Play from the controller.

5. **Edit the new notes.** Click back onto the cursor tool and begin editing the pitch values and duration of the notes to meet your needs.

Clearly, these techniques would be too cumbersome to create 100 measures or several minutes worth of music, but they are ideal for creating small, specific sections where you need pinpoint accuracy and don't have time or access to a keyboard controller. Try creating two-, four-, or eight-bar patterns this way. Then, use the copy and paste commands to make longer sections. If you go in and alter the pitch of few notes in every other section, you will achieve enough variation so that listeners won't know that you simply cut and pasted the same section multiple times, and they will be more likely to stay interested in the music. This is a great technique for creating looped sequences that repeat a certain section over and over, while giving a relative appearance of never repeating exactly or at least not boring the listening audience.

DLS: The future of MIDI

So if the big problem with MIDI is the lack of a standardized web sound engine, when are they going to settle on one format that will sound good on every machine? Fortunately a solution is near. Seeing the need for a web standard, the MIDI Manufacturers Association (MMA) has adopted a specification for synthesis and instrument sound storage. They called it downloadable sounds, or DLS.

DLS is a common language or set of instructions that MIDI synthesizer hardware manufacturers have agreed to incorporate into future devices in order to standardize sound synthesis. Where MIDI was a standard for note information such as pitch, duration, and volume, DLS is a standard for describing and reproducing specific instrument sounds. In other words, DLS will ensure that the MIDI composition you created in your home studio will sound roughly the same when it is downloaded from the Web and played back in a listener's home.

With the implementation of DLS, web sound design with MIDI should become a lot more compelling. Since DLS has already been adopted by Microsoft and Apple as the foundation of their next generation of built-in MIDI sound engines, the format should become available for practical use fairly soon.

Summary

After reading this chapter, you should have a better understanding of what MIDI is and some of the various methods available for use on your web pages. These methods include theme music, button sounds, and a MIDI soundtrack. You should also have an idea of how to use MIDI to tastefully enhance your site, as well as how to use MIDI files to generate the interest of visitors to your site. Finally, you should have learned how to create and edit MIDI files using Vision, Twiddly Bits, and the large MIDI file archives available on the Web. In the next chapter, we will look at Beatnik's RMF format, which combines a rich MIDI sound engine with the ability to tie playback to user events.

CHAPTER ELEVEN

DESIGNING AUDIO WEB SITES WITH BEATNIK

With its Rich Music Format (RMF), Beatnik is an active player in the future of interactive web audio. The Beatnik format generates compact file sizes that rival those of MIDI. Beatnik's advantages are its ability for intelligent interactivity with JavaScript, its standard set of instrument sounds for consistent playback across all platforms, and its Beatnik Editor for adding custom digital audio samples and instrument banks. Beatnik's interactive capabilities combined with its high music quality and small file sizes make it ideal for full-scale advanced sound design on the Web. Examples of web sites that have been "sonified" using the Beatnik System are shown in Figure 11-1. To hear a sample of RMF and the Beatnik System, visit the Beatnik web site at *http://www.beatnik.com.*

Beatnik Inc., a company co-founded by music legend Thomas Dolby Robertson under the moniker Headspace, developed the RMF format. Beatnik is significant because it's the first format that gives web audio producers the tools to create full-scale, high-quality interactive web soundtracks and the platform to deliver the music over limited bandwidths. Even though high-quality streaming audio has existed for a number of years, the interactive aspect has been absent. Other popular interactive technologies such as Flash do not offer as many controls over audio playback for traditional sound designers.

In this chapter

- New possibilities for interactive sound
- Beatnik authoring system
- Sonification tutorial
- Using the Beatnik Editor
- Summary

New possibilities for interactive sound

Seasoned audio professionals accustomed to delivering high-fidelity sound without bandwidth constraints often have found it difficult to engineer a compelling aural experience for the Web. Sound "design" for the web is frequently limited to creating low-quality sound effects for rollover buttons or composing background music with the same software-based, General MIDI instruments everyone is using.

Beatnik offers a new kind of aural experience by connecting a listener's interactions with what they hear. The Beatnik System allows for accurate music playback of the sounds created in the Beatnik Editor, regardless of the user's platform or machine. For sound designers, Beatnik's precise playback in cross-platform environments gives it an advantage over MIDI-based web music composition and playback. With a basic knowledge of JavaScript, audio professionals can build sophisticated interactive soundtracks. Much of the Beatnik toolset will be familiar to the modern audio engineer, and there are several applications that help generate the JavaScript you need, including Macromedia's Dreamweaver.

Beatnik allows you to:

- Orchestrate and deliver a complex, one-minute interactive soundtrack with multiple instrument sounds, rhythms, melodies, and JavaScript commands in a file size that's equivalent to a 10-second mono MP3 file.

- Create interactive soundtracks that unleash sound loops whenever a user clicks on a new location. The sounds are all sonically integrated components of one big groove.

- Use JavaScript to create interactive elements, such as buttons, mouseovers, and transitions, directly within a standard HTML page. This is an advantage over using a standalone authoring application. Beatnik also has a tool called the Beatnik Xtra for Director that adds Beatnik functionality to Director/Shockwave projects via Lingo scripting.

- Maintain precise control over fade-outs and transitions when a user leaves or enters a web page, clicks on a button or link, or rolls the mouse cursor over a specified area.

Figure 11-1. *Examples of sonified sites by Young & Rubicam (left) and 7-UP (center and right)*

- Control how instrument sounds and music tracks cross-fade and mix during playback.

- Build a soundtrack that is responsive enough to make people feel like they are jamming on a virtual graphic instrument.

While Beatnik is a powerful tool for building and delivering interactive soundtracks, the technology has several disadvantages:

- It's not yet tailored for streaming long-format audio files. For audio broadcasting applications, such as a radio show, live conference, or a 10-minute tutorial, RealAudio does a much better job. Beatnik expects to add streaming capability in 2000.

- The technology comes with a steep learning curve, which is well worth it for the serious web sound designer but can be a drawback for developers who just want to quickly add a few sounds to their web site. Both MIDI and JavaScript authoring can be fairly complex for the beginner.

- Beatnik does not have as large of a user base as RealAudio or Flash, which means you are more likely to encounter browser plug-in issues and errors.

- Previewing the Beatnik instrument sounds is difficult to do when composing your MIDI music. Although you can create a live MIDI connection with the Beatnik instruments and trigger them with a MIDI keyboard, there is a significant lag in the response time, which prohibits composing directly with the instruments in real-time. Instead, you must use the internal sounds of a separate General MIDI instrument to perform the various parts of a composition.

Beatnik authoring system

The Beatnik authoring system includes three elements: the Beatnik Player, the Beatnik Audio Engine, and the Beatnik Editor. All three work in conjunction to mix and play back music and sound effects that are composed of a hybrid of MIDI-based instrument sounds and web-optimized digitized audio samples.

MIDI forms the core of the Beatnik System. Beatnik uses MIDI-like messages to control the Beatnik playback sound engine. Other authoring systems such as Flash must compile and upload MP3-compressed sound files for playback in a browser. In addition to compressed MP3 audio files, Beatnik compiles and uploads text-based MIDI instructions that trigger the pre-loaded bank of Beatnik MIDI instrument sounds to play back your musical score or composition. Once these standard instruments are downloaded with the Beatnik Player and housed on a user's hard drive, little data needs to be sent

Beatnik versus MIDI QuickTime Musical Instruments

So what are the advantages of Beatnik over MIDI data using QuickTime Musical Instruments? There are two. The first difference is that the Beatnik System is tied to a robust web audio authoring environment that facilitates interactive audio programming using JavaScript commands. The second is that the Beatnik System allows users to add their own sound files and customized sound design via a user-definable bank of instruments.

over the Internet—just tiny instructions (compressed MIDI files) that instruct the Beaknik Player's tone generator/sequencer to play music. Later in this chapter, we will discuss the Beatnik Player's components in more detail.

Even though it relies on MIDI, the Beatnik System should not be confused with basic MIDI music on the Web. When a MIDI file is downloaded, it plays back using the General MIDI instrument bank pre-installed on most browsers and computer systems. General MIDI is a standard established by music equipment manufacturers that specifies that a given instrument bank number always represents a certain type of instrument sound, such as a horn or a drum. However, manufacturers are free to determine the synthesis algorithm used to create any given sound in their instrument bank. This leads to two problems: every instrument bank can have a different type of horn or drum sound, and there is no way to alter or customize the sounds in the instrument bank.

In addition to the General MIDI instrument bank, Beatnik allows you to customize and enrich its palette of high-quality, pre-installed sounds with your own digital audio samples. Once your custom audio samples and MIDI files are imported into the Beatnik Editor, the editor compresses everything into the proprietary Beatnik format for embedding into your web pages. The result is a General MIDI sound engine combined with a customizable digital audio sampler.

Mixman remixers are another compelling use of Beatnik technology. By clicking on different buttons, users can remix popular songs, such as "Maria" by Blondie and email their mixes to friends. The Mixman remixers itself is a multichannel *.rmf* composition and is typically only 250 KB in size. Smaller still is the emailed remix data, which is simply the instructions dictating which channels to play or mute. The *.rmf* file is not actually emailed, but instead is served from a central location. An example of a Mixman remixer is shown in Figure 11-2.

Beatnik sound banks also provide *Groovoids,* a set of musical snippets or compositions. Groovoids are premade miniature MIDI compositions or sound effects used for quickly and easily creating loops, button sounds, and transition effects. Later in this chapter, we will walk through the steps involved in creating Beatnik files and publishing them to a web page.

Beatnik Player

At the heart of the Beatnik System is the Beatnik Player, a browser plug-in that users must install. It's free, and it's a fairly small download (about 550 KB). Beatnik is working to have it included with other browsers, including Navigator and Internet Explorer.

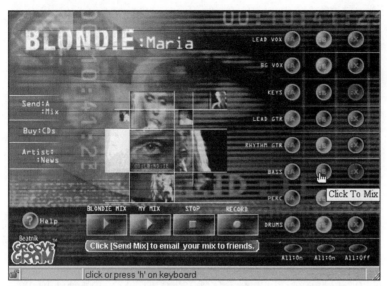

Figure 11-2. *By clicking on different buttons, users can remix popular songs, such as "Maria" by Blondie, and email their new "mix" to friends.*

The plug-in player allows the user's browser to play *.rmf* files (Beatnik's Rich Music File format). The Player also contains a software-based tone generator with two banks of 128 instruments each and a third bank for customized audio samples. The first of these banks comprises a standardized library of Beatnik instruments that map to the General MIDI specification. The second bank is a library of special Beatnik instruments. There is also a library of General MIDI percussion instruments and a library of special percussion instruments, which are assigned to MIDI channel 10 (the General MIDI drum channel). The third bank is empty and is used for receiving and storing any customized instruments contained within a given *.rmf* file. This user-definable bank of instruments allows sound designers to create custom instruments based on their own digital audio samples (or edited versions of the standard Beatnik library).

Although most designers will opt to keep the Beatnik player invisible to the end user, there are visible modes as well, which can be useful to provide end-user control. The visible Beatnik player features standard play, stop, and pause buttons, and more. You can toggle between the "meter" and "oscilloscope" visual modes by simply clicking on the lower part of the Control Player window. See Figures 11-3 and 11-4.

These two different modes provide alternate visual representations of a sound's playback. The meter mode displays a visual representation of the active channels producing sound. The oscilloscope mode dis-

Figure 11-3. *The Beatnik Player Control Panel's Meter mode displays flashing meters that show which of Beatnik's 32 voices are active.*

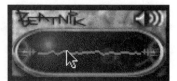

Figure 11-4. *Clicking on the lower part of the Beatnik Player's Control Panel displays the oscilloscope mode, which monitors Beatnik's total audio output.*

plays a line that changes according to the different frequencies being played back.

Clicking and holding (Macintosh) or right-clicking (Windows) the mouse button brings up a series of commands that allows the user to perform other actions, such as pause or stop, display song, and show copyright info and other relevant media information.

Beatnik Audio Engine

In addition to being a software-based tone generator, the Beatnik Audio Engine is a software audio mixer capable of mixing 64 discrete musical tracks in real time and playing back a mixed bag of file formats and sample rates. It is part of the core technology inside the Beatnik Player. The mixer's functions are controlled by JavaScript, so it is with JavaScript that you manipulate how the Beatnik Audio Engine responds when a user action occurs, such as rolling over an image or clicking on a link. While you will need to know some JavaScript, the mixer's ability to be controlled via JavaScript is key to the integration of the audio mixer's functionality with a predominant language used in web development. This helps facilitate and differentiate the Beatnik platform and makes the mixer useful and powerful to a web audio developer.

A basic understanding of JavaScript also lets you use Beatnik's ActionSets, which are available for Macromedia Dreamweaver and Adobe GoLive. ActionSets allows you to automate much of the JavaScript coding process. Beatnik also provides an integrated online tool called the Methodizer that automatically generates JavaScript code for the most common types of functions and user actions. You can then simply cut and paste the text code examples into your HTML pages. You can grab the Methodizer at Beatnik's web site, *www.beatnik.com*.

Beatnik Editor

The Beatnik Editor is the tool used for creating *.rmf* files. Unlike full-featured MIDI sequencers with multitrack editing and recording capabilities, the Beatnik Editor is primarily a content integration tool for combining MIDI scores with custom digital audio samples. The editor lets you import MIDI files from your favorite MIDI sequencing program and map the various MIDI tracks to the desired Beatnik instruments. The Beatnik Editor also allows you to input your own sampled recordings, such as a three-second vocal line or a guitar riff, and map it to the MIDI note ranges of your choosing. The editor accomplishes this by creating a third bank of sounds that resides in the *.rmf* file itself and is served to the user's browser along with the

.rmf file. The process is similar to working with a MIDI keyboard sampler to create custom patches. The Beatnik Editor audio samples can be musical instrument sounds, sound effects, or even short vocal samples.

It is important to note, however, that unlike the standard Beatnik instruments that reside on the user's computer (in the first two banks of the Beatnik Player), these custom instrument samples must be downloaded with the *.rmf* file over the Internet. So if you are using custom sounds, you will want to compress your audio samples using the Beatnik Editor's MP3 compression. The Beatnik Editor even allows you to mix and match variable encoding rates, sample rates, and bit depth, all in the same *.rmf* file. This allows you to "crunch" the file size of some sounds while allowing more fidelity (and file size) to more delicate sonic textures.

With these three elements of the Beatnik System, you can create customized, complex, responsive musical interaction with the graphical elements of your web site. You also can achieve extremely small file sizes if you are careful to crunch down your custom instrument sounds. And you have the tools to control all aspects of a sound's quality. Now let's get into the specific process of authoring with Beatnik tools.

First, we will discuss the basic skills you need to create Beatnik soundtracks, and then walk you through the step-by-step process of "sonifying" a web page, as Beatnik calls it. We will also introduce some basic concepts of "sonification," including the Music Object (Beatnik's API or library of JavaScript methods.)

The Beatnik web site

You can download the plug-in, the editor, and further documentation at the Beatnik web site, *www.beatnik.com/beatnik/*. The web site also contains Beatnik Production Music featuring over 120,000 *.rmf* sound effects and compositions developed by Beatnik and a host of other big name production music partners. These readymade *.rmf* files may be licensed for commercial use on the Web. The Beatnik web site also houses tutorials for Flash, Dreamweaver, Director, and other authoring tools.

Local serving

It's also possible to source the Music Object from your own server. Here's how:

1. Go to *http://www.beatnik.com/to/?music-object*.

2. Click on the Windows icon to download a zipped copy of the *music-object.js* file, or click on the Mac icon to download a stuffed copy of the *music-object.js* file.

3. Delete the piece of code you used before to source the Music Object and add this code just below the <BODY> tag in your HTML page:

```
<SCRIPT SRC="music-object.js"></SCRIPT>
```

That's it. You're now serving the Music Object yourself. (You will need to add this code below the <BODY> tag of *every* page you want to sonify.) A significant benefit to serving the Music Object this way is if the Beatnik Music Object server should go down, your site will still be sonified.

Remember your semicolons

You need to end most Java-Script commands with a semicolon, and "Music" must be capitalized.

Authoring with Beatnik

To sonify a web site with Beatnik sound, you need some basic experience in two areas:

Basic sound conversion
> Once you have sonified an HTML page with the standard sounds inside the Beatnik Player, you will be ready to add custom sounds to your site. This can be easily achieved by simply saving the sounds to standard *.wav* or *.aiff* files, and then importing them into the Beatnik Editor and exporting them as *.rmf* files.

Basic JavaScript skills
> Interactive sound and music is made possible by a set of commands or JavaScript methods on the pages you want to sonify. To begin sonifying, you don't need any sound or music software or custom sampled sounds; you can do it all with JavaScript by using the Beatnik Music Object and the sound bank that comes installed with the Beatnik Player.

Introduction to the Music Object

The Music Object is a class library written in JavaScript that lets you write your own JavaScript statements to control the Beatnik Player. It has two main functions:

1. It hides the differences between the various browsers and platforms your audience may use to view your web site.

2. It allows access to a set of methods and properties that you can use to make your pages come alive with sound.

More technically:

1. The Music Object wraps the Beatnik Player so that it works consistently with Netscape's LiveConnect API and with Microsoft Internet Explorer's ActiveX API, and it writes both EMBED and OBJECT tags for you.

2. The Music Object is also the Beatnik Player's JavaScript command set (or API). The Beatnik Player file sits on the user's computer, and the Music Object sits on a web server and is included with your sonified web pages. Interactive sound control is enabled when the two come together in a browser.

To begin authoring with the Music Object, follow these steps:

1. Source the Music Object into your HTML page.

   "Sourcing" a JavaScript file is the same idea as "including" a source file in other languages like C++ or C. While the script code resides in an external file, it's treated as though its contents actually appeared in the parent file.

Simply copy this bit of code just below the <BODY> tag in your HTML page:

```
<SCRIPT SRC="http://sonify.beatnik.com/music-object.js"></SCRIPT>
```

This code will retrieve the Music Object from Beatnik's servers whenever someone visits your site.

2. Create a Music Object instance.

   After sourcing in the Music Object, you need to instantiate a new Object of type Music before you can use it. This is your first Beatnik operation that requires actual JavaScript programming. To execute this operation, first open a new script tag and designate the language you will be working with:

   ```
   <SCRIPT LANGUAGE="JavaScript">
   ```

3. Provide a name for the new instance, then use the JavaScript keyword new, and the name of the object class Music. For example:

   ```
   theNameYouWantToUse = new Music ();
   ```

4. Embed an RMF file into the Music object using the preloadEmbed method, like this:

   ```
   theNameYouWantToUse.preloadEmbed ('yourRMFfile.rmf');
   ```

   Then end the script tag:

   ```
   </SCRIPT>
   ```

5. Set up the RMF file to play back when the user interacts with the page. This can be as easy as calling:

   ```
   <A HREF="JavaScript://" onMouseOver="theNameYouWantToUse.play();">
   your gif, link, or page element here</a>
   ```

6. Preview your file. Save your file and preview it in your browser.

Sonification tutorial

To learn how to add basic interactive sonification to a web page, let's build a version of the front page of the Sonicopia.com web site, *http://www.sonicopia.com* (see Figure 11-5). Sonicopia is a web design company that specializes in sound design using Beatnik authoring tools. Please note that all the content for this tutorial has been provided *http://www.designingwebaudio.com.*

Lesson 1: A simple mouseover

Here's a real basic use of Beatnik.

1. Start with a standard HTML page:

   ```
   <HTML>
   <HEAD></HEAD>
   <BODY BGCOLOR="black">
   ```

JavaScript tip

Once you have placed the JavaScript in your HTML page, try previewing the sound by opening the file in your browser and rolling your mouse over the page element you sonified. Make sure you have the Beatnik Player installed in your browser before you preview your *.rmf* file! This preview method can be used for all of the JavaScript examples in ths chapter.

```
<IMG SRC="images/home.jpg" width="600" height="400" border="0">
</BODY>
</HTML>
```

2. Source the Music Object into your HTML page:

```
<HTML>
<HEAD>
</HEAD>
<BODY BGCOLOR="black">
<SCRIPT SRC="http://sonify.beatnik.com/music-object.js"></SCRIPT>
<IMG SRC="images/home.jpg" width="600" height="400" border="0">
</BODY>
</HTML>
```

3. Create a Music Object instance:

```
<HTML>
<HEAD></HEAD>
<BODY BGCOLOR="black">
<SCRIPT SRC="http://sonify.beatnik.com/music-object.js"></SCRIPT>
<SCRIPT LANGUAGE="JavaScript">

listenPlayer = new Music ();

<IMG SRC="images/home.jpg" width="600" height="400" border="0">
</BODY>
</HTML>
```

Figure 11-5. *Mouseovers, audio navbars, background music, and automatic downloading of the plug-in are all included at the Sonicopia site. The lessons in this chapter take you through how to add these features to your own site.*

4. Embed an RMF file into the Music Object using the `preloadEmbed` method, like this:

```
<HTML>
<HEAD></HEAD>
<BODY BGCOLOR="black">
<SCRIPT SRC="http://sonify.beatnik.com/music-object.js"></SCRIPT>
<SCRIPT LANGUAGE="JavaScript">

listenPlayer = new Music ();
listenPlayer.preloadEmbed ('rmf/listen.rmf');

</SCRIPT>
<IMG SRC="images/home.jpg" width="600" height="400" border="0">
</BODY>
</HTML>
```

5. Set up the RMF file to play back when the user mouses over the *home.jpg* image with the page:

```
<HTML>
<HEAD></HEAD>
<BODY BGCOLOR="black">
<SCRIPT SRC="http://sonify.beatnik.com/music-object.js"></SCRIPT>
<SCRIPT LANGUAGE="JavaScript">

listenPlayer = new Music ();
listenPlayer.preloadEmbed ('rmf/listen.rmf');

</SCRIPT>
<CENTER>
<A HREF="JavaScript://" onMouseOver="listenPlayer.play();">
<IMG SRC="images/home.jpg" width="600" height="400" border="0"></a>
</CENTER>
</BODY>
</HTML>
```

6. Preview your file. Save your file and preview it in your browser.

Lesson 2: Building a sonified navbar

The best way to build interface sounds is by using the Beatnik Player's built-in sound bank as the source of those sounds. That way the sonification will add almost *no* additional download time to the page because the sounds are already in the Beatnik Player. If the user does not have the Beatnik Player, the site will work exactly as it did without sound; that visitor will not hear the sound.

1. Start with a standard HTML page:

```
<HTML>
<HEAD></HEAD>
<BODY BGCOLOR="black">
<CENTER>
<A HREF="about.html"><IMG SRC="images/about.gif" border="0"></A>
```

```
<A HREF="services.html"><IMG SRC="images/services.gif" border="0">
</A>
<A HREF="products.html"><IMG SRC="images/products.gif" border="0">
</A>
<A HREF="gallery.html"><IMG SRC="images/gallery.gif" border="0">
</A>
<A HREF="contact.html"><IMG SRC="images/contact.gif" border="0">
</A>
</CENTER>
</BODY>
</HTML>
```

2. Source the Music Object into your HTML page:

```
<HTML>
<HEAD>
</HEAD>
<BODY BGCOLOR="black">
<SCRIPT SRC="http://sonify.beatnik.com/music-object.js"></SCRIPT>
<A HREF="about.html"><IMG SRC="images/about.gif" border="0"></A>
<A HREF="services.html"><IMG SRC="images/services.gif" border="0">
</A>
<A HREF="products.html"><IMG SRC="images/products.gif" border="0">
</A>
<A HREF="gallery.html"><IMG SRC="images/gallery.gif" border="0">
</A>
<A HREF="contact.html"><IMG SRC="images/contact.gif" border="0">
</A>
</BODY>
</HTML>
```

3. Create a Music Object instance:

```
<HTML>
<HEAD></HEAD>
<BODY BGCOLOR="black">
<SCRIPT SRC="http://sonify.beatnik.com/music-object.js"></SCRIPT>
<SCRIPT LANGUAGE="JavaScript">

notePlayer = new Music ();

<A HREF="about.html"><IMG SRC="images/about.gif" border="0"></A>
<A HREF="services.html"><IMG SRC="images/services.gif" border="0">
</A>
<A HREF="products.html"><IMG SRC="images/products.gif" border="0">
</A>
<A HREF="gallery.html"><IMG SRC="images/gallery.gif" border="0">
</A>
<A HREF="contact.html"><IMG SRC="images/contact.gif" border="0">
</A>
</BODY>
</HTML>
```

4. Embed a "stub" RMF file into the Music Object using the
stubEmbed method:

```
<HTML>
<HEAD></HEAD>
```

```
<BODY BGCOLOR="black">
<SCRIPT SRC="http://sonify.beatnik.com/music-object.js"></SCRIPT>
<SCRIPT LANGUAGE=JavaScript>

notePlayer = new Music ();
notePlayer.stubEmbed ('http://sonify.beatnik.com/stub.rmf');

</SCRIPT>
<A HREF="about.html"><IMG SRC="images/about.gif" border="0"></A>
<A HREF="services.html"><IMG SRC="images/services.gif" border="0">
</A>
<A HREF="products.html"><IMG SRC="images/products.gif" border="0">
</A>
<A HREF="gallery.html"><IMG SRC="images/gallery.gif" border="0">
</A>
<A HREF="contact.html"><IMG SRC="images/contact.gif" border="0">
</A>
</BODY>
</HTML>
```

This Music Object instance will now be in a state where you can play notes through it.

5. Set up the page to play notes when the user mouses over the navbar with the page, using the PlayNote method:

```
<HTML>
<HEAD></HEAD>
<BODY BGCOLOR="black">
<SCRIPT SRC="http://sonify.beatnik.com/music-object.js"></SCRIPT>
<SCRIPT LANGUAGE="JavaScript">

notePlayer = new Music ();
notePlayer.stubEmbed ('http://sonify.beatnik.com/stub.rmf');

</SCRIPT>
<CENTER>
<A HREF="images/about.html"
onMouseOver="notePlayer.playNote(1,0,91,61,100,1000);return
    false;">
<IMG SRC="images/about.gif" border="0"></A>
<A HREF="images/services.html"
onMouseOver="notePlayer.playNote (1,0,91,64,100,1000); return
    false;">
<IMG SRC="images/services.gif" border="0"></A>
<A HREF="images/products.html"
onMouseOver="notePlayer.playNote(1,0,91,66,100,1000); return
    false;">
<IMG SRC="images/products.gif" border="0"></A>
<A HREF="images/gallery.html"
onMouseOver="notePlayer.playNote(1,0,91,68,100,1000); return
    false;">
<IMG SRC="images/gallery.gif" border="0"></A>
<A HREF="images/contact.html"
onMouseOver="notePlayer.playNote(1,0,91,71,100,1000); return
    false;">
```

```
<IMG SRC="images/contact.gif" border="0"></A>
</CENTER>
</BODY>
</HTML>
```

6. Preview your file. Save your file and preview it in your browser. Incidentally, the sequence of numbers enclosed in parentheses and separated by commas and following PlayNote, e.g., (1,0,91,71,100,1000), correspond to the MIDI channel, bank, instrument number, volume, and duration of the note respectively.

Lesson 3: Adding simple background music

Beatnik offers a variety of ready-made RMF music you can license for a web site—some on the Headspace label, some from various third-party music developers, and some from production libraries like Firstcom and Chappell. Of course, you may be strictly interested in creating your own original *.rmf* content. Here we will use a pre-existing background *.rmf* file. This script will play background music when the page is loaded.

1. Start with a standard HTML page:

```
<HTML>
<HEAD></HEAD>
<BODY BGCOLOR="black">
</BODY>
</HTML>
```

2. Source the Music Object into your HTML page:

```
<HTML>
<HEAD>
</HEAD>
<BODY BGCOLOR="black">
<SCRIPT SRC="http://sonify.beatnik.com/music-object.js"></SCRIPT>
</BODY>
</HTML>
```

3. Create a Music Object instance:

```
<HTML>
<HEAD></HEAD>
<BODY BGCOLOR="black">
<SCRIPT SRC="http://sonify.beatnik.com/music-object.js"></SCRIPT>
<SCRIPT LANGUAGE="JavaScript">

backgroundPlayer = new Music ();

</BODY>
</HTML>
```

4. Embed the background RMF file into the Music Object using the magicEmbed method, like this:

```
<HTML>
<HEAD></HEAD>
<BODY BGCOLOR="black">
<SCRIPT SRC="http://sonify.beatnik.com/music-object.js"></SCRIPT>
<SCRIPT LANGUAGE="JavaScript">

backgroundPlayer = new Music ();
backgroundPlayer.magicEmbed ('SRC="rmf/background.rmf"');

</SCRIPT>
</BODY>
</HTML>
```

5. Insert the HIDDEN parameter into the magicEmbed method so that the Beatnik Player control panel does not appear on the page:

```
<HTML>
<HEAD></HEAD>
<BODY BGCOLOR="black">
<SCRIPT SRC="http://sonify.beatnik.com/music-object.js"></SCRIPT>
<SCRIPT LANGUAGE="JavaScript">

backgroundPlayer = new Music ();
backgroundPlayer.magicEmbed ('SRC="rmf/background.rmf" HIDDEN');

</SCRIPT>
</BODY>
</HTML>
```

6. Preview your file. Save your file and preview it in your browser.

Lesson 4: Creating multiple Music Object instances on a page

In order to allow more complex interaction, you can create multiple instances of the Music Object in a single page. This allows separate *.rmf* files to play, depending on what the user does with his or her mouse. This example uses an image map to play different sounds when the user's mouse passes over parts of a logo.

1. Start with the final HTML from Lesson 1 earlier in this chapter:

```
<HTML>
<HEAD></HEAD>
<BODY BGCOLOR="black">
<SCRIPT SRC="http://sonify.beatnik.com/music-object.js"></SCRIPT>
<SCRIPT LANGUAGE="JavaScript">

listenPlayer = new Music ();
listenPlayer.preloadEmbed ('rmf/listen.rmf');
```

```
</SCRIPT>
<CENTER>
<A HREF="JavaScript://" onMouseOver="listenPlayer.play();">
<IMG SRC="images/home.jpg" width="600" height="400" border="0"></A>
</CENTER>
</BODY>
</HTML>
```

2. Create three new Music Object instances:

```
<HTML>
<HEAD></HEAD>
<BODY BGCOLOR="black">
<SCRIPT SRC="http://sonify.beatnik.com/music-object.js"></SCRIPT>
<SCRIPT LANGUAGE="JavaScript">

bePlayer = new Music ();
hearPlayer = new Music ();
nowPlayer = new Music ();
listenPlayer = new Music ();
listenPlayer.preloadEmbed ('rmf/listen.rmf');

</SCRIPT>
<CENTER>
<A HREF="JavaScript://" onMouseOver="listenPlayer.play();">
<IMG SRC="images/home.jpg" width="600" height="400" border="0">
</A>
</CENTER>
</BODY>
</HTML>
```

3. Embed the "Be Hear Now" RMF files into the Music Object by using the preloadEmbed method, like this:

```
<HTML>
<HEAD></HEAD>
<BODY BGCOLOR="black">
<SCRIPT SRC="http://sonify.beatnik.com/music-object.js"></SCRIPT>
<SCRIPT LANGUAGE="JavaScript">

bePlayer = new Music ();
hearPlayer = new Music ();
nowPlayer = new Music ();
listenPlayer = new Music ();

bePlayer.preloadEmbed ('rmf/be.rmf');
hearPlayer.preloadEmbed ('rmf/hear.rmf');
nowPlayer.preloadEmbed ('rmf/now.rmf');
listenPlayer.preloadEmbed ('rmf/listen.rmf');

</SCRIPT>
<CENTER>
<A HREF="JavaScript://" onMouseOver="listenPlayer.play();">
<IMG SRC ="images/home.jpg" width="600" height="400" border="0">
</A>
</CENTER>
```

```
</BODY>
</HTML>
```

4. Set up the RMF files to play back when the user mouses over the image map with the page:

```
<HTML>
<HEAD></HEAD>
<BODY BGCOLOR="black">
<SCRIPT SRC="http://sonify.beatnik.com/music-object.js"></SCRIPT>
<SCRIPT LANGUAGE="JavaScript">

bePlayer = new Music ();
hearPlayer = new Music ();
nowPlayer = new Music ();
listenPlayer = new Music ();

bePlayer.preloadEmbed ('rmf/be.rmf');
hearPlayer.preloadEmbed ('rmf/hear.rmf');
nowPlayer.preloadEmbed ('rmf/now.rmf');
listenPlayer.preloadEmbed ('rmf/listen.rmf');

</SCRIPT>
<CENTER>
<IMG SRC="images/home.jpg" width="600" height="400" border="0"
    usemap="#SonicopiaLogo">
</CENTER>
<map name="SonicopiaLogo">
<area shape="rect" coords="41,161,118,211" href="JavaScript://"
    onMouseOver="bePlayer.play ();return false;">
<area shape="rect" coords="121,162,198,211" href="JavaScript://"
    onMouseOver="hearPlayer.play ();return false;">
<area shape="rect" coords="202,162,278,211" href="JavaScript://"
    onMouseOver="nowPlayer.play ();return false;">
<area shape="rect" coords="306,136,558,214" href="JavaScript://"
    onMouseOver="listenPlayer.play();return false;">
</map>
</BODY>
</HTML>
```

5. Preview your file. Save your file and preview it in your browser.

Lesson 5: Putting it all together

Now you can add all the audio behaviors, such as those found on the Sonicopia home page, to your own page. The Sonicopia page is designed so the note numbers selected are part of a musical scale that fits nicely with the background *.rmf* file.

1. Start with the final HTML from Lesson 4 earlier in this chapter:

```
<HTML>
<HEAD></HEAD>
<BODY BGCOLOR="black">
<SCRIPT SRC="http://sonify.beatnik.com/music-object.js"></SCRIPT>
<SCRIPT LANGUAGE="JavaScript">
```

```
bePlayer = new Music ();
hearPlayer = new Music ();
nowPlayer = new Music ();
listenPlayer = new Music ();

bePlayer.preloadEmbed ('rmf/be.rmf');
hearPlayer.preloadEmbed ('rmf/hear.rmf');
nowPlayer.preloadEmbed ('rmf/now.rmf');
listenPlayer.preloadEmbed ('rmf/listen.rmf');

</SCRIPT>
<CENTER>
<IMG SRC="images/home.jpg" width="600" height="400" border="0"
    usemap="#SonicopiaLogo">
</CENTER>
<map name="SonicopiaLogo">
<area shape="rect" coords="41,161,118,211" href="JavaScript://"
    onMouseOver="bePlayer.play ();return false;">
<area shape="rect" coords="121,162,198,211" href="JavaScript://"
    onMouseOver="hearPlayer.play ();return false;">
<area shape="rect" coords="202,162,278,211" href="JavaScript://"
    onMouseOver="nowPlayer.play ();return false;">
<area shape="rect" coords="306,136,558,214" href="JavaScript://"
    onMouseOver="listenPlayer.play();return false;">
</map>
</BODY>
</HTML>
```

2. Copy the Music Object instances from Lessons 2 and 3:

```
<HTML>
<HEAD></HEAD>
<BODY BGCOLOR="black">
<SCRIPT SRC="http://sonify.beatnik.com/music-object.js"></SCRIPT>
<SCRIPT LANGUAGE="JavaScript">

bePlayer = new Music ();
hearPlayer = new Music ();
nowPlayer = new Music ();
listenPlayer = new Music ();
notePlayer = new Music ();
backgroundPlayer = new Music ();

bePlayer.preloadEmbed ('rmf/be.rmf');
hearPlayer.preloadEmbed ('rmf/hear.rmf');
nowPlayer.preloadEmbed ('rmf/now.rmf');
listenPlayer.preloadEmbed ('rmf/listen.rmf');

</SCRIPT>
<CENTER>
<IMG SRC="images/home.jpg" width="600" height="400" border="0"
    usemap="#SonicopiaLogo">
</CENTER>
<map name="SonicopiaLogo">
<area shape="rect" coords="41,161,118,211" href="JavaScript://"
    onMouseOver="bePlayer.play ();return false;">
```

```
<area shape="rect" coords="121,162,198,211" href="JavaScript://"
    onMouseOver="hearPlayer.play ();return false;">
<area shape="rect" coords="202,162,278,211" href="JavaScript://"
    onMouseOver="nowPlayer.play ();return false;">
<area shape="rect" coords="306,136,558,214" href="JavaScript://"
    onMouseOver="listenPlayer.play();return false;">
</map>
</BODY>
</HTML>
```

3. Copy the stubEmbed and magicEmbed lines from Lessons 2 and 3:

```
<HTML>
<HEAD></HEAD>
<BODY BGCOLOR="black">
<SCRIPT SRC="http://sonify.beatnik.com/music-object.js"></SCRIPT>
<SCRIPT LANGUAGE="JavaScript">

bePlayer = new Music ();
hearPlayer = new Music ();
nowPlayer = new Music ();
listenPlayer = new Music ();
notePlayer = new Music ();
backgroundPlayer = new Music ();

bePlayer.preloadEmbed ('rmf/be.rmf');
hearPlayer.preloadEmbed ('rmf/hear.rmf');
nowPlayer.preloadEmbed ('rmf/now.rmf');
listenPlayer.preloadEmbed ('rmf/listen.rmf');
notePlayer.stubEmbed ('http://sonify.beatnik.com/stub.rmf');
backgroundPlayer.magicEmbed ('SRC="rmf/background.rmf" HIDDEN');

</SCRIPT>
<CENTER>
<IMG SRC="images/home.jpg" width="600" height="400" border="0"
    usemap="#SonicopiaLogo">
<map name="SonicopiaLogo">
<area shape="rect" coords="41,161,118,211" href="JavaScript://"
    onMouseOver="bePlayer.play ();return false;">
<area shape="rect" coords="121,162,198,211" href="JavaScript://"
    onMouseOver="hearPlayer.play ();return false;">
<area shape="rect" coords="202,162,278,211" href="JavaScript://"
    onMouseOver="nowPlayer.play ();return false;">
<area shape="rect" coords="306,136,558,214" href="JavaScript://"
    onMouseOver="listenPlayer.play();return false;">
</map>
</CENTER>
</BODY>
</HTML>
```

4. Copy the navigation bar from Lesson 2:

```
<HTML>
<HEAD></HEAD>
<BODY BGCOLOR="black">
<SCRIPT SRC="http://sonify.beatnik.com/music-object.js"></SCRIPT>
<SCRIPT LANGUAGE=JavaScript>
```

```
bePlayer = new Music ();
hearPlayer = new Music ();
nowPlayer = new Music ();
listenPlayer = new Music ();
notePlayer = new Music ();
backgroundPlayer = new Music ();

bePlayer.preloadEmbed ('rmf/be.rmf');
hearPlayer.preloadEmbed ('rmf/hear.rmf');
nowPlayer.preloadEmbed ('rmf/now.rmf');
listenPlayer.preloadEmbed ('rmf/listen.rmf');
notePlayer.stubEmbed ('http://sonify.beatnik.com/stub.rmf');
backgroundPlayer.magicEmbed ('SRC="rmf/background.rmf" HIDDEN');

</SCRIPT>
<CENTER>
<A HREF="about.html"
    onMouseOver="notePlayer.playNote(1,0,91,61,100,1000);return
    false;">
<IMG SRC="images/about.gif" border="0"></A>
<A HREF="services.html"
    onMouseOver="notePlayer.playNote (1,0,91,64,100,1000); return
    false;">
<IMG SRC="images/services.gif" border="0"></A>
<A HREF="products.html"
    onMouseOver="notePlayer.playNote(1,0,91,66,100,1000); return
    false;">
<IMG SRC="images/products.gif" border="0"></A>

<A HREF="gallery.html"
    onMouseOver="notePlayer.playNote(1,0,91,68,100,1000); return
    false;">
<IMG SRC="images/gallery.gif" border="0"></A>

<A HREF="contact.html"
    onMouseOver="notePlayer.playNote(1,0,91,71,100,1000); return
    false;">
<IMG SRC="images/contact.gif" border="0"></A>
<IMG SRC="images/home.jpg" width="600" height="400" border="0"
    usemap="#SonicopiaLogo">
<map name="SonicopiaLogo">
<area shape="rect" coords="202,162,278,211" href="JavaScript://"
    onMouseOver="beHearNowPlayer.playNote
    (1,2,3,60,100,1000);return false;">
<area shape="rect" coords="121,162,198,211" href="JavaScript://"
    onMouseOver="beHearNowPlayer.playNote
    (1,2,2,60,100,1000);return false;">
<area shape="rect" coords="41,161,118,211" href="JavaScript://"
    onMouseOver="beHearNowPlayer.playNote
    (1,2,1,60,100,1000);return false;">
<area shape="rect" coords="306,136,558,214" href="JavaScript://"
    onMouseOver="listenPlayer.play();return false;">
</map>
</CENTER>
```

```
    </BODY>
    </HTML>
```

5. It is important to move the Embed commands to the bottom of the HTML page in their own JavaScript block in order to avoid a known page display artifact where the embed command shows up as a two-pixel by two-pixel dot in the finished web page:

```
<HTML>
<HEAD></HEAD>
<BODY BGCOLOR="black">
<SCRIPT SRC="http://sonify.beatnik.com/music-object.js"></SCRIPT>
<SCRIPT LANGUAGE="JavaScript">

bePlayer = new Music ();
hearPlayer = new Music ();
nowPlayer = new Music ();
listenPlayer = new Music ();
notePlayer = new Music ();
backgroundPlayer = new Music ();

</SCRIPT>
<CENTER>
<A HREF="about.html"
    onMouseOver="notePlayer.playNote(1,0,91,61,100,1000);return
    false;">
<IMG SRC="images/about.gif" border="0"></A>
<A HREF="services.html"
    onMouseOver="notePlayer.playNote (1,0,91,64,100,1000); return
    false;">
<IMG SRC="images/services.gif" border="0"></A>
<A HREF="products.html"
    onMouseOver="notePlayer.playNote(1,0,91,66,100,1000); return
    false;">
<IMG SRC="images/products.gif" border="0"></A>
<A HREF="gallery.html"
    onMouseOver="notePlayer.playNote(1,0,91,68,100,1000); return
    false;">
<IMG SRC="images/gallery.gif" border="0"></A>
<A HREF="contact.html"
    onMouseOver="notePlayer.playNote(1,0,91,71,100,1000); return
    false;">
<IMG SRC="images/contact.gif" border="0"></A>
<IMG SRC="images/home.jpg" width="600" height="400" border="0"
    usemap="#SonicopiaLogo">
<map name="SonicopiaLogo">
<area shape="rect" coords="202,162,278,211" href="JavaScript://"
    onMouseOver="beHearNowPlayer.playNote
    (1,2,3,60,100,1000);return false;">
<area shape="rect" coords="121,162,198,211" href="JavaScript://"
    onMouseOver="beHearNowPlayer.playNote
    (1,2,2,60,100,1000);return false;">
<area shape="rect" coords="41,161,118,211" href="JavaScript://"
    onMouseOver="beHearNowPlayer.playNote
    (1,2,1,60,100,1000);return false;">
```

```
<area shape="rect" coords="306,136,558,214" href="JavaScript://"
    onMouseOver="listenPlayer.play();return false;">
</map>
<SCRIPT LANGUAGE="JavaScript">

bePlayer.preloadEmbed ('rmf/be.rmf');
hearPlayer.preloadEmbed ('rmf/hear.rmf');
nowPlayer.preloadEmbed ('rmf/now.rmf');
listenPlayer.preloadEmbed ('rmf/listen.rmf');
notePlayer.stubEmbed ('http://sonify.beatnik.com/stub.rmf');
backgroundPlayer.magicEmbed ('SRC="rmf/background.rmf" HIDDEN');

</SCRIPT>
</CENTER>
</BODY>
</HTML>
```

6. Add in code to help your users who do not have the Beatnik
   Player. Once you've sourced in the Music Object, the Player
   installer automatically launches if your user's browser supports
   the Player and the Player is not yet installed. By default, it
   launches a slightly scary window. For this lesson, we have
   turned the default off and turned on the regular Beatnik Player
   Install Wizard. The installation process shuts down your user's
   browser and then automatically restarts the browser. If you specify a URL in the installerOptions.returnURL function, as follows,
   it then returns to the URL you specified. Usually this will be the
   page your user was just on.

```
<HTML>
<HEAD></HEAD>
<BODY BGCOLOR="black">
<SCRIPT SRC="http://sonify.beatnik.com/music-object.js"></SCRIPT>
<SCRIPT LANGUAGE="JavaScript">

bePlayer = new Music ();
hearPlayer = new Music ();
nowPlayer = new Music ();
listenPlayer = new Music ();
notePlayer = new Music ();
backgroundPlayer = new Music ();

Music.installerOptions.returnURL = "http://www.sonicopia.com";
Music.showCompatibilityPrompt = false;
if (Music.clientSupported && !Music.isPlayerCompatible ()) {
  (Music.installPlayer ());
}

</SCRIPT>
<CENTER>
<A HREF="about.html"
    onMouseOver="notePlayer.playNote(1,0,91,61,100,1000);return
    false;">
```

```
<IMG SRC="images/about.gif" border="0"></A>
<A HREF="services.html"
    onMouseOver="notePlayer.playNote (1,0,91,64,100,1000); return
    false;">
<IMG SRC="images/services.gif" border="0"></A>
<A HREF="products.html"
    onMouseOver="notePlayer.playNote(1,0,91,66,100,1000); return
    false;">
<IMG SRC="images/products.gif" border="0"></A>
<A HREF="gallery.html"
    onMouseOver="notePlayer.playNote(1,0,91,68,100,1000); return
    false;">
<IMG SRC="images/gallery.gif" border="0"></A>
<A HREF="contact.html"
    onMouseOver="notePlayer.playNote(1,0,91,71,100,1000); return
    false;">
<IMG SRC="images/contact.gif" border="0"></A>
<IMG SRC="images/home.jpg" width="600" height="400" border="0"
    usemap="#SonicopiaLogo">
<map name="SonicopiaLogo">
<area shape="rect" coords="202,162,278,211" href="JavaScript://"
    onMouseOver="beHearNowPlayer.playNote
    (1,2,3,60,100,1000);return false;">
<area shape="rect" coords="121,162,198,211" href="JavaScript://"
    onMouseOver="beHearNowPlayer.playNote
    (1,2,2,60,100,1000);return false;">
<area shape="rect" coords="41,161,118,211" href="JavaScript://"
    onMouseOver="beHearNowPlayer.playNote
    (1,2,1,60,100,1000);return false;">
<area shape="rect" coords="306,136,558,214" href="JavaScript://"
    onMouseOver="listenPlayer.play();return false;">
</map>
<SCRIPT LANGUAGE="JavaScript">

listenPlayer.preloadEmbed ('rmf/listen.rmf');
bePlayer.preloadEmbed ('rmf/be.rmf');
hearPlayer.preloadEmbed ('rmf/hear.rmf');
nowPlayer.preloadEmbed ('rmf/now.rmf');
notePlayer.stubEmbed ('http://sonify.beatnik.com/stub.rmf');
backgroundPlayer.magicEmbed ('SRC="rmf/background.rmf" HIDDEN');

</SCRIPT>
</CENTER>
</BODY>
</HTML>
```

7. An alternative to automatically launching the Player Installer (if the user does not have the Player) is to put a graphic or link on your page that notifies the visitor that the page is sonified and lets the user control the installation option. Simply call the Music.installPlayer() method when the visitor clicks on the link. In this lesson, we add a notice with a sonified Beatnik "Get the Player" graphic and remove the automatic installer code.

```html
<HTML>
<HEAD>
</HEAD>
<BODY BGCOLOR="black">
<SCRIPT SRC="http://sonify.beatnik.com/music-object.js"></SCRIPT>
<SCRIPT LANGUAGE="JavaScript">

bePlayer = new Music ();
hearPlayer = new Music ();
nowPlayer = new Music ();
listenPlayer = new Music ();
notePlayer = new Music ();
backgroundPlayer = new Music ();

Music.installerOptions.returnURL = "http://www.sonicopia.com";
Music.showCompatibilityPrompt = false;

</SCRIPT>
<CENTER>
    <A HREF="images/about.html" onMouseOver="notePlayer.playNote
    (1,0,91,61,100,1000);return false;">
    <IMG SRC="images/about.gif" border="0"></A>
    <A HREF="images/services.html" onMouseOver="notePlayer.playNote
    (1,0,91,64,100,1000);return false;">
    <IMG SRC="images/services.gif" border="0"></A>
    <A HREF="images/products.html" onMouseOver="notePlayer.playNote
    (1,0,91,66,100,1000);return false;">
    <IMG SRC="images/products.gif" border="0"></A>
    <A HREF="images/gallery.html" onMouseOver="notePlayer.playNote
    (1,0,91,68,100,1000);return false;">
    <IMG SRC="images/gallery.gif" border="0"></A>
    <A HREF="images/contact.html" onMouseOver="notePlayer.playNote
    (1,0,91,71,100,1000);return false;">
    <IMG SRC="images/contact.gif" border="0"></A>
<br>
<img src="images/home.jpg" width="600" height="400" border="0"
    usemap="#SonicopiaLogo">
<br>
<font color="white" face="Arial,Helvetica,Geneva" size=-2>This page
    is sonified. You will need the Beatnik Player to experience the
    interactive sounds</font><p>
<A HREF="JavaScript://"
    onMouseOver="notePlayer.playNote(1,1,112,60,100,1000)"
    onClick="Music.installPlayer ()"; return false>
<img src="images/getbeatnik.gif" width="90" height="30" border="0"
alt="Get Beatnik"></a>
</CENTER>
<MAP NAME="SonicopiaLogo">
   <area shape="rect" coords="41,161,118,211" href="JavaScript://"
   onMouseOver="bePlayer.play();return false;">
   <area shape="rect" coords="121,162,198,211" href="JavaScript://"
   onMouseOver="hearPlayer.play();return false;">
   <area shape="rect" coords="202,162,278,211" href="JavaScript://"
   onMouseOver="nowPlayer.play();return false;">
```

```
      <area shape="rect" coords="306,136,558,214" href="JavaScript://"
      onMouseOver="listenPlayer.play()">
  </map>
  <SCRIPT LANGUAGE="JavaScript"><!--
  bePlayer.preloadEmbed ('rmf/be.rmf');
  hearPlayer.preloadEmbed ('rmf/hear.rmf');
  nowPlayer.preloadEmbed ('rmf/now.rmf');
  listenPlayer.preloadEmbed ('rmf/listen.rmf');
  notePlayer.stubEmbed ('http://sonify.beatnik.com/stub.rmf');
  backgroundPlayer.magicEmbed ('SRC="rmf/background.rmf" HIDDEN');
  // --> </SCRIPT>
  </BODY>
  </HTML>
```

Preview your file. Save your file and preview it in your browser. Assuming you already have the Beatnik Player installed in that browser, the background RMF file should begin to play when the page loads, and the graphics and image maps play sounds when you mouse over them.

You've just built your first sonified site.

Using the Beatnik Editor

Now that you've worked with some premade content, let's take a look at how to create your own *.rmf* files. The Beatnik Editor is the primary tool for creating the *.rmf* files native to the Beatnik Player. This tool imports standard MIDI files and facilitates access and reassignment to the players built-in sound banks and patches. In addition, digital audio samples can be imported and assigned to various key ranges of a user-defined instrument patch within the custom user bank. After the samples are mapped to MIDI note ranges, they can be triggered by MIDI note commands just like the standard samples within the Player.

The Beatnik Editor is best used in conjunction with an OMS-compatible sequencing program such as Opcode's Vision, or Emagic's Logic Audio. OMS (Open Music System) acts as an intermediary translator between the sequencing software and the Beatnik Editor, allowing a "live" MIDI connection to the Beatnik instruments. Unfortunately, there is a significant lag in the response time of the Beatnik instruments, which makes it nearly impossible to compose directly with the Beatnik sounds. Although this is something Beatnik hopes to address, currently the best workaround requires the use of another general MIDI instrument to perform the input tasks and then audition the finished sequence with the various channels assigned to the instruments of the Beatnik Editor.

You can do this by choosing the File → Link to Sequence command. You must launch the Beatnik editor first and then your sequencer in order for the interapplication communication to work properly. This enables your sequencer to trigger the Beatnik player's multi-instrument tone generator, and to hear the composition exactly as the end user will hear it. The lag is actually still present, but all tracks are delayed by the same amount in this case, so it doesn't create any audible problem.

You can create MIDI sequences in any MIDI-sequencing program capable of exporting a standard type 1 MIDI file. You need to include the bank and patch assignments for the various MIDI channels in your exported file. This standard MIDI file is then imported into the editor, as shown in Figure 11-6. Note that your MIDI sequence will differ from what you heard when using the MIDI instrument you composed with. The best way to minimize the difference is to compose with a MIDI instrument that has banks and patch assignments that conform to the General MIDI specification. Since Beatnik instrument banks also map to this specification, your tracks will play with similar instrument sounds.

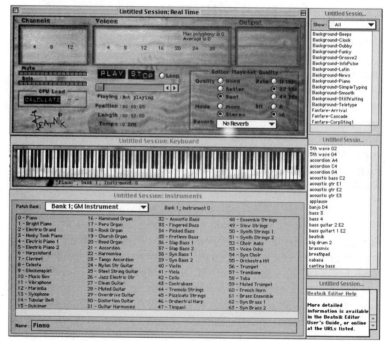

Figure 11-6. *The Beatnik Editor is useful for integrating different audio formats as well as editing custom samples.*

As of this writing, the Beatnik Editor was available only for the Macintosh. For Windows users, Beatnik has introduced the Beatnik Converter. The Converter does not allow the designer to create or assign custom instruments for the third bank, nor does it allow a live MIDI connection to the Beatnik instruments. It can import standard MIDI files or audio sample data and convert them to an *.rmf* file.

In order to run the Beatnik Editor, you will need a PowerPC-based Mac running System 7.1 or higher and Sound Manager 3.1 or higher. You should also have a MIDI instrument with a built-in General MIDI library. You will also want an OMS-compatible MIDI sequencing application and the OMS system extension(s). OMS is a MIDI utility that allows communication between an external MIDI controller, the computer itself, and other MIDI applications such as the Beatnik Editor or MIDI sequencer. If you want to create custom samples and instruments for the Beatnik Editor, you will also need a standard sound editing application such as Sound Designer II, Bias Peak, SoundEdit 16, or Sound Forge.

Getting started

When you first open the Beatnik Editor, you will be prompted to create a new session or open an existing session. You can think of a session as the workspace in which you collect and manipulate the various elements that will eventually be integrated and exported as an *.rmf* file. When you save a session file, it is important to understand that the elements remain in their native format. For example, a *.wav* file is still a *.wav* file, and a standard MIDI file is still a standard MIDI file. It is not an *.rmf* file until it is exported as such. This allows you to save your work in progress and to re-open a session file at a later time and manipulate the various files in their native format. Once the file is exported as an *.rmf* file, you cannot edit the individual elements.

When you create a new session, you can name it, and the program interface will display five windows: the Real Time window, the Songs window, the Samples window, the Instruments window, and the Keyboard window. Each appears with the session name at the top of its window. The Instruments window is a list of the instruments you have available to you. Likewise, the Songs and Samples windows show the songs and the samples that are available to you. Notice that the windows have pop-up menus that allow access to other banks. The Keyboard window is a graphical representation of a MIDI keyboard on which you can mouse-click to audition various instruments at different pitches, and also view MIDI key ranges, which you can map samples to. The Real Time window allows you to view important data such as CPU load, time, global reverb settings, and other graphical feedback in real time as you load and play with different elements.

Those who have worked with a MIDI keyboard or sequencer software will find the Beatnik Editor's interface familiar and intuitive. If you haven't worked with MIDI or a keyboard sampler, don't worry. The interface is still fairly easily understood and deals mainly with MIDI channel assignments, General MIDI patch assignments, and MIDI key note ranges. There is good documentation available for the Beatnik Editor, and the software may be downloaded free of charge at Beatnik's web site *www.beatnik.com*. The Pro Version includes MP3 compression and is moderately priced.

Importing MIDI and audio files

To import a MIDI file into your session, select File → Import. From the dialog box, select the MIDI file and click the Import button (the editor also supports dragging and dropping your standard MIDI files on the Song window). Your MIDI file will now appear in the Song window. Once it's displayed in the Song window, you can highlight the name of the song and then manipulate the MIDI file by opening the song item of the menu bar.

To import an audio file or sample into your session, select File → Import as shown in Figure 11-7. From the dialog box, select an AIFF, WAV, or a Sound Designer II file if (you are a user of Digidesign's Pro Tools Software), and click the Import button (you can also drag and drop these file types directly into the Samples window). Your sample will now appear in the Samples window. As with MIDI, once it's in the Samples window, you can now manipulate the audio sample file.

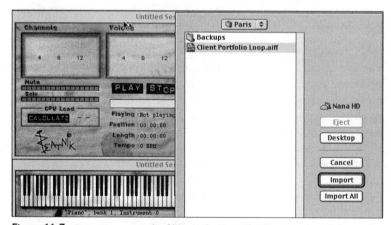

Figure 11-7. *Importing an audio file into the Beatnik Editor is a straightforward process.*

Manipulating the files

The Beatnik Editor menu bar allows you to manipulate songs, instruments, and samples. The appropriate menu will become activated or grayed out depending on type of file you have highlighted (and in which window).

Working with songs

Let's start with songs. Standard MIDI files can be imported into the editor where they will appear in the Songs window, as shown in Figure 11-8.

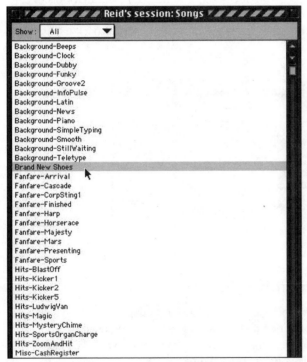

Figure 11-8. *The Songs window displays the audio and MIDI files you have imported into the editor as well the Groovoids currently installed in the Editor.*

The pop-up menu at the top of the Songs window has four possible choices: All, Groovoids, User Songs, or Imported *.rmf*s. As explained earlier in this chapter, Groovoids are small, premade MIDI compositions that are built into the Beatnik Player, so you can experiment with these files immediately. Some are stingers and cues, and some make great interface sounds. Groovoids cannot be edited or changed in any way. However, any user-imported file that appears in the User Songs view can be edited. You can listen to any of the songs by double-clicking them, by using the keyboard shortcut Command-T, or by highlighting the name of the song and then clicking the Play button in the Real Time window.

When you have highlighted a song in the Song window, you can change the song's tempo, volume, and reverb settings by choosing Song→Song Settings from the menu bar. This displays the window shown in Figure 11-9. The value in the Tempo field represents a percentage of the tempo for the song, where 100% is normal speed. Percentages over 100% will cause the song to play at faster than normal speed; values of less than 100% play at slower than normal speed. You can select one of several different reverb types to be associated with the song. You can also set a "Volume gain" setting for each song. Note that these settings will be saved with the song and will be reflected on the web page when the song is played back using the Beatnik plug-in.

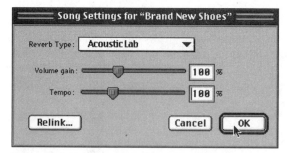

Figure 11-9. *The Song Settings window*

Digital watermarking and copyright protection

The copyright and media information are watermarked and encrypted within the Beatnik file so no matter where the file goes, the appropriate information and credits follow. As with Liquid Audio, digital watermarking is an essential feature for professional musicians, producers, and music industry professionals, as it guarantees proper copyright information and necessary security features to protect the rights of songwriters and publishers.

Most artists make a living from royalties paid by people who use and enjoy their music. Artists are accustomed to being paid royalties by certain agencies such as ASCAP or BMI, which collect the money and distribute it to the artists. However, one of the fundamental flaws or assets of the Web, depending on which side of the fence you sit, is that media on the Net is easy to download without proper permission. With the 40-bit digital encryption and watermarking included with Beatnik, artists, publishers, and sound designers can be secure that their music is protected from piracy.

You can also edit the copyright information for a song by selecting the song and then choosing Song → Copyright. The information that you enter in the copyright window can be accessed by the user via the Beatnik plug-in. As copyright protection with electronic music becomes increasingly important, this is a welcome feature for those of us who wish to protect our hard work from being copied and pasted into a web site that didn't bother to pay for it. It also lets you reassure your clients that the sound design you create for them won't be available to everyone else free of charge. The copyright information in a Beatnik .rmf cannot be edited by the user. Tampering with it will cause the file to be unplayable. In addition to this watermarking, .rmf files are also scrambled with 40-bit digital encryption, which affords further protection to the creative community.

The copyright window contains the following fields:

Title

    The title of your piece of music

Composer(s)

    The composer of your piece of music

Copyright

    The music's copyright line, e.g., © 2000 CS Audio Visual, Inc.

Performed By

    The performer of your piece of music

Composer Notes

    Any notes about the music, such as special commentary, thanks, etc.

Once the copyright information and song settings have been adjusted to your needs, you can export your song as a Beatnik .rmf file, which maybe embedded in a web page for playback with the Beatnik Player plug-in.

Working with instruments

There are three banks of sounds to compose with. As previously discussed, two of the banks are contained in the Beatnik Player; the third must be created in the Beatnik Editor and attached to the .rmf file. You do not have to create any original instruments to compose high-quality original music. Furthermore, if your final .rmf file uses only the standard instruments of the Beatnik Player's first two banks, you gain the advantage of extremely low data rates and quick download times for the end user. However, the option of custom instruments and samples affords the sound designer/composer powerful and unique creative possibilities (with the consequence of larger file sizes and longer load times).

What is that song called?

You don't have to remember its name. The song title, composer, copyright, and composer fields associated with each song in the copyright settings are displayed as the music is played.

Lets take a look at the three banks:

Bank One (the General MIDI bank)
> A complete set of 128 General MIDI instruments and a full GM percussion set

Bank Two (the special bank)
> 128 special instruments and a special percussion set

Bank Three (the user bank)
> Room for 128 user instruments and a user percussion set

The General MIDI bank, shown in Figure 11-10, ensures almost universal compatibility with all standard MIDI files. The special bank provides an extended set of instruments created specially for the Beatnik System by Beatnik composers and sound designers, including numerous sound effects customized for the Web.

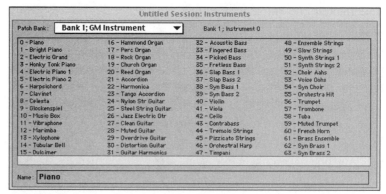

Figure 11-10. *The Instruments window displays the available instruments in Beatnik's Audio Engine, including a General MIDI bank, a special instrument and percussion bank, and a user bank that can be filled with customized instruments, samples, and percussion instruments.*

In addition to importing your own samples, you may also use the user bank to create custom-edited versions of the pre-existing Beatnik instruments by making a copy and altering the instrument settings to your specific needs. These options are described later.

You can view all of these instruments by opening the Instrument window from the Windows menu. The pop-up list in the top of the window allows you to select the different banks for viewing and editing. The instruments in the GM and special banks cannot be edited, deleted, or changed; you can, however, copy and paste them into user bank slots if you would like to modify them or create new instruments using them as a starting point.

The Instrument menu includes the following options:

Keymap

Allows you to define the MIDI note range for individual samples of a multisample instrument.

Modulation

Uses LFOs (Low Frequency Oscillators) to effect various parameters of the sound.

Volume

Creates and changes the instrument's envelope (attack, sustain, decay, and release).

Filters

Uses dynamic low-pass filters to change the instrument's sound.

Instrument Settings

Tweaks an instrument's reverb, looping, pitch, and pan settings.

Experiment with these different options and various settings. Altering pan settings and LFO modulation can have a striking effect on your music. In fact, a relatively simple sound, such as a bell chime or a spoken word, can be altered to sound very complex using combinations of these choices, and entirely new instruments can be created.

Working with samples

The Samples window shows an alphabetical list of all the samples associated with the current Beatnik session. The samples used by the built-in General MIDI bank and the special bank are displayed in italics while user-imported samples are displayed in plain text. Again, the built-in samples cannot be edited or deleted until they are copied and pasted in to a user-definable slot. They are automatically duplicated if you make a copy of a General MIDI or a special bank instrument in the Instrument window. If you want to view only the custom samples you have imported, select User Samples from the Sample window's pop-up menu.

If you select a user sample, you can then edit it by selecting choices from the pull-down Sample menu. The following options are available:

Sample Settings

Allows you to view basic information about the selected sample and change the sample rate, root key, and loop start and end points.

Compression

Allows you to select between None, IMA, Sun, MPEG (with the Beatnik Editor Pro), and Beatnik compression types.

Including web links

You can enter URLs in the composer notes field. This allows listeners on the Web to link directly to a web page of your choosing from the copyright display window of the Beatnik plug-in. To enter a URL, type it in simple text form and the Beatnik plug-in will resolve it automatically. Do *not* enter complete HTML. For example, type in *www.raspberrymedia.com,* not *http://www.raspberry-media.com.*

Making a custom instrument from your imported samples

After you have the samples imported and compressed, they are eligible to become part of a custom instrument. To do this, move the mouse into the Instrument window, and select the user bank from the pop-up menu. In a newly created session, you will see that the bank is empty. Double-click on the first empty instrument. This brings up a keymapping tool (shown in Figure 11-11) that allows you to create zones (or keymap ranges) and assign individual samples to the various zones. If you have worked with a MIDI keyboard sampler, you will be familiar with this tool. This is the standard method in which instrument designers create a full range of chromatic notes with as few samples as possible. A sample usually sounds its best at the pitch it was sampled at (this is called the *root pitch*), but it is possible to "stretch" the sample across a limited note range before it starts to lose its quality. You can easily verify this by assigning one sample to the entire 88-key range of a piano and auditioning the sample at various places on the keyboard. The trick is to determine the exact range of notes where an individual sample sounds reasonably good, and to record new root samples for the note ranges where the sound quality falls apart. If you use at least one or two root samples for every octave, that is sufficient. For example, you may use root samples at C and F in every octave you intend to use. This is a common practice of sound designers who routinely create their own customized mappings of samples on an 88-key keyboard controller.

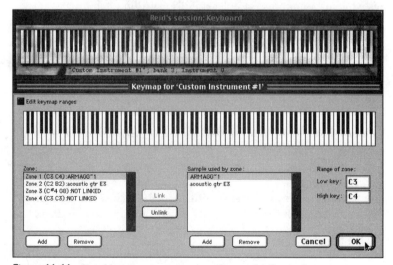

Figure 11-11. *To add custom instruments to the user bank, use the keymapping tool.*

Dreamweaver, Flash, Director, and Beatnik

Dreamweaver, Flash, and Director let you create Beatnik actions within their authoring interfaces. The Beatnik ActionSet for Dreamweaver versions 2 and 3 adds the functionality of the Beatnik Music Object directly into the Dreamweaver tool palette. The Beatnik ActionSet lets you create Beatnik rollovers and sound effects without having to write code. Using the Beatnik ActionSet allows you to set Beatnik playback parameters such as Autostart and Display. The Beatnik Action-Set extension is bundled with the latest version of Dreamweaver and is available free of charge from the Beatnik web site for earlier versions of Dreamweaver.

You can integrate Beatnik into your Flash movies by using a special extension of the *music-object.js* file, called the *music-object-x-flash.js* file. This extension file allows you to "wire" FS commands from within the Flash movie to trigger standard Beatnik Music Object JavaScript methods.

The Beatnik Xtra for Director provides Beatnik functionality for your Director and Shockwave projects. The Beatnik Xtra encompasses a set of specialized Lingo scripts that allow you to control the special Beatnik Xtra player (sonified Director and Shockwave projects do not make use of the standard Beatnik browser plug-in).

The keymapping tool is easy to use. You simply add as many zones as you need by clicking the Add button below the zone field. Next you add the individual samples of the instrument you are building by clicking the Add button below the samples field. You then link the samples to the various zones, and define the keymap ranges by highlighting the notes of the keyboard graphic in the top of the window. By moving the three small arrows, you can determine to which notes the root pitches for the individual samples and the overall instruments are mapped. When you have finished, you can name the instrument in the Name field at the bottom of the window. You now have a custom instrument containing multiple samples that can be triggered by MIDI note on commands—just like the standard Beatnik instruments.

Exporting an RMF file with the Beatnik Editor

After you have brought all the various elements together and have a song in your session sounding just the way you like it, you should save your session. After saving the session, you can export your composition as an *.rmf* file. To export the song as a Beatnik file, select the song in the Song Window and choose File → Export Beatnik. A dialog box (as shown in Figure 11-12) gives you the option of including the instruments and samples used in the song as part of the Beatnik file. If you are not using custom samples, you do not need to include any instruments because they are already built into the plug-

in. If you are using custom instruments, include them in your Beatnik file. When you have selected the instruments you want to
include, click OK, and then save your file. Remember that after you
create a *.rmf* file, it cannot be edited. In order to make changes, you
must go back to the original session document, make changes, and
export a new Beatnik file. Note that after a song is exported as a *.rmf*
file, it is encrypted and cannot be re-opened and edited. If you want
to make changes to the file, you must edit the song and re-export it
as a *.rmf* file.

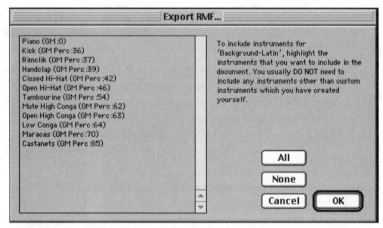

Figure 11-12. *After you have finished creating your Beatnik file and custom sound
bank, use the Export dialog box.*

Summary

In this chapter, we examined the Rich Music Format and Beatnik's
authoring tools to deliver interactive sound over the Web. While
other audio delivery methods are currently more suitable to certain
tasks, such as streaming audio, Beatnik has evolved into a capable
toolset for interactive sound design on the Web. Its tools, especially
the interactive command set via JavaScript, allow for a lot of creative
freedom. The small file sizes and interactive capabilities make it an
ideal format for bringing high-quality, fast-downloading audio to your
web site.

Although learning the JavaScript language is not appealing to some
audio professionals, there are some easier alternatives, including the
availability of ActionSets for both Macromedia Dreamweaver and
Adobe GoLive, which automate most of the coding process. There is
also Beatnik's online tool—the Methodizer—which can generate specific coding for most common functionalities.

As connection baud rates and Internet bandwidth increase, you can expect the software instrument sets to get fairly robust and audio fidelity to increase. There is the possibility of extending the standard instrument libraries now offered. And Beatnik is committed to building a comprehensive authoring platform for interactive audio. Audio design for the Web is still in a primordial stage. However, it is the type of skill that is likely to become an important component of web productions.

CREATING THE ULTIMATE WEB SOUND STUDIO: BUYERS GUIDE AND WEB RESOURCES

This buyers guide was developed as a result of the many interviews we conducted with web audio experts. The feedback was unanimous: with high-fidelity audio frequently compressed and degraded during conversion to web audio formats, the need to capture high-quality source material is essential.

Using the proper equipment and tools is one sure way to increase the quality of your source material. If you are a web professional with little audio engineering experience, the information in this appendix will help you purchase and configure the best possible audio production equipment and software suited to your needs.

Not all audio equipment is created equal. There is a big difference in quality between the inexpensive audio equipment found at your neighborhood electronics shop versus the high-end professional audio gear found at retailers catering exclusively to audio professionals. It is no coincidence that audio professionals highly value their tools. It takes good equipment in the right studio environment to consistently capture a great musical performance or a voice-over take. It is nearly impossible to take a bad recording with noise and distortion and turn it into a pristine, professional-sounding masterpiece, especially when faced with the compression formats used for web delivery. The proper web sound studio will help you achieve more professional results. For more tips on creating a suitable studio, see Chapter 3, *Capturing Original Source Material.*

It's the technique, not the tools

Although this buyers guide emphasizes the importance of having great equipment, you do not always need the most expensive gear to get the results you want. Good recording and editing techniques are often far more important than expensive equipment. Some of the best web audio was produced on inexpensive "prosumer" gear. So if you have a limited budget, you can still get high-quality results with a little ingenuity and skill.

However, if you are not sure you can pull recording miracles out of a custom, re-engineered $30 Radio Shack microphone, then spend the money and use professional grade equipment.

Creating the ultimate web sound studio

The key to building the ultimate web sound studio is to select professional-grade equipment that captures the highest fidelity audio while avoiding equipment that adds noise and low-level distortion. Professional gear should have balanced XLR inputs (large, three-pin connectors) instead of 1/4-inch or RCA jacks, built-in power supplies instead of external "wall warts," and high-grade, sturdy electrical components that resist age and rust.

This appendix outlines the standard equipment, software, and accessories used for professional web audio production and sound design. Where appropriate, each featured professional grade studio component is listed with a "pro option," along with its manufacturer's "list" price versus its "street" price. Keep in mind that these prices are as of June 2000. The professional grade equipment listed in this appendix is targeted at a reasonable, small-scale audio production studio budget of $25,000. Many professional studios used for film scoring and music recording spend hundreds of thousands or millions of dollars on equipment. If you just want to add some audio to your site, the budget option targets the home studio builder with a budget of a few thousand dollars.

Street value prices are constantly fluctuating and may vary from store to store depending on the retailer's wholesale purchase price. Many retail chains offer "loss-leader" discount prices on certain items to get you into the store so they can sell you other, more expensive items. The street value prices in this appendix do not reflect this pricing.

Designing a studio with proper acoustics

The first and largest component of the ultimate web sound studio is the room itself. A proper recording environment with pleasing acoustics and no echo or noise is essential to high-quality recording. (For more information about optimum room acoustics, see Chapter 3.) Successfully building a great sound studio depends largely on having the proper budget to design and remodel a room from scratch or the ingenuity to repurpose an existing room on a budget.

Pro option

Money and space permitting, most professional recording studios are customized from the ground up to have the ideal acoustics and optimum recording functionality. Professional studios generally have a minimum of two rooms: a control room for mixing and monitoring and a soundproof recording room for capturing the audio signal. The control room is where the audio engineer resides during a recording or mix-down session and contains mixing boards, a digital audio workstation, studio reference monitors, and so on. The recording room is where the musicians, voice-over artists, and microphones reside. Generally, the control room is directly adjacent to the recording room with a soundproof window built in-between so the engineer can supervise microphone placement and communicate with the recording artists.

Professional studios optimize good room acoustics by placing high-frequency-absorbing audio-grade foam on the walls and ceilings, bass baffles and traps on the floors and corners, and reflective hardwood floors for warmth and pleasing reverberation.

Budget option

Building a sound studio on a shoestring budget takes ingenuity and resourcefulness. Most web professionals and audio enthusiasts will have neither the luxury of building a room from the ground up nor an extensive budget to equip it with acoustic foam, bass traps, or sound isolation booths. For people with a limited budget, converting an existing square or rectangular room in their home or production offices into a dedicated sound studio is their only option. If you have one room for recording, mixing, and monitoring, the first step is to isolate and place any noisy, fan-cooled hard drives or power amps into a padded box or a closet with enough air circulation around the components.

Once you reduce any extraneous noise that can leak into your microphones during recording, place bookshelves, file cabinets, wall hangings, or other large objects against the walls to reduce echo and slap-back. If the ceiling and floor are parallel, place a rug on the floor or a tapestry on the ceiling to further reduce slap-back and echo.

Microphones

Microphones capture and convert sound waves into electrical impulses. A good microphone is one of the first components you will need if you plan on recording voice-overs or live music. You will want to choose a microphone that has an extended high-frequency response and a low signal-to-noise ratio. A high-quality microphone should capture the entire audio spectrum of the human hearing range from 20 Hz to 20 kHz with a low 11dB of self noise. Inexpensive microphones generally only capture the frequencies between 50 Hz to 15 kHz and add a lot of noise into the audio signal.

A note about prices

Prices are current as of June 2000. While the prices listed in this appendix will change over time, the pricing information is included to provide you with an overall picture of the general retail markup of each make and model.

Pro option

Generally speaking, the more expensive the microphone, the more accurately it reproduces sound waves and the more features it contains. A large diaphragm condenser microphone with at least two or three polar patterns, preferably omni and cardioid, is the industry standard for recording voice-overs and acoustic instruments. As far as all-around performance, reliability, and sound, there are several good condenser microphone options available in the $700 to $1,300 range, including:

- Rode NT2 large-diaphragm condenser mic* (list $749/street $595)
  Best Buy
- Audio-Technica AT4050 multipattern condenser mic (list $995/street $650)
- AKG C3000B large-diaphragm (cardioid) mic (list $520/street $350)
- CAD Equitek E200 condenser mic (list $749/street $550)
- AKG Solid Tube large-diaphragm tube mic (list $1,195/street $999)
- Neumann TLM 193 large-diaphragm mic (list $1,495/street $1,199)
- Neumann TLM 103 large-diaphragm mic (list $995/street $900)

Professional versus consumer grade equipment

Bear in mind that professional gear, as the name implies, is designed for people who are making money from audio production. This means at minimum a studio with at least $20,000 to $50,000 worth of equipment. Professional gear is expensive for a reason—it is generally not mass-produced and contains electrical components that have been handcrafted and oft-tested.

If you find an inexpensive piece of equipment that claims to do everything, the price is probably too good to be true. Most likely the manufacturer is cutting corners with low-grade electrical components or simply misleading the consumer. The recent trend in consumer-grade audio equipment is to pack every piece of gear with the most possible features—compression, EQ, reverb, and so on. This often leads to more system noise and makes the piece of equipment more difficult to use when trying to get a quick task done under pressure.

Look for equipment that is known for doing one thing really well. You will find the audio quality is better, and the tool is easier to use.

Budget option

If you cannot afford to spend $1,000 on a large diaphragm condenser microphone, some of the small diaphragm electrets give fine sound at a budget price. (The disadvantage of an electric condenser is that it will only last a few years.) A few to consider are:

- Sure SM81 condenser microphone (list $529/street $300)

- AKG C1000 condenser microphone* (list $350/street $160–$180)
  Best Buy

- Shure BG5.1 condenser microphone (list $220/street $149)

- CAD 95 condenser microphone (list $239/street $199)

There are occasions when dynamic microphones are an advantage over more expensive, sensitive condenser mics. They are nearly indestructible, and they do not capture as much distant ambient room noise or feedback from studio speakers. To get the best recording quality from less-sensitive dynamic microphones, place the mic within six inches of the sound source and make sure you are getting the "hottest" or loudest possible signal going into the mic.

Pro option

- Electrovoice RE-20 large-diaphragm dynamic (standard radio announcer mic) (list $665/street $479)

- Shure SM-7 Warm, big dynamic (list $450/street $349)

Budget option

- Shure SM58 dynamic microphone (list $150/street $119)

- Peavy PV520—similar to RE-20 (list $300/street $200)

- Electro-Voice RE-50 omni dynamic—used on TV news programs (list $299/street $299)

- Electro voice RE-635 omni (list $178/street $119)

Mic pre-amps

A mic pre-amp boosts the weak output signal of a microphone, just as a telephoto lens magnifies the image of a regular camera lens. A good mic pre-amp is the most overlooked component in the recording studio. Novices and beginners alike usually find it easy to understand why a good microphone is necessary for high-quality recording, but few comprehend why mic pre-amps are just as important.

When it comes to choosing one or the other, the microphone always comes first. But a high-quality outboard mic pre-amp should always accompany your investment in a good condenser microphone.

Additional resources

How to Build a Small Budget Recording Studio from Scratch, Second Edition by Frederick Alton Everest (Tab Books, 1998) is an excellent, practical handbook on acoustics that is suitable for both professional and beginning engineers.

Without a mic pre-amp, you will not reap the full benefit of a professional-grade microphone.

Pro option

Most professional studios utilize separate, high-quality outboard mic pre-amps, or expensive mixing consoles, which have built-in high-quality mic pre-amps. These components start at $30,000.

The difference between a high-quality mic pre-amp and a poor-quality one is the output clarity and purity of an amplified low-level microphone input signal. A high-quality mic pre-amp magnifies every nuance and subtlety of a microphone signal without introducing noise. A cheap mic pre-amp, like the ones found in most 16-channel mixers, introduces system noise into the signal path and easily overloads and distorts loud input signals.

A few good mic pre-amps include:

- A.R.T.-Pro MPA Stereo Tube mic pre-amp* (list $599/street $495) *Best Buy*

- Millennia Media HV3B Stereo solid state mic pre-amp (list $1,895/street $1,700)

- Joe Meek mic pre-amp and compressor (list $600/street $450)

Budget option

If you cannot afford a professional grade outboard mic pre-amp, use the built-in mic pre-amps on your mixing board. The Mackie MS1202 12 channel mixer has four built-in mic pre-amps and sells for only $369. If you have to use the built-in mic pre-amp on your mixing board, try to ensure that the signal going into the microphone is as "hot" as possible. The "hotter" (or louder) the signal entering the microphone, the less the mic pre-amp has to boost the signal. Move the microphone closer to the sound source or ask someone to speak or play louder. A few to consider are:

- A.R.T. Tube mic pre-amp direct box with phantom power* (list $189/street $139) *Best Buy*

- A.R.T. Tube mic pre-amp (list $250/street $199)

- Mackie-MS1202-VLZ 12 channel mixer with built-in mic pre-amps (list $400/street $359)

- Aphex 107 "tubessence" (list $449/street $299)

Compressor/limiters

A compressor, as the names implies, is used to even out and compress incoming audio signals that vary greatly in dynamic range. An example is a singer going from a soft whisper to a resounding scream. A compressor allows for the hottest incoming signal possible to your sound card without distorting it by limiting the sounds that peak above the 0dB-distortion range. By reducing the amplitude of the loudest sounds with a compressor you can increase the input level of your microphone to get a hotter recording. Compressors are used widely in pop music where the aesthetic dictates that the overall volume and presence of each instrument remain consistent throughout the mix. Compressors are not as ubiquitous in classical or jazz music, where a wider dynamic range is preferable. However, in the age of hard-disk recording, compressors have become a necessity to avoid digital distortion.

Pro option

A high-quality compressor will produce a more natural, pleasing sound and will accept a higher-level input signal before reaching the distortion point. The ultimate choice in compressors is the dbx blue series or the TC Electronics Finalizer, which both feature 24-bit digital outputs. The digital outputs on the dbx 160S allow you to take the incoming signal from your mic pre-amp directly into the compressor and straight out to your sound card digitally!

- A.R.T.-Pro VLA compressor/limiter* (list $349/street $289)
  *Best Buy

- TC Electronic-Finalizer compressor/limiter 3-band compression (list $2,495/street $1,995)

- dbx-160S compressor/limiter (list $2,495/street $1,995)

- Aphex Systems-651 Expressor Mono compressor/limiter (list $495/street $350)

Budget option

Less expensive dynamics processors generally offer the same features as the high-end models but with poorer sound quality. If you cannot afford a compressor or limiter, you will have to watch your incoming recording levels closely and make sure to normalize your sound files once they have been recorded.

- dbx 262 Stereo compressor/limiter* (list $269/street $130)
  *Best Buy

- A.R.T. Mono Levelar Stereo Tube compressor/limiter (list $349/street $249)

- Alesis 3630 Stereo compressor/limiter with gate (list $300/street $199)

Digital audio workstation/recording editing software

The digital audio workstation is the centerpiece of the web sound studio. Audio workstations contain special DSP chips for audio processing and analog-to-digital conversion, as well as recording and editing software. Most sound cards have at minimum one pair of digital inputs and outputs as well as analog stereo inputs and outputs. More expensive systems have 8 to 16 direct inputs and outputs.

Low-end systems generally offer software-only solutions and rely on the internal DSP of your CPU to process audio. Along with a sound card, you will need a computer with a 2 GB or larger AV hard drive, 120 MHz CPU or faster, plenty of RAM, a 17-inch monitor, a proper universal power supply unit, and a backup storage system large enough to store the contents of your hard drive.

Note that a few packages listed in the budget option are two-track stereo editors designed for audio mastering, editing of final mixes, and two-track recordings.

Pro option

A professional system such as Digidesign's Pro Tools system or Sonic Solutions' Sonic Studio have outboard DSP components as well as internal PCI cards for faster processing, playback, and output of 16 or more simultaneous tracks. High-end systems have better built-in analog-to-digital converters, higher signal-to-noise ratios (93dB), and more bulletproof sophisticated software code.

*   Digidesign Pro Tools-24 MIX with 882-20 Interface (list $8,240/ street $7,500). System features eight channels of analog input and two channels. Pro Tools 24 features 64 tracks of simultaneous 20-bit 44.1 kHz playback and recording (Macintosh).

*   Sonic Solutions Sonic Studio Hardware/Software (list $7,999/ street $7,999). Sonic Studio features 24 tracks of 24-bit 96 kHz recording and playback (Macintosh).

Budget option

Low-end hardware/software systems generally feature only two analog inputs and outputs on one PCI card and fewer simultaneous playback tracks. Some recording and editing software applications are standalone packages that do not come with any hardware components. Note that MIDI-sequencing software packages now support digital audio recording and playback (see the following section).

- Event Darla Hardware/Software* (list $500/street $429). Two analog inputs (PCI card), eight analog outputs (standalone box), digital SPIDF inputs and outputs, 20-bit A/D. *Best Buy

- Digidesign Pro Tools-24 with Audiomedia III/ToolBox Digital Audio Card (list $1,200/street $900). The AudioMedia III/ToolBox features two analog inputs, two digital outputs, digital SPIDF inputs and outputs, 20-bit A/D, easy-to-use software interface (Macintosh and Windows 98).

- CreamWare U.S. Masterport Hardware/Software (list $998/street price $900). 16 tracks of 18-bit playback and 2 RCA analog recording inputs and outputs (Windows 95).

- Metalithic Systems Digital Wings for Audio 1.4 (list $1,195/street $999). 16 tracks of 18-bit A/D and 2 RCA analog recording inputs and outputs (Windows 95).

- Korg 1212 Digital SPIDF I/O 20-bit A/D with Deck II 2.6 multitrack software (list $1,200/street $900) (hardware only list $1,000/street $750) (Macintosh).

- Macromedia, Inc. SoundEdit 16 2.06 Stereo Mastering software only (list $299/street $250). Two tracks recording and playback, unlimited work tracks, numerous DSP effects, Shockwave Audio support (Macintosh).

- Sonic Foundry, Inc. Sound Forge 4.0 Stereo Mastering software only (list $495/street $349). Two tracks recording and playback, numerous DSP effects, and RealAudio support (Windows 95).

Sequencers: MIDI and digital audio recording and editing applications

A MIDI sequencer is an important component to the web audio studio if you plan to compose music with several synthesizers or tone generators. In the past few years, the industry has seen a convergence between MIDI and digital audio applications. It is now standard to buy one application, such as Studio Vision Pro or Logic Audio, that records both MIDI data and digital audio. The number of simultaneous MIDI and audio playback tracks depends on your computer hardware, CPU speed, and external I/O sound card.

The MIDI component of a sequencer functions like a standard digital audio application with all the familiar controls—record, stop, play, fast forward, rewind, loop mode, and so on. However, a MIDI sequencer does not actually record the sound output of a synthesizer. It merely records the actions that triggered certain sounds, much the same as an old-time piano role.

Because a sequencer records actions only as text-based commands, it has many speed and editing advantages over hard-disk recording. A 10-minute MIDI composition with 4 separate playback tracks takes only 40 KB on your hard disk, while the same digital audio file requires a giant 200 MB in disk space.

The main disadvantage to MIDI is that you can playback and record only the limited palette of sounds stored inside your synthesizer. MIDI cannot store, record, or transmit digital sounds. If you record voice-overs or live instruments, you will have to use the digital audio hard-disk recording feature of your MIDI sequencer. Note that most companies offer free trial demos of their MIDI software packages on the Web.

Pro option

High-end sequencing packages offer professional I/O support for Digidesign's Digital Audio Engine or other proprietary systems, real-time effects plug-ins, and unlimited simultaneous MIDI tracks. Note that each package listed in both the pro and budget options includes the compatibility information with Macintosh and Windows operating systems.

- Steinberg Cubase Audio XT 3.5 MIDI* and multitrack digital audio with real-time effects and EQ (list $799/street $550) (Macintosh and Windows 3.1, 95, 98) *Best Buy

- Opcode Studio Vision Pro 3.5 MIDI and multitrack digital audio, easiest MIDI application to use (list $995/street $700) (Macintosh only)

- Emagic Logic Audio 3.0 MIDI and multitrack digital audio (list $799/street $550) (Macintosh and Windows 95, 98)

Budget option

Low-end sequencing packages provide few effects-processing features, no I/O support, and in some cases no digital audio recording or editing.

- Steinberg Cubase AV* no frills MIDI and multitrack digital audio, 8 audio tracks, 16 MIDI tracks (list $99/street $79) (Macintosh and Windows 3.1, 95, 98) *Best Buy

- Emagic, Logic Audio Discovery 1.1 MIDI and digital audio (list $299/street $199) (Macintosh and Windows 95, 98)

- Opcode, Vision 3.5 MIDI and multitrack digital audio (list $395/street $279) (Macintosh only)

Synthesizers and tone generators

Even the most rudimentary forms of sound design require some type of musical element or ambient background texture. The easiest way to generate different background washes and musical sounds is with a MIDI synthesizer or tone generator. If you plan on doing sound design and music composition, you will need to purchase a synthesizer keyboard or a MIDI controller with an outboard tone generator.

Avoid synths that have built-in sequencers; you will not need them if you use a computer-based MIDI sequencer application. There are a huge variety of keyboards on the market that cater to a wide range of tastes. Spend a good amount of time listening to the built-in presets and features before you buy. If you are purchasing your first keyboard, buy one that produces a wide range of sounds, from piano to strings to percussion.

Pro option

Professional keyboards have weighted piano keys, extra RAM for longer-playing waveform samples, a minimum of 64 voice polyphony (64 simultaneous MIDI instruments), additional DSP chips for ultrarealistic audio replication, and some method or form of input card for importing custom digital samples. If you have several synthesizers, as is common in professional studios, you will need to purchase an additional MIDI patchbay to route the MIDI signals to your MIDI controller.

- Korg Trinity Rack Synth,* 48 kHz samples, best prestocked in-house sounds (list $1,400/street $1,200) *Best Buy*

- Kurzweil K2500, no specs or pricing provided

- Korg Z1 Analog Synth* with physical modeling (list $2,800/street $2,000) *Best Buy*

- Yamaha EX-5

- Emu Esynth

Budget option

Low-end synthesizers have nonweighted keys and fewer DSP chips and RAM. Fortunately, synth technology has improved dramatically over the past few years, enabling low-end models under a $1,000 to closely meet professional standards.

- Alesis QS6 Synth*, 64 voice polyphony, aftertouch, 48 kHz samples (list $1,100/street $799) *Best Buy*

Mixers

The mixer is the Grand Central Station of the sound studio. Audio mixing boards connect and route all the input and output signals from one component to another. Mixing boards also have signal processing capabilities such as equalization and effects for outboard reverb and delay. Mixers save you from the headache and hassle of patching together different pieces of equipment for common, day-to-day studio tasks. Mixers are often used for routing output signals from a DAT machine, CD player, or microphone into a sound card and back out to a set of studio reference monitors.

Five tips for selecting the best audio equipment retailer

1. Get a recommendation from someone you trust. When you get a good recommendation, make sure to get the name of a specific salesperson. When you speak with the salesperson, mention the name of the customer who referred you.

2. Check to see if the company has a high employee turnover rate. Ask the salespeople how long they have worked at the company.

3. Go in with a question you know the answer to, to see if the salesperson gives you an honest response. The salesperson should be knowledgeable enough to properly answer your questions. Especially make sure they are up-to-speed on digital audio. Ask a salesperson what MIDI stands for and see if they give you an informative answer. They should at least tell you that MIDI stands for Musical Instrument Digital Interface.

4. Call the Better Business Bureau to find out if any complaints have been filed against the company.

5. Finally, check out a music retailer's commitment to customer service. A good music retailer will help you buy the product you need, even if they have to refer you to another retailer who has the item in stock. An honest retailer will ask questions to find out what components suit your needs instead of only pointing you in the direction of overstocked items the store wants to push. Ask the salesperson if he or she has to meet sales quotas. A consumer-friendly retailer will not have sales quotas. (Remember that all sales people have some type of commission plan, but not all stores implement sales quotas.) Generally, the large nationwide retail outlets have high sales quotas and heavy employee turnover. Finally, call them on the phone before you go in and see if they are responsive to your questions.

Once you find a good audio equipment dealer and have purchased your gear, stay in touch with the salesperson. A good salesperson will be more than happy to provide information and technical help. The more a salesperson gets to know you, the more likely he or she will give you honest and straightforward answers. Do not ask 30 minutes of questions and then run across town to buy the same item for 5 bucks less elsewhere.

The key component of a mixing board is the signal-to-noise (s/n) ratio, measured in dB. A good mixer will introduce less noise into the signal than a poor one. The best way to tell if a mixer has low noise is to plug in some headphones or monitor speakers, turn up all the faders on the board without turning on any sound, and then turn up the main output levels. If you hear excessive hiss and noise, then the mixer has a poor s/n ratio. If you hear only a little or none at all, then the mixer has a good s/n ratio.

Pro option

Professional-grade mixers use good electronic components for every knob, circuit, and switch to avoid adding system noise into the audio signal. One of the key components of good mixer is high-quality mic pre-amps. Expensive mic pre-amps can drive up the price of a good mixer considerably because a mixer needs a mic pre-amp for every input channel.

- Allen & Heath Mix Wizard 20 Analog 20×8×2* mixer with eight mic inputs, four-band EQ with sweepable mids (list $1,295/street $1,100), 101dB signal-to-noise ratio *Best Buy*

- Mackie CR1604-VLZ Analog 16×4×2 mixer with 16 mic inputs (list $1,199/street $899), 90dB signal-to-noise ratio

- Alesis Studio 32 Analog 16×4×2 mixer with 16 mic inputs, 16 inline tape returns (list $1,200/street $1,000)

Budget option

Low-end mixers use cheaper components and produce more system noise. Even a relatively small 12-channel mixer has over 400 knobs, switches, and inputs alone, excluding the internal circuitry. Unless manufacturers are paying pennies for these components, they cannot make a profit on a $500 mixer. Compared to 10 years ago, the gap in sound quality between super high-end models and low-end models is closing. Most studios, with the exception of a few high-end venues, use Mackie mixers.

- SoundCraft Spirit Analog 12×2×2 mixer* with four mic inputs (list $350/street $295), 90dB signal-to-noise ratio *Best Buy*

- Mackie MS1202-VLZ Analog 12×2×2 mixer with four mic inputs (list $429/street $349), 88dB signal-to-noise ratio (The 1402-VLZ offers linear faders for a little bit more money.)

Digital mixers

Any of the new digital mixers can boost the audio quality of a studio. One reason for this is that the audio signal remains entirely in digital form once it enters the mixer and is routed through various internal effects without the degradation caused by repeated digital-to-analog (D/A) and analog-to-digital (A/D) conversions. Although the price tag may seem hefty, digital mixers are a bargain for a new installation because they include many channels of high-quality compression and other effects that otherwise would have to be purchased as separate pieces of gear. They also offer snapshot and synchronized automation features that make recording sessions very efficient.

Pro option

More and more manufacturers are producing all-digital mixing boards with superior built-in effects and super-high signal-to-noise ratios. Mixing digitally avoids the danger of getting analog system noise. If you have a high-end Pro Tools system with digital inputs hooked up to a digital mixer, you can stay entirely in the digital realm, from multitrack to mix-down.

- Mackie Db8 72 input channels (list $10,000)
- Panasonic DA-7* 48 input channels (list $5000) *Best Buy*
- Yamaha O3D Digital 26×4×2 mixer with eight mic inputs (list $3,699/street $2,999), 110dB signal-to-noise ratio

Budget option

Cheaper digital equipment means more system noise and less inputs and outputs.

- Tascam DM-1000 16-channel digital mixer with 6 analog inputs and 6 digital inputs, 4 XLR mic inputs with phantom power (list $1,299/street $995), 80dB signal-to-noise ratio

Studio reference monitors

High-quality studio reference speakers, or monitors, accurately reproduce a "flat," transparent representation of your audio without adding coloration, distortion, noise, or equalization. Consumer stereo speakers, by contrast, are designed to boost the high and low audio frequencies to sound good on the sales floor. Unlike home stereo speakers, reference speakers are designed to give you the most accurate sound, not the most pleasant.

Experienced engineers rely on their favorite reference speakers to give them a consistent reference to their sound. They rely on the same reference speakers or a set of speakers every time they mix-down their audio tracks. Serious engineers will even bring their favorite reference monitors along from one recording studio to another. Just as every computer monitor screen displays colors slightly differently, every brand of studio "near field" reference speakers produce a slightly different sound. Most good-quality reference speakers give an accurate, "flat" representation of the audio frequency spectrum.

The most important step is to use the same set of speakers every time you listen to your audio mixes. A favorite trick of savvy recording engineers is to play popular CDs on their reference speakers to hear how other mixes sound on their system.

Pro option

The professional choice is to use self-powered studio speakers. A self-powered, gnarled monitoring system contains a power amp built into each speaker. There are several advantages to using self-powered speakers: you eliminate the need for a noisy standalone power amp; you are guaranteed that the power going to your speakers is always the right amount (often standalone power amps deliver too much or too little power to your speakers); and it's easier to transport self-powered speakers if you travel to another studio.

- Event 20/20 Self-powered,* nearfield monitoring system (list $1,000/street $999) *Best Buy

- Genelec 1029A Self-powered, nearfield monitoring system (list $2,000/street $1,800)

- Hafler Self-powered, nearfield monitoring system (list $1,400/street $1,200)

- Mackie HR 824- Self-powered nearfield monitoring system (list $1,500/street $1,000)

Budget option

The standard option is to use a pair of reference monitors powered by a standalone power amp. Alesis sells the relatively inexpensive RA-100 power amp for $299.

- Event 20/20 reference speakers* (list $400/street $340) *Best Buy

- Tannoy SBM reference speakers (list $295/street $250)

- KRK K-ROK reference speakers (list $500/street $425)

Effects processors

Ever since the first spring box reverb unit took the rock world by storm, effects processors have become the all-powerful magic box of the sound studio. Instantly replicating the sound of huge cathedrals, concert halls, and echoing canyon walls, effects processors offer the sound designer a world of possibilities that were once cost-prohibitive or completely impossible. As more recording and editing is performed on the computer, effects processing will be performed solely through software plug-ins instead of outboard gear. For the time being, most people find it more convenient to use both outboard effects processors and internal software plug-ins.

Pro option

High-end effects processors give you better overall audio fidelity and longer, more accurate reverbs and delays. A rich sounding 10-second delay or reverb requires tremendous processing power and RAM.

- TC Electronic, Wizard/M2000 Reverb,* delay, chorus, flange, and more (list $1,995/street $1,600), 20-bit/20-bit ADC/DAC, max delay time 1,200 ms, XLR AES/EBU digital outputs *Best Buy*

- Lexicon, PCM90 Reverb, delay, chorus, flange, and more (list $2,995/street $2,500), 18-bit/18-bit ADC/DAC, max delay time 2500 ms, RCA S/PDIF digital outputs

Budget option

Low-end processors produce more noise and have less RAM for long reverb and delay effects. Effects boxes such as the Alesis Microverb loop a two-second portion of the reverb in order to produce a long decay.

- Alesis, Microverb Reverb,* delay, chorus, flange, and more (list $299/street $225), 18-bit/18-bit ADC/DAC, max delay time 1,300 ms, no digital outputs *Best Buy*

- Alesis, Q2 Reverb, delay, chorus, flange, and more (list $799/ street $675). 18-bit/18-bit ADC/DAC, max delay time 5,400 ms, no digital outputs (mid-range effects processor)

- A.R.T. Effects 1 Reverb, delay, chorus, and flange (list $169/street $135), 18-bit/18-bit ADC/DAC, max delay time 1,300 ms, no digital outputs

DAT (digital audio tape) recorders

A DAT is a miniaturized version of a VHS tape and is the professional recording standard for stereo mix-downs and mastering. Even if you choose to store your stereo master recordings as audio files on a hard disk or CD-ROM instead of a DAT tape, it is certain that clients will bring you their audio source materials on a DAT at some point in time. If you are creating a professional studio, you will need a DAT player.

If you are on a tight budget and do not plan on working with high-end clients, you can skip the DAT player and mix-down your audio to stereo master files for storage on a hard disk or backup storage media. As the prices of CD recorders keep dropping, more and more digital audio professionals are switching from DAT stereo masters to CD-ROM audio masters. However, most professional recording and mastering engineers still prefer to use DAT for final mix-down masters.

Pro option

DAT machines feature high-speed tape reel mechanisms that are prone to stop working, or worse, eat your tape and ruin a good recording session. With high-end machines, you are more likely to get reliable playback and recording over time as well as higher-quality analog to digital converters.

- Panasonic SV 3800 DAT* (list $1,695/street $1,400). 18-bit/20-bit ADC/DAC, 92dB signal-to-noise ratio, XLR inputs. *Best Buy

- Sony PCM R500 DAT (list $1,695/street $1,400), 20-bit/16-bit ADC/DAC, XLR inputs.

- Tascam DA-45 MKII DAT (list $2,500/street $1,900), 24-bit/20-bit ADC/DAC, 113dB signal-to-noise ratio, XLR inputs.

Budget option

The following options contain lower-quality components (higher system noise) and lower-quality RCA inputs instead of XLR inputs:

- Sony R300 DAT* (list $1,000/street $799), 20-bit/16-bit ADC/DAC, RCA inputs. *Best Buy

- Tascam DA-20 DAT (list $999/street $850), 20-bit/16-bit ADC/DAC, RCA inputs

Sound studio accessories

The following accessories are essential to good recording and production in the studio. Since these accessories are not the big-ticket items, they are often overlooked. Do not make the mistake of spending a few thousand dollars on mixers and microphones and then get cheap cables or headphones.

Headphones

Good studio reference headphones let you hear subtle details and noises that are difficult to detect with studio monitors. Several sets of high-quality headphones that completely cover the ears are necessary for voice-over recording sessions and critical sound-editing applications. Headphones also serve as a monitoring system during recording sessions where a live microphone is in the same vicinity as your studio reference monitors. Do not use cheap headphones. For under $100, buy the industry favorite, Sony MDR-7506 or AKG headphones.

Six ways to get the best deals every time

Getting the best deals and service is an art form. Everyone knows that music retailers never sell for list price, but how far they will come down is anyone's guess. All audio equipment manufacturers offer retailers different wholesale percentage discounts. High-end specialty companies such as Mesa-Boogie generally sell their gear to retailers at only 30% off list, while other companies such as Alesis sell their low-end items to retailers at 40% to 50% off list. There is no formula to wholesale pricing in the music retail business. Do not expect to get the same percentage discount for every brand. Generally, retailers are making less of a profit than you think. The average markup on products is 20% to 27%. In many cases, their sale price might be only 5% to 10% above cost. That 10% to 27% margin is what keeps the music store alive.

1. Research prices before you buy. Do your homework. Before you buy equipment, look at a few mail-order catalogs and make a few phone calls to get an idea what the going rate is for the particular item you are looking to purchase.

2. Look for overstocked blow-out items. Music retailers give greater discounts on items in stock. Watch for blow-out sales when retailers have too many items in stock and need to move inventory.

3. Look for old demo models. Music retailers as a rule do not always give discounts on demo models. But on occasion, if you think the model has been on the floor for a long time and it has a few nicks or dings, it is worth asking for a small discount. Also look for last year's models. Most manufacturers update their models periodically. Often retailers are forced to discount previous models if newer versions have arrived.

4. Shop at the end of the month. If you are shopping at a large retail chain, go at the end of the month when salespeople have to meet their sales quota, or better yet, shop at a store where salespeople don't have quotas.

5. Mention the competition. Before you discuss specific prices with the salesperson, let him or her know in a tactful manner that you are aware of the competition. In passing conversation, drop a name or two of the other retail stores in town. Where appropriate, be direct. If another store gives you a good price, ask the salesperson to beat or match it.

6. Buy all your gear at one time. If you are buying several items at once, retailers will give you a few extra percentage points off as a package deal, as well as discounts on accessories such as cables.

High-quality cables

Cables are the last item anyone wants to spend money on, but considering that they transmit all the electrical signals in the studio, it is worth the extra money to buy high-quality cables with reinforced connectors and proper shielding. Cheap, poor quality cables produce noise and interference, and they break frequently.

Do not buy cheap cables. One bad cable can ruin an entire recording session and render all your high-quality gear useless. If you are adept at electronics and soldering, the best option is to buy long runs of specialized audio cables for all your studio components and attach the appropriate XLR or 1/4 connector yourself for each length of cable. This is generally the technique for large professional studios where hundreds of audio cables are needed. Look for Mogami audio cables—they have a reputation for manufacturing the best cables in the industry.

If you are configuring a large-scale studio, you will have to special-order audio cables direct from the manufacturer or from a distributor such as Markertek at *http://www.markertek.com*. For small studios, it is easier to buy premade high-quality cables. For premade cables, you should expect to pay anywhere from $20 to $30 each.

Sound libraries

A set of sound effects CDs is an indispensable tool for any sound designer under tight deadline or budget constraints. We cannot tell you the number of times that a soundtrack called for a particular, hard-to-capture sound that would have been nearly impossible to get ourselves if it were not for sound libraries. It may be a bus traveling down the street, or a bird singing on cue for exactly 11 seconds, or even a particular door slam or footstep sound. For each of these noises, we could go right to our sound libraries, import the desired sound into our editor, and be done.

You can purchase high-quality, royalty-free professional sound effects CDs for $50 to $100 for approximately 90 minutes of sounds or upwards of $1,000 for an entire collection. The Hollywood Edge offers some of the best production sound libraries in the industry. In fact, we use The Hollywood Edge "Premiere Edition" sound effects for all our sound design projects at Raspberry Media. A sampling of 80 royalty-free sounds can be found at *http://www.designingwebaudio.com*.

For a low-cost alternative, you can download audio clips from a variety of web sites that provide free or low-cost sound effects. A few are listed in the "Web resources" section in this appendix. Beware: cheap sound effects packages generally contain poorer-quality audio files with more noise and glitches than high-end packages.

Disk repair and optimization utilities

If you do any hard-disk recording, you will need to optimize your hard drive at least once a month, if not every week. It is always a good idea to optimize your hard disk before an important recording session. Due to the speed that hard drives read and write digital audio files, it is highly critical that there is enough contiguous hard disk space for each recording session. Fragmented disks are the leading cause of audio system crashes and error warnings. Norton Utilities is the industry standard for hard drive repairs and optimization.

Audio plug-ins and utilities

With the steady rise of hard-disk-based recording and editing, more and more effects processing is being done internally with software. An ever-increasing number of outboard analog equipment manufactories, such as Lexicon, Focusrite, and dbx, and traditional audio software companies, such as Waves and Audio Ease, have introduced digital software plug-ins for Pro Tools and other hard-disk recording applications. Internal software plug-ins allow you to keep the audio signal entirely in the digital domain from recording to editing to final mix-down.

The most useful plug-in or utility you will want to purchase is a batch conversion and processing application such as Waves' Wave Convert Pro or Audio Ease's BarbaBatch. Both batch processors convert Macintosh and PC audio files between sample rates, word lengths, channels (stereo/mono) and file types (AIFF, SDII, *.wav*, *.ra*, *.swa*, QuickTime) while retaining optimal sound quality. As well as converting sound files to alternate file formats, they perform dynamics effects such as normalization, equalization, and peak limiting.

Wave Convert Pro from Waves runs native on Macintosh and is available for Windows 98 (*http://www.waves.com*). BarbaBatch runs on Macintosh (*http://www.audioease.com*).

Pop screens

Pop screens are essential for reducing wind and explosive P's and S's in voice-over recording sessions. A pop-screen is a circular hoop with a thin nylon material that rests directly between the speaker's mouth and the microphone. Pop screens may be found in most music stores. In a pinch, you can get away with using a homemade method that many engineers have used in the past before pop screens were manufactured. Take a nylon stocking and stretch it over a framing device, such as a bent metal clothes hanger or embroidery hoop, and then tape it to the mic stand with duct tape.

Web resources

For those on a tight budget, you can download shareware audio applications, MIDI files, and sound effects. We have provided a list of web sites that offer audio resources.

Digital audio software

The following sites contain software for writing, editing, and playing music, including analysis utilities and programs for generating effects, tuning instruments, learning music, converting file formats, printing scores, and many other handy utilities:

Shareware Music Machine (http://www.hitsquad.com/smm)
  Shareware Music Machine claims to be the largest music software site on the Internet for free and shareware music programs for music-making professionals, enthusiasts, and listeners. Indeed, they have a wealth of interesting programs for Macintosh, Windows 95 and 3.0, OS/2, DOS, and even Atari.

Cool Edit for Windows (http://www.syntrillium.com/cool.htm)
  Cool Edit by Syntrillium Software Corp. is a sound editor for Windows available as shareware for $25 and $50. Cool Edit provides a variety of special effects: reverberation, noise reduction, echo and delay, flanging, filtering, and many others.

Computer Music Programs for the Macintosh (http://shoko.calarts.edu/ ~tre/CompMusMac)
  This site features various shareware and freeware sound utilities, editors, and processors for the Macintosh.

MIDI files and sequencers

The following sites contain information on MIDI shareware and freeware, MIDI-sequencing software, and public domain MIDI files for Macintosh and Windows:

MIDIWeb (http://www.midiweb.com)
  The MIDIWeb™ contains a huge resource of information on MIDI-related subjects including many interesting DIY projects and some demo-, share-, and freeware programs. The MIDIWeb also features a discussion forum and links to other MIDI resources.

MIDI Farm (http://www.midifarm.com/midifarm/free.shtml)
  The MIDI Farm offers resources and information about all things MIDI including a helpful links page.

Music Machines (http://www.hyperreal.com/machines/)

Music Machines claims to be the home of musical electronics on the Web. Music Machines offers images, software, schematics, and lots of tips and comments from electronic musicians all over the Internet. You will find information about MIDI, synthesizers, effects, drum machines, and recording equipment.

Shareware Music Machine (http://www.hitsquad.com/smm)

Shareware Music Machine claims to be the largest music software site on the Internet for free and shareware music programs for music-making professionals, enthusiasts, and listeners. Indeed, they have a wealth of interesting programs for Macintosh, Windows 95 and 3.0, OS/2, DOS, and even Atari.

MIDILink Musician's Network (http://www.xnet.com/~midilink/)

Another useful site with MIDI resources, information, and links.

Classical MIDI Archives (http://www.prs.net/midi.html)

This site offers thousands of public domain classical MIDI files.

Sound effects and samples

The following sites contain free sound effects and digital samples for a variety of keyboards in *.wav, .aiff,* and other file formats:

Sound Central (http://www.soundcentral.com)

Sound Central contains samples for computers (*.wav, .au, .aiff,* etc.), samples/sounds for keyboards (Ensoniq, Korg, etc.), MIDI files, and many freeware and shareware programs for all platforms.

Sound FX Page (http://www.vionline.com/sound.html)

This site offers an archive of useful sound effects including animal sounds, bells and whistles, body sounds, car sounds, clock sounds, drum sounds, gun sounds, horns, laugh sounds, multi-FX sounds, and miscellaneous sound FX in *.wav* format.

Summary

The information in this appendix is intended to take some of the anxiety, confusion, and mystery out of buying audio gear. Creating the ultimate web sound studio should be an exciting adventure, not a frightening journey into the great unknown. As you configure your system, remember that achieving high-quality web audio is the end result of superb talent, engineering skill, and excellent equipment. Good equipment alone will not produce great audio. Take time to read the equipment manuals and try to get the best possible voice or musical talent available. Pay a little extra money to hire an experienced voice-over artist or musician. Read Chapter 2, *The Science of*

Sound and Digital Audio, Chapter 3, *Capturing Original Source Material*, and Chapter 4, *Optimizing Your Sound Files*, to learn the basic engineering concepts and skills required to properly use your equipment.

AUDIO FORMAT COMPARISON

The following tables will help you select the web audio broadcasting format appropriate for your needs.

RealMedia

Capability	Rating
Browser compatibility and percent of browsers with Plug-in	Excellent.
Interactive sound design capabilities	Fair. Format is designed primarily for streaming media. Simple synchronized media presentations such as slide shows, audio with moving text, captions, and pictures.
Software cost for encoding and streaming	Free to $695 to $21,595+. Basic Server with 25 simultaneous streams is free. Basic Server Plus (60 streams) costs $695. The full-featured Internet Solutions Server (400 streams) costs $21,595.
Level of documentation and support	Outstanding.
Audio encoding and content generation	Easy.
Audio authoring and delivery	Medium to Easy. Medium difficulty to set up dedicated RealServer. Easy to post RealAudio files on standard web server for playback without bandwidth negotiation and other dedicated server features, etc.
Audio fidelity and compression	Excellent.
Low-bandwidth performance	Good/Excellent. RealNetworks' RealServer provides bandwidth negotiation for all types of bandwidth connections from 14.4 Kbps modems to T1 lines. RealMedia is designed to look at the user connection speed and then serve a stream that is optimized for that user's connection.
Server performance and quality of software tools for large-scale streaming	Outstanding—RealServer. RealNetworks has the most sophisticated servers, hands down. RealMedia running on Unix is the preferred method for the most robust and reliable streaming possible.

MP3

Capability	Rating
Browser compatibility and percent of browsers with Plug-in	Excellent.
Interactive sound design capabilities	Limited/None. Technology is a compression format, not a multi-media authoring environment.
Software cost for encoding and streaming	Free to inexpensive. Small licensing fee may apply for professional applications. No dedicated server required for posting downloadable files.
Level of documentation and support	Limited.
Audio encoding and content generation	Easy.
Audio authoring and delivery	Difficult to Easy. Installation of SHOUTcast server for MP3 streaming requires Unix programming expertise. Posting MP3 files on a standard web server for downloading is easy.
Audio fidelity and compression	Outstanding. Depends on the rate.
Low-bandwidth performance	Excellent. MP3 shines in low-bandwidth environments. To the discerning listener, the MP3 encoding algorithm produces the most ear-pleasing and natural form of audio degradation after compression for 28.8 bandwidth environments.
Server performance and quality of software tools for large-scale streaming	Good—SHOUTcast Server. But primarily a downloadable format. Streaming options such as SHOUTcast are becoming more widespread. Currently very few tools available for large-scale broadcasting.

Windows Media

Capability	Rating
Browser compatibility and percent of browsers with Plug-in	Excellent.
Interactive sound design capabilities	Fair. Format is designed primarily for streaming audio. Simple synchronized media presentations such as slide shows, audio with moving text, captions, and pictures.
Software cost for encoding and streaming	Free. Must have NT/Windows 2000.
Level of documentation and support	Good.
Audio encoding and content generation	Easy.
Audio authoring and delivery	Medium. Requires Windows NT expertise. Windows Media Server comes pre-installed on NT.
Audio fidelity and compression	Good.
Low-bandwidth performance	Good.
Server performance and quality of software tools for large-scale streaming	Excellent—Microsoft NT/Windows 2000 Server. Windows Media provides good support for large-scale broadcasting of thousands of simultaneous steams. Does not support the Unix platform.

QuickTime

Capability	Rating
Browser compatibility and percent of browsers with Plug-in	Excellent.
Interactive sound design capabilities	Fair. Technology is a compression format and widely used playback standard, not a multimedia authoring environment.
Software cost for encoding and streaming	Free to $1,000+. Free to encode QuickTime and place downloadable files on web server. Large-scale managed streaming requires Mac OS X Server, which starts at over $1,000.
Level of documentation and support	Fair.
Audio encoding and content generation	Easy.
Audio authoring and delivery	Easy. No programming expertise is required to set up Mac OS X Server.
Audio fidelity and compression	Excellent. Q Design Music encoding technology.
Low-bandwidth performance	Excellent.
Server performance and quality of software tools for large-scale streaming	Good—Mac OS X Server. QuickTime support large-scale broadcasting. Number of streams depends on hardware configuration and bandwidth capacity.

Liquid Audio

Capability	Rating
Browser compatibility and percent of browsers with Plug-in	Poor.
Interactive sound design capabilities	Limited/None. Format is designed solely for music distribution. Audio synced to video or text for music video simulation.
Software cost for encoding and streaming	$1,000+. Basic starting level software package costs about $1,000.
Level of documentation and support	Good.
Audio encoding and content generation	Medium.
Audio authoring and delivery	Medium. As a format designed for specific professional applications, Liquid Audio provides detailed support and automated setup functions.
Audio fidelity and compression	Excellent. Supports MP3 compression.
Low-bandwidth performance	Fair. Although Liquid Audio is designed for previewing audio files in low-bandwidth environments, downloading large Liquid Audio files is best suited for high-bandwidth connections.
Server performance and quality of software tools for large-scale streaming	Good—Liquid Server. Note that Liquid Server is primarily designed for secure music sales and distribution.

Flash

Capability	Rating
Browser compatibility and percent of browsers with Plug-in	Excellent.
Interactive sound design capabilities	Excellent. Format is both a popular playback standard and a multimedia authoring environment. Button rollovers, transitions, sound effects, loops, and audio synced to animation.
Software cost for encoding and streaming	$200+. Must purchase Flash application to export Flash files. Format does not require dedicated server.
Level of documentation and support	Excellent.
Audio encoding and content generation	Easy.
Audio authoring and delivery	Medium to Easy. Easy to encode Flash audio and place on standard web server for HTTP delivery. Medium difficulty to author Flash content.
Audio fidelity and compression	Outstanding/Poor. Embedded sound effects and loops compressed with the MP3 compression technology sound great. Longer-playing streaming files tend to drop out.
Low-bandwidth performance	Poor. Flash is not designed as a streaming playback medium. Flash streaming audio does not perform well in low-bandwidth environments. In contrast, Flash sound effects and loops work great with Flash's compact vector animation.
Server performance and quality of software tools for large-scale streaming	Poor/Fair. The Flash format does not support large-scale broadcasting. RealFlash does support large-scale broadcasting when used with Real Networks RealServer.

Director Shockwave

Capability	Rating
Browser compatibility and percent of browsers with Plug-in	Fair.
Interactive sound design capabilities	Excellent. Technology is designed to compress multimedia files as well as create them with advanced Lingo scripting. Advanced button rollovers, transitions, sound effects, loops, audio synced to animation, scriptable fade-ins and fade-outs, and more.
Software cost for encoding and streaming	$900+. Must purchase Director to export Shockwave files. Format does not require dedicated server.
Level of documentation and support	Good.
Audio encoding and content generation	Easy.
Audio authoring and delivery	Hard. Director is a powerful multimedia authoring environment that takes time to master.
Audio fidelity and compression	Excellent. Shockwave audio files compressed with the MPEG codec in Director sound great.
Low-bandwidth performance	Poor. Shockwave files often drop out if a user's bandwidth fluctuates. Shockwave and Flash audio streaming works best for users with 56 Kbps or DSL modem speeds.
Server performance and quality of software tools for large-scale streaming	Poor/Fair—HTTP Pseudo-Streaming. The Director Shockwave format does not support large-scale broadcasting.

Beatnik

Capability	Rating
Browser compatibility and percent of browsers with Plug-in	Fair.
Interactive sound design capabilities	Outstanding. Format is built for sound designers. Advanced button rollovers, transitions, sound effects, and loops.
Software cost for encoding and streaming	$10 to $100. Inexpensive to purchase Beatnik software package. More expensive if you want direct consulting and support from Beatnik engineers.
Level of documentation and support	Good.
Audio encoding and content generation	Difficult. Must have familiarity with composing MIDI scores and editing digital audio samples.
Audio authoring and delivery	Difficult. Beatnik requires a fairly complex setup and testing process to encode hybrid MIDI audio files into the Beatnik format and to develop the Java-Scripts necessary for synchronized playback.
Audio fidelity and compression	Outstanding/Good. Supports MP3 compression. Overall playback sound quality is phenomenal relative to file size. Note, Beatnik is not a format for encoding streaming audio files.
Low-bandwidth performance	Outstanding
Server performance and quality of software tools for large-scale streaming	Poor/Fair—HTTP Pseudo-Streaming. However, Beatnik files are generally very small so they download quickly making true streaming not as necessary as with other more bandwidth intensive formats.

MIDI

Capability	Rating
Browser compatibility and percent of browsers with Plug-in	Excellent.
Interactive sound design capabilities	Limited. Format is designed for song compression and to allow electronic devices to communicate, not as a multimedia authoring environment. Button rollovers.
Software cost for encoding and streaming	Free to $100+. If you already have MIDI files, you can post them to a web server for free. To create your own MIDI, files you will need to purchase a MIDI editor such as Vision or Cubase.
Level of documentation and support	Limited/None.
Audio encoding and content generation	Difficult. Must have familiarity with MIDI authoring environments such as Vision, Cubase, Performer, etc.
Audio authoring and delivery	Easy. Easy to place MIDI files on a standard web server for playback.
Audio fidelity and compression	Fair. Note, since MIDI is not a digital audio format but a form of music notation, audio fidelity is dependent on the user's sound card and sound engine.
Low-bandwidth performance	Outstanding
Server performance and quality of software tools for large-scale streaming	Poor/Fair—HTTP pseudo-streaming from a standard web server.

WAV and AIFF

Capability	Rating
Browser compatibility and percent of browsers with Plug-in	Excellent.
Interactive sound design capabilities	Limited. Simply a file format for playback over PC (WAV) and Macintosh (AIFF). Button rollovers.
Software cost for encoding and streaming	Free. Can export WAV or AIFF files from any standard audio editing application including free Open Source audio editing applications.
Level of documentation and support	Limited/None.
Audio encoding and content generation	Easy. Easy to export AIFF or WAV files from any standard audio editing application.
Audio authoring and delivery	Easy. Easy to place WAV or AIFF files on a standard web server for downloading.
Audio fidelity and compression	Poor/None. Large WAV and AIFF sound files sound good when uncompressed. Neither offer elegant compression for high fidelity with small file sizes over limited bandwidths.
Low-bandwidth performance	Poor. WAV and AIFF work best as uncompressed 16-bit 44.1 kHz or 22.5 kHz sound files and are thus not suited for playback in low-bandwidth environments.
Server performance and quality of software tools for large-scale streaming	Poor/None. WAV and AIFF are merely audio file types—not proprietary formats such as RealMedia that include server-side technologies.

GLOSSARY

Acoustics

Term used to describe the science of sound as well as how sound travels through particular environments. Sound waves reflect and disperse off of various surfaces in our environment, such as a wall or trees or even people. These sound waves travel through the air, bouncing off objects before they reflect back to our ears. We rarely ever hear the pure direct vibration of a sound wave before it is masked or altered by the coloration of thousands of small reflections.

Active Streaming File (ASF)

Microsoft's proprietary streaming media format.

AIFF (Audio Interchange File Format)

Standard Macintosh file format commonly used on the Internet.

Aliasing

A type of quantization error or digital distortion that occurs during analog to digital conversion. Sampling rates that are too low to accurately reproduce a sound often cause aliasing or unwanted sound artifacts such as a low rumbling or "woosh" noise.

Ambient Soundscape or Loop

The term applied to a background audio track or continuous loop that helps set a mood behind the visual content.

Amplitude

The maximum change in air pressure. Amplitude is universally measured in decibels (dB). The metric is used both to measure the loudness of a sound signal and to mark the maximum cut-off point for analog and digital recording. This cut-off is the maximum level before distortion and is called the 0dB point.

Analog Distortion

The term commonly used in analog tape recording or tube amplification when a signal goes above the "red" or maximum recording level. Low-level analog distortion, in contrast to digital distortion, enriches a sound with harmonics and compresses an audio signal, raising the level of quieter sounds.

Auditorials

An online tutorial with an accompanying audio track.

Bandwidth

The term used to describe a range of frequencies. Often bandwidth determines the range of frequencies being amplified or reduced by an equalizer. Generally, you are never boosting or reducing one single frequency but instead a range of frequencies.

Bandwidth Negotiation

A feature of RealNetworks' RealServer 5.0 that ensures that all users receive the appropriate encoded content for the best audio quality at their available bandwidth, from 28.8 Kbps modems to dual ISDN connections.

Batch Processor

A software utility for converting and processing multiple sound files. A batch processor such as Wave Convert Pro (Mac, Windows) or BarbaBatch (Mac) will import an entire folder of audio files, normalize them, perform EQ enhancements, and convert them on the fly to any popular format such as RealAudio.

Beatnik Editor

An application for converting WAV, AIFF, SDII, AU, and standard MIDI files into RMF files. The Beatnik Editor allows you to import unique instruments or sounds to create an entirely new collection of sounds in the Beatnik sound engine.

Beatnik Plug-in

A plug-in that manages the playback of RMF files within a web browser. The plug-in is available free at the Beatnik web site and is supported by Netscape Navigator 3.0 and higher or Internet Explorer 3.0 and higher on both Macintosh and Windows platforms.

Bidirectional Microphone

The term used to describe a microphone that captures sound directly in front and in back of the capsule. For example, a bidirectional mic can be used for recording a duet with musicians on both sides of the microphone.

Bit-Depth

The size of the binary numbers assigned to describe the dynamic value of each sample. The higher the sampling rate and bit-depth, the more accurate the sound reproduction. In particular, higher bit-depths reproduce quieter sounds more accurately.

Cardioid Microphone

A microphone that captures sound directly in front of the capsule, providing maximum noise rejection. Cardioid mics are primarily used for live concert vocal recording and amplification because of the pick-up pattern's excellent feedback-rejection characteristics.

C-events

A RealAudio 3.0 utility that enables the creation of a binary event file for synchronizing web pages with audio.

Clustering

A RealMedia feature that allows multiple RealServers to be configured in a cluster to work as a single machine, exceeding the connection load of a single CPU.

Codecs

An encoding algorithm that compresses and optimizes audio for Internet transmission.

Compressor

A dynamics processor that evens out and compresses incoming audio signals that vary greatly in dynamic range, such as a singer going from a soft whisper to a resounding scream. A compressor allows for the hottest incoming signal without distortion to your sound card by limiting the sounds that peak above the 0dB distortion point. By reducing the amplitude of the loudest sounds with a compressor, you can increase the overall input level of your microphone to capture a "hotter" or louder signal.

dB SPL

Decibels of sound pressure levels, a unit of measurement for the loudness of sound.

Decibel (dB)

A logarithmic unit of sound loudness, audio power, or audio voltage.

De-esser

A dynamics processor or plug-in used to reduce sibilance, or the high frequencies that contain excessive hissing or "S" sounds. De-essers are commonly used to clean up voice-over recordings.

Delay

Sound wave reflections or echoes that strike the ear drum after 40 milliseconds of the original sound. Delay, as opposed to reverb, can be heard as a second distinct sound or echo.

Desktop Audio Recording

The term for hard-disk audio recording and editing on a desktop computer as opposed to an outboard tape recording device.

Destructive Editing

The process of permanently changing or altering the original master file. When a destructive edit is performed, the sound file is permanently altered and then rewritten to disk. In contrast, nondestructive forms of editing never alter or rewrite over the original sound file.

Digital Audio

The term applied to sound that has been digitized into binary code. Sound waves are converted to digital code by means of a circuit that assigns a value or binary set of numbers that correspond to the shape of the incoming electrical wave or current.

Digital Audio Tape (DAT) Machine

A recording device for digital stereo mix-downs and mastering. DAT two-track tapes look like miniaturized VHS tapes and are smaller and more affordable than cumbersome and expensive analog tape reels.

Digital Distortion

The term used to describe a signal that rises over the maximum 0dB point. Digital distortion produces unpleasant noise and unwanted "clicks" and "pops," which are also known as artifacts. Digital encoding, unlike recording to analog tape, cannot quantify signals above 0dB.

Directionality

A microphone's capability to reject unwanted sounds coming from off-axis directions. Each type of microphone has a particular recording range or pick-up pattern.

Director Shockwave

The term applied to Shockwave content authored with Macromedia Director. Director Shockwave leverages the Lingo scripting language to directly interact with the operating system and multimedia functionality of a PC, enabling such capabilities as audio fade-ins and fade-outs, volume and panning control, and audio synchronized with animation and mouse rollovers.

Dry

An adjective used to describe an original sound or audio signal that has not been processed or enhanced with effects such as reverb and delay.

Dynamic Range

The difference between the loudest point of a sound passage and the softest point. Audio systems also have a dynamic range: the difference between the loudest sound the system can record before distortion and the softest signal that can be recorded without introducing noise. This range is measured by the signal-to-noise ratio. The signal is the actual sound you're after; noise is any hiss or other artifact introduced by the amplifier, microphone, or other electrical components of the audio system.

Emblaze

A file format developed by Geo Interactive that allows the playback of any type of media without plug-ins. Emblaze media playback is controlled by a small Java applet that automatically downloads when viewed in 3.0 and later browsers. When a visitor enters a site containing Emblaze content, the small, platform-independent, 50 KB Java applet or Emblaze Player automatically downloads to the user's computer, completely transparent to the web visitor.

Envelope

The term used to describe the shape or contour of the initial attack or ending decay of a sound. Each instrument or sound has a unique envelope or fade-in and fade-out.

Equalization (EQ)

The process of boosting or reducing the amplitude of particular sound frequencies. All sounds are made up of an overall spectrum of frequencies that are simultaneously resonating. Equalization is used to boost or reduce a range of frequencies within the full sound spectrum.

Event Sounds

Short sounds embedded in an interactive movie or web page as opposed to longer streaming audio tracks. Event sounds are triggered by user input and are most commonly used as rollover button sounds.

Fader

A type of volume control knob or slider commonly found on mixing boards.

Feedback
> The term used to describe the wailing or piercing sound that results from a signal loop that occurs when an output signal is fed back into its input.

Field Recording
> The term used for capturing sounds on location with portable recording equipment, as opposed to studio recording in a controlled environment.

Flash
> An authoring environment and file format developed originally by FutureWave Software and later by Macromedia for multimedia creation and delivery over the Web. Macromedia Flash has become the de facto standard for full-scale, high-impact web multimedia. Flash features vector animation technology ideally suited for low-bandwidth connections.

Foley
> The art of providing audio realism to visuals in post production. Foley sounds are often the first sounds added to a film soundtrack and generally include footsteps, sounds of the actors' clothing, and prop movements onscreen such as a closing doors or an object falling to the floor. Foley artists try to emulate the sounds of real life. The term foley artist originally comes from the time when real life actors performed in a recording room making sounds and noises, with various objects, to simulate the sounds of the action on screen.

Frequency
> Rate or speed of a repeating waveform. A sound's frequency determines its pitch. The faster the frequency, which is measured in hertz (Hz) or cycles per second, the higher the pitch.

Frequency Response
> The range of frequencies that a device can reproduce or record. The human ear has a frequency response of roughly 20 to 20,000 Hz.

Frequency Spectrum
> The complete range of frequencies audible to the human ear. Frequency spectrum also refers to the range of frequencies present in a particular sound.

Fundamental
> The lowest harmonic of a given tone or musical sound. A pitch consists of a dominant frequency, as well as multiples of this frequency. These additional frequencies are the harmonics. It is the number and characteristics of the harmonics that help create timbre.

General MIDI

A MIDI standard developed to alleviate the problem of unpredictable playback of MIDI compositions. General MIDI specifies that certain note numbers or MIDI channels will play the same type of instrument, such as a drum or piano, across various devices or synthesizers.

Graphic Equalizer

A machine or dynamics processor that boosts or reduces the amplitude of a range of frequencies. Graphic equalizers generally have sliding levers, known as faders, representing the different ranges of frequencies between 20 and 20,000 Hz— the normal hearing range of a human.

Groovoids

The term for small, premade sound effects and clips that are built into the Beatnik plug-in.

Harmonics

The multiples of a given fundamental frequency. Harmonics affect the characteristics of a particular sound.

Hertz (Hz)

The basic unit for measuring frequency. One hertz is equal to one cycle per second.

High-Pass Filter

An equalization effect that removes all frequencies below a specified point while preserving those that are above the cut-off point. This effect is often used to remove lower bass sounds, such as a rumble of an automobile engine or the sound of a jet plane flying overhead.

HyperText Transfer Protocol (HTTP)

An Internet transmission protocol designed for transferring documents, files, and email over the Internet; primarily suited for the transfer of web pages.

Impedance

The resistance to current flow. Sounds are colored by the material and substances they travel through. A voice projected through a wall will sound different than a voice projected directly into the ear. As sound travels through the dense materials of a wall, the high-frequency energy is absorbed into the wood leaving behind only the lower frequencies. A voice spoken directly into the ear, on the other hand, will produce an unbearably loud sound. Without the impedance of a wall or other sound-absorbing materials, the energy of the higher frequencies of the voice travel straight to the ear drum.

Interactive Sound Design

    The term applied to integrating sound into a non-linear interactive media format such as a Flash movie or a CD-ROM.

IP Multicasting

    A RealServer feature that allows all users of a network or intranet to listen to a single live stream, making efficient use of network resources. Multicasting, instead of many simultaneous point-to-point connections, delivers a stream to a certain point in the network where it knows other users are requesting the same file.

Java

    A cross-platform programming language developed by Sun Microsystems.

LAN (Local Area Network)

    A computer network designed to serve a local facility that is no larger than a few square miles.

Lavaliere Clip-on Microphone

    A thumbnail-sized microphone designed for inconspicuously capturing close-proximity voices. Lavaliere microphones are commonly used for video shoots and TV talk shows where the use of a large microphone on a bulky stand is unacceptable.

Limiter

    A dynamics processor that limits or prevents signals from peaking above a specified amplitude level. A limiter works by compressing all sounds that peak above a specified threshold point. The average levels of your sound files can be raised several dB beyond the regular normalization level by using a limiter to compress the highest volume peaks. Using simple normalization alone to maximize the dynamic range has limitations. Because the normalization process simply calculates the available headroom, you are limited by the proximity of the loudest peak to the maximum cut-off point.

Lingo

    Macromedia Director's proprietary scripting language for creating sophisticated interactive games and presentations.

Liquid Audio

    An Internet file format and suite of software applications that provide a complete end-to-end solution for secure music delivery over the Internet.

Liquid Express

A software package specifically designed for audio professionals in film, radio, television, music, and advertising that allows for the secure real-time preview, approval, delivery, and archiving of broadcast-quality audio.

Liquid Music Player

An application that allows users to preview and purchase CD-quality Liquid Tracks on a Macintosh or Windows PC. It also allows you to see album graphics, lyrics, liner notes, and promotions while listening, as well as easily record an actual Red Book audio CD playable on any home, car, or portable stereo system.

Liquid Music Server

An application that lets you publish and host Liquid Tracks on the Web. The Liquid Music Server also includes an SQL database and can even hook into larger, industry-standard SQL databases, such as those from Informix and Oracle.

Live Encoding

The process of capturing and converting a live event for broadcasting over the Web.

Lossless Compression

A type of compression that squeezes or stuffs data into smaller-sized data packets without permanently discarding information. Compared to lossy forms of compression, lossless compression offers superior audio quality but larger file sizes.

Lossy Compression

A type of compression that intelligently discards data to achieve smaller file sizes. Lossy forms of audio compression, similar to JPEG image compression, permanently discard frequencies above and below specified points by removing "unnecessary" or redundant sound information. The client-side decoder or player then decompresses the compressed file as the audio downloads to a user's computer and fills in the missing information according to the instructions set by the decoding algorithm.

Loudness

The perception of the strength or weakness of a sound wave resulting from the amount of pressure produced. Sound waves that have more intensity or larger variations in air pressure produce louder sounds. Low-intensity sound waves with smaller fluctuations in air pressure produce quieter sounds. Loudness is not to be confused with amplitude. Loudness refers to the human perception of sound; amplitude refers to quantifiable measurements of air pressure variations.

Low-Pass Filter

An equalization effect that allows all the frequencies lower than a specified frequency to pass through unaffected while filtering out everything above the specified frequency cut-off point.

Mic Pick-up Patterns

The term used to describe the three-dimensional area or range of a microphone recording capsule. All microphones have a variation of one or more of the following patterns: omnidirectional, bidirectional, cardioid, and shotgun. Certain recording situations call for the use of different pick-up patterns.

Mic Pre-Amp

A device that boosts or amplifies the inherently weak signal of a microphone for output to a mixer or sound card.

Microphone (Mic)

A transducer device that converts air pressure waves into electrical signals.

MIDI (Musical Instrument Digital Interface)

A language originally developed to connect various electronic music devices. MIDI has since grown into an important compositional language and tool. MIDI contains no sound data but merely describes in the form of a "composer's score" how a device should playback music. MIDI files are ideally suited for web transmission since they are small, text-based "scores" and not actual representations of sound itself.

MIDI Sound Engine

Software that provides the necessary sound synthesis to generate musical tones for MIDI playback.

MPEG (Moving Pictures Experts Group)

A group of people that meet under ISO (the International Standards Organization) to generate standards for digital video and audio compression. The term MPEG also represents a multimedia compression scheme and format.

MPEG-4

A new MPEG format for low-bitrate coding of audio-visual presentations. The MPEG-4 standard was designed for a spectrum of new applications, including interactive multimedia communications, videophone, mobile audio-visual communication, multimedia electronic mail, remote sensing, electronic newspapers, interactive multimedia databases, and games. MPEG-4 targets the very low bitrate applications defined loosely as having sampling dimensions up to $176 \times 144 \times 10$ Hz and coded bitrates between 4,800 and 64,000 bits/sec.

Mixer

A device that connects and routes all the input and output signals from one component to another. Mixing boards also have signal-processing capabilities such as equalization and reverb. Mixers save you from the hassle of patching together different pieces of equipment for common, day-to-day studio tasks.

Multitrack Recording

The process of recording or capturing several simultaneous tracks of audio.

NetShow

A component of Windows NT Server and Microsoft's Windows Media Technologies. NetShow services include a comprehensive suite of authoring tools and streaming services for delivering audio, video, animations, and other multimedia over the Internet. NetShow presentations are played back with the Windows Media Player, a universal player that plays most local and streamed media file types including NetShow's native file format, Advanced Streaming Format (ASF), as well as MPEG, WAV, AVI, QuickTime, and RealAudio/RealVideo.

Noise

The term applied to non-musical sounds that are mainly comprised of random chaotic frequencies at random amplitudes, such as the roar of a crashing wave or the sound of a computer hard drive.

Noise Floor

The inherent background noise level in an audio signal. Poor-quality audio equipment produces a higher noise floor.

Nondestructive Editing

A form of audio editing that preserves the original sound file and does not permanently change or rewrite over the original master file but instead merely alters its playback. Nondestructive edits become permanent once the final mix is recorded or "bounced" to disk. With nondestructive editing, the original source files are always preserved as separate sound files.

Normalization

The process of increasing the overall level of a sound file by boosting the loudest peak in the file up to the maximum 0dB point. If you are working with pre-recorded material, you will want to normalize your sound files before converting them to web formats. Normalization maximizes the dynamic range of a sound file, enhances a sound by making it more present or clear, and sets a uniform volume or amplitude level for a group of sound files recorded or mixed at different volume levels.

Omnidirectional Microphone

A device that captures sounds from all angles. This type of mic is commonly used for recording multiple instruments and voices.

Panning

The term used to describe the action of placing or mixing sounds in the left or right channels during stereo playback. All mixers feature a pan knob for adjusting the stereo playback parameters of an audio clip.

Parametric Equalizer

An equalizer that allows you to specify the bandwidth and range of the frequencies you want to boost or lower. Unlike a graphic equalizer, parametric equalizers feature several knobs for adjusting bandwidth and gain instead of a horizontal row of faders. Parametric equalizers provide greater flexibility for altering specific frequencies.

Pitch

The sensation of how high or low a sound is perceived. Pitch is determined by a sound's frequency, or rate of repetition. The faster the frequency, which is measured in hertz (Hz) or cycles per second, the higher the pitch. The slower the frequency, the lower the pitch. On home stereo equipment, high-frequency sounds are often referred to as "treble" and low-frequency sounds as "bass." Piercing sounds such as a siren or whistle are composed of extremely rapid vibrations of air molecules. Lower-pitched sounds such as a bass guitar consist of slower vibrating sound waves.

Pitch Shifting

The process of raising or lowering the pitch of a sound file. Use time correction with pitch shifting if you want to preserve the same length and file size as the original sound.

Pop Screens

A circular hoop with a thin nylon material that rests directly between the speaker's mouth and the microphone. Pop screens are essential for reducing wind and explosive P's and S's when recording voices.

Pseudo-Streaming

A term for HTTP streaming from a standard web server as opposed to UDP or RTSP streaming from a dedicated audio server.

QuickTime

Apple Computer's technology that enables the delivery and playback of video, sound, music, 3D, and virtual reality on Macintosh and Windows computers. QuickTime is also the leading video production platform for both Windows and Mac.

RealEncoder

A RealNetworks' utility that enables you to compress audio files or input from an audio device into RealMedia clips.

RealFlash

A RealNetworks' format that works in conjunction with the Real-System 5.0 to enable broadcasting of streaming Flash vector animation synchronized to RealAudio.

RealMedia Clip (.rm)

The term used to describe media content such as audio or video, encoded into the RealAudio, RealVideo, RealFlash, RealPix, or RealText formats.

RealMedia Metafile (.ram)

A metafile located on your server that connects a web page to your RealAudio, RealVideo, or RealFlash clips. The metafile contains the URL of one or more clips located on the RealServer.

RealPlayer

A RealNetworks' application that decodes incoming audio packets that have been compressed with the RealEncoder back into the original audio signal. The RealPlayer features random access controls such as scroll, stop, start, and pause.

RealPlayer Plug-in Metafile (.rpm)

The RealPlayer metafile is the same as the RealMedia metafile but used with the RealPlayer plug-in for Netscape and Internet Explorer.

RealPublisher

A RealNetworks' utility that enables you to compress and convert video as well as audio files or live input from a video device. RealPublisher is an enhanced version of RealEncoder and offers web publishing features such as automatic HTML page creation and easy uploading of HTML pages to either a standard HTTP web server or a RealNetworks RealServer. RealPublisher is especially useful for creating web pages that display an embedded RealPlayer.

RealServer

RealNetworks' streaming media delivery system that works in conjunction with a standard web server to stream encoded audio and multimedia content over the Internet.

RealSystem

RealNetworks' streaming media software that allows users, equipped with conventional multimedia PCs and voice-grade telephone lines, to browse, select, and play back streaming multimedia on demand.

Real-Time Audio Captions

Long-playing streaming audio clips placed in a web page.

Reverb

Rapid sound wave reflections that strike the ear drum within 40 milliseconds of the original sound. If a sound reflects off of a wall that is close to our ears, we hear the reflections or reverb instantly as part of the richness of the original sound wave decay. If a sound bounces off a hard reflective surface that is far away, we hear the reflection as a second distinct sound or echo. This type of reflection is known as "delay."

RMF (Rich Music Format)

A hybrid format developed by Headspace that offers the best of MIDI, digital audio, Java, and JavaScript technologies. An RMF file is a small, efficient music file that contains MIDI, sample, and copyright information in a compressed, encrypted form optimized for playback on the Web. RMF offers the universality, convenience, and small file sizes of MIDI, the interactivity of Java, and a playback sound engine that delivers superb audio quality.

Room Tone

The natural ambient background sound in a given environment such as subtle wind outdoors or the distant hum of an indoor generator or fan.

RTSP (RealTime Streaming Protocol)

An open, standards-based protocol for multimedia streaming. RTSP supported by RealSystem G2 provides several advantages over UDP transmission, including better support for synchronized media playback.

Sample

A value assigned to represent a portion of an electrical waveform.

Sample Rate

The number of samples of an electrical waveform taken per second.

Shockwave

A term used to describe Macromedia Director or Flash content that has been converted for delivery over the Web with the Shockwave utility.

Shotgun Mic

A microphone that contains a recording capsule embedded in a long hollow tube. The capsule picks up a highly exaggerated hyper-cardioid pattern of sounds far in front and back of the microphone.

Sibilance

Overemphasized or particularly loud high frequency noise such as the sounds produced when annunciating S's, P's, and T's. Cutting specific higher frequencies can usually lessen the unwanted effect.

Signal-to-Noise Ratio (SNR)

The difference in dB between the maximum input signal level and the system noise level that is introduced to the output signal. High fidelity audio equipment has a higher signal-to-noise ratio.

SMPTE

A time code standard for synchronizing audio to visuals set by the Society of Motion Pictures and Television Engineers.

Sound

The vibration of air molecules in the atmosphere that can be sensed by the ear. A sound wave is produced by a force that vibrates the surrounding air molecules, such as a stick striking a wooden surface or a guitar string being plucked. As the air molecules are set in motion, they radiate outwards, colliding into other air molecules like a chain of falling dominoes, until they strike the ear drum. Each type of disturbance in the atmosphere produces a distinct pattern of vibrations. These patterns of vibrating air molecules give a sound its unique loudness, pitch, and timbre.

Sound Design

The process of orchestrating all sounds including the dialogue, music score, and sound effects into one cohesive soundtrack. Full-scale film sound design came about in the late 1970s when film producers and directors realized they could put a sound signature on an entire film by hiring one person—a sound designer—to orchestrate all the various audio components into one cohesive soundtrack.

Soundtrack

The audio accompaniment to film, graphics, or text.

Speed of Sound

The speed of sound is 770 MPH.

Splitting

A RealSystem feature that enables you to split and route the audio signal from one RealAudio Server to several other RealServers located at different strategic points across the Internet. By allowing users to connect to the closest RealServer, you ensure better quality and performance.

Studio Reference Speakers

Professional monitoring speakers that accurately reproduce a "flat" transparent representation of a sound without adding coloration, distortion, noise, or equalization. Home stereo speakers, by contrast, are designed to boost the high and low audio frequencies to provide a richer sound. Unlike home stereo speakers, the goal of reference speakers is to give you not the most pleasant sound, but the most accurate.

SureStream

A RealSystem G2 technology for dynamic bandwidth allocation for more efficient and reliable streaming. SureStream switches down to a lower bandwidth without rebuffering the clip when a user's Internet connection degrades or, presumably, if the user's bandwidth was misjudged. RealEncoder G2 with SureStream generates one master file that includes several different bandwidth settings.

TCP (Transmission Control Protocol)

A protocol that emphasizes the reliable transfer of data between computers. TCP functions much like an error-correction traffic cop methodically directing the flow of data packets to the same destination, while making sure that everything that was sent arrives at the proper address. TCP, as opposed to UDP, resends lost packets.

Threshold of Compression

A term used to describe the point at which a signal rises above a determined amplitude level or threshold setting and a compressor or limiter begins to compress or reduce the signal.

Timbre

The tone, "color," or texture of a sound. The term timbre encompasses all of the qualities of a sound besides loudness and pitch, such as smooth, rough, hollow, peaceful, mechanical, etc.

Transients

The attack and decay (or beginning and ending) characteristics of a sound such as the quiver of a violin bow as it strikes the strings or the brief squawk of a saxophone as the air begins to vibrate the reed.

UDP (User Datagram Protocol)

A protocol that facilitates the rapid transfer of data between computers. UDP, unlike TCP, keeps directing traffic and does not retransmit packets when data is lost or damaged. When a UDP audio packet drops out, the server keeps sending information causing only a brief glitch instead of a huge gap of silence.

Vibrato
> A slightly tremulous effect imparted to a vocal or instrumental tone for added warmth or expressiveness by slight and rapid variations in pitch.

Voice-Over Artist
> An artist who specializes in voice recording. A voice-over artist is generally someone with a nice quality voice, good microphone technique, and previous theatrical or radio experience.

WAVE (.wav), Waveform Audio File Format
> The native audio format for Windows developed by Microsoft and IBM.

Waveforms
> The patterns of air pressure variations that move outward from a point of impact. Waveforms are the "substance" of sound.

Web Mastering
> The discipline of optimizing sound files for Internet delivery. Mastering for the Web is the final optimization process before converting sound files to their respective web formats.

Wet
> An adjective used to describe a processed audio signal.

About the Authors

Josh Beggs is co-founder and president of Raspberry Media, a design firm in the San Francisco Bay Area specializing in web-smart architecture, interface design, and brand development for Internet start-ups. Josh began his career in the multimedia industry as a recording engineer and sound designer. In 1995, he produced the interactive soundtrack for EMI Records flagship CD-ROM, Queensrÿche's "Promised Land." After receiving impressive reviews from *Billboard Magazine* (March 1996) for the soundtrack, Josh went on to explore interactive media design with Raspberry Media (*http://www.raspberrymedia.com*). In addition to designing some of the top web sites on the Internet, he also follows his musical passions as a pianist and recording artist.

Dylan Thede's multimedia experience began in the cultural mecca of the San Francisco Bay Area in 1985. At a young age, he was designing sound systems and multimedia presentations for the University of California at Berkeley. At the University of California at Santa Cruz, Dylan became a pioneer in the emerging fields of digital audio, digital video, and multimedia and later graduated with a degree in multimedia and psychology. He was one of the pioneers in web design when the World Wide Web burst onto the scene in 1994. In 1995, Dylan founded Audio-Visualize, a multimedia consulting company that caters to companies who wish to implement multimedia into their web sites and corporate operations. Besides writing and creating multimedia projects, he is also a musician and is currently composing and recording music for an upcoming multimedia CD release. Dylan can be reached at *dylan@usa.net*.

Colophon

Our look is the result of reader comments, our own experimentation, and feedback from distribution channels. Distinctive covers complement our distinctive approach to technical topics, breathing personality and life into potentially dry subjects.

Melanie Wang was the production editor and proofreader, with support from Nicole Arigo, Jane Ellin, and Emily Quill, for *Designing Web Audio*. Nicole Arigo was the copyeditor. Mary Sheehan and Colleen Gorman provided quality control, and Nancy Williams, Matt Hutchinson, Leanne Soylenez, and Lucy Muellner provided production assistance. Pamela Murray and Ellen Troutman-Zaig wrote the index.

The cover of this book was designed by Edie Freedman, with help from O'Reilly's Creative Services Group. It was produced using QuarkXPress 4.11 and Adobe Photoshop 5.5, with Adobe Formata fonts.

Alicia Cech and David Futato designed the interior layout based on a series design by Nancy Priest. Mike Sierra implemented the design in FrameMaker 5.5. The text and heading fonts are ITC Garamond Light and Gill Sans. The illustrations that appear in the book were produced by Robert Romano and Rhon Porter using Macromedia FreeHand 8 and Adobe Photoshop 5.

Whenever possible, our books use a durable and flexible lay-flat binding. If the page count exceeds this binding's limit, perfect binding is used.

How to stay in touch with O'Reilly

1. Visit Our Award-Winning Web Site

http://www.oreilly.com/

★ "Top 100 Sites on the Web" — *PC Magazine*
★ "Top 5% Web sites" — *Point Communications*
★ "3-Star site" — *The McKinley Group*

Our Web site contains a library of comprehensive product information (including book excerpts and tables of contents), downloadable software, background articles, interviews with technology leaders, links to relevant sites, book cover art, and more. File us in your Bookmarks or Hotlist!

2. Join Our Email Mailing Lists

New Product Releases

To receive automatic email with brief descriptions of all new O'Reilly products as they are released, send email to:
ora-news-subscribe@lists.oreilly.com
Put the following information in the first line of your message (*not* in the Subject field):
subscribe ora-news

O'Reilly Events

If you'd also like us to send information about trade show events, special promotions, and other O'Reilly events, send email to:
ora-news-subscribe@lists.oreilly.com
Put the following information in the first line of your message (*not* in the Subject field):
subscribe ora-events

3. Get Examples from Our Books via FTP

There are two ways to access an archive of example files from our books:

Regular FTP

- ftp to:
  ftp.oreilly.com
  (login: anonymous
  password: your email address)
- Point your web browser to:
  ftp://ftp.oreilly.com/

FTPMAIL

- Send an email message to:
  ftpmail@online.oreilly.com
  (Write "help" in the message body)

4. Contact Us via Email

order@oreilly.com
To place a book or software order online. Good for North American and international customers.

subscriptions@oreilly.com
To place an order for any of our newsletters or periodicals.

books@oreilly.com
General questions about any of our books.

software@oreilly.com
For general questions and product information about our software. Check out O'Reilly Software Online at **http://software.oreilly.com/** for software and technical support information. Registered O'Reilly software users send your questions to: **website-support@oreilly.com**

cs@oreilly.com
For answers to problems regarding your order or our products.

booktech@oreilly.com
For book content technical questions or corrections.

proposals@oreilly.com
To submit new book or software proposals to our editors and product managers.

international@oreilly.com
For information about our international distributors or translation queries. For a list of our distributors outside of North America check out:
http://www.oreilly.com/distributors.html

5. Work with Us

Check out our website for current employment opportunites:
http://jobs.oreilly.com/

O'Reilly & Associates, Inc.
101 Morris Street, Sebastopol, CA 95472 USA
TEL   707-829-0515 or 800-998-9938
          (6am to 5pm PST)
FAX   707-829-0104

O'REILLY™

International Distributors

http://international.oreilly.com/distributors.html

UK, EUROPE, MIDDLE EAST AND AFRICA

(EXCEPT FRANCE, GERMANY, AUSTRIA, SWITZERLAND, LUXEMBOURG, AND LIECHTENSTEIN)

INQUIRIES

O'Reilly UK Limited
4 Castle Street
Farnham
Surrey, GU9 7HS
United Kingdom
Telephone: 44-1252-711776
Fax: 44-1252-734211
Email: information@oreilly.co.uk

ORDERS

Wiley Distribution Services Ltd.
1 Oldlands Way
Bognor Regis
West Sussex PO22 9SA
United Kingdom
Telephone: 44-1243-843294
UK Freephone: 0800-243207
Fax: 44-1243-843302 (Europe/EU orders)
or 44-1243-843274 (Middle East/Africa)
Email: cs-books@wiley.co.uk

GERMANY, SWITZERLAND, AUSTRIA, LUXEMBOURG, AND LIECHTENSTEIN

INQUIRIES & ORDERS

O'Reilly Verlag
Balthasarstr. 81
D-50670 Köln
Germany
Telephone: 49-221-973160-91
Fax: 49-221-973160-8
Email: anfragen@oreilly.de (inquiries)
Email: order@oreilly.de (orders)

FRANCE

INQUIRIES & ORDERS

Éditions O'Reilly
18 rue Séguier
75006 Paris, France
Tel: 33-1-40-51-52-30
Fax: 33-1-40-51-52-31
Email: france@editions-oreilly.fr

CANADA (FRENCH LANGUAGE BOOKS)

Les Éditions Flammarion ltée
375, Avenue Laurier Ouest
Montréal (Québec) H2V 2K3
Tel: 00-1-514-277-8807
Fax: 00-1-514-278-2085
Email: info@flammarion.qc.ca

HONG KONG

City Discount Subscription Service, Ltd.
Unit A, 6th Floor, Yan's Tower
27 Wong Chuk Hang Road
Aberdeen, Hong Kong
Tel: 852-2580-3539
Fax: 852-2580-6463
Email: citydis@ppn.com.hk

KOREA

Hanbit Media, Inc.
Chungmu Bldg. 210
Yonnam-dong 568-33
Mapo-gu
Seoul, Korea
Tel: 822-325-0397
Fax: 822-325-9697
Email: hant93@chollian.dacom.co.kr

PHILIPPINES

Global Publishing
G/F Benavides Garden
1186 Benavides Street
Manila, Philippines
Tel: 632-254-8949/632-252-2582
Fax: 632-734-5060/632-252-2733
Email: globalp@pacific.net.ph

TAIWAN

O'Reilly Taiwan
First Floor, No.21, Lane 295
Section 1, Fu-Shing South Road
Taipei, 106 Taiwan
Tel: 886-2-27099669
Fax: 886-2-27038802
Email: taiwan@oreilly.com

INDIA

Shroff Publishers & Distributors Pvt. Ltd.
12, "Roseland", 2nd Floor
Mumbai 400 050
Tel: 91-22-641-1800/643-9910
Fax: 91-22-643-2422
Email: spd@vsnl.com

CHINA

O'Reilly Beijing
SIGMA Building, Suite B809
No. 49 Zhichun Road
Haidian District
Beijing, China PR 100080
Tel: 86-10-8809-7475
Fax: 86-10-8809-7463
Email: beijing@oreilly.com

JAPAN

O'Reilly Japan, Inc.
Yotsuya Y's Building
7 Banch 6, Honshio-cho
Shinjuku-ku
Tokyo 160-0003 Japan
Tel: 81-3-3356-5227
Fax: 81-3-3356-5261
Email: japan@oreilly.com

THAILAND

TransQuest Publishers (Thailand)
535/49 Kasemsuk Yaek 5
Soi Pracharat-Bampen 15
Huay Kwang, Bangkok
Thailand 10310
Tel: 662-6910421 or 6910638
Fax: 662-6902235
Email: puripat@.inet.co.th

ALL OTHER ASIAN COUNTRIES

O'Reilly & Associates, Inc.
101 Morris Street
Sebastopol, CA 95472 USA
Tel: 707-829-0515
Fax: 707-829-0104
Email: order@oreilly.com

AUSTRALIA

Woodslane Pty., Ltd.
7/5 Vuko Place
Warriewood NSW 2102
Australia
Tel: 61-2-9970-5111
Fax: 61-2-9970-5002
Email: info@woodslane.com.au

NEW ZEALAND

Woodslane New Zealand, Ltd.
21 Cooks Street (P.O. Box 575)
Waganui, New Zealand
Tel: 64-6-347-6543
Fax: 64-6-345-4840
Email: info@woodslane.com.au

ARGENTINA

Distribuidora Cuspide
Suipacha 764
1008 Buenos Aires
Argentina
Phone: 5411-4322-8868
Fax: 5411-4322-3456
Email: libros@cuspide.com